KU-112-611

ENVOY TO MOSCOW

Memoirs of an Israeli Ambassador
1988–92

The Cummings Center for Russian and East European Studies
The Cummings Center Series

ENVOY TO MOSCOW
Memoirs of an Israeli Ambassador, 1988–92

Aryeh Levin

ENVOY TO MOSCOW

Memoirs of an Israeli Ambassador
1988–92

ARYEH LEVIN

FRANK CASS
LONDON

First published in 1996 in Great Britain by
FRANK CASS & CO. LTD.
Newbury House
900 Eastern Avenue, London IG2 7HH, England

Copyright © 1996

British Library Cataloguing in Publication Data
A catalogue record for this book is available from the British Library

ISBN 0-7146-4597-4 (cloth)
ISBN 0-7146-4268-7 (paper)

Library of Congress Cataloging-in-Publication Data
A catalog record for this book is available from the Library of Congress

All rights reserved. No part of this publication may be reproduced in any form or by any means, electronic, mechanical, photocopying, recording or otherwise, without the prior permission of Frank Cass and Company Limited.

Typeset by Marty Bokel, Tel Aviv, Israel
Printed in Great Britain by
Bookcraft (Bath) Ltd, Midsomer Norton

To Aliza

Contents

List of Illustrations

Acknowledgements

The idea of writing a book about my experiences in the Soviet Union and Russia was urged on me by many friends and well-wishers throughout the unique four years I spent there at the head of Israel's Mission. I never related to it seriously during my stay, as the pressures of work were far too great to indulge in keeping a detailed diary. Nor could I sustain the effort of methodic note-taking in meetings and conversations with the many interesting people and situations that I encountered.

Upon returning home from Moscow I soon resigned from the Foreign Ministry. I thought the forty-two years of service in government had earned me the right to devote a few years to other activities: among them, writing an account of the extraordinary events my companions and I had gone through in those tumultuous concluding years of the Soviet state and of the massive immigration to Israel.

I had thus to rely on my personal appointment books and letters home, which amounted to a description of the life and times that I lived through in Moscow. The rest came from the pages of a vivid memory still fresh with the images of those unforgettable days. The great upheaval in the life and times of both Israel and Russia have left deep impressions. I have written this book in the hope of sharing them with the public and with specialists who wish to gain insight from a participant, like myself. My book is a personal memoir, not an endeavour at historical or political analysis, which must be left to the scholars.

Professor Gabriel Gorodetsky, Head of the Cummings Center at Tel Aviv University, encouraged and helped me to bring this task to completion. I shall be forever in his debt. I wish to express my thanks and appreciation to Deena Leventer, who edited the text. A number of friends, among them Newton Frohlich and Dr Avraham Ben-Yaacov, read the manuscript and offered valuable suggestions. My family was there as always, optimistic and supportive to the end.

Aryeh Levin
Jerusalem, 1995

Foreword

One of the most spectacular features of the Communist collapse was the change that ensued in the Middle East. The huge weight and bulk of the Soviet Union was suddenly transferred from the negative to the positive scale of the strategic balance. No longer the Soviet Union as the spoiler, the supplier of arms to radical Arab countries and the instigator of hostility between Israel and its neighbours. There was now Russia as a partner of the peace process and an ally of the United States in the promotion of stability.

This change led to a wider opening of the gates, enabling a massive emigration of Soviet Jews, mainly to Israel. Opportunities for creative diplomacy were now available for the Israeli diplomats who had previously led an embattled existence in an atmosphere of tense hostility.

Aryeh Levin straddled the transition between the two eras. He used his enhanced fortune with good effect. He has a dramatic story to tell in this book and he tells it with style and passion.

Israel was fortunate in having one of its most talented emissaries in such a central post.

Abba Eban

Preface

Of all my travels in the service of the Israeli government, the Russian interlude still seems to be the most extraordinary. There was a great deal of drama: I witnessed the demise of the communist state; I stood at the floodgates when a sudden wave of Jewish immigration rose, crested and subsided with a burst of tremendous energy. But above all, this was a very personal experience. I lived through all these events, not as an outsider, a foreigner shielded from the populace by the conventions of diplomatic practice, but rather as an individual deeply involved in the texture of life around him. The circumstances in which I first found myself in Moscow were quite unconventional. Lack of access to the upper echelons of the state was largely compensated by an easy rapport with the people around me. And as so often in one's life, many things just happened. Destiny, it seemed, had brought me to the very heartland of Russia at a crossroads in its complex history.

It was also fate that led me to learn a number of languages. In large measure they dictated the course of my life and career. I was born and raised in Tehran as a Farsi and Russian speaker. My father came from an observant family of Hasidic Jews in the Ukraine and longed to 'ascend to Jerusalem', though it took him many more years than he had planned. He had no knowledge of spoken Hebrew. To him it was the 'holy tongue', not to be used for vulgar speech but a language in which to study the Talmud and to pray. A fervent Zionist, he vowed to raise me in Palestine. Times were difficult, we could not travel and my father failed to fulfil his pledge. To allay his feelings of guilt, he made me learn Hebrew. There was an assortment of teachers available in Tehran, all zealous but sadly underqualified. One of them was an old cantor from Vilnius, who would translate the text of the Torah, chapter by chapter, and assign me to repeat the translation at a second lesson during the week. My father felt satisfied that I was being educated in the language of the prophets and would summon me twice a year to check on my progress. He would inquire if I already knew Hebrew. I did not, but would weakly reply 'yes', inwardly trembling at the consequences. To verify my statement, my father would fetch a volume in Hebrew with silver-embossed letters on a light blue cover and command me to read and translate into Russian. The book was a condensation of Daniel Defoe's *Robinson Crusoe*, written in a style far removed from the religious writing I had been studying. As I stammered, my body wet with perspiration, my father's rage surged, along with his parental voice. When we both approached the breaking point, Father warned that I would 'bleat like a sheep' when I arrived in Jerusalem and shame the family. At this point, the storm would subside, I would promise to pay greater attention to Hebrew and could count on an additional six months' grace. This association of pervasive fear with the Hebrew language did not prevent me from settling in Israel and integrating Hebrew into my system, although my children sometimes catch me counting in Farsi.

As we spoke Russian at home, my father never checked my proficiency in that tongue. He possessed a sizable Russian library which contained, needless to say, an unabridged version of *Robinson Crusoe*. There was also a large émigré library in Tehran, most of which I went through before I had reached the age of 13. The classics were my favourite reading. Their language became indelibly imprinted on my mind. The first time I ever stepped on Russian soil was in 1988, when I arrived for a brief six-week tour of duty. I heard myself attempting to revive my memory of Russian from past readings of Leo Tolstoy, Ivan Turgenev and Nikolai Gogol — hardly the medium of modern diplomacy. After a time, daily perusal of the Soviet press, attentive viewing of television and repeated ventures into Russian conversation brought my speech closer to the modern-day idiom.

Since the age of 30, I have reaped the benefits of my earlier encounters with languages. In army intelligence my duties required me to read a great amount of material in the languages I had learned in my early youth. When I joined Israel's foreign service I was posted to Paris, where I polished the French which I had learned in a private kindergarten and high school and which I had never forgotten. I was assigned as deputy chief of our diplomatic mission to pre-Khomeini Tehran because of my knowledge of the country and of its tongue. At the United Nations in New York, I returned to the American English I had learned at the Community School, an American secondary-school establishment in Tehran, which has left its mark on me until this very day.

The Six-Day War of 1967 was to be a turning point in my life. The war caught me in Kigali, Rwanda, at the head of our embassy there. I had poor communications with Jerusalem and heard of Israel's victories over a shortwave radio, a possession which placed me very much in demand among Rwandan ministers and my fellow diplomats. I heard of the severance of relations with the Soviet Union but was astonished when the local Soviet ambassador demonstratively ignored me at official functions and averted his eyes when we met on the only paved street in Kigali. It must have been difficult for him, as he did not know a single language except Russian and I was the only diplomat who could help him out at receptions. The other envoys in the small African city joked about the official, fierce expression he would affect when he saw me appear.

In Israel, we had become used to the quirks of Soviet international politics and to its propaganda — ever more strident — against us. The Soviet severance of relations with Israel was reminiscent of Khrushchev's shoe-banging at the UN. It was a typical manifestation of Soviet political culture. In light of the severe deterioration in Soviet-Israeli relations, Israel became deeply concerned about the fate of Jews in the Soviet Union, who, to an extent, had to bear the consequences of these international developments. Few people thought it would take the Russians over two decades to renew diplomatic relations, and I never imagined that I would be the one running up the flag in Moscow when they did.

My proficiency in Russian was only one of the reasons I found myself in Moscow. Beyond the professional considerations of my ministry, which found me suitable for the task, I always liked working in new and exceptional situations. Ethiopia, Rwanda, Iran and Russia stand out, from that point of view. I knew I would be exposed in Moscow to the elements of the Soviet system, *a priori* hostile and unwelcoming to an Israeli diplomat; none of us had any inkling of how matters would turn out, but my curiosity prevailed, and I assented to my minister's bidding. An assignment to the Soviet Union was considered a challenge. It was also very important politically. For all these reasons, I considered a first Moscow trip, late in 1988, an opportunity not to be missed. This was a mission for which, subconsciously, I had been preparing myself. After my first weeks there, I became increasingly hesitant about remaining in Moscow as I realized our goals would take much longer to attain than I had originally thought. In the end, I stayed four years and have never regretted it.

I

Into the Breach

1 · *Preparations*

I had never enjoyed as much popularity as when I returned from my first trip to Moscow at the end of December 1988. I was inundated with phone calls and requests for interviews, appointments and lectures. Israel's Ministry of Foreign Affairs had sent me out on an exploratory assignment to the Soviet capital to see if I could hold out as head of our temporary consular mission.

The assignment was unusual; after all, we had not had a mission in Moscow for well over 20 years and relations with the Soviet Union were still cool. The first group of consular workers we had sent out was headed by a junior official. They reported difficult living conditions and official ostracism. Our ministry concluded that a diplomat of ambassadorial rank could perhaps improve the mission's stature, and I was asked to head the group in Moscow for six weeks. My presence would probably not have had the desired impact had it not been for a lucky and entirely unforeseen incident: the hijacking of a Soviet airplane to Israel and its prompt return made world headlines and extricated the Israeli mission from the isolation to which it had been relegated by the Russians. The Israeli public, used to Soviet churlishness, was elated at the unexpected 'breakthrough'. This optimism was not fully justified, but even so, I found myself very much in the news.

I was frankly relieved to be back behind my desk as head of political research. This post afforded great insight into our external affairs. It was far more enjoyable than being an unofficial Israeli representative in Moscow, under constant scrutiny by the KGB. Still, I had difficulty in getting back to my department, prominent and thriving though it was. I had to make up for the six weeks I had spent away from my job. I found myself constantly reliving the extraordinary events that had made that initial sojourn so memorable in my own mind, as well as in the perception of numerous friends and colleagues. In the eyes of the Israeli public, thirsty for news about Russia and its Jews, the unexpected nature of the events made them even more remarkable.

It had taken the Soviet government almost a year to agree to our demands for a reciprocal presence in the respective capitals. They had requested permission in 1986 to post a group of consular officials in residence at the Finnish Embassy in Tel Aviv. The Finns had been looking after Soviet interests ever since the break of diplomatic relations in 1967. We asked for a *quid pro quo*, but the Soviets demurred. They used all the tricks of the trade: they broke off the negotiations, toughened and relaxed their positions. At one point we suggested setting up consulates-general, which would have the virtual authority and privileges of embassies, but the Russians turned us down flat. Finally, they did allow us to establish a presence symmetrical to theirs in Israel and to maintain a group of 'consular workers' at the Netherlands Embassy in Moscow. The Dutch had been looking out for Israeli interests since the Six-Day War.

The Russians were making great efforts to convince us that their only interest in Israel was to oversee the real estate of the Imperial Russian family and the Orthodox Church, which they considered 'Soviet property' in the Holy Land. Since the 1967 War, most, but not all of this, was being administered by the Israeli Custodian for Absentee Property. They were indeed interested in laying hands on property they considered their own, but this was hardly the reason for sending a consular mission to Israel. It may have been a pretext for the Politburo's sudden change of policy in this regard. The professionals in the Foreign Ministry, the KGB and the research institutes, all with a great deal of influence over the Soviet decision makers, had a different argument. They were beginning to realize that the Soviet Union was losing out in the peace process unfolding in the Middle East. The Soviets wanted to force the participants into a peace conference, with the USSR present as a referee alongside the United States. In the Soviet view, the two superpowers, each protective of its clients' interests, would help steer the course of the negotiations. Israel was convinced this approach would subject the peace conference to superpower dictates, and rejected the Soviet scheme.

As the breezes of perestroika began blowing in earnest in the second half of the 1980s, the need for a reappraisal of the USSR's strategy *vis-à-vis* Israel became more apparent. The Soviet government, due to its lengthy absence from the political scene in Israel, was rather ignorant of internal developments and political life. Their intelligence inside the country was spotty, and they had difficulty making realistic assessments. The Soviets did maintain unofficial contacts, both with individual politicians and with communists and other fellow-travellers. In secret meetings with Israeli officials such as Peres's assistant Nimrod Novik, Soviet diplomats would often direct the conversation to the political scene in Israel, revealing their naïveté about its complexities. Even knowledge of Hebrew, a key to studying the political and social life in Israel, was lagging behind intelligence needs. This was hardly satisfactory for a great power with ambitions in the area. In time, as the signs of reform became more concrete, the Soviet establishment, including the Ministry of Foreign Affairs, decided to cautiously begin reshaping policy.

The Israeli government and public opinion were responsive to the first signs of Soviet interest in contacts. Israel was eager to establish a presence in the USSR, above all to assist Soviet Jews in any way possible and facilitate their immigration to Israel. We also wanted to work toward the eventual re-establishment of diplomatic relations. Nevertheless, Israel had to abide by the conventions of Soviet diplomacy and play at their game of dissimulation and secrecy. The Soviet government declared its interest in establishing a small team of officials in Tel Aviv to help Soviet citizens residing in Israel and to maintain Soviet property. Israel announced it wished to inspect its embassy building and observe the issuing of visas to Israel by Dutch consular officials.

The Soviets were stubborn in refusing to consider Israeli requests for reciprocity. Their leadership feared they would lose international prestige if they allowed Israeli diplomats into their country. An Israeli presence in their capital, they argued, might harm ties with the Arab states. The initial negotiations on allowing a Soviet consular group into Israel opened in Helsinki in summer of 1986. Israel demanded the release of all prisoners of Zion, free emigration for the 11,000 refuseniks and the lifting of restrictions on Jewish education. The Russians immediately halted the meeting. They then haggled and procrastinated for many months until they finally, begrudgingly, agreed to Israel's terms. Israel was permitted to send a consular group to Moscow. The Soviet team in Tel Aviv anticipated the Israelis by something like a year. The Israeli group arrived in the Soviet capital at the end of July 1988.

This whole move had been discussed and planned by Israel's Foreign Ministry well ahead of time. Israel had been waiting for just such an opportunity. The meetings between Israeli and Soviet leaders had been infrequent. Yitzhak Shamir met Gromyko in 1981 and again in 1984. As prime minister, he met Shevardnadze in 1988; Shimon Peres, in his capacity as minister of foreign affairs met Shevardnadze in 1987 and then again in 1988. There were sporadic lower-level meetings as well. The questions of Jewish education, freedom for prisoners of Zion and emigration of refuseniks were always raised by the Israeli side, as was the subject of normalization of diplomatic relations. The habitual Soviet response was that relations would be resumed when the peace process was well under way and when Israel retreated from the occupied territories and recognized the Palestine Liberation Organization. With the beginning of Gorbachev's perestroika, hopes ran high for a different approach. The Politburo, however, had the decisive voice and was chary of giving the impression — to the Arabs and the Soviet public alike — that the Soviet government was giving in. Voices calling for a change of attitude toward Israel could already be heard in the Soviet establishment, and there was a certain softening in the tone at the end of the 1980s. Nonetheless, the higher echelons of power in the USSR attempted at all times to 'maintain the dignity of a great power', which slowed down progress on relations with Israel. The Helsinki meeting in 1986 and its follow-up later in 1987 signalled a change in the pace.

The Israeli government never removed the subject of the Soviet Union from the agenda. The Russians were a most important element in the map of the Middle East and had been active there since the establishment of Israel. The Israeli cabinet's intelligence briefings often related to the subject of the USSR's presence and activity in the area. The issue of Soviet policy was broached on many occasions in the discussions that I participated in as head of political research. Gorbachev's ascent to power and the changes in the international climate made the USSR an object of great curiosity and closer scrutiny. Israelis had a very special interest in Russia because of their emotional and cultural connections.

One briefing with Foreign Minister Peres stands out in my mind because of its somewhat unusual character. Peres demanded that we role play in order to prepare him for a meeting with his Soviet counterpart, Shevardnadze, at the General Assembly session which was to take place in autumn 1987. Peres was to play 'our' part, while we interpreted Shevardnadze's. But our foreign minister did not have the patience required for such a rehearsal. He snapped at us and interfered with our acting, claiming we did not reflect the Soviet minister's thinking or behaviour. Roles got mixed in the process and so we did not get very far that day, but we remained intrigued as to how things would work out at the actual meeting.

When he returned, Peres did not call us in to say what had transpired during his talks with Shevardnadze, but he did hand out the minutes of his meeting, albeit under seven seals of secrecy and only to a select few in his bureau. The transcript, by the way, was not dissimilar to the rehearsal, barring the fact that the parties did not for a minute forget who they were. Shevardnadze turned out to be a little more positive that we expected. He showed an inclination to pursue a political dialogue and expressed readiness to look into our requests on freeing Jews from detention and instituting direct flights for immigrants. None of these points were actually concluded until much later. At the same time, the Soviet minister complained about Israel's vociferous propaganda against the Soviet Union on the subject of Jewish emigration and its cooperation with the US in the Star Wars programme. Still, Shevardnadze was certainly an improvement over his predecessor, the dour and dogmatic Gromyko.

When the Israeli team finally arrived in Moscow, we started getting back reports of material hardships and of the inaccessibility of government agencies to our diplomats. The Moscow Ministry of

Foreign Affairs housed our officials at the Ukraina Hotel, a once attractive place of residence for officials of the Soviet bloc. It was built in the early 1950s, with a tall spire and huge stone urns on the roof, a flight of Stalin's personal architectural fancy. I was soon to discover at first-hand the lifestyle imposed on its lodgers.

At the Netherlands Embassy, where some of us were to work, three members of our delegation (those helping the Dutch with consular work) shared a room with four Russian secretaries, experienced and friendly consular workers who made us feel at home in the cramped space. It was hardly comfortable, but we were thankful, as the Dutch themselves were working out of a badly constrained chancellery.

Our diplomats were slowly getting used to their tasks and carrying them out with patience and good humour, mindful of the importance of the assignment. They were not fazed by the many recurrences of harassment, clearly committed on orders from above: slashing our car tyres, open and aggressive surveillance, and hovering when mission members were visiting acquaintances. We were denied contact with the Ministry of Foreign Affairs. The tactic was to assign our official meetings, those deemed absolutely necessary, to a functionary of the consular department of the Foreign Ministry. This official essentially acted as a post-office box for our messages. We were told to maintain all our contacts only through the good offices of the Royal Netherlands Embassy. We were not allowed to visit, or entertain the thought of using the Israel Embassy building, still under lease by us. The Soviet Foreign Ministry would not even allow the flag of the Netherlands to fly on that building, in spite of the fact that the Netherlands Embassy was officially representing Israel. When once the Dutch had the temerity to run up their flag at Israel's former embassy, they were immediately called on the carpet. Later applications in that regard were rather impolitely turned down — this notwithstanding the fact that Israel had contributed over two million dollars' rent to the Soviet treasury over the 20 years of its absence from Moscow. The Russians made it quite plain that the Israeli mission was not wanted in the capital, but since we had somehow managed to find our way in, they intended to keep us out of sight.

On balance, the experiment was considered positive from our

point of view. The Jewish population of the USSR had become aware of our presence in their midst and were not strongly hindered in making contacts. The Israeli government's inclination was to maintain and widen the scope of the mission.

Early in October the time had come to rotate our team and it was thought that higher visibility should be given to the head of mission. The foreign minister reconsidered his earlier reservations about sending his ministry's head of intelligence to the Russian capital, for fear of a protest, and I was asked to go to Moscow. As I was eager to continue my duties as head of political research until we knew where we were heading in Moscow, I was assured my sortie would be over in six weeks. In the meantime, I was to leave for the Soviet capital to get my bearings.

Although I had been following the Soviet scene for years, I had never dreamed that my first trip to the Soviet Union would be at the head of my country's mission. When I was informed of the decision and had given my consent, I went home feeling slightly giddy and a little worried about the days ahead. The Soviet Union in October 1988 was not the country it is today. I could not imagine how the Soviets would behave toward me and my colleagues, and what we could do to establish better working relations with them.

A year earlier I had received in my office at the ministry a man of some notoriety: Victor Lewis, the Soviet journalist who was purported to have special contacts with the KGB and the Soviet leadership. He was one of the most active sources of extraordinary news leaks to the West and had carved himself a special niche in the grey area of unofficial East-West relations. His visit to Israel was unusual but had no special significance. We had a long conversation in Russian about the Middle East and the Soviet Union as well as about the future of the Russian presence in Afghanistan. As he was leaving my office, he turned around and said: 'You know, I wouldn't be a bit surprised if sometime very soon I will see you as your country's ambassador in Moscow.' I laughed. The thought of Israel renewing its ties with the USSR was unrealistic enough at the time, to say nothing of the possibility of my own appointment. I put the thought quite out of my mind. The memory of those prophetic words came back to me as I was on my way home to announce the news to my family.

I wanted to obtain as much practical information as possible before I flew out to Russia. The reports we were receiving from our mission in Moscow were skimpy. Communication problems and the heavy workload our officials had to bear left little time for observation and less for writing reports. I called on a number of specialists and former Soviet citizens for consultations. Some were well-known and well-connected in the Soviet Union before their emigration to Israel. They described what they remembered of life in Moscow and compiled long, outdated lists of telephone numbers and addresses. It was evident I would have to be very much on my own and I began preparing myself for the worst.

My wife and children were not particularly pleased about my departure to the USSR, but they threw a big farewell party and all made light of the six weeks that awaited me. On the weekend before my departure, some friends and I drove out to the Diefenbaker forest on the road to Jerusalem for a picnic and talked about my assignment. Most of us were experienced diplomats, but not one of us knew anything about daily life in the Soviet Union. Neither did we understand what perestroika really meant or where it was heading.

The following week I took the KLM flight to the Hague, where our embassy was running the Moscow mission with the help of the Netherlands government. I saw a number of officials at the Dutch Foreign Ministry and had a briefing with our staff, one of whom, Danny Megiddo, had just returned from a stint in Moscow.

One tends to forget how little we knew at that time about the Soviet Union, Gorbachev and his policy of perestroika. The many accounts I heard at the Hague, though intelligent and well-informed, were somewhat at variance with the hard truth I discovered for myself in the course of my first six weeks in Moscow. They simply did not reflect the confusion, the cross-currents inside the Soviet establishment, and the growing instability and loss of confidence that I was to witness. The predominant theme which emerged in my talks at the Hague was the unpredictability of the Soviet Union and the inscrutability of its leading personalities, including Mikhail Gorbachev. It goes without saying that I was also thoroughly briefed on the efficiency of the KGB and alerted to the necessary precautions I had to take to be on my guard. The security people did not bolster my self-confidence.

The other challenge I knew I would face was Russian weather. Images of vast steppes under layers of deep snow in sub-zero temperatures led me on a vast shopping spree for woolen underwear, fur hats and other paraphernalia which I thought was essential. Indeed, all this equipment proved invaluable since Moscow had run out of everything. And so, on 1 November 1988, with bags laden with clothes and food, I took off on the flight to Moscow.

At the stopover in Warsaw we were asked not to leave the plane. My heart beat faster when I saw Polish soldiers boarding the plane. Inspection? I was relieved to discover they had only come to collect their ration of western cigarettes, nonchalantly handed out by the steward. That small incident put politics into its proper perspective and made my journey into the Soviet sphere less awesome.

Finally, we landed at the snow-covered Sheremetyevo airport. It was dimly lit and uninviting. The KGB border guard examined my diplomatic passport with great thoroughness. The suspicious-looking document was turned over and over. After what seemed an hour, the soldier's telephone rang and a lengthy conversation ensued about 'him' and 'his' with repeated stares and comparisons to the passport photo. 'Israel' and 'Israeli' were words that went back and forth many times. Obviously, a very dangerous individual had landed. Just when I was planning to camp there overnight, the soldier slapped my documents down and curtly informed me I could go. I went to collect my luggage in the mound of suitcases and cartons of every description piled high on the conveyor marked KLM HAGUE, only to discover that my suitcases were being fed into the conveyor marked JAL TOKYO. A member of our mission whisked me out into the daylight and put me into our official car, bearing Dutch license plates. The sound of Russian broadcast over the public address system still rang in my ears as we started out of the airport on the road to Moscow.

The sights were all new to me, but very much what I had imagined. Several kilometres out there was a giant 'dragon's tooth', an iron tank obstacle symbolizing the limits of the German advance on Moscow in the Second World War. I remembered the days of my childhood in Tehran, when my father, back from work late in the evening, his cigarette held in his tobacco-stained fingers, would look into my 'situation room'. I had a large-scale map pinned on the wall, where I would daily mark the German advance with a black ribbon. Later, a red ribbon was used to pinpoint the Russian counter-attacks. My father was worried about the progress of the war — for personal reasons, among others. There had been no news at all about his family in the Ukraine since the outbreak of hostilities. The only message we had was a single letter from Uncle Lev, who was a colonel in the tank corps. He was fighting in the Moscow region and was apparently killed defending the city, as we never heard from him again. The rest of the family disappeared as well. They had all been evacuated from the Ukraine into the Russian hinterland at the outset, but the letters my father had been receiving before the German invasion stopped coming altogether. In all my years in Russia, I could not find any trace of his family.

The mission's car finally entered the city and drove down Gorky Street, approaching Manezh Square. The store windows and shelves appeared to be empty. Yet there were crowds milling about on the sidewalks. People looked sullen and purposeful, going about in endless processions, very much like Van Gogh's depiction of convicts exercising in the prison yard. I found this first impression of Moscow striking. As we drove on, my companion busily explained the rules and regulations of traffic: no left turns except at points marked overhead, and long detours in search of exits. Pedestrians were taught not to infringe on the prerogatives of vehicles. A truck drove by, raining a mixture of sand, pebbles and salt to de-ice the road. A small rock hit the windshield, luckily just a scratch. Broken glass would have meant putting the car in a garage for over a week and ordering a spare from Finland.

Finally, we made it to the Ukraina, a hotel characterized by worn Victorian splendour. A large red plaque in the lobby announced the patrons' order of precedence: heroes of the Soviet Union had access to rooms without prior notification; invalids of the Great Patriotic War could get a room after three days' notice. Ordinary people, depending on their institutional connections, had to make alternative arrangements. We faced the hotel reception's bureaucrats. They wanted to know if we had applied to the Tall

Buildings Administration for permission to reside at the hotel. It appeared there was a separate bureau that ran tall buildings (up to 20 floors) in the city, of which the hotel was one. Of course, we had forgotten to ask their permission beforehand. But for two cartons of Marlborough cigarettes we were given leave to produce such a permit the next day. In the meantime, I could use the room that had been illicitly reserved for me. I was thoroughly exhausted and overwhelmed with first impressions of an incomprehensible Soviet Union.

2 · Reconnaissance to Confrontation

The long trajectory in space and time, from modern-day Hague to the faded glory of the Soviet capital, made for an exciting but exhausting journey. I fell into a deep and sound sleep that first night at the Ukraina Hotel. However, the realization that I was actually in bed under a Soviet roof awakened me in the middle of the night. I approached the window and observed the dimly lit streets below. Across, I could see the white marble building of the Russian Socialist Federated Soviet Republic (also known as the White House), scene of many exciting and unusual events yet to come. It was slumbering under its large golden clock tower. The Moscow River had frozen over with thin ice. There were trucks on the bridge that connected the two banks and fed the wide avenue beyond. Workers in heavy clothing were unloading and fixing multicoloured flags to the railings in preparation for the November festivities marking the 71st anniversary of the October Revolution. It was snowing, not the big flakes I always thought blanketed the steppes, but a thin powder, which kept falling slowly for days on end, until it built up to a uniform, thick cover of crisp, crunchy snow.

My mind went back to a meeting I had attended in autumn 1984 between the then Foreign Ministers Yitzhak Shamir and Andrei Gromyko. Bibi Netanyahu had just been appointed our ambassador to the UN. He was the Likud Party's great hope and already, in the minds of some, the heir apparent to Shamir, who headed the party. I was deputy ambassador to the UN. A meeting with the Soviets had been organized at our request. Shamir, like other ministers of foreign affairs of Israel, was always eager to meet with his Soviet counterpart. The results of these interviews were virtually predetermined by the rigid Soviet Middle East policy and close alliance with the Arabs. Still, our ministers insisted on having the Russians hear them out.

We arrived at the appointed hour at the Soviet UN Representation in New York and were received at the door by a short young lieutenant in uniform. He led us to a reception room and after a while a small group of people walked in. I recognized Anatoly Dobrynin and Oleg Troyanovsky, Soviet ambassadors to the US and the UN, respectively. An assistant told us Andrei Gromyko was in another meeting and would be joining us soon. We sat down in two rows, facing each other in heavy silence, broken only by words whispered by members of both parties among themselves. Tea arrived and was consumed, and Gromyko was still absent. I thought we had better get some conversation going. As New York was going through a beautiful Indian summer, I asked Dobrynin when snow fell in Russia. I hoped that Dobrynin, the great and experienced diplomat that he was, would take up the cue. 'Snow usually starts falling toward the end of October', he said, but in 1941, when the Germans were in the full swing of their attack against his country, Dobrynin added, it unexpectedly fell in September, bogging down the German advance and making life much more difficult for the Germans than they had expected. Dobrynin went on from there, speaking in fluent English, and needing no encouragement to continue the story until Gromyko finally walked in.

When I arrived in Moscow in early November snow had already covered much of the ground. I was concerned how things would turn out for my mission and for our ambition to get the Russians moving away from the ironclad position they had been maintaining toward us. Would perestroika and *détente* affect the Soviets' behaviour? There were many attempts to get them to change their sullen attitude. Western governments and considerable public activity had not made a dent; nor had efforts of influential individuals to approach Gorbachev and other members of the Politburo. However, I refused to give up hope. My main concern was to establish an operational base from which we could widen our presence in the Soviet Union and achieve our goals. With no friends or influence in the top echelons of power, or even access to government, we had to build our contacts from the ground up. I hoped I would be able to penetrate the barriers around me. That first night in Moscow, I had no idea how to proceed.

I woke up early, to a snowy morning. At the bank in the hotel lobby, I was advised that the 500 dollars I wanted to change was a lot of money, and that I would not be needing it. In the street, my first encounter with *sama zhizn'* (real life) was highly instructive. I stood in line for milk and was told, impatiently, to go pay for it first. Then I had to stand in line again to collect the purchase. Triumphantly, I emerged from the store and came into our rooms to discover the milk had turned. We gathered to breakfast on some of the food brought from the Hague and from Vienna, our convenient havens from the inadequacies of Moscow.

Miron Gordon, who had preceded me as temporary head of mission, had been the first trail-blazer into Soviet territory when the mission arrived. I was now relieving him and we sat down to talk about the situation in Moscow and our relations with the Soviet government officials, which were practically non-existent. Miron was born and raised in the USSR and had studied Soviet affairs at the Hebrew University in Jerusalem. Because of his Russian inflection, as well as his considerable girth and scraggly beard, many people mistook him for a Russian Orthodox priest — a fact which had led to many amusing incidents. On one occasion, when Miron was at the Intourist office, a female receptionist whispered into the phone that the priest had arrived for his appointment and was impatient to be received. Over the next few years, Miron came to Moscow on different occasions to help us out. Being very knowledgeable about life there and a specialist on Russian balladeers, he was always in contact with a segment of the population that others among us missed, and was popular among artists, singers and people of that genre. It was always a great pleasure to have him aboard and see him behind his desk, into the small hours of the morning, struggling with the Russian phone system or trying to answer the hundreds of letters that mercilessly landed on top of our tables every day. After a time, Miron was appointed ambassador to Poland, a position well earned. He subsequently ran the Russian desk at the ministry in Jerusalem.

Miron showed me the office in the hotel suite I was to inherit from him and the meagre archive he had put together, which was purposely open to possible scrutiny by the KGB during our absences. He briefed me on his activities and contacts in the three months he had spent in Moscow. The Soviet Foreign Ministry was unavailable and non-committal. The foreign diplomats, however, were curious, as were the journalists of the international press. Most read into our mission's presence a sign of changing times.

After a brief conversation, Miron and I rode out to the Royal Netherlands Embassy, which was giving us diplomatic cover and providing the framework for our activity. The sight that greeted me on my arrival at the embassy was that of an immense Dutch flag flying over a crowd of people standing in the snow, waiting for their turn at the consular offices. The militiaman at the gate sternly asked for my papers, and having examined them to his satisfaction, waved me in. We walked up the steps into the office, brushing against people standing in line and came into a room where four Russian women and three Israelis were handling documents and talking with the applicants through a small window. The Israelis in the room were members of our mission. They were not allowed by the Soviets to issue visas to Israel. This work was done by the Dutch consuls, who stamped and signed the documents. In contrast to procedures for all other countries, this was merely an intermediary step in the process eventually leading to exit from the Soviet Union.

Ambassador Petrus Buwalda and his staff were ideal hosts, trying to respond to all our needs, encouraging and helping us to the best of their ability. The Dutch had been acting on our behalf for many years, tending to the requirements of the Jewish exodus, in good times as well as bad. They eventually developed close contacts with the Jewish refuseniks. The embassy's Jewish contacts were a major source of information about life in the USSR, a point not lost on the European diplomats in general, as contacts with the Soviet population were sparse. The effort on behalf of Jewish

15

emigration and interests was a considerable political commitment for the Dutch government. It also appeared to be the mainstay of their diplomatic work in the Soviet Union in those years. The goal of my mission was to take over this activity and develop it into a full-fledged Israeli undertaking. With any other government we might have had a good share of tension and friction. These were reduced to a minimum with the Dutch — testifying to their indulgence more than ours. We were driven by our Mediterranean temperaments and our impatience to forge ahead in an area which constituted one of the main pillars of our state, Jewish immigration.

After years of pressure and negotiations, the USSR finally found it in its own interests to make certain concessions in the procedures to be followed by the emigrants. Israel was providing *vizovs* from relatives in Israel to families in the USSR. These were invitations either for visits or for permanent residence, mostly the latter, duly stamped and verified by a notary public. The forms, officially, were provided by the Israeli Ministry of Foreign Affairs, but in actual fact they came from Lishkat Hakesher, the Liaison Bureau, a special office in Tel Aviv dealing with questions pertaining to Soviet emigration. The Lishka was established in 1953 to deal with problems of Jews inside the eastern bloc countries. Until the collapse of the Soviet Union, its operations were covert and it was known by the code name 'Nativ'.

Vizovs were sent by mail to the Soviet Union. To my unending surprise over the years I spent in the Soviet Union, these letters regularly reached their destinations. There were few cases of sabotage, mostly perpetrated by local people, motivated by anti-Semitism or, at later stages, envy at the supposed ease with which Jews could leave the Soviet Union. The recipients of *vizovs* then applied to the local OVIR — the visa and registration department run by the Soviet Ministry of the Interior. The regulations said the papers should take two months to be processed but in fact they took a lot longer. In the general relaxation engendered by perestroika, the waiting period was reduced. In the meantime OVIR checked on the applicants to see if there were any objections to their departure. These were usually based on a tacit quota system, which eased up gradually as time went on. The other filtering system widely used by the authorities was security, often a euphemism for other considerations such as suspected political or Zionist activity. Obstacles were put in the way of anyone who was even remotely connected with the defence establishment in either industry, research or administration. Objections to granting an exit permit could be and were numerous. An application for emigration could bring dismissal from employment and systematic harassment. In late 1988 this type of brutality had been curbed but had not disappeared altogether.

After OVIR ascertained, with the KGB's help, that the applicant was quite harmless, he would be issued a so-called triptych. This was a document consisting of OVIR permission to begin the process: the person in question would have to go to the Netherlands Consulate to get his Israeli visa and then purchase his airplane ticket. Jews were required to prove that Israel was ready to allow them in. Since there were no direct flights to Israel, the tickets would be made out to Austria or Italy, which meant standing in line for visas to one of those countries as well. This would allow OVIR to grant an exit visa, for which the applicant had to pay a tax, usually unfeasible for the average Soviet citizen to raise, and provided by the government of Israel through the Dutch Consulate. Upon issuing the exit visa, the authorities automatically annulled the emigrant's Soviet citizenship, rendering him stateless. The Jews had to pay for this 'service'. Those who emigrated to Israel received Israeli citizenship upon arrival. However, since the large majority of about ten to one usually went to Austria or Italy and were processed there for onward travel to the US, they were left high and dry, without an international status that could protect them in case of need. These excesses were maintained by the Soviet government until late into the 1980s. They were slowly changed as a result of external pressures and of developments inside the Soviet Union, where appeals for human rights were gradually gaining recognition.

This process was not only a prolonged test of patience and tenacity for those who became entangled in it. It was also a reflection of the arbitrariness of the Soviet regime. In our many efforts to modify and change this unnecessary and humiliating bureaucratic procedure we always came up against the basic inhumanity of the communist regime. For over 70 years the Soviet system had subjected the inhabitants of the Soviet Union to hardship and degradation, sapping their strength and self-confidence. In the case of the Jews, there were doses of anti-Semitism accompanying other improprieties. Whereas the regulations governing the exit of emigrants were more or less uniform, only Jewish citizens had to pay a tax for an exit visa and no other emigrants had their citizenship revoked.

The workload generated for the Dutch Consulate by these convoluted requirements of the Soviet administration was heavy. Over the years from 1967, the Royal Netherlands government had borne this burden. Hundreds of thousands of Jews left the Soviet Union through the doors of its embassy in Moscow. We covered the costs involved, the salaries of the personnel and the expenses incurred: exit permits, material help where required when people were discharged from work, air tickets and other ancillary outlays of money. However, since we were not on the spot, we had no control over the actual issuance of visas, and had to leave it to our friends the Dutch to take the proper decisions in the framework of Israeli laws and regulations.

With our arrival in Moscow an increasing number of technical tasks were taken over by three members of our mission. The other three were occupied with diplomatic aspects of our assignment and security. All the official paperwork was done by the Dutch consuls and their Russian assistants. The end result of the effort involved in this emigration process was the exit of Soviet Jews primarily to the West and not to Israel, as we had dreamed for decades. Yet the growing number of emigrants was an encouraging sign in itself. We were hopeful that the day would come when Jews would change direction and come to Israel. The main reason for the *neshira* or 'drop out' of immigrants from their 'rightful path' to Israel was considered to be the ease with which Jews could obtain the status of political refugee, which greatly facilitated their entry into the US. This situation was to change toward the end of September 1989, but in November 1988, when I first arrived, the problems still looked formidable.

The Israeli government was motivated, at this point, by a desire to increase the *aliyah* ('ascent' to Israel) of Jews from the Soviet Union. The number of emigrants was still low and *neshira* did not seem to be a major problem. Toward the end of 1988 and the beginning of 1989, attention to it increased as restrictions were gradually relaxed and the number of emigrants began mounting. The transit stations for Jewish emigrants in Italy and Austria began to overflow. The Hebrew Immigrant Aid Society (HIAS) and other Jewish organizations were handling their end of processing the would-be refugees, but US officials could not keep pace.

Beyond the work done at the Netherlands Embassy, members of the mission dealing with emigration spent their time meeting Jews — prospective emigrants, who would be instructed on applications procedures. With time, word got out that there was an Israeli mission in Moscow. Contacts began developing with a growing number of Jewish communities over the vast map of the Soviet Union. The difficulty in maintaining such contacts was in the absence of feasible points of congregation beyond the Dutch Consulate in Moscow.

Gradually, members of the mission began fanning out, visiting other areas and setting up lines of communication. The telephones at the Ukraina Hotel rang constantly, mainly late at night. The usual question was why the *vizov* had not arrived. The reason was usually the inaccuracy of addresses or names, or the tremendous backlog in the Lishka office in Tel Aviv.

Toward the end of 1991 over a million of these *vizov*s were floating about, giving us an excellent assessment of the number of potential emigrants and their state in the exit pipeline. I had the impression, however, that the Lishka at times preserved the backlog, hoping for an improvement in the situation of *aliyah* to Israel and the opening up of direct flights — something that appeared rather remote at the time. Everywhere I went, I received complaints about delays. The Lishka people explained they lacked manpower and that there were too many *vizov*s for the processing to be handled more efficiently. On special occasions, when I thought it necessary for humanitarian reasons, I would make a special request and the Lishka would deliver the *vizov* in record time. I never asked for special privileges for people who were not going to Israel.

My initial discussions with the Dutch Embassy officials did not go beyond preliminaries. Our main difficulties at the time were logistics, an almost total lack of communication with Israel, the inadequacy of housing and absence of offices. The Dutch could not offer any help, tied up as they were with problems of their own and dependent as all foreign missions on the goodwill of the Soviet government. The official arm of the Soviets was the totally inefficient and frustrating UPDK, the Directorate for Servicing the Diplomatic Corps, affiliated with the Foreign Ministry. This was an organization whose task, to provide housing and other facilities, was carried out only in accordance with official policy. The Soviet government was highly uncooperative with Israel on the question of our mission's presence in their capital, and we had to make do with bare necessities. The Dutch did have a telephone line that connected them with the outside world and we were allowed to use it, sparingly, and at assigned times. We used the phone to get to our embassy in Vienna, which acted as a forward post and logistics centre for our mission. We had no expectations of being allowed to use our old embassy building on Bolshaia Ordynka Street.

The line of Jews standing outside in the snow, waiting for their exit papers, left an indelible impression. I recalled the very large demonstrations I had participated in and observed in New York and other cities for the freedom to emigrate. I believe they contributed a great deal to the relaxation of Soviet policies. I wondered, as many of us did, if the small group of Jews going to the US on Israeli visas was all we would be able to show for the huge effort that had been invested. From all we knew, things were about to change, but the direction and speed of these developments were unclear.

After my first visit to the Dutch Embassy, Miron took me on a tour of Moscow, showing me the two most exciting spots — the Kremlin and Red Square — and the special hard currency stores where we could buy food and other necessities not available to ordinary Soviet citizens. We had no staff or help at that point and had to do everything for ourselves, including cooking meals. The large suite I had at my disposal at the Hotel Ukraina had no cooking facilities. I prepared my own meals on a small electric hot plate from the provisions we bought at the dollar stores. Some of us were better cooks than others. In the evenings, when we had time, we would make the rounds, exchanging the tidbits we had accumulated. There were few restaurants into which we dared venture, although there were some among us brave enough to try the *pelmeny* (dumpling) parlours — reminiscent of Fellini films — with corpulent Russian women, decked out in soiled aprons, fishing *pelmeny* out of boiling soup with large ladles. One of the most important quests in this city of ten million inhabitants was for decent places to eat. In this regard, diplomats, journalists and other foreigners cooperated fully, exchanging addresses and culinary critiques. Gradually, the situation improved, our restaurant intelligence expanded the number of eateries on our lists, and we began suffering less from the inadequacies of home cooking.

A long weekend began on the eve of celebrations commemorating the October Revolution. Long lines of people with flags, balloons, paper flowers, large banners and streamers trudged through the sleet toward Red Square to rehearse their roles in the upcoming parade. Television programmes were festive, in heavy Soviet fashion: classical music and theatre, and marathon speeches. There was also a lot of unexpected discussion on topical questions, including pornography and Afghanistan. In interviews, so-called *afgantsy* (soldiers who had fought in that country) spoke their minds on the pain, the drudgery, the cruelty of the unnecessary war and on the need to terminate it. I thought of how the 1970s had seen most unexpected upheavals — coups and revolutions — in many countries where they were least expected. Such was the case in Spain and Portugal, Ethiopia and Iran. Would the USSR's turn come too?

As we were not a full-fledged mission, and were consequently not invited to Red Square for the parade, we watched it on television. There was nothing new: well-fed Soviet marshals in light-blue parade dress drove around in open Zil limousines, receiving permission to proceed from the minister of defence, who wore an enormous peaked cap and stood on the balcony of the Lenin Mausoleum together with the other leaders. The units then marched down Red Square in exemplary order, if not with outstanding enthusiasm. Gorbachev and his companions saluted from the Mausoleum and we wondered how a group of elderly men could stand the piercing cold and hold their water for such a long time.

The first days spent in Moscow made me realize what a terrible waste it would be if we did not use the opportunity to try to improve our official contacts with the Soviet government. The political departments of the Foreign Ministry refused to see or talk with us. We could not go very far if we did not have their backing or approval in our relations with the official organizations. The only contact we had was Ivan Pogrebnoy, a deputy head of the consular department. From the reports I had seen, he did not appear to be very forthcoming. I decided to confront him anyway and pass on a message to the higher political echelons requesting discussion of the current political problems of the Middle East. I requested a meeting through the Netherlands Embassy. A few days later we received word that we could come over to the consular department. I arrived with the minister of the Royal Embassy of the Netherlands, Willem Bentinck.

Pogrebnoy received me courteously. He complimented me on my Russian. His own vocabulary was limited: 'I shall pass on your remarks to the proper authorities.' I pointed out that we were lacking the minimal necessities to conduct our work in Moscow, and I requested to be received by the heads of the political departments of the ministry since I had messages to give them on behalf of the government of Israel. Pogrebnoy repeated his dogmatic refrain. He would not be moved to add anything more substantial. After an hour of pleasantries and general observations, I was satisfied that I had at least told him what I thought. I was certain Pogrebnoy would indeed pass my words on to the proper authorities. This tactic was to become the pattern of my contacts for many days to come.

3 · Moscow–Zagorsk–Leningrad

In those early days of November 1988 I found Moscow very much alive with glasnost and struggling with perestroika. I spent a lot of time watching television. The talk shows were overwhelming, not only because of their ponderousness but also because of the unfamiliar freedom of expression. The shackles were being discarded and almost everything was coming into the firing line of criticism and 'new thinking', an expression introduced by Gorbachev and used widely by the media. The Voice of Israel broadcasts were jammed by the Soviets and we had to struggle to make sense of the weak signals we received from the BBC and the Voice of America. Russian radio was expanding its coverage beyond the prescribed limits of strict censorship, but its foreign news was still highly unreliable and slanted. The press, too, was still largely muzzled. The exceptions were the so-called 'thick magazines' or monthlies — Soviet outlets for literary activity and social commentary — which were beginning to question the purity of the Communist Party and the cult of Lenin. Everyone was assessing Gorbachev's chances for political survival. His rush for reform and his opposition to the conservatism of the Politburo and the Central Committee were considered a threat to his longevity. Doubts regarding Gorbachev's own good intentions began cropping up later. Toward the end of 1988 Gorbachev was being commended for his gift of avoiding confrontation and cleverly outmanoeuvring the opposition.

Gorbachev had adopted a high profile and was travelling around the country pushing for his reforms. He was invariably accompanied by television crews. Private initiative was widely discussed and rarely understood, as people had forgotten what it had been like before the revolution. On one occasion, when Gorbachev was visiting the vicinity of Orel in the heartland of Russia, he met members of a very large kolkhoz or state farm, whom he questioned about the economic situation. 'Oh yes, things are much better now, as a result of party initiatives', they declaimed in unison. Figures on milk and meat production were quoted, but Gorbachev wanted to know if income had risen as well. The voices trailed off and became indistinct. Finally, someone said: 'We haven't earned any money yet, but there will be some next year.' Gorbachev beamed.

On this and similar trips around the country the first secretary was never shown speaking to 'farmers' (a euphemism for private dairy farmers) because of a great deal of public resentment and active opposition to private initiative in agriculture. There was public interest in obtaining land from the government or from the state farms, but the little that was being granted was of poor quality, with no financial support. There was no legislation governing private land ownership and property. In cases where such initiatives did work out and private farms became successful, sabotage, including arson, was frequent. It was evident that forced collectivization in the early 1930s had severely curbed appetites for private ownership in the rural areas, depopulated of traditional peasants. Agriculture had become a state enterprise and agricultural workers were employees, with a very low work ethic. As a result of Gorbachev's tampering with the accepted scheme of things, agriculture too became disoriented. State farms and other enterprises did not know what to expect and how to react. The bosses were of the opinion that Gorbachev wanted more of the same — but with a dash of modern efficiency. The workers were disgruntled because more was expected of them, as always, with fewer incentives.

Salt, matches and cigarettes, sewing thread and clothes, even vodka, were getting scarcer by the day, especially in the countryside. Andrei Fedorov, one of my first acquaintances, was the owner of Kropotkinskaya 36, a restaurant frequented by foreign dignitaries and nouveau riche Russians. President Mitterand, Secretary Shultz and President Carter, all visited Fedorov's restaurant. The food was typically Russian, with the whole gamut from blini to *morozhenoe* (ice cream) available at all times and served in a clean and pleasant environment. One could dine in an intimate space with large mirrors and porcelain candelabras upstairs, or in a large red-brick room that was probably once the cellar of a merchant's mansion. There were burnished brass samovars and authentic-looking Russian bric-à-brac in each of the many niches. Fancy china was set on crisp white tablecloths, and the list of wines included California and French, in place of the vinegary concoctions usually served in other establishments. The patron himself hovered over his guests and tended to their needs. Fedorov's place was considerably more welcoming than the cavernous but lifeless halls of official restaurants, with their bevy of listless waiters bunched up at the entrance, smoking cigarettes. To Soviet citizens this restaurant was dreamland — private enterprise at its best, although inaccessible to most budgets.

Fedorov, a man of great perspicacity regarding business in the Soviet Union, told me a story to illustrate the peculiar attitude the Russians had toward private enterprise. When, because of the growing supply problems, it became difficult for him to buy dairy and meat products for his restaurant, he decided to try to organize supplies directly from a kolkhoz in the vicinity of Moscow. He made an appointment with the kolkhoz management at ten o'clock one morning and rode out with his partner to talk to them. When he noticed only a few people in attendance, he surmised that the rest were already drunk. He told those present he could offer them ten times the pay they were getting from the government if they agreed to provide him with the fresh food his restaurant needed. Whereupon one of the women got up and said: 'You expect me to get up at the crack of dawn to slave for you. For money? What the devil do we need your money for? Better tell us if you can get us blouses, skirts ...' Others had a similar reaction. They could not see any reason to work more. They were quite satisfied to put in the usual few hours and be done with it. Housing, medical care, education and food were provided by their kolkhoz. They were not interested in more. Improving their lot meant a much greater workload. They did not believe they would be compensated for the greater effort with consumer goods. Fedorov gave up on his idea of working with the kolkhoz and sought out private entrepreneurs. He has not lacked supplies since.

The diplomats that I began visiting at this juncture to announce our active presence in Moscow were rather more optimistic about perestroika than the Soviet intelligentsia and public. The ambassador of Norway, rounding off his fifth year, was fluent in Russian and known to be knowledgeable about the country. He told me that Kremlin watchers inside and outside the USSR were either optimists or pessimists, depending more on their own disposition than on an objective reading of facts. The ambassador was among the optimists. Gorbachev will succeed, he said, as he was supported by a large number of technocrats and administrators who had seen the failure of the Soviet system back in the days of Brezhnev. Gorbachev was in his intellectual and physical prime and the Russians would eventually be infected by his enthusiasm. The Russians had hidden potential and ability and would forge ahead in spite of their inherited pessimism. He also quoted Abel Aganbegyan, Gorbachev's close associate at the time. Aganbegyan was a foremost economist, who was a member of the Novosibirsk Economic Institute, set up in the 1960s. The institute was involved in formulating several plans of economic reform on orders of the Politburo itself, but these plans were not acted upon because they were considered to be too radical and too encumbering on the leadership of the party. Toward the end of 1988 Aganbegyan was quoted as having said: 'We have retreated but a little from the edge of the abyss.' The other economists, as I could see, were no more enthusiastic than Aganbegyan about the course of developments. Those who understood the realities of the situation were highly pessimistic and fearful of the reforms, though they could see no other way out. Those who did not know the truth, like the general public, were even more worried and sceptical about Gorbachev's ability to maintain himself in power.

Diplomats believed the army was behind Gorbachev and would back him up against the diehards, should the need arise. Some western ambassadors thought their countries should support

Gorbachev and his reforms. They even advocated extending financial help to improve the theoretical and practical knowledge of the administrators, in order to apply the 'new economic thinking'. Others told me the USSR was concerned about Europe's rapid development and eventual economic unification in 1992. The Soviet Union's marked trend towards becoming a Third-World country would then become more obvious. Consequently, the argument went, Europe should support the Soviets in their economic development as this would have a positive world-wide effect. These sentiments were not shared by the American Embassy in Moscow, which, at the time, seemed to have a more detached approach.

Many of the people I met during those first days in Moscow spoke about an impressive return to religion. Property taken over under Stalin was being slowly but systematically returned to the Russian Orthodox (Pravoslav) Church. Church officials were beginning to fill a very strong need for spirituality and religion, methodically suppressed throughout the years of communist rule. The rapid deterioration of political authority and the gradual weakening of the Communist Party's hold over the population were leaving a void that was being readily filled with the traditional trappings of the Russian Orthodox establishment.

There were no parallel Jewish bodies. Unlike the Russian Orthodox who had been able to preserve a skeletal organization, albeit riddled with agents of the KGB, the Jews had lost all of their extensive pre-revolutionary network of synagogues and cultural and 'national' organizations. Since the October Revolution in 1917, under Lenin, Stalin and Khrushchev, all synagogues but a handful had been turned over to party and municipal organizations. One of the biggest, in the city of Kuibyshev (Saratov) on the Volga, housed a bread factory. The rabbinical schools had been closed, Hebrew and religious education had been proscribed. The few rabbis who remained were entirely subservient to the Central Committee and the KGB and had to report on the activities of their parishioners and events in the synagogues, including visits of foreigners.

The Soviet government was reluctant even to discuss returning property to the Jewish communities, which had virtually ceased to exist. Toward the end of 1988, important Jewish personalities, such as Edgar Bronfman, president of the World Jewish Congress, Rabbi Arthur Schneier of New York City, Rabbi Adin Steinsaltz, a great religious scholar from Jerusalem, Albert Reichman, the financier from Toronto and others, were actively engaged in trying to recover at least some of the buildings in question. Their goal was to renew Jewish cultural activity, including the study of Hebrew. Since the beginning of perestroika, prospects began to look a bit more promising, but there were still no concrete results.

Yet, the Soviet Union seemed to be changing. There was movement in the hearts and minds of the population and the Brezhnev period of stagnation was thought to have come to an end. However, as difficulties increased, Brezhnev's era was being remembered with nostalgia. My new acquaintances insisted the shops had been full of food, clothing, furniture and other necessities, at least in Moscow. Most would add: 'Well, maybe we had to use some connections, but the goods were there.' This was difficult to believe, but I discovered it was not always far from the truth. Many of the items I saw in some of the shops on my first trip were left over from the former supply network and had vanished on my subsequent visits.

The population was increasingly worried about the forced march toward a market economy. Every day brought new hardships in the process of transmutation from Soviet socialism. In spite of all the suffering and the tragedies of the past, the long periods of hunger and KGB horrors, this society had been protected from the bane of consumerism and a monetary economy. Basic food, lodging, education and employment were undisputed rights. Even though the government did not always provide these in sufficient measure, it was considered obligated to do so. As the impact of perestroika was felt and reforms began to bite into these accepted norms, many people, especially the very poor and the very privileged, began idealizing the past. Obstinate communists and establishment loyalists were worried about their privileges and their sacrosanct positions on the *nomenklatura* lists. The threats to the position of the privileged had not begun materializing yet, but concern over the future was already gripping their hearts.

I thought I should do some travelling before I concluded my term. The only city outside of Moscow which one could visit without a permit was Zagorsk, some 70 kilometres away. This was the seat of the Russian Orthodox Church, the Soviet Vatican. Once there, I was immensely impressed at the sight of soldiers in uniform at prayer. Soviet campaigns against all religion and mockery of religious trappings had given way to tolerance and even respect. To see soldiers crossing themselves, even bashfully, in front of the iconostasis in a church in Zagorsk was a revelation. For me, this was the first sure sign that communist power was collapsing. I remembered how suprised I had been, one day late in 1943 at the time of the defence of Stalingrad, when I saw a group of Soviet officers in Tehran wearing golden shoulder boards. Throughout the days of the Bolshevik Revolution and the Civil War, shoulder boards had been a mark of the tsarist anti-revolutionary White Army. White officers were executed for wearing these distinctive insignia. But in the dramatic days of 1943 Stalin suddenly restored the traditional shoulder boards to evoke greater patriotism and unity among the Russians. My whole conception of the Soviet Union was devastated, seeing those soldiers in their greatcoats, meekly standing in an ornate Russian church and making the sign of the cross.

Months later, Mikhail and Raisa Gorbachev went to visit West Germany. The Metropolitan Pitirim, a well-known Russian Orthodox clergyman, with his flowing beard, golden cross and tall white headgear, accompanied them to consecrate a Second World War Red Army cemetery. I sensed, once again, that the changes coming over the Soviet Union were more than just cosmetic.

After my trip to Zagorsk, I asked the protocol department of the Foreign Ministry to provide us with permission to visit Leningrad. After a while, our passports came back appropriately stamped and my assistant Yoav Baron and I took the 'Red Arrow' night train to Leningrad. We reserved a two-bed sleeper. After the stewardess brought us tea, we bolted the door against thieves and fell asleep as the train rushed past dimly lit villages under a blanket of heavy snow.

After a few hours I woke to the sound of a drunken male voice in the next compartment. It had a heavy Caucasian accent: 'You're shit', the man kept saying to someone. This went on for about a half hour, increasing in volume. From time to time another voice mumbled in reply, meant to calm his companion. After a time, in an alcohol-induced paroxysm, the man next door shouted: 'The Soviet Union is shit!' This was followed by long minutes of dreadful silence. Then, the train made an unscheduled stop at the nearest station. Someone burst into the neighbouring compartment and there was a loud argument. The drunken voice trailed away, protesting, through the corridor. As the train got under way, the same voice could be heard shrieking from the station at which we had stopped.

Leningrad was full of contrasts. The old Romanov palaces in the suburbs, full of grandeur, had been repaired and made to look as beautiful as in the days of Peter the Great and his heirs. The Germans had destroyed most of them, in a savagely vandalistic rage over their failure to take the city. Russian artisans had lovingly restored the lot over time and at tremendous expense. The population, however, looked bedraggled. People stood in lines in the snow, some for transportation, others for food or anything else that might be procured. The shortage of salt, matches and cigarettes was as acute in Leningrad as in Moscow. Other 'fancy' goods, such as meat and vegetables, were difficult to come by, in spite of our guide's assertions that Leningrad had thousands of acres of hothouses that 'supplied the city and its environs with all its needs'. In the evenings at the hotel I felt conscience-stricken eating the rich food laid on the tables for foreign tourists.

Our young guide, who had been showing us around, all the while extolling the virtues of communism, said we should visit the Nikolsky Church, 'to experience the majesty and the peace which embraces you as you enter and the expression of religious belief in the singing of the choir ...'. We went to Nikolsky and found all the guide's descriptions to have been true. The young administrator of the church shooed the beggars out. The lights were low and an atmosphere of mysticism set in during the vespers. Then the lights came on and the worshippers lustily joined the choir: 'Rejoice, oh Jesus / For we have kept our faith / For we have not transgressed / Rejoice, Jesus, we truly believe in your miracles / Rejoice, oh Doer of Great Deeds!' Young people were crossing themselves with a practised hand, and kissing the icons with marked devotion. I could not believe my eyes. Some 21 churches had been returned to the Leningrad patriarchate and more were on their way. I also saw a number of Hare Krishnas on the streets of the city and learned that they had been active for years at the universities. These were signs of a spiritual earthquake in this bastion of atheism.

Leningrad, the majestic capital of the Romanovs, was unkempt and badly in need of repairs. Its streets were full of giant pot-holes and the taxis careened to and fro to avoid them. A western city in architecture and layout, its population included many survivors of the long siege in the Second World War when nearly two million of its citizens died of starvation and bomb attacks. After the war nearby villagers were moved into the city to provide the workforce for the large industrial enterprises that make this city one of the most important economic centres of Russia. Most of these newcomers were housed in enormous blocs, ugly and rundown 'monsters', as the locals called them, at the outer periphery of this beautiful city. In spite of the hardships and difficult times and Leningrad's shabby appearance, a sense of pride and aristocratic tradition were noticeable in the behaviour and speech of some of the old-timers.

We went to see the central synagogue, a remnant of former days of glory, built at the turn of the century by a famous Jewish industrialist, Baron Horace Ginsburg. The synagogue was deserted. We had to hunt for the official caretaker and wait while he brought the keys and looked us over with great suspicion. He seemed to be quite disturbed about meeting the head of the Israeli mission, and I had a difficult time persuading him to show us the inside of the synagogue, a large and impressive building. In my childhood in Tehran I had lived with the Kotlers, St Petersburg Jews who had left the city for Berlin after the Revolution. Elisabeth Kotler was the daughter of the Chief Sephardic Rabbi of St Petersburg, himself a scion of an ancient Spanish family, the Don Yikhyas. Elisabeth had been married in the special wedding chapel of the Ginsburg synagogue and I was deeply moved to see that it was still intact and as beautiful as she had described it to me.

The Jews of Leningrad were in flux. Everyone was talking about emigration, though at that time most were leaving for the US. I had introductions to a number of Jewish activists. In spite of the attractions of the US, many were engaged in the study of Hebrew, an activity just emerging out of clandestinity, to which many young and older people had taken with enthusiasm. Hebrew teachers had materialized from nowhere, usually knowing just enough to teach rudiments to others. There was a dearth of textbooks and literature on Israel and few details on the immigration process. I was swamped by hundreds of questions regarding problems such as how much baggage was paid for by the government, how to get official personal documents such as diplomas through the customs, the status of non-Jewish members of family, what pensions would Soviet war veterans receive and many more.

Everywhere I went, I was met by large numbers of Jews, though at that time it was still considered risky to consort with the head of the Israeli mission. Members of our mission in Moscow who were sent out by the Lishka had growing contact with the Jews of Leningrad as well as many other cities, but communication was still a problem and every opportunity was being used to spread the word. Yoav Baron and I visited a number of Jewish families, but in spite of their goodwill, there were still many signs of apprehension, a lot of looking about, checking of doors and a general fear of exposing themselves to the scrutiny of the ever present KGB and the neighbourhood informers. Although we were evidently followed around by members of the security services, they were not apparent to our untrained eyes. On one occasion, however, while we sat in an apartment deep in discussion over Israel and the prospects of immigration, there was a knock on the door. No other guests were expected and our host paled as he got up to answer. There was a longish, calm, but insistent, conversation and when he came back he looked confident. A captain of the militia had called to find out what the gathering was all about. Our host told him, politely but firmly, that it was not his business to knock on the door and inquire, and that Stalin's days were over. The militiaman was so taken aback by this statement that he just nodded and left.

I had very much wanted to see the official museum of the city's defence during the siege. It was closed that day for 'sanitary inspection'. We took the 'Red Arrow' back to Moscow and arrived there the next morning, this time with no incidents.

4 · Access through Research

My requests for contacts at the political level continued to be rebuffed. This was not really surprising, as the whole nature of our relations with the Soviet government were still *sub rosa*. The Russians kept insisting their consular group's presence in Israel was non-political and was necessary only in the interests of taking care of their property. They wanted to avoid unnecessary embarrassment *vis-à-vis* the Arabs and quietly establish a political dialogue with Israeli leaders through informal channels. The Israeli public, however, was awarding the Soviet consular group full recognition and acceptance. Fraternization with Israelis was discouraged by higher authorities, but the Soviet group slowly gained enough confidence to make contacts with Israeli leaders and public figures. The Russians were sought after and wined and dined. Although Yevgeny Martirosov, the head of the group, conscientiously kept his prescribed low profile, he could pick up the phone and call anyone he wanted.

There was a clear imbalance in this situation, and I tried my best to persuade our officials to demand reciprocity. I was convinced the Russians needed a presence in Israel at least as much as we needed one in Moscow, even if for entirely different reasons. In a country as small as Israel where most people knew each other, it was inadvisable and virtually impossible to force the Russians to lower their profile. It was also impractical to limit their travel in Israel, in retaliation for the severe restrictions imposed on us, as on all foreigners. Yet contacts with government officials and the granting of privileges could be used to equalize our status. It was well-known that the Russians were extremely sensitive about their diplomatic privileges and would go to great lengths to defend and maintain them. There was, however, little response in Israel to my persistent requests, though everyone knew there was no other leverage we could use. Our officials were so elated over the opportunity of seeing and speaking with 'real live' Soviet officials in Israel that they threw all good sense to the wind. In Moscow, we were living in a run-down hotel, had no international communications, no diplomatic identity cards and could not work out of our own embassy, for which we were paying rent. The Russians could live anywhere they chose. They could receive identity papers, but refused our offers to grant them out of fear we would demand ours. In Israel they could pick up the telephone and reach someone in the USSR or anywhere else in the world. This possibility was not accorded to us in Moscow: the government controlled all communications. We spent literally days on end trying to order calls to Israel with a 24-hour delay or more, and having our requests sidetracked by the operator. There were other problems, all stemming from the inability of the Russians to accept our presence on their soil.

In Moscow, Soviet leaders and officials refrained from meeting members of our mission. When I phoned government agencies and asked for information or requested appointments, there was palpable fear at the end of the line. 'And what is your status?' was the usual question. When I attempted to explain, 'a representative of Israel, attached to the Dutch Embassy', there would be hesitation, tinged with fear and resolved in a string of predictable excuses. This was not true of my contacts with foreign diplomats and the press corps, but that was not what I was after in those first days. The Dutch Embassy was unrelenting in its efforts to make the Russians change their sterile attitude and establish contacts between me and the political departments of the Foreign Ministry, to no avail. The US Embassy was supportive as well, in imparting a sense of security and advising on contacts. American Embassy staff carefully monitored Middle East and Jewish affairs, and were good listeners and responsive when we needed their help. On occasion they would put questions to the authorities regarding some of the issues that concerned us, which made the Soviets aware of American interest.

The American Embassy advised me to try to establish a working relationship with the political research institutes. In fact, I had already, inadvertently, made one such contact. Gideon Rafael, a former director-general of the Israeli Ministry of Foreign Affairs, who had contacts with Soviet researchers, had been invited with Professor Galia Golan, a sovietologist of the Hebrew University of Jerusalem, to an international conference in Pushchino, near Moscow, in November 1988. The minister of the Dutch Embassy, Willem Bentinck, invited us both to a luncheon at his home with some people from the Institute for Oriental Studies of the Academy of Sciences, which were acting as the government think-tank on the Middle East. The institute was headed for years by Professor Mikhail Kapitsa, a Middle East expert who had been the front-man for various Soviet 'peace initiatives' and contacts with the Arabs. Kapitsa, a cantankerous defender of the party line, was given to outbursts of self-righteous temper.

I arrived at Bentinck's apartment on the appointed day only to discover that Rafael had departed for Leningrad. When the members of the institute heard of Rafael's absence and saw me, they refused to sit down to lunch and wanted to leave. Bentinck had to use his best powers of persuasion to convince the Russians to get acquainted with the representative of the Israeli government or at least sit down at the table for a few minutes. The Russians reluctantly agreed but sank into a torpid silence. I knew they could resist anything but a provocation. That I had learned over my four years at the UN in New York, when, on many occasions, I crossed swords with them. I made a few remarks about Soviet responsibility for the 1967 war and their mistakes following it. This the scholars from the Oriental Institute could not ignore and a hot, loud debate ensued, especially with Irina Zviagelskaya, deputy to the head of Middle East affairs. The other participant, Vladimir Nosenko, who dealt with Israel and Jordan, appeared to be less disputatious. Nosenko was transferred to the Foreign Ministry in 1992, and in summer 1993 was appointed minister plenipotentiary of the Russian Embassy in Tel Aviv.

After a while, as lunch was served, we began conversing in more civil tones; maybe it was the excellent meal itself, served in the typically West European setting of the Bentincks' apartment, so different from the usual Moscow décor. The Dutch minister's diplomatic skills were also helpful in putting the Russians in a more conducive mood, though we all energetically defended our points of view over the Middle East conflict. This unintended confrontation turned out to be the beginning of a long-lasting contact. Eventually it grew into a solid connection and friendship with the institute's members, including Zviagelskaya, Nosenko and others. I also developed excellent relations with the head of the institute's Middle East studies department, Vitaly Naumkin, a brilliant scholar, very well versed in the problems of our area. Having studied at the University of Cairo, Naumkin had a feel for the region that grew out of his first-hand knowledge and many personal connections. He has been at the institute for many years and at the time of writing is using his considerable expertise, with his other colleagues, in researching Central Asia and the Middle East.

I was surprised to discover that the institute followed Middle East developments almost exclusively through Arab sources. At first I ascribed this to its evident political leanings. The material it was publishing had for many years borne a decidedly anti-Israeli and anti-Zionist character. I soon realized, however, that the institute also suffered from professional weaknesses. It did not have a regular supply of unclassified information from Israeli sources, its newspapers were outdated, and its Hebrew-speaking researchers few. That having been said, one of the staff, Nina Sementchenko, raised in Petah Tikva near Tel Aviv, spoke fluent Hebrew with a strong colloquial flavour that was delightful to hear. Nina came from a family of Subbotniki who came to Palestine in the 1920s. The Subbotniki were a Russian sect which first emerged in the eighteenth century and which observed the Jewish Sabbath as well as other customs and traditions. Subjected to cruel persecution at the beginning of the twentieth century, a number of them adopted Judaism and settled in Palestine. I met her many times when she was acting as interpreter, and at every encounter with Israelis someone would remark on her local Petah Tikva accent, so typical of the town where she grew up.

In those first days, the Bentinck luncheon served to introduce me to an organization with close ties to the Ministry of Foreign Affairs and other departments — such as the KGB and GRU — which dealt with Israel-related questions. I was thus satisfied that our point of view might now begin to get across.

In the first weeks of my stay in Moscow I realized how dependent Soviet official thinking was on experts of the party Central Committee, who guided by ideology, drew their information largely from intelligence sources and research institutes. So important was the role of these research institutes, that their directors were represented at summit conferences. Georgy Arbatov, director of the Institute for the Study of the USA and Canada, and Yevgeny Primakov, head of the International Relations and Economics Institute (IMEMO), were present at the Reykjavik summit in 1986. The institutes' recommendations, however, did not always end up as policy, which was determined by the complex interrelationships between the leaders of the Politburo, the Central Committee and government agencies. The Soviet positions on the Middle East, on Israel and the PLO, at the time of my arrival, reflected stilted and regurgitated thinking, in reality a resistance to badly needed change. Soviet Middle East experts, aware of the regional realities, could not bring themselves to forcefully recommend changes; at least, such recommendations were not reflected in Soviet Middle East policy. A tradition of close contacts with the Arabs and none with Israel over the 20-odd years after 1967, as well as an exaggerated sense of personal loyalty toward some Arab leaders, strongly affected Soviet behaviour. The other considerations centred around the Middle East as a pawn in the wider international game. This was true especially of the USSR's stance with regard to the US. It was quite clear that Soviet Middle East policy reflected perceived western attitudes toward the region, rather than of bilateral considerations between the Soviet Union and individual Middle Eastern countries. A clear indication was the existence of a 'desk' on American Middle East policy at the USA and Canada Institute.

After an initial meeting with the American deputy chief of mission, John Joyce, I was invited to dinner at Eric Edelman's residence. Edelman was first secretary in charge of Middle Eastern affairs at the embassy. His house was in a row of smart brick duplexes situated within the new US Embassy compound, notorious for the electronic bugs discovered in the main chancellery building before its completion. At that dinner I became reacquainted with Judith Kipper of the Brookings Institution in Washington DC. I had met Kipper before in Jerusalem when I was head of political research. She was well-known there for her extensive knowledge and connections in the Middle East. Andrei Shumikhin, head of the Middle East 'desk' at the USA and Canada Institute had also been invited. He was an old UN hand, had worked in New York as a translator, travelled widely in the US and had written a doctorate on US-Israel relations. Eventually, he was transferred to the USA and Canada Institute to replace Alexander Kislov, who was returning to IMEMO, an institute with considerable influence in government. Kislov became Yevgeny Primakov's deputy at IMEMO.

This group of Soviet scholars, whom I was getting to know during my first stint in Moscow, were all very deeply engaged in the problems of the Middle East and were on call by the agencies which dealt with the region. This was a sort of 'old boys' network, all graduates of the same schools, closely connected and aware of the general trend of affairs and developments in the countries of the Middle East. There was a grapevine that kept everyone abreast of news. For that reason, I was certain that every word uttered by me would be passed around. The first appearance of a senior Israeli Foreign Ministry official in Moscow aroused curiosity.

At the Edelman dinner I achieved two very important objectives. First, after gentle nudging by Edelman and Kipper, a meeting was arranged with Andrei Shumikhin, who suggested I come to the USA and Canada Institute and talk to the researchers about Israel and our view of the Middle East. This was an invitation very few Israelis had received. My second achievement, perhaps less important but not less complicated, was obtaining a list of restaurants in Moscow.

After frustrating attempts to reach my new acquaintance, Shumikhin, on the phone, I finally fixed a date for my visit to the institute. When I arrived, Shumikhin brought me into a long conference hall on the second floor and sat himself down across from me at an empty table. For some reason the promised meeting with the scholars of the institute had not materialized. Shumikhin devoted the following two hours entirely to me. From his numerous and largely naïve questions about the political scene in Israel I could surmise that Israel was not his favourite topic of research and that the Soviet authorities knew little enough about it. Shumikhin freely admitted to this fact: Hebraic and Jewish Studies had been almost completely abandoned over the years in most universities and research institutions. Experts were now being sought to revitalize this area of research.

The lack of information and the weak analysis of the Israeli political scene were unexpected. The Soviet Union had been depicting us for years as one of the chief culprits in the West, arrayed against the USSR. Even if this line of propaganda was only for the masses at first, in later years the Soviets began believing in their own fabrications, judging by the amount of attention paid Israel as a mini-superpower in the Middle East. Israel was in fact caught in the East-West confrontation, and Soviet policy toward it was an expression of the USSR's international strategies. I found it difficult to understand the exaggeration of our importance, on the one hand, and the dearth of research devoted to us, on the other.

Shumikhin answered a number of questions himself. Maybe he too felt my queries reflected a lack of understanding of life in the USSR. He gave me some definitions which were very curious indeed. These descriptions and assessments of Soviet practice served me as guidelines, as I delved deeper into life in the Soviet Union. Among other things, he said everyone in the USSR realized that the 1967 decision to severe relations with Israel had been a mistake. However, the USSR would not act like a western country; it had a conservative outlook on the world and hated change or abandonment of advantages in foreign policy garnered over a long period of time. The Soviet Union, he added, was wary of adopting new and untried methods that might weaken its assets without necessarily gaining new ones. This was true of the USSR's economy, military, its international relations as well as its relations with the Middle East. As to Israel, he added, to my incredulous ears, the USSR believed the US and its Jews would never allow an improvement of relations with the Soviet Union in the areas of culture, economy, academia, and certainly not in international relations. The Jewish lobby would exert great political and financial pressures on Israel not to change its inimical attitude toward the USSR. To this Shumikhin added a request: would I please provide him with information on the Israel lobby in the US, its organization and the methods it uses in gaining influence. The only other example of such a direct, head-on request for information on the Israel lobby in the US that I could remember was thrown at me in Tokyo, at the Foreign Ministry's Political Research Institute. The question was abrupt in both cases and contained a great dose of *chutzpah*. I referred Shumikhin, as I did my Japanese friends, to open sources on the subject.

Shumikhin then gave an example to back up his theories: Israeli President Herzog's congratulatory telegram on 9 May, the anniversary of victory over Nazi Germany, was prominently publicized in the Soviet press. Initially, it was widely believed to signal a warming of relations between the two countries. Many regretted that the government of Israel did not follow up this encouraging message. Now the Soviets were expecting a new, conciliatory message to the USSR, accompanied by a gesture of magnanimity to the PLO. It was true, he added, everyone knew about the mistakes of the past, 1967 and the rest of it, but the Russians would love to be able to show substantive political and economic gains in return for the renewal of ties. Shumikhin finally stated that he would be eager to help in changing the impressions we had of the USSR, by exchanging visits — delegations, researchers, individuals. He himself was looking forward to a possible visit, although there were 'bureaucratic difficulties'.

In the course of this long and revealing conversation, a General Radomir Bogdanov popped his head through the door and said he wanted to see me in a few days, after he returned from his trip abroad. I had had no knowledge of Bogdanov, deputy to the head of the USA and Canada Institute and a professor at the Diplomatic Academy of the Foreign Ministry. A former high official in the KGB, Bogdanov had the distinction of being named in *KGB*, John Barron's book about that organization, first published in 1974. The book's revelations about the inner workings of the KGB were considered sensational at the time. Bogdanov had served in Poland

and some ten years in India. Toward the end of his stay in India, he had acted as KGB station chief. He was dismissed from India, apparently as a result of Svetlana Alliluyeva's elopement with an Indian citizen during an official tour in Delhi. Stalin's daughter was watched over by a large group of KGB agents specially detailed to follow and 'protect' her but she managed to disappear nonetheless, embarrassing her chaperons. In Barron's later book, *The KGB Today*, Bogdanov was described as a typical functionary of the twelfth department of the First Chief Directorate. This department was staffed with senior KGB officers, who had gained experience abroad, and their assignment was the recruitment of foreigners living in the USSR. Barron claimed that Bogdanov was using the USA and Canada Institute as a cover.

Bogdanov presented himself as an expert on questions of disarmament. He had written articles on this issue in specialized journals and taught the subject at the Foreign Ministry's Diplomatic Academy. The academy had conferred on him the title of 'Professor'. Whatever his professional qualities as a KGB officer, Bogdanov was also a man of the world, with great reserves of caustic humour and an appetite for good food and good times, although he suffered from a severe heart condition. He displayed a good deal of interest in pushing 'business' (an English word he used with great relish in Russian conversation). He was trying to use his connections to that end, and 'helping out friends', he said. He was connected with some international Jewish personalities, such as the president of the World Jewish Congress, Edgar Bronfman, and later kept me abreast of the latter's comings and goings in Moscow. This seemed to be flying a bit high for the twelfth department, but who knows, I thought. In any case, Bogdanov never tried to recruit me. He seemed quite a sick and spent KGB officer who was, in any case, not trying to hide his identity. In fact, I found him quite useful.

In Moscow of the early perestroika days there was a widening circle of former KGB, Central Committee and other personalities from Soviet institutions who were beginning to look beyond their occupations, searching for connections and contacts with the outside world. Their main pole of attraction was usually moneyed foreigners who could assure a steady income or occasional

41

remuneration for services rendered. When I arrived in November 1988 the appetites of these individuals had not yet reached the proportions of today. Western businessmen had their favourite influence peddlers or gate openers — Russians who were working for the benefit of their patrons while still continuing their employment in various government or other offices. The ethics of these contacts were open to interpretation. There was no clear-cut opprobrium attached to involvement with foreigners. What probably started out as assignments by the KGB or other organizations for initiating contacts with moneyed foreigners, gradually turned into private projects for the individuals involved. This development reflected a general deterioration of discipline. It was, however, foolhardy to forget the bonds that continued to exist between people like Bogdanov and their former employers. I always assumed that most of my remarks would be reported. With a certain amount of caution, these channels could be used to transmit desired messages.

In time, as the erosion of authority increased, so did the manoeuvrability of those who were acting on behalf of foreigners. People like Bogdanov became more driven by their own interests, which was only natural. The number of people who were involved and the area of their activity were increasing with the arrival of perestroika. I came across these people in many walks of life, including government agencies, the Academy of Sciences, the arts, commerce and others. As notions of market economy began coming into their own, the atmosphere changed, and the secret services relaxed their surveillance, or did not follow through with the intelligence they were collecting.

One often had the impression that people on the inside were either simply jealous of their enterprising colleagues or wanted to share in their good fortune, and sometimes did. At the end of 1988 and in 1989 logistics in Moscow were extremely problematic. Connections and contacts, as well as bribes — ever on the increase — were used to rent offices, provide telephone lines, and obtain airplane tickets and hotel rooms payable in roubles. Introductions to industrialist bosses were also important. In this way raw materials or semi-finished goods could be obtained for markets in the West. This caused great chagrin to diehard communists or devotees of the Soviet system in industry. The idea of exporting raw materials, rather than finished goods, was understandably unattractive. Many of the captains of Soviet industry that I met often said the needs of the Soviet Union were so great in reconstruction and the renewal of infrastructure, that export was a waste of resources and time. These attitudes began changing, but at a slow pace. The grip of the so-called administrative and command system over the Soviet economy was far too great. On the other hand, the 'joint venture' theme in business, so popular with the Soviets, was not backed up by solid legislation and rarely fared well. Flights coming into Moscow from Europe were full of optimistic businessmen who wanted to exploit the grey areas and what seemed like good opportunities. Most of these fortune seekers usually returned to their countries disappointed. Even so, the seeds of the growing turnover in trade with the outside world were sown several years before, when these connections were just being established.

After that first meeting with Andrei Shumikhin, I was invited out to lunch by Bogdanov. Shumikhin and Alla Bobrisheva were also there, the latter a veteran of the USA and Canada Institute and the spouse of a Soviet writer and war hero, Ovidi Gorchakov. We talked at great length about Bogdanov and Shumikhin's upcoming visit to Israel. The tour was finally organized and they set out for Israel in early March 1989, via Cyprus. The official host was the Israel-USSR Friendship League — a Communist Party front organization — though Shumikhin swore it had nothing to do with the Israeli Communist Party. The Israel Foreign Relations Association was also involved, but I had asked the Foreign Ministry to look into the programme, to guide our guests to get better acquainted with Israel's human and economic landscape.

Bogdanov and Shumikhin were the first important guests to arrive in Israel from the Soviet Union, who were not communist activists or hostile journalists. In the years that preceded 1989 most visitors were invited by the Israeli Communist Party and came to support their activities in Israel. I knew Bogdanov had to report back to the KGB or the Central Committee about the state of affairs in Israel. I was convinced that the information Bogdanov would take back with him would be positive and help change the adverse image of Israel imprinted on the minds of the professionals who dealt with Israeli affairs. I managed to be present in Israel when these two gentlemen arrived, and although I could not participate in their activities, I tried to keep track of them. Shumikhin told me the USSR was mainly interested in learning about Israel's ability to invest in the Soviet Union. He said his country wanted to obtain modern technology and produce goods which might eventually be sold on the American and European markets using Israel's privileged status in those areas. The Russians also wanted to know more about Israel's modern agriculture and its possible benefits to the USSR.

When Bogdanov arrived in Israel, however, he settled in at the Dan Hotel, situated on the Tel Aviv beach, and declared himself perfectly satisfied spending his time watching the pretty girls. He refused to leave the hotel. He said he had absolutely no interest in seeing the country, only getting acquainted with prominent businessmen. This sounded the alarm for me. I was certain he had received orders from some agency in Moscow to limit his movement to business contacts only. On one of his first mornings in Tel Aviv I found him having breakfast with David Kimche, a former director-general of the Foreign Ministry and the vice-president of our Foreign Relations Association. I noticed Bogdanov wearing a skull-cap and asked him if he was Jewish. 'No', he said, 'I'm just wearing it to protect my bald spot from the draft.' It took us another two days of effort to persuade Bogdanov to leave the hotel and see the kibbutzim and some of the country. He was more than pleased to be introduced to important financiers like Shaul Eisenberg, with whom he discussed large-scale business opportunities.

When the trip was nearing its end, I asked Bogdanov what his impressions were. 'I am completely overwhelmed', he answered. 'They have been feeding us lies and criminal propaganda all these years. This is a modern, vibrant, strong and expanding country the like of which I have but rarely seen. When I return I shall write a big article to present the real picture. You can count on that.' I consulted with Shumikhin, who was rather concerned about Bogdanov's reactions at first, but agreed with every word he had said. Shumikhin had gone off on his own and met some people in academia to discuss possible joint plans for research and exchanges of visits. Our guests departed with their conceptions of Israel completely transformed. Bogdanov did send an extensive article to *Argumenty i Fakty*, a bi-weekly that had an unbelievable circulation of over 26 million and was respected for its truthful presentations of current and popular themes. The journal printed Bogdanov's article only a year later and then in much abbreviated form. By that time Israel had shed its taboo status and Bogdanov's impressions were not news.

After this trip Bogdanov and I became good friends. He still had the aura of a former important KGB 'general' about him. In fact, he was a colonel. His small entourage respected and feared him, but were also extremely loyal to him, for he looked after their interests. Bogdanov's rougher edges were smoothed when he left the institute and became a business consultant.

The other research institute I made a point of visiting, and was allowed to do so after what appeared to have been consultations with the Soviet Foreign Ministry, was IMEMO. This institute was headed at the time by Yevgeny Primakov, himself very close to the decision makers of the Central Committee and the intelligence organizations. He had had a considerable number of meetings with Israeli political leaders, including Begin and Peres, and had visited Israel on several occasions. Primakov was appointed head of the foreign intelligence arm of the security services in 1991.

I was received by Robert Markaryan, a relatively young researcher (later Primakov's personal assistant), who was also a member of this inner circle of people in government think-tanks. The conversation did not go beyond the declarative positions of the Soviet government: the PLO had become more flexible and wanted peace, Arafat had taken great strides towards peace and should be negotiated with, and the like. Markaryan added a new point: the Soviet government was drawing closer to the US on the subject of the Middle East, one of the last and most important areas of discord between the powers. I detected a subtle tone in Markaryan's words that was slightly more positive than most on the questions of the region. There was greater openness and willingness to listen, the responses were not harsh and dogmatic and the reception more friendly.

These meetings were extremely important for me in those initial days in Moscow. I was discovering more and more that to the Soviets, Israel was *terra incognita*, a fact that surprised me and gave me an excellent opportunity to explain our positions. With the attitude the Foreign Ministry had taken of isolating our mission completely from the government and the public, I could at least depend on the 'research channel' to pass on important information, of which few seemed to be aware. With time, the research institutes proved to be useful in many other ways.

5 · An Introduction to Shevardnadze

By the end of November 1988, Soviet stonewalling of our requests for political contacts and exchanges of visits had become a stumbling block to improving relations with the USSR. We thought better contacts in Moscow might help in furthering freer emigration to Israel. The important matter of inaugurating direct flights also was being constantly put off, evidently for political reasons. This was all a heavy burden imposed on relations between the two countries. The world around us was becoming more communicative in international relations and old prejudices were fading like dying leaves. Soviet stubbornness was counter to the spirit of perestroika that the Russians were crowing about. People abroad, in their naïveté, were giving exaggerated credence to perestroika and its spirit. After the bloody history of Russia in the twentieth century, Gorbachev and his policy of perestroika were a sight for sore western eyes. Political leaders and public servants in Israel, too, were captivated. They were confident that, given half a chance, they could now persuade the Soviets, through unassailable logic, to change their demeanour toward us. The ambition was understandable but the way some went about it was, at times, undignified.

There were many attempts to crash the Soviet gates. Two stand out in their tragi-comic nakedness: the uninvited visits to Moscow of the Foreign Ministry's director-general, Abrasha Tamir, and of the minister of agriculture, Avraham Katz-Oz. The latter arrived in

1989 and I will relate it in a different context. Tamir's visit came in November 1988, just a few weeks after my own arrival in Moscow.

General Avraham (Abrasha) Tamir is well-known in Israel and abroad as a brilliant strategist and a highly original, resourceful and versatile thinker. He was one of the first people to conceptualize and openly promote the idea of possible territorial and political compromises in our ongoing conflict with the Palestinians. At the time of his arrival at the Foreign Ministry in 1987 he was already a self-proclaimed dove. Abrasha was an appointee of Ezer Weizmann, the former commander of the air force, future Israeli president and a political ally of Shimon Peres. Peres was foreign minister in 1987 as part of the 'rotation' arrangements of the coalition with the Likud Party.

I had never worked with Tamir, though I knew him when he was head of the planning division of the General Staff. He was never an easy person to get along with, but I always enjoyed reporting to him in his office at the ministry and would leave enriched with new ideas and perspectives on problems that seemingly defied solutions.

Tamir had an uncontrollable desire to visit the Soviet Union. As a military man and strategist, he felt compelled to see the lay of the land. First and foremost, however, Abrasha felt that he could find political understanding in the USSR regarding prospects for future relations with the Palestinians. Abrasha was wrong. The Soviets did not want to talk politics with him. They must have known he did not represent anyone but himself, and perhaps Ezer Weizmann. At this time the Soviet Foreign Ministry was already having an 'affair' with Shimon Peres, in secret meetings held between assistants of Peres and Foreign Minister Eduard Shevardnadze.

Thus, Tamir's attempts to obtain a visa through the usual channels failed, but he persisted. He decided on a direct course of action. He requested a visa from the Soviet Embassy in Denmark, where he was on a staff visit. In those days the Soviets wanted to avoid any implications of political contacts with us and were extremely stringent in permitting entry to Israeli visitors. They refused to grant General Tamir a diplomatic visa. After negotiations, however, they stamped a businessman's visa into his diplomatic passport. I had no warning of Abrasha's arrival, only frantic last minute telephone calls from various embassies announcing his flight. The story was leaked to the Israeli press, which hysterically attacked Tamir for going to Russia without an official invitation.

This was not the visit I had been praying for at that time. I certainly could have done without the adverse propaganda which accompanied it. I had just enough time to rush to Sheremetyevo airport and catch Tamir going through customs. I stood dutifully in line with him for inspection as he had no diplomatic privileges with his businessman's visa. The customs inspector mercilessly demanded to be shown the cash Tamir had declared on his customs declaration and Abrasha had to dig into his pockets, fish the money out and count the bills one by one, all of which was most embarrassing and enervating. We finally got through and I took him to our Ukraina Hotel. He had no reservation, but there was no alternative. We had to double up in one of our rooms to let him use a bed reserved for our mission. Tamir disappeared into his room, only to emerge a few minutes later, naked, shouting that he had no soap. 'What is this, the days of Palmach* all over again?'

Not a single official agreed to meet Tamir, in spite of my repeated pleas. It was against policy. The spokesman of the Foreign Ministry was asked by reporters about the Tamir visit and all he had to say was that Tamir was an uninvited guest and would not be seeing anyone. Our own journalists had a field day with the visit, going out of their way to say nasty things. Personally, I liked neither the cynicism of the Soviets nor the Israeli press's greediness for scandals, but there was nothing I could do for Abrasha, much though I wanted to.

With nothing else more substantive on our schedule, I took my director-general to the opera. Tamir's first night in Moscow was extremely cold and damp. He did not have the right clothes. He was hatless and wearing thin-soled oxfords; he stubbornly refused to put someone else's hat on his head. That night they were performing Borodin's *Prince Igor* at the Kremlin Congress Hall. As we crossed the stone bridge leading into the Kremlin, Abrasha

---

* Jewish commando units which operated during the Mandatory period in Palestine, known for their spartan training.

slipped on the ice-covered cobblestones and started loudly complaining about the extreme cold. 'Mummy, I'm going to die', he whimpered. I told him it would not do for him to die. Making arrangements for the transportation of a coffin containing the body of a director-general out of Soviet Russia, I said, was a costly and most complicated affair. It was quite beyond my capabilities at that time. But all these problems were promptly forgotten once the curtain went up. Abrasha loved the performance and completely identified with the heroes. In one scene the Polovets Tatars burned Prince Igor's city, Putivl, while he was away campaigning against them. The flames shooting up around the houses were so realistic that Abrasha worriedly asked me if the stage was not on fire. I reassured him. A few moments later, with Igor still away fighting the enemy, Abrasha was desolate over Prince Galitsky's cavalier behaviour toward Prince Igor's wife Yaroslavna. His lively commentary became explosive when he realized Prince Igor was coming back from captivity without his son, Vladimir (who had fallen in love with the Polovets Khan's daughter). 'How dare he leave his son in captivity!' I must say I fully shared the sentiments of my director-general although I was a trifle less carried away, due perhaps in part to our neighbours' constant attempts to calm the disturbance we were causing. At the intermission I was asked where we were from. 'Afghanistan', I replied.

The behaviour of the Soviet authorities toward General Tamir was shameful and politically foolish. They had an excellent opportunity to discuss mutual points of interest with an authoritative, perspicacious and friendly Israeli official. They risked nothing and could have gained a great deal of important information and insight into the strategic outlook of Israel, and a better understanding of its genuine concerns. It was typical of the Foreign Ministry to arrogantly reject Tamir and prefer to talk clandestinely with politicians of their own choosing. When they later agreed to talk with Ezer Weizmann on his visit to Moscow, they had apparently learned this lesson but applied it in a heavy-handed and self-defeating manner.

Toward the end of November 1988, there was a great earthquake in the Republic of Armenia. Whole cities and villages were ravaged, some wiped off the map. Scores of people were killed, thousands rendered homeless. It was a disaster on a mammoth scale and international offers of aid started coming in right away. Israel also volunteered help, proposing to send in a military field hospital with personnel, food and a team of experts with dogs to search for survivors buried under the debris. This was a humanitarian gesture, proffered in spite of the harsh attitude of the Soviet government and the absence of official relations. After some initial hesitation, a decision was made by the Soviet government to accept our contribution, even if it did originate in Israel. Our aid was to be flown in directly from Israel in a military airplane and all of us in Moscow awaited it with excitement. I was afforded an opportunity to make contact with the Ministry of Foreign Affairs in order to formally offer this aid, and later to coordinate landing arrangements for our plane. This was also done through the Soviet representation in Israel.

I asked the Foreign Ministry for permission to be on hand as the representative of the state when our transport plane landed in Armenia. Whether for logistical or political reasons, this request was denied, as indeed it was for other embassies in Moscow. The difficulty, the Foreign Ministry said, was the lack of proper facilities to service the diplomats and journalists who wanted to go out there. This was hardly credible. While it would have been complicated to handle visitors, we all suspected that in fact the Soviet government did not want foreigners to see the extent of the disorder and the bitterness of the Armenians. The operation was complex. Most of the infrastructure had disappeared in the initial tremor and the ones that followed. In Israel we are relatively well prepared for such eventualities, having had considerable experience in similar disasters resulting from terrorist acts. Our representatives were very warmly received by the Armenian population and gave an excellent account of themselves. The field hospital we put up remained on the spot for a number of months. A year later, the American Jewish Joint Distribution Committee (JDC) opened a children's hospital in Stepanakert and staffed it with Israeli doctors. Israel's activities in Armenia were widely publicized in the USSR, where the population had been used to hearing only negative reports and had been conditioned to identify Israel as an enemy state.

Several months later, I flew to Erevan from Moscow to join up with the first plane load of wounded Armenians being transported to Israel to be fitted with artificial limbs. We were flown down in an El Al plane — the Israeli air carrier's first flight ever to Erevan. The Armenian government warmly welcomed us. We were given an official lunch, with Israeli and Armenian flags decorating the tables and words of appreciation to the State of Israel — an act of courage in those days. I was especially cognizant of the Armenians' political dilemma: some weeks before, in the aftermath of the earthquake, Gorbachev had been prevailed upon to fly out to see the carnage with his own eyes. In the process, he responded with great brutality to questions about Armenia's dream of political independence. He strongly implied that those who dared to pursue such ambitions would be severely punished.

It was widely rumoured that the hasty apartment-building activity in the Khrushchev era was responsible for the massive damage to housing. At that time, as a result of pressure from Moscow, government contractors had had to complete their jobs in record time and were not overly mindful of building standards. In addition, there was a lot of pilfering of cement and iron reinforcements. The construction activity advanced rapidly and there were celebrations as thousands of people were given keys to the first apartments they had ever owned. The deficiencies, however, made the houses topple like dominoes at the first serious earthquake, which occurred in 1988. The recurrent shocks took additional victims and the situation was bitterly exacerbated by the advent of winter. The Soviet government made inefficient use of the generous aid given by many foreign countries. There was a great deal of mismanagement in handling funds, food and building materials. Armenian friends from the US, passing through Moscow on their way to Erevan, told me of the complete unpreparedness of the country to receive help and the incompetence in dealing with it. People had nowhere to seek shelter. Armenia was, unfortunately, in the news for quite a number of weeks. As misfortune brings people together, so did this tragedy. Israel's active participation in the rescue operations, and its subsequent relief to the suffering population became widely known and acknowledged.

At this point, my endeavours were beginning to have some

limited effect in getting the Soviet government to soften its resentment toward our mission. I was not hindered from broadening my contacts with the research institutes and with many private individuals. Foreign Ministry officials were not very happy about my good connections with the diplomatic corps in Moscow, but I would not have been interfered with in that respect. These positive changes were more theoretical than practical, however. The absence of direct, working relations with the government was untenable. I had a strong feeling it was not going to change. Our working and living conditions did not improve. KGB surveillance was less noticeable, though undoubtedly ever-present. We could not keep any records, write any reports or communicate classified information. We had to carry every piece of paper on our bodies or in our bags, wherever we went. Since telephone numbers were a commodity hard to come by and there were no directories, we had to collect and collate all numbers and store them in our pockets. This was impractical. Writing official letters home was also a problem; it had to be done just before the departure of members of our mission to Vienna. Sometimes, when I was particularly wary of the watchful eyes of the KGB, I wrote under an opened umbrella to dodge unseen equipment that could photograph the writing. This was an unusual precaution, perhaps, directed mainly at protecting my sources of information.

Toward the end of 1988 Gorbachev was proclaiming the need to widen contacts, inviting foreign representatives in Moscow to rub shoulders with government and party officials, as well as to increase exchanges and broaden understanding. Israel was evidently not included in the list of 'normal' countries, and we were still left out in the cold. We had no dialogue with the government. The Russian attitude was frustrating and pointless. At the end of my six-week tour, I was getting ready to return to my duties in Jerusalem, when an unforeseen event radically and swiftly changed the parameters of our work in Moscow.

On the afternoon of 2 December, when I was at the airport welcoming our volleyball team from Kiryat Ata (a suburb of Haifa), I heard a rumour: a group of Soviet Jews had kidnapped schoolchildren, held them hostage, and demanded an airplane to take them on a direct flight to Israel. This sounded bad enough in itself, but the long-term implications could be disastrous. It could affect the mission's efforts to control the emigration process. Such an incident might deal a further blow to the Soviet Jews who were only beginning to raise their heads from years of government oppression. Later, I received reports which indicated how concerned Soviet Jews had been that this development might become a pretext for new restrictions. I did not mention anything to our volleyball team, which had come to compete in the European cup. They were scheduled to play the next day and it would not do to upset them.

The hijacking itself sounded like an inexplicable act of desperation. It had happened once before and had resulted in the much publicized Leningrad trial. The sentencing of the Jews involved to long prison terms had created an international scandal. As the Soviet government could be rather unpredictable in such cases and the members of our mission were exposed to all manner of pressures, including a major media campaign, I thought we should all adopt a wait-and-see attitude. That evening I tried in vain to reach Israel on the phone from the hotel. Our telephones in the USSR could receive foreign calls but not reach numbers abroad. I could not understand Jerusalem's silence. It could not be that difficult to get in touch and share information with me or at least suggest what we might do if the situation really turned ugly.

The following day we all turned out for the game, with great pride at seeing the name of our team on the electronic scoreboard at the Dynamo stadium in Moscow. This had never happened before, certainly not in recent years. The game itself was not very inspiring, since our players were not as professionally trained as the Russians and were inferior in height by a good number of inches. The Russian hosts, however, were courteous and received the Kiryat Ata team warmly. By this time, the news that we were hearing from the local radio stations indicated it was not a group of Jews, but a gang of criminals that had hijacked young schoolchildren in the town of Mineralnye Vody in the south of the Russian Federation, exchanged the children for an airplane and a huge pile of ransom money and were making their way to Israel. No one knew why they chose this destination. The media were suggesting that Israel was somehow at fault.

It was already dark when I made my way back to the Ukraina Hotel. Carrying a large carton of groceries I had just purchased, I struggled to pull open the monumental oaken entrance door. A large splinter lodged under my thumbnail. In excruciating pain but without dropping the precious carton, I reached my room on the seventh floor. As I unlocked the door, I heard a long and insistent ringing of the telephone. With the hijacking in the back of my mind, I had a premonition that I was being called by the Ministry of Foreign Affairs. As I picked up the receiver, I heard the polite Russian phrase: 'This is Alexei Chistyakoff of the foreign ministry disturbing you. I have been looking all over Moscow for you and am glad to have finally located you. The foreign minister requests that you meet him in his office in an hour's time.' I did not ask what the nature of the request was or what the foreign minister had on his mind. It was clear it was the hijacking. I was already trying to figure out how to contact my ministry and consult on what I should say. I picked up the telephone and got through to the operator of the international lines. 'Would you please get the following number in Jerusalem, Israel, on a matter of highest governmental priority.' I was expecting the usual impolite refusal, but the girl said, 'Please hold the line, I'll make the connection right away.' Before I knew it, I was talking to Director-General Abrasha Tamir.

'We're returning them without further delay', Tamir shouted into the phone. 'It's all settled and don't worry about a thing.' I told him I was about to meet with the Minister of Foreign Affairs. 'Then tell him the government has decided to return the hijackers. There might be a few hitches because of the legal aspect of things and international law. We must make sure they will not get the death penalty. Negotiations are going on right now between the legal experts, but it's going to be all right.' As I knew nothing at all about the developments, Tamir had to fill me in. It transpired that the hijackers and the airplane had already landed in Israel on the previous day, the air force had escorted them in and they were immediately taken into custody. The minister of defence, the chief of the general staff, the commander of the air force as well as officials of the Ministry of Foreign Affairs were all at the airport. The Soviet consular group in Israel was very much in evidence, using the airport communications system to talk to Moscow. Tamir was in a great hurry to tend to the problems connected with this affair and wished me luck on my meeting with Shevardnadze. I was amazed. Over the last 24 hours my ministry had not even tried to contact me. They knew perfectly well what we must have been going through in Moscow.

It took another day and a half for me to get the full details of this extraordinary event. The first contact was established before the arrival of the airplane, through international telex. The Soviet Ministry of Civil Aviation had sent an urgent message to Israel's Ben-Gurion airport authorities requesting landing rights for a Soviet Ilyushin 76 transport plane. The information said that 'bandits' had hijacked a group of schoolchildren, that they were armed and were going to land the airplane in Tel Aviv. This message was so unusual that the airport authorities had to contact the Ministries of Defence and Foreign Affairs to check its veracity. Just to make sure, an inquiry was sent to the Soviet Civil Aviation Ministry, after the telex number was discovered in an international directory found in the airport offices. An hour later the original message was confirmed. No one at the airport remembered ever receiving a request so direct and bizarre from a superpower that had no diplomatic relations with us. A senior Soviet Ministry of Foreign Affairs official then telephoned his Israeli counterpart in Jerusalem and briefed him on the events in the south of Russia that led to the flight to Israel. The children had been freed. The Soviet government asked that the criminals be extradited and the plane be returned. Even before our government had time to consider this request, the airport was put on full alert. Police and ambulances were called in and it was decided to direct the incoming aircraft to a remote runway. The authorities at Ben-Gurion airport had had sufficient experience with hijackers and emergency situations and knew what to do. Permission was granted and the plane landed in a military zone of the international airport.

My thumb was throbbing again with the pain suppressed by the excitement of the past two hours. A colleague drove me out through the snow-covered streets to the Foreign Ministry, another of Stalin's architectural aberrations, which I now entered for the first time. Alexei Chistyakoff was downstairs, waiting for me. He was all smiles. As we were going up in the elevator he asked me if the Netherlands ambassador's invitation to lunch with Gennady Tarasov, the official in charge of Israeli affairs at the ministry, had been coordinated with me. I confirmed that it had. Chistyakoff said that in that case we would be meeting at lunch in a few days. I felt my luck was changing; but one could not be sure of anything in Moscow, I told myself.

As I entered the Foreign Minister's secretariat on the seventh floor, I was taken aback. On a television screen in the room, staring me right in the face, was Yohanan Bein, our ambassador to the UN in New York, being interviewed on CNN. He was commenting on the hijacking of the Soviet plane. We were not hooked up to CNN at the Ukraina Hotel and there were no foreign papers available in Moscow in those days. From this brief glance at Bein in New York, I understood the world-wide repercussions of this seemingly limited incident. Silently saluting my far-off colleague, I listened to his words, which helped me get my bearings on this affair, as seen from the UN headquarters at Turtle Bay.

The Foreign Minister's secretariat looked drab, a far cry even from the utilitarian decor of our own ministry. After a few minutes, I was led into the presence of Eduard Shevardnadze. 'Well, have you completely frozen in Moscow?' the Soviet minister asked. 'There is so much warmth in the heart of the Muscovites, one hardly feels the cold outside', I answered. 'That's an excellent reply', said the minister, broadly smiling, and sat me down on the sofa next to him. I glanced at the carpets. They were the usual soulless, machine-woven style one saw in all Soviet offices. My mind wandered for a split-second to a meeting in the office of the Iranian prime minister, Fereydoun Hoveyda, in 1975. Then, as now, my eyes were riveted to the carpet. What a difference: in Hoveyda's office I longed to roll it up, put it nonchalantly on my shoulder and walk out of the room. Shevardnadze's rug hardly merited such daring daydreams.

'You probably have been following the painful events the Soviet people have been subjected to in recent days, and there is no need to expand on this barbaric deed', Shevardnadze said. 'The Soviet government has authorized me to express the deep gratitude of the people and the government of the Soviet Union to the people of

Israel and to its government. We are appreciative of your humane and noble gesture and happy that it was a direct and independent decision, not a result of long and difficult negotiations. We are glad that all developments occurred within the bounds of normal civilized behaviour between countries. I have been receiving reports on how pleased international public opinion is with the goodwill shown by your country. I wish to add my personal opinion in saying the actions of the government of Israel reflect the will of the Israeli people.'

I understood the reason for this profuse expression of gratitude. In March 1988, there had been a similar incident. A family of 11 from Novosibirsk had hijacked an airplane and demanded to leave the country. At a small airport near Leningrad, the plane was attacked by a KGB anti-terrorist unit. Five members of the family, in addition to three passengers and a stewardess, were killed. The media, free of former restraints thanks to glasnost, severely criticized the government for its brutality.* The Soviet authorities acted more prudently this time. Besides, Gorbachev was about to visit Great Britain, the US and Cuba. He had to be true to his new image, less savage than that of his predecessors. The minister of foreign affairs himself had lived through a similar, unpleasant incident. As first secretary of the Communist Party of Georgia, before his promotion to the Politburo, some members of his family were abducted for ransom. The kidnappers were found and severely punished.

The minister turned to reminiscing about the meetings he had had in the past with Prime Minister Yitzhak Shamir and Foreign Minister Shimon Peres. He also expressed his appreciation for the assistance the Soviet group was getting in Tel Aviv toward fulfilling their tasks 'normally' (a word denoting 'well', in Soviet Russian). 'And what about you?' he queried. I told him about our difficulties in housing, communications and of his ministry's refusal to supply us with diplomatic identity cards. I also told him about the disagreement over the use of our embassy, for which we had been

---

* See Amnon Kapeliuk's article from Moscow in *Yediot Aharonot*, 4 Dec. 1988.

paying rent for over 20 years. Shevardnadze said: 'We shall consider these requests and do our best to fulfil them.' He turned to his three aides at the table busily taking notes: 'Let's urgently consider all these problems, keep me informed and don't procrastinate!' I then touched upon the question of access to the political echelon. Shevardnadze said: 'But we have been meeting from time to time with your leaders and discussing our views'. I retorted that dialogue and consultation were necessary in Moscow, as changes were rapid, opportunities many. 'All right', he said, 'we shall discuss this problem too, after our meeting. I know you are concerned. We shall consider it and let you know.' I glanced at Chistyakoff, Stepanov, the minister's personal assistant, and Filev, deputy to head of the Near East and North Africa department. They looked surprised.

Shevardnadze then spoke at length about his views on the Middle East. A historic compromise should be found, he said. It should reflect the interests of all sides. A serious approach should be adopted. He then repeated what he had often said to Shamir and Peres: 'Why then should we not all meet together, permanent members of the Security Council and the parties involved, to find solutions in a common effort. Every one of us could contribute. Perhaps it would be wise to have a preparatory meeting to plan an international conference.' I was familiar with this line. In our political research department at the ministry we had analysed the question of the international conference and come to the obvious conclusion that preliminary meetings and Security Council involvement were contrary to Israel's interests. This had been Israel's position for many years.

I told the minister there was no real need for a preliminary conference since the outstanding issues between the protagonists were already being discussed. The involvement of outside powers would only be detrimental to a resolution of the problems and to the process of negotiations, something we were certain the USSR would be eager to help avoid. I knew the fear my government had of Soviet intrusion. The Russians' total lack of objectivity and poor record in relations with Israel made it hard for us to trust their offers of assistance.

Shevardnadze insisted that he would not want to harm the

negotiations in any way. However, his ministry had to to work out as many alternatives as possible, in order to come up with a feasible one. He now turned to his assistants and said: 'Let us see what we can come up with; every suggestion we have offered should be reviewed again and new ones should also be put forward. We should be doing our utmost to bring this region to a normal state of affairs.'

At this point, Shevardnadze took me into his confidence regarding the visit of the Chinese foreign minister. This was the first visit since 1949, he told me. Of course, he added, Chou En Lai had visited Moscow before the foreign minister. They had discussed many bilateral and regional problems and he hoped the Chinese minister's visit would remove some of the obstacles between them. They saw this as an extremely important and positive development. I offered my best wishes for success.

As I got up to leave, Shevardnadze said: 'I know you are troubled with the difficulties of your situation here. We shall discuss the different aspects of these problems among us and shall contact you soon. I wish you lots of luck and success in your work.'

When I returned to the hotel I tried the international telephone operator again. She was immediately at my service, and connected me to Shimon Peres. I told him about the meeting, but said that I would have to go to Vienna to send him an encoded report. 'That's not important now. Tell me everything right away', he said, impatiently. So I told him the substance of my conversation. I think he was rather pleased. We both understood that in a country like the USSR a single conversation on secondary issues with one of the members of the ruling ten — the Politburo — might cause things to happen faster than numerous conversations with lesser officials. It now only remained to be seen whether Shevardnadze's instructions to his staff would be carried out.

The immediate results of this meeting were rather different than I had imagined. I was thinking of the political dimension of our mission and its anticipated upgrading to an official one. But the direct and immediate result was that my name and face became known, overnight, all over the Soviet Union. The meeting with Shevardnadze was shown at prime time on the main television channel. Journalists who had shied away from me until then devoted whole columns to the meeting and to the airplane hijacking. Later, three documentary films were made on the subject in Israel and the Soviet Union. Strangers would stop me in the streets and shake my hand for my 'noble gesture'. Policemen, who used to recognize the Netherlands license plates of our Volvos and unceremoniously try to scrounge 'souvenirs' from us or harass us, would now salute smartly and congratulate us. And the Jews of Moscow glowed with pride, which was the most satisfying result of all. Had things turned out badly, they would have been the first to suffer. Now, they could not only look back with dignity on the events of the past days but also look forward to greater relaxation of Soviet emigration policy. In fact, this incident and the meeting with the minister of foreign affairs was to become a milestone in our mission's work in Moscow. The conditions of our life and activity did not change dramatically overnight. But this was a new beginning, on an entirely new basis. We were no longer incognito. Everyone was convinced that our promotion to a full embassy was only a few weeks away. In fact it took much longer. But at least we felt more confident.

A few days after my meeting with the minister, some of our mission members were about to enter the slow elevator to the seventh floor of the Ukraina Hotel. As they got in, a fellow passenger looked at them and asked: 'Italian?' No. 'French?' No. 'British?' No. 'Ahhhh', he said, as it suddenly dawned on him, 'Commando Levin!'.

6 · The Thaw Begins

There seemed to be continued stubborn resistance in the Politburo and within the administration to the idea of moderating the USSR's stance toward Israel. The express orders of the foreign minister following the hijacking incident were slow in execution. Still, as the year came to an end, we could register a number of improvements in our relations with the government and greater exposure to the Soviet public as well as to the Jewish population. Continued international pressure and the expectations that small gestures of goodwill might loosen the purse-strings of Jewish money and influence to the benefit of the Soviet Union, brought continued relaxation regarding the Jews. The loss of self-confidence within the Soviet Union and the growing emphasis on human rights were propelling the question of free Jewish emigration toward a more decisive resolution. The pace of these developments, however, was excruciatingly slow. The mission suffered the strain of every passing phase.

Although dispersed over the vast expanses of the USSR, most Jews knew about the presence of the mission at the Dutch Embassy and the Ukraina Hotel almost from the moment of its arrival. The members of the mission who dealt with emigration, representatives of Lishkat Hakesher in Tel Aviv were making ever-wider contacts. The Jewish Agency, whose duty it was to tender to the needs of open immigration into Israel, still lacked official status and could not begin its operations. Consequently, most of the work was still in the hands of the Nativ people, who had been responsible for the emigration of Jews from Eastern Europe over the long, difficult years since the lowering of the Iron Curtain.

NATIV PICKS UP MOMENTUM

There was no doubt that the Soviet security services identified the members of Nativ in the mission very quickly, for they had known about its existence and activities and were aware of its *modus operandi*. Nativ (the Route) was established in 1953, in the wake of the deterioration in Israel's relations with the Soviet Union and the eastern bloc. Access to Jews in these countries became highly problematic and immigration was restricted. The prime minister of Israel at that time, Moshe Sharett, organized Nativ on the lines of a covert organization, endowing it with sufficient means to allow clandestine operations. Nativ became indispensable after the severance of diplomatic relations in 1967, when no Israeli representative could maintain contacts openly with the Jews of the Soviet Union or Eastern Europe.

As soon as Nativ officials arrived in Moscow as members of our first mission, they began feverish activity. They developed existing contacts with members of the Jewish community, established ties and communications with areas which had sizable Jewish populations and helped them in promoting Jewish education and the study of Hebrew language. They began supplying information on immigration and prospects for integration in Israel. In short, they disseminated the information that had been lacking for over 20 years and had been obtainable only at great risk. Nativ officials were constantly on the phone, planning, discussing and coordinating their operations all across the Soviet Union. After we started having access to an international telephone line, they would call Tel Aviv to get instructions and provide their staff with up-to-the-minute reports. Nativ tried to overcome obstacles as they arose and to take advantage of opportunities as they developed. Yet the activity of the mission in this sense was kept within the limits of accepted regulations. Our firm policy was never to cross the boundaries of Soviet law. This having been said, it is clear that the tremendous and rapid rise in emigration was, to an extent, a direct result of the mission's presence in the Soviet Union. The mission was there to give encouragement to Jews to use its widening services. In previous years a continuous trickle of books (usually prayer books), prayer shawls and other religious articles had been smuggled into the country. On at least one occasion, a well-known Soviet personality, an ambassador to Canada, helped pass indispensable objects of Jewish ritual. It was said that he unabashedly used the diplomatic pouch to do it.

On several occasions Israeli organizations participated in book fairs in Moscow — an excellent opportunity to distribute books in large numbers. In September of every year, the large and well-organized Israeli stand attracted tremendous attention. The shelves were loaded with books of every description published in Israel. As soon as the fair opened the shelves would be ransacked by the many Jews who rushed in. When the shelves emptied, the books were replaced from the stocks kept in large boxes. Often, visitors were so eager to take possession of books that they went directly to the boxes and had to be restrained. The KGB kept close watch throughout. A telescope observing the goings-on at the Israeli stand was very much in evidence and there were numerous plain-clothes agents circulating among the thick crowd. Interference, however, was rare, as it risked scandalizing the many other exhibitors.

The September fairs were also occasions to raise the Israeli flag, show videotapes on the computer stand that dispensed information on Israel, and bring Israeli intellectuals to Moscow to mingle with the many Jews who were drawn to the gathering.

One of the numerous mysteries in the Soviet attitude toward the mission was the inexplicable fact that nothing significant was really done to place obstacles in the way of Nativ's operations. This was especially strange as there were no serious attempts to hide or to cover up this work from the host government. The KGB followed us around like hawks. They tapped our telephones and checked and double-checked every lead they had about our contacts, our conversations and our activity. This we knew from the many 'interviews' our friends were being subjected to. Yet, in spite of what must have been a large-scale effort on the part of the Soviet intelligence services, the government did little if anything to curtail the movements of our immigration agents or make life difficult for them, beyond the ordinary limitations that were imposed on all the members of the mission and the diplomatic corps in general. The Soviets carried out their regular policy of heavy-handed administrative restrictions, easing up as time wore on, and eventually lifting virtually all limitations toward the end of 1991. This was a blessing, but also a source of bewilderment. On the other hand, it was clear to us then as it is today, that had the Soviets been able to pay the political price of active interference in the work of the mission, they would have had no compunctions about doing so. The international situation and the internal difficulties the regime was facing were too great to allow the conditioned reflexes of the Soviet system to bear down on the emigration of Jews. The Soviets were stymied because of international pressure, their own internal weakness and their need for economic aid. Their growing leniency regarding emigration was in fact not restricted to Jews but was applied to other minorities as well: Germans, Armenians and Greeks. The lines at the embassies and the consulates eloquently testified to this new situation.

LUNCHEON AT TCHAIKOVSKY'S HOUSE

Our mission was settling in. A number of 'firsts' following very soon after my dramatic meeting with Shevardnadze. Heading the list was a luncheon that Petrus Buwalda, the Dutch ambassador, organized in his home. He had invited the head of the Near East and North African Department of the ministry, Vladimir Poliakov, to participate in this first meeting with the representative of Israel. Poliakov, however, was at the UN in New York with Gorbachev. The luncheon was attended instead by Gennady Tarasov (later Russian ambassador to Saudi Arabia), Poliakov's assistant and head of the Foreign Ministry's sub-department for Israel, Jordan and the Arab-Israel conflict, and Alexei Chistyakoff, Tarasov's aide.

Tarasov was a well-known *apparatchik* in the Soviet bureaucracy that dealt with the Middle Eastern region. I never did find out what his institutional alma mater was, but he was acquainted with some of the problems connected with Israel. In my four years at the UN in New York, as ambassador and deputy chief of mission, I very often came across this tall and self-assured man, always on hand at meetings of the Security Council and constantly shuttling between the various Arab delegations and his own. He frequently helped the Arabs in drafting resolutions, mostly condemning Israel, that being part of Soviet strategy at the UN and in the world at the time. He studiously avoided contact with us. He always accompanied the suave Soviet ambassador, Oleg Troyanovsky, at meetings dealing with the Middle East conflict. He used to hover and whisper advice into the ears of Arab delegates. As there were a great number of such meetings, I ran into him quite often. He was purposefully distant and unfriendly. The absence of diplomatic relations did not prevent courteous exchanges between our delegation and the Soviets, but Tarasov was too involved with the Arabs. He seemed to lack a sense of humour. I now had to deal with him in Moscow. His behaviour and manners bore out the impressions I had formed.

Both Tarasov and I were aware of another problem. For over a year, Tarasov had been having unpublicized meetings discussing the Middle East scene with Nimrod Novik, a Shimon Peres aide. As head of political research I was privy to the substance of these meetings, but not always to the details. Gennady Tarasov was the man the Soviet Foreign Ministry had delegated — with the approval of other agencies, no doubt — because of his rich background in Middle Eastern affairs. In his conversations with Novik, Tarasov seemed to be especially interested in exploring the complexities of the Israeli political scene. One such Tarasov-Novik meeting lasted 11 hours. These meetings never took place in either capital city, underlining their confidentiality and the Soviet insistence on informality.

The fact that Yitzhak Shamir was about to be appointed prime minister and the Likud Party's clear-cut and aggressive anti-PLO stand would become official policy, hung like a cloud over the Buwalda luncheon meeting. Tarasov knew perfectly well that I would be arguing against the Soviet insistence on contacts with Yassir Arafat. The Soviet government had had many dealings with Arafat over the years but hesitated to recognize him as the sole representative of the PLO. Rumour had it that Arafat had been recognized as such after his meeting with Gorbachev in Berlin in April 1986. The Soviets maintained their ties with other underground and above ground Palestinian groups and terrorists. They supplied them with weapons and funds, fully aware of the subversive and terrorist nature of their activities against Israel and the West. Documents that have come to light in recent years show that Palestinian terrorism was not only helped materially, but was coordinated at the planning stage with the KGB and other secret Soviet organizations. Extensive training was given to these terrorists in the Soviet Union and the East European countries. The KGB even accepted stolen archeological artifacts from the Beirut museum in partial reimbursement for the funds supplied to terrorist groups.

The luncheon at Petrus Buwalda's residence on that day in December 1988 was the first contact I had had with a Foreign Ministry political officer. The setting itself was remarkable. The Dutch residence was located in the old town house of composer Petr Ilich Tchaikovsky. The Dutch maintained the building very much in the old style. However, neither the remarkable venue nor the amiability and diplomatic flair of the host could overcome the haughtiness of Comrade Tarasov. The Russian guest was making a concession by attending this lunch. He seemed to be doing it under duress and would not let us forget it for a minute. The conversation revolved around questions concerning Soviet insistence on Israel's meeting with the PLO and negotiating with the Palestinians. At the time, just after the 1988 Israeli elections and well into the difficulties over the formation of a government, the invocation of this sacrosanct Soviet theme was an outright waste of time. It was evidently ordained by the Soviet ideologists of Middle East affairs. The Soviets must have known the Likud position of not dealing with the PLO under any circumstances. Tarasov and I had a dutifully long and strained discussion on this subject. It was, however, rich in political content and important for that reason, though the Dutch ambassador must have been rather bored.

In the course of the conversation, Tarasov conceded that the absence of diplomatic relations between Israel and the USSR was wrong, but implied that the establishment of such relations would be dependent on Israel's willingness to negotiate with Arafat. He said contacts were being maintained with Israelis (the Novik-Tarasov talks), but that both governments should be 'creative', meaning that Israel must be more forthcoming and receptive to the Soviet point of view. This remark was aimed not only at the government soon to be inaugurated, but also at Peres, whom the Soviets were not finding pliant enough. Incidentally, Tarasov was convinced that the Likud government would not last and that Peres would soon be returning to power at the head of the government. Tarasov went on to state that his country was concerned about the problems of nuclear proliferation and thought the situation would greatly deteriorate in three to five years. He was obviously warning of the advancing nuclear capability of Iran, Iraq and Pakistan and suggesting that Israel sign the Non-Proliferation Treaty (NPT), thereby freeing the Middle East region of a nuclear threat (with the help of the USSR). These were well-rehearsed, standard Soviet arguments. Negotiations with the Palestinians and the PLO had been a Soviet theme for many years, raised in all of the Soviet meetings with Israeli political leaders since the 1970s (with Rabin during his posting to Washington as ambassador, Abba Eban, Yigal Allon, Yitzhak Shamir, Shimon Peres and others).

I should point out that these two fundamental questions, relations with the Palestinians and the NPT, have transcended all the upheavals in the Soviet Union and the changes that have come over the Middle East. They are still on the political agenda in the region, as of summer 1995.

After coffee was served, Tarasov excused himself to the Dutch ambassador and took me aside. He expressed thanks for our offer of help for the victims of the earthquake in Armenia and said his government was considering it (I had however already received word it had been officially accepted). Tarasov then went on to discuss the importance of Israel handing over Soviet property to the government. He explained that the revolutionary government had declared immediately after the establishment of Soviet power that all property of the Romanov dynasty was to be expropriated by the state. This was embodied in Soviet law and consequently such property, located abroad, had to be handed over as well. The Politburo had agreed to send a delegation to Israel, only in order to receive these assets, and were extremely concerned that its mission was not being accomplished. I retorted that Israel was not subject to Soviet law and asked if there had been a precedent in the West. Tarasov did not answer my question but said: 'A great deal could be achieved if you restituted this property. This would make a very good impression.'

A rather droll incident occurred at this juncture. After coffee, Mrs Vilma Buwalda, the Dutch ambassador's wife, came in to join us for a few moments. Mrs Buwalda is a kind and caring person, who demonstrated great compassion for the people standing in long lines outside her embassy, just under the windows of her residence. When she would see an old woman standing a long time in the sun, she would rush out with a chair, or with a glass of water. Mrs Buwalda thought nothing of giving the policemen at the gate a piece of her mind if she thought they were getting too rough with the callers. When Mrs Buwalda joined us, there was a conversation in progress about the transfer of the Israeli mission to its embassy compound. Tarasov indicated to us that a positive response would not be forthcoming soon. Mrs Buwalda took Tarasov by his sleeve and led him to the window overlooking the street. There were tens of men, women and children standing in the snow, shivering, waiting to come into the consulate to get their papers. 'How can you tolerate seeing all these people standing out there in the cold and not let them move to an area where they could be treated as human beings?!' Tarasov did not bother to look outside. He just snorted and turned away.

My meetings with Tarasov were far less exploratory than the ones he had had with Novik because the administration I represented was simply not interested in Soviet brokerage of a deal with the PLO; nor was Peres, as far as I knew. But the Novik conversations, informal and unofficial, were not as binding as an exchange of positions at the Foreign Ministry in Moscow. Tarasov was unbending. On the personal level, the atmosphere of our many conversations was heavy and unpleasant. Alexei Chistyakoff, who sat in on the meetings, later became the head of the Soviet mission in Israel and minister plenipotentiary when embassies were established. When the Israeli ministry gave him a farewell luncheon in the autumn of 1993, in the presence of Russian ambassador Alexander Bovin, Chistyakoff proposed a toast and said he wanted to apologize for the heavy-handedness of their attitude toward me at the time. I thought this admission was a belated gesture of recognition, amusing in that it came from

Chistyakoff and not Tarasov, who would have never expressed such words of regret. Chistyakoff, though given to pro-Arab sympathies, was always very correct in his attitude toward me.

The report on the long conversation with Tarasov caused a ripple of excitement at home in Jerusalem, when I went there for a few weeks to resume my research duties. This contact, albeit irregular and forced, was seen as the beginning of a normalized mode of relations with Soviet officialdom. The question of tsarist property was being dealt with very seriously by the minister of justice, Dan Meridor, with whom I met and considered the case. The inclination of the Justice Ministry was favourable toward the Russians, even though some hard-liners, like Plia Albeck, wanted the Russians to first return all the synagogues that they had confiscated over the years. This was not unreasonable, but hardly feasible.

A few weeks after the Buwalda luncheon, after I had returned from a trip to Jerusalem, I requested a meeting with Tarasov and was invited to come to the ministry — my first official business visit to the Near East Department. I told Tarasov about my meetings with the prime minister and the minister of foreign affairs and transmitted their messages. Tarasov returned to the question of property. I explained the legal difficulties and the procedure that we would have to go through. In principle, our government was not against having the real estate handed over to the Soviets. The decision, however, would have to be left to the courts. Since the government was willing to indicate its favourable predisposition, the court's ruling would in all probability be positive. Tarasov insisted on a political decision to return the property. As the Soviets were adamant on this point, we could not resolve the issue.

Tarasov then announced the decisions reached at the ministry with regard to our mission: we were to be granted permission to use the first floor of the former Israel Embassy building as the consular branch of the Dutch Embassy. However, we would not be allowed to stamp our own visas yet. We were to have one telephone line which could communicate with the outside world. Instead of our usual visitors' visas, we would be granted resident visas for the duration of six months, but would not be given diplomatic identity cards (since these could be issued only to diplomats residing in the USSR for over a year). Shevardnadze had kept his promise.

Tarasov then went on to say that the very fact that we were meeting at the Foreign Ministry was an upgrading of the mission's status and that a political dialogue was thus being held. 'The political dialogue is now being transferred to Moscow', he announced, haughtily. However, he asked me not to divulge our meeting to the media. 'If Israel shows readiness to be more flexible toward the PLO and suggests new ways to solve Middle East problems, relations could be expanded', he asserted.

The Soviet position had not improved on the substance of the important issues, but at least we had overcome our first big hurdle in Moscow. We were beginning a dialogue with the political echelon. Its sterility was evident, as was the Soviets' unadorned support for the PLO. I was far from elated: I felt that the official position of the Soviet government was not liable to change in the near future. Still, we were getting back our embassy building and would have a link with the outside world. In practice, Soviet efficiency being what it was, it took a good six months to reach this goal.

At this time, a whole series of other events affecting our mission and Jewish life in Moscow symbolized the great transformations taking place in the Soviet Union. I have already described my entry into the Foreign Ministry. In February, an incident occurred that reflected both the cynicism and the fickleness of the Soviet system toward its Jewish population.

7 · Jewish Culture Reinstated

THE OPENING OF THE MIKHOELS CENTRE

I have already touched upon the personal relations that existed between a number of foreign Jewish leaders and Soviet officials. Some of these contacts evolved over many years, such as the ties established between Rabbi Arthur Schneier of New York City and various personalities in the higher reaches of the Soviet government. A relationship also developed between the president of the World Jewish Congress, Edgar Bronfman, and certain Soviet officials, including Foreign Minister Eduard Shevardnadze.

Elsewhere, an interesting role was played by Rabbi Adin Steinsaltz. Through an organization called the World Laboratory and the Chief Rabbi of Holland, Rabbi Abraham Suttendorf, Rabbi Steinsaltz befriended members of the Soviet Academy of Sciences. This was accomplished through the good offices of academician Yevgeny Velikhov, the noted atomic scientist and a great initiator of projects far afield from his area of specialization. There were others, like Isi J. Leibler, president of the Executive Council of Australian Jewry, who had also established links with the Soviet government. All these people enjoyed international prestige and connections, and some possessed considerable wealth. All had their own favourite projects, which they pushed and promoted with exemplary determination through the thick and thin of Soviet bureaucratic fluctuations.

A subject of concern to all was the question of Jewish education and the study of Hebrew, long subjected to strict proscription. With the coming of perestroika, these regulations were relaxed and prospects for a renewal of Jewish culture improved. There was a great deal of activity concerning the opening of Jewish day schools, *yeshivot* (seminaries) and Hebrew classes. Hebrew language study was slowly being activated, informally at first. One of the first regular after-hours Hebrew language schools was opened at the Soviet Academy of Atheism, of all places. However, the project that appeared most prestigious and attractive in those final days of 1988 was the re-establishment of the Jewish theatre.

There was no organized 'National' Jewish theatre before the Revolution, although there was a long tradition of itinerant theatrical troupes. The Soviet government, having recognized the Jewish people as a nation within the Soviet system, set up the first of such companies. They reached their artistic pinnacle in the 1920s and 1930s. At that time a number of talented artists led by Solomon Mikhoels organized the State Jewish Chamber Theatre in Moscow and began playing to large and enthusiastic audiences. The theatre performed in Yiddish, a language recognized by Soviet law as the national language of the Jewish minority. The theatre's director, Alexander Granovsky, declared that it was to be a temple of beauty in which prayers would be said in Yiddish. Marc Chagall painted beautiful murals for the State Theatre on Malaia Bronnaia Street. Mikhoels stayed on as performer and director and was recognized as an outstanding theatrical personality. With the outbreak of the Second World War, Stalin recruited him and a number of other outstanding Jewish writers and artists to head the Jewish Anti-fascist Committee and organize an appeal for funds in the West. The Soviet government also sent Mikhoels and the Yiddish poet Itsik Fefer to the US to support a drive for contributions and help Soviet propaganda — a part Mikhoels performed as brilliantly as his others. His charismatic personality, however, was too much for Stalin. In January 1948, Stalin secretly ordered his 'liquidation' and the great artist was murdered. The other members of the Anti-fascist Committee were jailed, tried and shot four years later, and the committee was disbanded. Most of the Jewish theatres that had been playing to large audiences in the 1920s, 1930s and even after the war, were eventually closed, 'for lack of attendance'. This official pretext was an expression of the regime's anti-Jewish policy. Mikhoels's murder caused great pain and frustration to all those who had heard and seen him. When the idea of establishing a Jewish cultural centre was taken up by Isi J. Leibler in Australia, together with Mikhail Gluz, a well-known musician who had worked in the Jewish theatre, it seemed natural that it would be named after the great actor.

The idea behind this initiative was to create a centre where young people would meet, study Hebrew, hear lectures on Jewish culture and history, watch films and visit a book and video library. The propaganda department of the Central Committee sanctioned the project and the Moscow municipality allocated a small abandoned movie theatre seating 500. After solicitation of support and promises, the dilapidated building was finally remodelled. The halls were literally plastered with large framed posters of the Second World War and the Holocaust. This was hardly appropriate as the sole decoration of a new Jewish cultural centre. Photographs of Mikhoels and of the many actors who were loved and remembered by their audiences were hidden away in a special room, while the foyer featured a wall covered with photographs of Soviet Jewish generals, including the notorious chairman of the anti-Zionist committee, General David Dragunsky. Little money was in fact contributed, some by the Marc Rich Foundation, some by Edgar Bronfman and a small amount by other philanthropists. The date of the inauguration was finally set for 12 February 1989.

The centre promised to be a new beginning, a departure from the long years of stagnation in the cultural life of the Jewish population of Moscow that numbered somewhere around a quarter of a million souls. The inauguration turned out to be a very important international media event. Prime Minister Shamir and Foreign Minister Moshe Arens sent their greetings, and I was to read them out. I decided to present them in the original language, Hebrew. This was to be another 'first' — the public appearance of the Israeli head of mission.

We arrived at the Mikhoels Cultural Centre that evening together with over a thousand other people and found it difficult to get in. Finally recognized and admitted, I found myself in the company of the ambassadors of Great Britain, Australia, France and the Netherlands, Canada and the US chargé d'affaires. Bronfman, Leibler and others arrived especially for this inauguration. The foreign ambassadors read out the messages of their heads of state or prime ministers. As I was not a recognized ambassador, my country having no relations with the Soviet Union, I was last in line to read my messages. It was also evident that the master of ceremonies, Mikhail Gluz, the director of the newly established centre, was rather nervous over the fact that an Israeli representative was there, and making a speech to boot. Among the Soviet personalities present were the well-known theatre director Yuri Lyubimov, and the actress Natalya Mordyukova. Mordyukova is famous for her role in Askoldov's film on the Civil War called *The Commissar*. The director was ostracized for his portrayal of Jews in that film as ordinary people, suffering from the tragedy of war and treating their fellow Russians with compassion. *The Commissar* was made just after the Second World War but was only released years later. Askoldov and I became good friends in Moscow.

Lyubimov and Mordyukova spoke very movingly. The many speeches and greetings expressed fresh hopes and praised the Soviet leadership for allowing this centre to be opened. The official part of the programme was followed by a performance of Jewish music. The Soviet press gave a brief account of this cultural event, but said nothing about the presence of foreign ambassadors and obviously not a word about the messages of the Israeli leaders. Contrary to promises made to prominent Jewish friends of the Soviet establishment, no official Soviet personality was present, either from the Foreign Ministry or from any cultural organization.

Reports on the opening of the Mikhoels Centre were printed in papers all over the world. It was indeed exciting news to that segment of the international public interested in Soviet policy on Hebrew and Jewish culture. The event was trumpeted as yet another great achievement of perestroika, an unprecedented gesture of good will on behalf of its leader, Mikhail Gorbachev.

The expectations for the future of this centre were great. The Jews of Moscow hoped it would become a pole of attraction for young and old Jews alike. However, as time wore on it became clear that the municipality of Moscow and the cultural bosses of the government had no intention of satisfying the needs of this new Jewish enterprise. There was a great deal of negotiating over the lease of another building to house a club and a restaurant serving kosher food. Moscow had no kosher restaurants save one, which was 'kosher-style' — less 'kosher' and more 'style'. Gluz complained to me very often about the broken promises of the various Jewish philanthropists, who, he maintained, had cashed in on the publicity but were not underwriting the operations. He said his Jewish supporters were not coming through with the film and video equipment. These supporters, on the other hand, were complaining about technical and organizational mismanagement of the centre which apparently led them to hold back on their contributions. Gluz eventually resigned his position as director of the centre. He organized a Jewish troupe of musicians and entertainers — the Tum Balalaika — which had considerable success within the Soviet Union and in engagements abroad. Our mission often invited Gluz's artists to perform Jewish music and songs on festive occasions.

Many months later, on one of my periodic visits to the centre, I found the doors locked and had to invoke my ambassadorial authority to enter the premises. The place was in a shambles. No one had been there for some time.

Luckily, Jewish culture was not limited to state initiative. From 1989 on there was continuing establishment and expansion of institutions, all private and supported with outside help, promoting various aspects of the Hebrew language and Judaic studies. Schools or classes were organized at different levels, mostly in existing synagogues or in rooms in private homes. In none of these was there any evidence of government assistance. Where Soviet official bodies were involved, they were erratic and unreliable, even when the intentions of some were honourable.

Two examples stand out. First is the story of Rabbi Arthur Schneier, president of the Park East Synagogue of New York City. Years ago, Rabbi Schneier launched a campaign for the return of the northern wing to the Arkhipova Choral Synagogue — the main synagogue in Moscow. This space had been a *yeshiva*, or seminary, before the Second World War. During the war, the synagogue was forced to offer this wing as a hospital for the Red Army. The war having been won, the synagogue applied to the authorities to have its property restored. In the meantime, the government had assigned the disputed rooms to the Ministry of Health, which established a part of its offices there. Rabbi Schneier, who had access to very important Soviet personalities because of his involvement in international philanthropic and cultural work, pleaded insistently over the years for the return of the *yeshiva* area to the synagogue to which it belonged. The synagogue's rightful ownership was never denied, but the struggle for the restoration of this space took many years and traversed various epochs in the history of the Soviet Union. Rabbi Schneier showed extraordinary patience and indulgence in addition to his inordinate diplomatic skills. He knew how to talk to the Russians and he was also armed with an unshakable belief that he would win out in the end. When there was no other retreat for the authorities, they declared the Ministry of Health would move out only after it was provided with alternative housing. When this was done, they had to make repairs on the building. This painful process came to a final conclusion only after the fall of the Soviet Union. When the official transfer took place, the mayor of Moscow, Yuri Luzhkov, handed over the keys of the building to Rabbi Adolph Shayevich of the Choral Synagogue. Many speeches were made and glasses of kosher vodka raised, to mark the long-awaited occasion. Rabbi Schneier was there too, of course, but his face did not show the effects of the long haul and the tortuous paths he had had to tread to reach that summit.

The other example is the Adin Steinsaltz *yeshiva*. As I have already mentioned, Yevgeny Velikhov of the Academy of Sciences was deeply impressed with the personality of this outstanding Talmudic scholar. He invited Rabbi Steinsaltz to Moscow in October 1988 to appear before a select audience of Soviet scientists, including the famous astrophysicist Roald Sagdeyev, who later married Dwight Eisenhower's granddaughter. Rabbi Steinsaltz so impressed the members of the academy with his erudition and integrity that he was allowed to establish a small seminary within one of the buildings of the Academy of Sciences.

Already in the first years of perestroika many were attempting to fill the great spiritual void that had been created in the communist state over the 70 years of its existence. This was true of the leading scientists of the country as well as of the man in the street. Rabbi Steinsaltz appeared before this group of thinkers, which included world-renowned names, and spoke about the universal values of Judaism and their place in the world of today. His appearance met with great appreciation and success. It also initiated a friendship with these men of science, born and raised in a world of atheism, equipped with Marxism-Leninism as their sole guiding light, and inculcated with discipline and blind loyalty to the state. Evidently, there was a great deal more to life than the jargon of the communist paradigm. The study and observation of nature alone, could not wholly satisfy the curiosity of these intelligent people. The tribulations and suffering experienced by the population of this great land evoked profound questions which required answers. That is why the appearance of Rabbi Adin Steinsaltz was so welcome. He was a novelty, a man of unimposing physique but imbued with an inspiring presence; a man of a different culture and background, but captivating nevertheless.

Steinsaltz's *yeshiva* had to vacate the academy building after a year, and there were enormous difficulties in procuring alternative housing. There was a danger of the *yeshiva* closing its gates. Velikhov turned to many influential people and after a time found a solution. The *yeshiva* moved to the *dacha*, or country house, of the mayor of Moscow. Once situated on the outskirts of the city, the metropolis had eventually spread and encompassed the area with enormous residential complexes. This was a very modern wooden structure, with all the amenities granted to a communist boss, including a hidden movie projector in the large bedroom. The small group of students was garnered from the Moscow area. They would attend classes in the evenings at first, later extending into the daytime hours as well. The *yeshiva* soon became an attraction for foreign visitors. One evening in autumn 1989, I met Prime Minister Mulrooney of Canada there. Mulrooney had been on an visit to Gorbachev and had been invited to the *yeshiva* by Albert Reichman, the well-known financier and real estate developer of Toronto. Reichman was one of the people who supported the *yeshiva* financially and used his important connections in the Soviet

Union to protect and promote the interests of this as well as several other *yeshivot*, opened in subsequent years in Russia and in Ukraine.

The signs of relaxation increased as 1989 advanced. Continued pressure by the West, especially by the US and its Secretary of State George Shultz, were having a cumulative effect on the Soviet government. It was, nonetheless, far easier for the Russians to satisfy their newfound western friends with small gestures in favour of Jewish culture and tradition, than approach the problems of diplomatic relations with Israel.

It was becoming clear that the Soviet Union was not about to change the nature of its official relations with Israel. I had been traveling back and forth to Jerusalem, trying to run both my jobs, the Political Research Centre as well as the Moscow Mission. My personal life was suffering. I was seeing very little of my family. The idea of bringing my 13-year-old daughter, Yael, over to Moscow, even if she were to study in the American school, was not terribly appealing. It would take her at least a year of very hard work and emotional upset to get used to a different social group and make friends. Having already subjected our older children to this traumatic experience, we thought it would be criminal to go through it again. It was, in any event, categorically overruled by Yael, busy with her life in a far more friendly environment. The ministry wanted me to remain in Moscow. I would have to pick one of two alternatives: either abandon Moscow altogether or give up my Jerusalem job and stay in Moscow alone, with periodic visits home. This was a most difficult solution, hard on all of us, but I felt I had no choice. The Moscow challenge was far too great for me to turn my back on. This was a historic opening, a time of titanic movement. Would I not be there to witness it? I gave up my job in Jerusalem.

On Bastille day, 14 July 1989, I saw Gennady Tarasov at the French Embassy reception. I presented my wife Aliza, who had brought Yael with her to see Moscow. Tarasov said, 'I hear you have been relieved of your duties as head of the Political Research Department.' He never had to try hard to be unpleasant. He added as an afterthought, 'I understand you're now going to stay permanently in Moscow. Congratulations.' I thanked him for his politeness. Silently telling him to go to hell, I walked away, and found Boris Yeltsin. Very unpopular at the time, having been ousted in February as a candidate member of the Politburo and at odds with Gorbachev, Yeltsin was busy forming a party, and it was obvious that it would oppose the establishment. I talked with him at length, finding solace in speaking with a member of the opposition. Yeltsin said, among other things, 'Why don't you come to terms with these Arabs? Make a compromise, but don't drag it out any longer!' This fellow is belligerent all right, I thought, but at least he is sincere — a breath of fresh air after the vinegary vapours of the Smolensk Square Foreign Ministry bureaucrats.

8 · Duologue in Cairo

THE SOVIETS MAKE A SORTIE

The month of February 1989 was notable not only for the opening of the Mikhoels Centre: it was also the time when the Soviets again attempted to attain equal status with the US in the important region of the Middle East. Minister of Foreign Affairs Shevardnadze, prompted by his advisers to take a more active position, decided to try his hand at Middle East mediation. However, the Soviets gave the strong impression that they were primarily interested in establishing themselves as a point of reference for the Arabs. Operationally, the idea was floated around that Shevardnadze would probably be leaving on a tour of the Middle East, visiting Syria, Jordan, Egypt and Iraq. The Soviets were not pinning their hopes on Israel, which was not included in the list of countries Shevardnadze would visit. They had not had relations with Israel for many years, had little possibility to influence its policies, and in any case wanted to avoid close association with it for fear of damaging their ties with the Arab states.

The Israeli government, through the mission in Moscow and other channels, sent word to Shevardnadze that he would be welcome to include Jerusalem in his itinerary. The Soviets declined. If mediation was their goal, they were hardly demonstrating equal consideration for the interests of Israel and the Arabs. Whatever it was Shevardnadze was seeking to achieve, outwardly it appeared like an attempt to refurbish Arab connections. Insofar as we could judge by the wealth of information streaming in from open sources and from diplomatic and private contacts, the Politburo and the Central Committee realized that if negative economic trends continued much longer, the results might be catastrophic for the regime. It thus appeared that the overriding Soviet interest at the time was to attract investments. The Soviet Ministry of Foreign Affairs was attempting to bolster its international position in the Middle East and attract Arab investments in the Soviet economy by projecting greater understanding of Arab positions.

After a repeated exchange of messages, a meeting between Shevardnadze and Israeli Foreign Minister Moshe Arens was scheduled in Cairo. The thoughts and the attitude of the Soviets seemed clear. Their plan for a solution of the Middle East crisis, reminiscent of the one they proclaimed in 1984 at the UN, was structured on the principle of an international conference, with the participation of the five permanent members of the Security Council and the belligerents. Shevardnadze had repeatedly proposed this scheme in his meetings with Israeli leaders. In all of my contacts in Moscow, including my interview with Shevardnadze and the talks I had with Tarasov, this position stood out in sharp relief.

The Russians' self-esteem had been badly damaged in 1973 when Henry Kissinger deftly excluded them from the peace process. Kissinger left the machinery of the Geneva conference on the Middle East an empty shell, while he conducted shuttle diplomacy between the parties. The Russians wished to redress the situation but went about it in ways contrary to their own interests. They kept insisting on reviving the idea of an international conference, when the real activity was taking place elsewhere, under the aegis of the Americans. By 1989, the Soviets realized perfectly well they had been outmanoeuvred, but they needed to make their presence felt in the Middle East arena.

The time was ripe for finding a solution to hard core international conflicts, the Soviet government declared. As long as the Afghan crisis persisted and the Soviets had an extremely negative international image, they had not been too eager to show their hand. With the end of the Afghan conflict, they felt confident enough to make a sortie. In marketing their plan to the Arabs as that of a supportive friend, the Russians were implying that the US was a superpower with an Israeli slant. Besides, this tactic of friendship did not preclude an approach based on 'new thinking'. In the Israeli view, 'new Soviet thinking' was old thinking in the new context of the Middle East: the aim was to get all the Arabs to sit across the table from Israel in a conference supported by the UN and the European powers. On the Damascus leg of his Middle East tour, Shevardnadze encouraged Syrian President Hafez Assad to patch up his long-standing quarrel with the PLO in order to help present a united Arab front. The Russians would gain an equal status at the conference table as champions of the peace process, together with the Americans, if the Arabs were amenable.

Israel was fundamentally opposed to this whole approach. Ever since the end of the War of Independence, Israel's leaders had refused to face an array of Arab states sitting across the same table, where the presence and the power of the strongest Arab party would intimidate the others. A united Arab front would end all hope of reaching an understanding with the Arab countries. Egypt already had a peace agreement with Israel. It would not go to the conference as part of an Arab delegation. As a result, the Syrian line of greatest resistance and least complaisance would prevail. The Arabs would goad each other to greater heights of intransigence, only willing to accept superpower decisions foisted on the participants. The presence of the Palestinians would be meaningless, for they would have to toe the line of the strongest Arab delegation. Israel preferred to deal with its neighbours separately, where the national interests of each party would be considered and negotiated on a mutual basis, without the interference of outside powers.

The Soviet plan had two additional objectives: to stop nuclear proliferation in the region and to set up peacekeeping machinery. One of the authors of this idea was Sergei Rogov of the USA and Canada Institute, a former official of the Soviet Embassy in Washington DC. He had been the embassy's Middle East expert and did much to set up contacts both with the Israelis and the Jewish community in the American capital. When Rogov left the US, he was assigned to the disarmament desk at the USA and Canada Institute. A very able and articulate professional, Rogov had unorthodox ideas which he did not find necessary to conceal.

He was usually in demand because of his involvement with disarmament. I always enjoyed meeting him, though I often felt he advertised his understanding of Israel's problems a bit too strenuously. Apparently, he had his own pet disarmament projects that he was promoting, hoping to gain Israeli support.

Thus, when Shevardnadze set out on his trip to the Middle East, he had a whole basket of goods prepared for sale to the Arabs. The Israelis seemed to be less of an object of his courtship. Israeli minister Moshe Arens met Shevardnadze at Soviet ambassador Alexander Zhuravlev's residence on the Nile, on 22 February. I was there with my minister, as the man-on-the-spot, an ambassador without an embassy, as one of the leading Israeli papers called me. Accompanying Arens were Bibi Netanyahu, then deputy-minister of foreign affairs, Yeshayahu Anug, the deputy director-general and a few others. Zhuravlev and Tarasov assisted Shevardnadze.

The meeting opened with a very friendly exchange, including remarks on the population explosion in Egypt. When Arens asked his colleague about similar problems in the USSR, Shevardnadze said, 'We have reached a certain equilibrium. The Russians, Belorussians, Baltic peoples and Georgians are not working very hard, but there is a considerable overload in the Central Asian republics.'

The meeting in Cairo lasted over two hours. It was an extremely open and friendly juxtaposition of two entirely different approaches that could not possibly merge. Shevardnadze opened with a general assessment of the world situation and the need for conventional and nuclear disarmament. At times he spoke of American positions as though they had been coordinated with him. The Soviet foreign minister broadly hinted about his knowledge of Israel's capabilities and warned about proliferation. He kept harping on the theme of an international conference. Arens repeatedly asserted that the PLO was a terrorist organization. Shevardnadze said at one point that the USSR would have no objections to Israel's meeting with the PLO through the good offices of a country other than his own — there would be no competition on that score with the Americans, he remarked, tongue-in-cheek.

Arens went into a historical exposé on the years of struggle Israel had experienced and dwelt on the incompetence of the UN.

He described the complications that PLO terror caused. Shevardnadze countered that he simply could not understand why Israel, which had declared it favoured direct negotiations with its adversaries, refused to talk to the PLO. He thought Israel should think things over, as should the US. Israel, he warned, might find itself politically isolated. Arens suggested that the solution of the Palestinian problem had to be reached in conjunction with King Hussein of Jordan, as most of the West Bank inhabitants were Jordanian citizens and the population of Jordan included a majority of the Palestinians west and east of the river Jordan. Arens warned that if Soviet insistence on the PLO continued, there would not be much left to talk about. Shevardnadze retreated somewhat. He said visits with Israel could be exchanged if Israel agreed to meet the PLO.

Toward the end of this long conversation, Arens and Shevardnadze seemed rather weary of their own repetitions. The latter started nervously fiddling with his pen. Arens said time was too short for him to fully explain his position. The suggestion then arose spontaneously that experts should be exchanged to deepen the understanding of mutual views.

In summing up the meeting, the Soviet foreign minister said he was going public with his plan in Cairo and would speak about the USSR's greater involvement in the Middle East. He promised he would describe his meeting with his Israeli counterpart in positive terms. Finally, he said he would appoint someone knowledgeable about the area as his special representative on the Middle East crisis. Someone we knew, he added.

In spite of the many cups of strong Russian tea (with accompanying rock-hard Russian biscuits), we all came out of the meeting in a daze. The conversation had been too strenuous and meandering. We were greeted with the perspiring but expectant faces of a small army of journalists and television cameramen downstairs in the front yard, all of whom were convinced that the two-hour long conversation was going to end in an agreement on the resumption of diplomatic relations. Their disappointment was great when the only thing the two ministers could announce was their agreement to exchange experts at a future date. I asked Tarasov if he was the 'someone we knew'. He said he had no idea.

But he was, of course. I asked if Shevardnadze's insistence on the PLO's inclusion in a conference we were not prepared to enter into, was part of the 'new thinking' in Soviet foreign affairs. He assertively replied that it was.

Our delegation returned to Jerusalem that same day. The next morning Shevardnadze appeared before the Egyptian ruling party, and in the presence of many invited Egyptian personalities, proclaimed the new Soviet doctrine for the Middle East. The speech sounded a great deal more aggressive than the friendly persuasion we had encountered at the meeting in Cairo.

While disclaiming any magic formula, Shevardnadze said in his public address that the conflict boiled down to the Palestinians' right to self-determination and Israel's right to exist within secure borders. Israel had the USSR's support in 1947 for gaining its self-determination through the UN, he continued. Now, Israel was preventing the Palestinians from obtaining theirs. In so doing, Israel was undermining its own security and the legitimacy of its own self-determination. Israel was the only country that opposed an international conference on the Middle East. It could continue in its refusal, but would then run the risk of political isolation and legitimate international sanctions.

As there had been a lot of homework done in Moscow on the peace machinery that would be set up, Shevardnadze dutifully raised the issue. It would include a package of guarantees, he said, mutually assured surveillance and control of armaments including nuclear weapons. He renewed his call for an international conference, saying all Arab countries were agreed on that point. The USSR had encouraged the Arab leaders to exchange visits at the highest level, in order to discuss the subject.

The Soviet foreign minister called for an end to the 'enemy' image which prevailed between Israel and the Arab countries of the Middle East. Shevardnadze concluded his speech by saying that relations between Israel and the USSR were dependent on Israel's recognition of the PLO. The launching of the international conference would begin the countdown.

The Soviet press ecstatically applauded full Arab support for Shevardnadze's plan. However, the Arab position was not entirely clear. Jordan would run the danger of sublimating its interests to those of Syria; the PLO hardly could be expected to accept Syrian dominance at the conference table. This mattered little to the Soviets. The important thing was to get their feet in the door. It should be noted that Israel was also uncomfortable about a certain political understanding between the USSR and France on the issue of an international conference, but this was nothing new. France too had its own well-defined interests in the Arab world. The statement that Israel was 'endangering its own self-determination' was found to be offensive. Israel was not on trial as a state and the Russians were not there to decide our fate. The words about possible sanctions, too, were entirely unnecessary. Our reaction was one of disappointment. I do not remember what we really expected the Russians to say, but Shevardnadze had, perhaps inadvertently, placed an additional obstacle in the way of improving relations.

To many of us old enough to remember, Shevardnadze's speech brought back memories of the Suez Canal crisis in 1956, when Britain, France and Israel launched a joint attack against President Abdul Nasser of Egypt. Nasser had nationalized the canal and blocked it against its British and French owners. Israel occupied the Sinai peninsula and the Gaza strip. At the time, the Soviet prime minister, Marshal Nikolai Bulganin, sent an ultimatum to Ben-Gurion saying there would be an intercontinental ballistic missile attack against Israel if it did not comply with the UN resolutions on withdrawal from the Suez Canal and Sinai. Prime Minister Ben-Gurion read that 'subtle' message out in the Knesset and concluded it by reading the signature, N. Bulganin. Bulganin was on everyone's mind when we read the text of Shevardnadze's Cairo speech.

The reason I describe at length this ill-fated meeting in Cairo is to show how little the Soviets understood us, or the Middle East, for that matter. Their whole approach was condemned to failure from the start. It should have been amply evident that Israel would not accept the terms of the Soviet propositions. Anyone seriously wishing to mediate had to have equal credibility with both the Arabs and the Israelis. The Soviets failed in winning over Arab support as well. They had lost their prestige with the Arabs long before Shevardnadze set out to recruit them by offering the tainted goods of an international conference. In 1989, Egypt was already refitting its military equipment with western parts. It did not need more Soviet arms, for whose past deliveries it had a huge debt pending. Syria still needed Soviet *matériel*, but was no longer granted credit. Both Egypt and Syria, the leading countries of the Arab Middle East, well understood the facts of economic life: the USSR could be of no help to them; they did not need arms as much as they needed financial aid, which the USSR was unable to furnish, itself experiencing a major economic crisis. Syria was seeking a rapprochement with the US but was unable to achieve it because of its own intransigence, fuelled by internal and inter-Arab considerations and its support of terrorism.

The Cairo session of the two foreign ministers had been preceded, less than two months earlier, by a Paris get-together. The agenda in the French capital had been similar: there were propositions quite unacceptable to Israel and a demonstration of naïveté about the new rightist Likud government. Soviet experts, after many years of isolation from Israel and close contact with Arab politicians and officials, were unable to comprehend the Israeli mentality, formed in the context of the continuous state of war with the Arabs and Palestinians. It was difficult for us to understand Soviet stubbornness in declaring Israel-Soviet relations to be a function of Israel's attitude toward the PLO. There may have been additional reasons for this lack of insight. At times, a literal reading of the Israeli press or too impressionable an opinion about the influence of various Jewish leaders, added to the Soviet officials' confusion.

On the eve of the Mikhoels Centre inauguration on 12 February 1989, there was a meeting between Shevardnadze and Edgar Bronfman, president of the World Jewish Congress. At this meeting Bronfman recounted the conversation he had had with Larry Eagleburger, then US deputy secretary of state, at which matters concerning direct Jewish emigration to Israel were discussed. Eagleburger also announced the US intention to alter the practice of awarding emigrants automatic refugee status. This was an important point. The Soviet authorities were perfectly aware that large numbers of Soviet Jews were arriving in the US with Israeli visas and claiming refugee status, and they were interested in perpetuating that process: the Kremlin was concerned about Arab criticism of the inflow of large masses of Jewish manpower into Israel. Bronfman said, further, that Eagleburger would be supportive of the demand that Israel issue its visas from its own embassy in Moscow, implying the time had come to re-establish official relations, at least in some form. However, Shevardnadze swiftly swept this last point under the rug, saying it would have to be discussed with the Israelis.

Bronfman went on to say that he would like to discuss the Middle East. He related to pressure 'being brought to bear for direct negotiations between the Palestinians and Israel'. Bronfman elaborated a suggestion: the UN should make an accord under which the US and the USSR would shuttle back and forth, together or separately, to bring the parties together. Then, if an agreement could come about on Gaza and the West Bank, an international conference could make the peace comprehensive for the whole area. So there would be no doubt as to the support this idea had in Israel, Bronfman told Shevardnadze he had delegated his assistant, Israel Singer, to discuss this issue with Prime Minister Shamir. The prime minister commented to Singer that he would be willing to discuss this question with any person necessary.

The fact was that the idea of an international conference was abhorrent to Shamir. I have no idea what Shevardnadze really thought of Bronfman's suggestion. He told the president of the World Jewish Congress that he agreed that a Palestinian-Israeli dialogue was an interim stage toward a conference and comprehensive settlement, but did not know how the Arabs would respond to it.

After a time, when I visited Prime Minister Shamir, I asked him about his position on Bronfman's proposal. He had no recollection of having had such a conversation with Singer. Shamir's memory, selective or not, is not the point. Bronfman was conveying the impression that his ideas had been coordinated with the Israeli prime minister. In essence this made Bronfman, who is a highly respected Canadian citizen, a representative of Israel on an important matter of state. Yet, the particular notion Bronfman brought up was quite contradictory to declared Israeli positions. Edgar Bronfman was acting in good faith, but he seems to have been poorly advised. Shevardnadze was not well-versed on the intricacies of Jewish politics and was taking Bronfman's declarations at face value. All of which must have undoubtedly increased Shevardnadze's confusion regarding Israeli positions. Shevardnadze's staff were probably as perplexed as many others in the Soviet Union who could not, for the life of them, distinguish between Jews and Israelis. As I became more deeply involved in Israel's positions in the USSR, I often came across this desire to project leadership, without prior consideration for the fallout.

9 · A Dutch Consulate at the Israeli Embassy

Tarasov's official announcement allowing us back onto the first floor of the embassy building was made in January 1989. We thought it would be a matter of a few weeks. I had visited the embassy with the members of my mission and found that a thorough clean-up was all that was needed after the 22-year absence. The large garage was filled to the brim with furniture and bric-à-brac left over from 1967. Judicious use of these remnants could help us get started. The Netherlands deputy chief of mission Willem Bentinck and I divided up the rooms between the Dutch Consulate that would open in the building and our own staff. We would be ready for business by 1 March, we thought. In fact, it took us until the first days of summer, almost 22 years to the day after we were expelled by the Soviets.

In my endeavours to organize the first floor for consular business, I had to deal with the UPDK. In the good old days of the Soviet Union this organization, affiliated with the Soviet Ministry of Foreign Affairs, provided housing, food, fuel, and vacations for the diplomatic corps. It was also one of the instruments of KGB intrusion into the personal and professional lives of foreigners. I had thus to deal with the extensive bureaucracy of UPDK in all things connected with the repairs of the embassy building as well as the installation of a telex, telephones and the rest. The UPDK people were very cooperative and polite, but their inefficiency was astounding. I could not help suspecting that there were sinister motives behind their snail's pace. All they had to do was sand the walls here and there, repaint and repair the sanitary installations. But they had just run out of toilet bowls; then they had no white paint; afterwards, there were difficulties with the electrical wiring; and finally, they had no telephones. When, in desperation, I found an Austrian contractor who promised to do the job, though for a much stiffer price than the Russians, problems arose in transporting the fittings from Vienna. When the Russians found out we were dealing with Austrians, they were terribly offended. How could we? We had signed a contract with the UPDK! By the way, they had just run out of lighting fixtures. Could we get them from Israel? And so it went.

As I flew into Moscow from Vienna in the first days of May, I was pleasantly surprised at the transformation that had taken place. My previous visit had been in early November, when the ground was covered with snow, the skies were overcast and the disposition of the Russians doleful. The grim looks had etched themselves into my mental picture of the city. Now people appeared more relaxed, the trees were green and the banks of the Moscow River were covered with fresh grass.

We were certain that in a few weeks we would be past all the procrastination and would be able to open the embassy. As the celebration of our first Independence Day in Moscow approached, I decided to give a reception, come what may. I consulted the Dutch ambassador, who did not have any objections. I contracted the 'Russian Restaurant' hall at the Armand Hammer Centre, and we were off to a flying start. This was the only western-style enclave in the city, with several restaurants, not at all bad, a hotel and offices in a separate wing. The industrialist Armand Hammer had dreamed up this project years back. It was his genius and influence in high places that carried it through, much to the relief of many foreigners in this dilapidated, gloomy capital.

The Hammer Centre operated in a distinctly different manner from the rest of the hotels and restaurants in Moscow. It was built as a large, self-contained complex, with its own heating, air-conditioning and other systems, plust elements of a mall — a non-existent concept in the USSR in those days. Guards posted at the doors checked passports, and denied entry to Soviet citizens. The restaurants, primarily for foreign residents of the hotel, were as ridiculously cheap as the others in the city, all controlled and subsidized by the government. I remember one occasion when we went in to have lunch at the Hammer Centre. We were asked if we were residents. We said we were, and ordered the usual plentiful Moscow meal. The bill for the three of us, including hors-d'oeuvres, soup, large steaks, and dessert came to just over nine dollars. This was the usual bill in public eating places, unless the waiters got wind of your being a foreigner, which would raise the price considerably. The Japanese Sakura restaurant at the Hammer Centre cost 300 dollars for lunch, for two. It was *the* prestigious place to which Russians wanted to be invited.

AFFIXING THE MEZUZAH

On the eve of Israel's Independence Day, which fell on 10 May that year, I went to affix the mezuzah* on the doorpost of the embassy building. I meant for this to be a public act symbolizing our return, but this could not be arranged without first gaining the agreement of the Dutch ambassador, who was our official caretaker. I went over to his office and we had a most unusual conversation.

Petrus Buwalda listened with great interest to what I had to say on the plans to refurbish the embassy building. There was a great deal of impatience at the Dutch Embassy. They were badly cramped themselves and needed additional space. The Dutch consul Robert Lanschoot was constantly asking us when the repairs would be completed so that they could move in with their staff, since their own consular traffic would be handled from our embassy as well. I told Ambassador Buwalda that everything was ready and that we would be moving in shortly. I added that I wanted to carry out an ancient Jewish rite of affixing a mezuzah to the doorpost.

The Dutch ambassador looked concerned and said he might

---

* A small parchment scroll inscribed with a portion of the Old Testament and attached in a case to the doorpost of a Jewish house as a sign of faith.

have to consult with the Hague. I was taken aback. There was something amiss. I carefully explained about the mezuzah again and pointed out that it had no legal effect on the ownership of the building or the fact that we were still under the auspices of the Netherlands. Ambassador Buwalda seemed relieved, but not fully. He said the problem was of a different nature. Under Dutch law and practice, there was no custom of praying or making a blessing, either Catholic, Protestant or otherwise, on such occasions. The government was secular and there was a total separation of church and state. If prayers were to be said, then all denominations would have to be present. He would have to consult. A number of days later Buwalda called me in and said it was all right, I could go ahead with the mezuzah ritual and, although he was not terribly happy with it, he would not make any objections. It was my turn to be relieved, but not fully. It was, after all, our embassy and it was strange to have to get approval for this innocent rite. There is no separation of church and state in Israel, but I could understand his point in this case.

When it was all over, I heard remarks from Tarasov, too. I had to tell him not to worry about the legal implications; it was only between man and God and since the Soviet Union was swiftly returning to old religious customs, I was certain there would be no misunderstandings on that score. Tarasov looked at me with distaste. He was, after all, a devout communist.

On the Day of Independence, I invited Rabbi Adolf Shayevich of the Moscow synagogue to come and officiate. Word had got out and there was a small group of excited people watching the proceedings with undisguised emotion. We screwed the mezuzah securely to the iron doorpost (which did not prevent it from being lifted as a souvenir by the first wave of callers who rushed to the embassy). There were some photographers present and journalist Amnon Kapeliuk of the Tel Aviv daily paper *Yediot Aharonot*, who recorded the event for posterity. Officially, Kapeliuk was the representative of *Le Monde Diplomatique* of Paris, as Israeli journalists were not allowed into the USSR. I considered him a friend and fellow sufferer in Moscow, with whom I shared many joys and frustrations. Directly after the mezuzah ceremony, I went to our reception at the Armand Hammer Centre. I stood at the entrance welcoming Israel's first guests in 22 years with Soviet champagne and red caviar (which is considered kosher, as opposed to black, which is not).

Elsewhere in the eastern bloc similar receptions were taking place for the first time in many years. The Soviet decision to sever ties with Israel in the wake of the Six-Day War had damaged the whole fabric of Israel's relations with the East European countries under the tutelage of the USSR. As I stood at the entrance to our own reception, I thought of my colleagues, Shlomo Marom in Budapest and Mordechai Paltzur in Warsaw. They too probably had 'butterflies' in their stomachs. They had also waited for this Independence Day with a great deal of impatience, after suffering many months of frustrations and setbacks and fighting heavy-handed communist bureaucracy. Still, the situation in Moscow was unique. In the excitement of that first large reception, my mind could not but recall Israel's first diplomatic mission as an independent Jewish country in the Soviet Union.

GOLDA'S LEGACY

The Israeli ten-shekel banknote carries a likeness of Golda Meir, surrounded by thousands of Jews welcoming her on her first visit to the central synagogue in Moscow, after her arrival to head the new legation in 1949. Golda is depicted on this bill because the plight of Soviet Jews, kept as hostages by the Soviet government, had become a national and later an international issue. The illustration symbolizes the world-wide campaign which came to be called 'Let My People Go'. Its goal was to persuade the Soviet government to allow free emigration. Golda had purposefully gone to visit the single place of worship left to the quarter of a million Jews in the capital. Thousands congregated in the aisles and in the doorways, trying to reach out, touch her clothes and pass handwritten notes. There was perceptible, pervasive fear that forbidden ardour shown an emissary representing the Jewish state would be avenged by the KGB.

From 1927 on, when Stalin completely took over the reins of the Communist Party, the lot of Soviet Jewry was painful and bitter.

Jews lived with growing discrimination. Administrative repression could be turned off and on by the government at the slightest whim. The presence of an Israeli embassy in their midst somehow gave a ray of hope for intercession and help — a connection, albeit fragile, to the Jewish world at large. Jews were not allowed to visit the Israeli Embassy and avoided it even when invited to receptions. Soviet personalities of Jewish background rarely responded to invitations out of fear of being persecuted or of falling under suspicion of committing the deadly sin of collaboration with Israel. The Israeli Embassy, like all western embassies, was almost totally isolated from the public. But whereas most embassy diplomats did not have kinsmen in Moscow, the Israelis did. And Jews kept abreast of events in Israel, a difficult and risky effort though it was. I remember the late General Yosef Avidar, one of the ambassadors who served in Moscow before 1967, once telling me how, while walking in the street, he was passed by a young man who distinctly said, in Hebrew: 'The temperature in Eilat will be 32 degrees'. This was to confirm that Israel radio was being listened to, even though it was forbidden. The message was that whatever the danger, Soviet Jews would always be with us.

Golda Meir arrived in Moscow only a few years after the Second World War, the Holocaust, and the renewal of Stalin's repression against the Jews. Stalin's recognition of Israel and the material help given the young Jewish state in its war against the Arabs had no bearing on the leader's anti-Semitic policies. The Jews in Moscow knew Golda was one of the leaders of the new country, that she was Ukrainian-born, and that her family had fled the pogroms early in the century. Her presence in Moscow, as a legitimate representative of the state that had been helped by Stalin, awakened a feeling that times might change. They did not, of course. The persecution and the anti-Jewish campaigns continued and grew more intense. Many of the people who had welcomed Golda Meir at the synagogue were identified by the KGB and later interrogated or jailed. After a while, a heavy curtain descended on the Jews. Most contacts with relatives abroad were cut. It was politically unwise even to admit one had relatives outside the country. My own cousins, I later discovered, destroyed letters and pictures my father had sent them, or carefully crossed out the words on the photos, for fear of an 'unexpected visit' to their home. The very phrase 'relatives abroad' was feared as it was considered equivalent to an admission of anti-Soviet activity. A friend once showed me a postcard he had received from a cousin in the USSR. It was sent from the Republic of Georgia, although the cousin was a resident of Moscow. 'Al Tikhtevuli' was given as the sender's name. It sounded Georgian, but meant, in Hebrew: 'Don't write to me'.

INDEPENDENCE DAY IN MOSCOW

All this belonged to the past. In May 1989, the situation was different. The fortunes of the communist regime were considered unpredictable, but everyone felt its end was near. Perestroika was still a new and promising phenomenon. While the sad demise of Khrushchev's Thaw in 1965 was vividly remembered, hope seemed to be edging out fear. Spring was in the air, there was great enthusiasm, an expectation of better days and the anticipation of a Jewish exodus. These sentiments led the representatives of the Jewish communities all over the Soviet Union to come to Moscow to identify with us at the reception. We were conscious of the important times ahead. We knew we would eventually open our embassy and organize direct flights of immigrants to Israel. We did not know these hopes would take two years to be fulfilled.

The Israeli flag at the entrance was small, but there was no mistaking the nationality of the hosts. The Israeli Mission reception to mark its country's Day of Independence had become the talk of the town. Over 150 people, from the Academy of Sciences, the research institutes, the press, personal friends, painters, actors and other artists as well as a relatively large number of heads of diplomatic missions from western countries, attended the event. Considering the fact that we were not allowed to send out written invitations and had to spread the word by telephone, the reception was well attended, though it clashed with a more important event, a reception at the same hour for the US Secretary of State James Baker. I had invited people from the Soviet Foreign Ministry. After promising to send a representative, they made sure no Soviet official attended. The absence of Soviet diplomats was more than compensated for by the many Jews from all over the Soviet Union who had received personal invitations. This became a tradition at every reception we had in the Soviet Union afterwards.

Later in the day, there was a large gathering at the Mikhoels Centre, organized by the Jewish Historical Society. An overflow crowd came to mark Israel's Day of Independence. I addressed them from a rostrum draped in a large Israeli flag, an act of daring on the part of the organizers. Jewish folklore ensembles, Klezmers, played traditional tunes. Elsewhere, there were large picnics in the forests around Moscow. In the past, these outings in the forest had been confrontational — the KGB and the police often arresting the celebrants. Now the atmosphere became so relaxed that a newly formed political group organized by a rightist Israeli party used the occasion to carry out paramilitary exercises in the woods, training young people to carry a wounded man on a stretcher over rough terrain. When I later inquired, I was told this was in preparation for their immigration and induction into the Israeli army. Marking Israel's independence in May 1989 was the first tangible proof of the mission coming into its own in the unfriendly territory of the Soviet Union.

CAMPING WITH THE DUTCH

We opened the embassy for official business on 5 June 1989. The sign at the gate said 'The Royal Netherlands Embassy, Consular Department'. There was a large official Dutch coat of arms at the entrance to the building. The only indication that this compound had anything at all to do with Israel was an additional plaque at the gate that simply said: 'Visas to Israel'. I had insisted it should be there, for want of an acceptable alternative. The sanctioned first floor was all spruced up, the parquet floors waxed, the furniture and decorations left over from the closing day in 1967 distributed to the various offices. Our immediate preoccupation would now be the processing of emigrants, including the verification of their identity and eligibility for an Israeli visa. There were a great many other activities that my lone assistant and I still had to attend to in setting up the rudiments of a soon to be embassy: political contacts, public relations and press and logistics. In reality, we knew we would have little opportunity to organize our time. The number of visitors promised to be overwhelming.

On opening day the Dutch ambassador Petrus Buwalda arrived in his official car, proudly flying the flag of the Netherlands. Together, we went from room to room on an inspection tour, to make sure everything would function as planned. Members of the mission broke out bottles of champagne and the gates were thrown open. A considerable crowd had been waiting outside since dawn. All rushed in and sat down on the few available chairs and on the steps of the staircase to fill in their questionnaires. So great was the enthusiasm of the callers that an elderly man walked right through one of the very large glass doors. He got up, smiling, with only a few cuts and bruises.

In a few days' time we had the telex in place and I sent a triumphant first message to Jerusalem. The response was dampening. Jerusalem simply could not fathom what the mission in Moscow wanted. ('So you have telex; big deal!') I could not believe it. The telex was a major achievement after all those long frustrating months of no communications at all. This dichotomy — the high praise we were getting for our efforts ('Continue your sacred work'), struggling days and nights to keep afloat in the face of a great deal of hostility, and, on the other hand, the native-Israeli rudeness of 'You're not the only ones' — always left us bewildered. But these were only momentary aggravations. In most cases the bureaucrats at home extended us a helping hand.

Soon after opening day, crowds began forming in ever-growing numbers at the gates. They would start arriving in the early morning and organize into queues, a conditioned reflex in the Soviet Union. Brokers would appear when numbers became unmanageable. For a fee, they would organize the line, write up a list and trade off places between the applicants. There were separate lines: emigration, visitors and Dutch visas for Holland. The latter were usually Africans or Asians, studying in Moscow under Soviet state scholarships. They were seeking tourist visas to work in Holland or another European country during their summer vacations. They would then return with replenished purses for the following semester.

One other category of people who received Israeli visas from the Dutch Embassy were the Pentecostalists, Baptists and other non-Jewish Soviet dissidents who were emigrating on the basis of invitations from Israel. These applicants also suffered persecution for their religious beliefs and there was no other way for them to leave the Soviet Union. As the Dutch Embassy was representing Israel, it began issuing Israeli visas to members of these communities, on the understanding they would not settle in Israel but go on to other countries. This too was an aberration of international understandings. The Soviet government knew these people were leaving, but did not want to let them go to countries other than Israel. The probable reason was that the Russians feared that the exit of non-Jews in large numbers would reflect negatively on their public image. It was natural for the Jews to want to leave, but not others.

This procedure continued until the early 1990s, when emigration was shorn of its many earlier limitations. The Israeli government was not terribly happy over this evident misuse of its visas by people who were not entitled to them by Israeli law, and representations were made to the Dutch, but to no effect. Prime Minister Shamir once inquired of Ambassador Buwalda, visiting in Jerusalem, if the practice could not be changed. Buwalda refused, as the Dutch were acting on the basis of agreements with other European countries. There was also pressure from the US government not to change the routine that had been established and for the consular delegation not to urge the Soviet authorities to deny Pentecostalists and others exit permits issued on the basis of Israeli visas. Israeli objections were not too strenuous and the matter was not pursued.

The increasing number of callers soon began evolving into a whole new embassy compound subculture. The embassy was the only spot in the 23 million square kilometre territory of the USSR where a visa to Israel could be obtained and the supporting papers checked and verified. The grounds became an open-air meeting place for Jews from all over the Soviet Union. As applicants for visas were usually accompanied by relatives or good friends, the prerequisite visit to the embassy was becoming somewhat of a social event as well. For those out of town, there were relatives, friends or even mere acquaintances helping with lodgings, information and advice on how to surmount the difficulties. Our policy was to issue the necessary papers on the same day insofar as possible. This meant longer dalliance on embassy grounds of people who had to have their papers handled. The small number of our officials was an impediment to efficiency. After a time, some 20 young Jewish 'volunteers' were taken on and paid to help manage the crowds. The Soviet government did not interfere in this arrangement, perhaps because they were using some of these non-mission employees to keep a vigilant eye on the proceedings.

The business of emigration kept us occupied and alert. The great wave that washed over us in the latter part of 1989 had not begun yet, but our hands were already full. We had taken over from the Dutch the procedure of checking the *vizovs* and handing them back after correction. As there were tens of thousands of these, it was a time-consuming affair and had to be done almost around the clock. The Dutch personnel were also swamped with work as they had the sole authorization to stamp the visas.

One other service our mission had taken over from the Dutch was the collection of the immigrants' personal documents, such as professional diplomas, driving licences and even marriage certificates. The authorities did not allow the emigrants to take their personal documents with them, and we had to put them in special envelopes with personal details and send them all by Dutch diplomatic mail to the Hague, where they were redirected to the emigrants' final destinations. The expense was enormous, but we thought it only fair. Emigrating to a new country without one's papers is tantamount to losing one's identity and creates enormous difficulties upon arrival. This 'punishment' was certainly unnecessary but was part of the contorted logic of Soviet bureaucracy. It took us several years of unending negotiations to cancel the ruling on taking personal documents out of the country. The Soviets were perfectly aware of the fact that we were sending hundreds of kilograms of documents by diplomatic mail, yet there was never a question raised on this subject at any level. On the contrary, on many occasions I personally talked with Foreign Ministry officials and others about the superfluous activity and expense involved and requested cancellation of the restrictions. I was consistently told the practice would be changed, but no decision had been taken by the end of 1990.

Emigration visas to Israel are granted under the Law of Return. Promulgated in the first days after the establishment of the State of Israel, this law permits any person of Jewish origin (on the side of either parent), to settle in Israel. It also recognizes as eligible, applicants with Jewish grandparents or spouses. The provisions of this law widen the framework of legitimate immigrants. The result of this liberal approach was that some 20 per cent of those who received Israeli visas were non-Jews. The social, religious and political problems that ensued have not been solved and will hound us for many years to come. On many occasions, visitors from Israel would inquire into this aspect of the emigration process. Mostly, these were representatives of parliamentary, religious or political organizations, who expressed concern over the number of non-Jews slipping in under the provisions of the Law of Return. The majority of non-Jews obtaining immigration visas did so lawfully. An extremely low percentage got in illegally, usually on forged documents. In 1990 we set up an unofficial committee to monitor these infractions by receiving access to the Ministry of Justice's population registry department, the only agency in the Soviet Union authorized to maintain and issue birth certificates going back several decades. This department became the final arbiter in disputed cases over questions of parentage, but insofar as I can recall, their advice was sought rarely. The forgeries were usually discovered on the spot and we took care of them by ourselves.

The number of applicants for emigration from the Soviet Union was growing rapidly in other embassies as well. The chanceries of Germany, Austria, the UK and Greece, to name the popular ones, were being besieged. Greece was attractive to citizens of Greek background who had settled in Russia several generations earlier. They were now eager to use their connections to escape. Yet, the fastest growing numbers of applicants were at the Israel Embassy/Dutch Consulate. An Israeli visa was an easy conduit to the US. Nonetheless, it was our policy not to set limitations on this practice in the hope that the long-awaited exodus to Israel would finally begin.

10 · Visitors and Natives

Through spring to early autumn of 1989 the workload of the mission was increasing steadily. This was a period of heightened activity and expectations of greater things to come with regard to *aliyah* and to my widening scope of contacts. The Americans had been liberally granting refugee status to Soviet citizens of Jewish origin, faced with prevalent anti-Semitism and prejudice. However, the US government was soon to change its practice of processing applicants from the USSR in Italy or Austria. Applications would be reviewed by the US Consulate in Moscow. In the middle of summer 1989 I got word to that effect from the US ambassador, Jack Matlock, and from senators and congressmen visiting Moscow. The reason was that the relaxation of emigration regulations engendered by perestroika reduced the need for refugee status being granted by the US government. There was also the high cost to the US taxpayers, as the Jewish communities in the US were apparently unwilling to reimburse the government for all the costs involved. Jews would still be admitted into the US as refugees, but not as freely as before. There was also continued pressure in Washington on behalf of Israel, to discontinue an arrangement which diverted immigrants from that country. Processing of emigrants in Rome and Vienna would be abandoned and the American Consulate would gear up in Moscow to take care of the increased numbers of prospective immigrants to the US. This development represented a substantive change in the direction of emigration for the near future. By the end of summer we realized at the mission that a very sharp increase in emigration to Israel, for which we had been hoping all along, was just around the corner. At the same time, such an increase would strain our resources even more, if relations were not restored and additional officials not permitted by the Soviets to be added to the mission roster.

The relaxation of international tensions and the continued loosening of the political vice were beginning to dispel the trauma of the Stalinist years — still noticeable at the end of 1988, when I arrived in Moscow. The population's pervasive fears of eavesdropping, control and persecution, were beginning to fade. People were regaining their voices. Russians were more willing to meet and talk with Israeli diplomats, which considerably eased the environment in which we were living and working. On a personal level, my relations with the establishment and the public in general were improving steadily.

A POLE OF ATTRACTION

At the height of summer, after we had moved into our own offices, contact with the Jewish population strengthened and developed. The mission's presence within the old embassy building on Bolshaia Ordynka Street was widely publicized. Those who needed consular help were perfectly well informed of our working and sleeping hours, but the telephones never ceased ringing, day and night, at our rooms in the Ukraina Hotel. Moreover, the well-known Soviet government limitations on entry into the territory of a foreign mission were becoming a thing of the past. The embassy grounds, rooms and corridors were crowded with people who came to consult, request assistance, offer their imagined or real scientific inventions or industrial technology, their books and their advice or simply get acquainted, open their hearts and pour out their pent-up feelings. It was impossible to satisfy or seriously relate to the desires and the requests of all our visitors, but it was important to hear them out: our mission had become an important address, psychologically and materially, for Jews all over the country. There had never been another place for them to turn to. Our rule was to receive as many as was humanly possible. This was probably counterproductive, but unavoidable. We had to remain accessible to our callers virtually around the clock, at our offices and at home. Our ministry had thus to relieve us every six to eight weeks and give us an opportunity to live at home for a few days before we went back to our posts. The Nativ officials did longer stints because of their exceptionally heavy workload. As head of the mission I had to create a sense of permanence, and was only permitted brief leaves of absence.

JERUSALEM WATCHES AND WAITS

The Israeli Ministry of Foreign Affairs maintained a heightened interest in our Moscow existence. My periodic presence back home enabled me to meet and talk with many of the political leaders of the country. The reason I had such a captive audience was the continued absence of daily communications with Moscow, where we still had no cipher or dependable telephone lines. There was plenty of international reporting, but no first-hand, eyewitness information. My presentations received ever wider exposure as many new friends appeared in my life, all exceptionally curious about the Soviet Union — still a love-and-hate object to many in Israel.

I had served President Haim Herzog as aide-de-camp when he was head of military intelligence in the 1960s, on his trips to Haile Selassie's Ethiopia and the Shah's Iran, and I had briefed him when I was head of political research. He was keen to listen to the latest reports about the Russian scene. Prime Minister Shamir, always hungry for news about what he liked to call 'Soviet Russia', asked me to report to him personally whenever I was in Jerusalem. Foreign Minister Arens expressed great interest in the work of the mission, although he seemed powerless to accede to my requests that Nativ be brought into line. This agency was already displaying growing unruliness, soon to develop into a confrontation.

The situation in the Soviet Union was fluid. There was no clear indication as to where that country was heading. On the other hand, there was no attempt made to discuss or plan our own actions or possible initiatives ahead of time. I was not given strict political parameters or instructed to attain definite goals. It was self-evident that planning would be a complete waste of time. Meetings with the director-general were conducted on the basis of pragmatic views of the situation in Moscow, never a discussion of long-term perspectives, insofar as I can recall. It was difficult to project ahead with only two Foreign Ministry men on the spot and Herculean tasks on their hands. The Foreign Ministry had a wait-and-see attitude toward developments. The initiative was in the hands of the Soviet government. In the final analysis, it fell to the mission itself to try and establish its presence in the Soviet capital.

In the vastness of the city around me, amid the feverish agitation at the mission from the early morning hours when I would arrive at work until the small hours of the next day, there was no person with whom I could consult or share my burdens and doubts. Nor was there anyone whose advice I was prepared to seek or take. In my office, intruded upon constantly by outsiders coming to see me personally or to use our only telephone line, I could rely only on myself. It was inadvisable to speak out even in the presence of close associates. I had to take into consideration, as did all members of the mission, that the KGB was trailing us and that we had to be constantly on guard against the Soviet 'dirty tricks department'. Our security was not capable of giving us any protection — only advice. We were still a group under the auspices of the Dutch Embassy, with no defensive perimeter of our own. Poor communications virtually cut us off from our headquarters and homes. These severely limiting factors, however, did not decrease the tempo of the mission's activity nor prevent it from carrying out its functions.

In March 1989 the new coalition government in Israel presented a peace plan for the Middle East. I was now able to brief the Foreign Ministry and the media, to whom we were gaining greater access. We were also engaged in expanding the reach of the mission, getting to know people and officials, projecting Israel's political personality and its character as a modern state. My task of making friends and influencing a great number of often suspicious and uncooperative people, in a disoriented and complex country where I had never set foot before, was indeed a challenge.

A LINK WITH GORBACHEV

My repeated attempts to reach the Central Committee's shamans on the Middle East and Israel were not terribly successful. Valentin Falin, head of the International Department, responsible for planning, coordinating and conducting active measures against foreign countries, was a great specialist on Germany and was also dabbling in the Middle East. His counsel carried great weight with the Politburo. He never returned my calls. This appeared to be common Soviet practice. Karen Brutens, a well-known Central Committee specialist on the Middle East, was unavailable. When I once finally got through to his secretary, she told me Brutens had instructed her to tell me he would call me. After many attempts and false starts, I finally got an appointment with Vadim Zagladin, one of Gorbachev's closest international advisers. Zagladin was a professional. He knew the international scene from his long involvement in Soviet propaganda. His frequent trips abroad and contacts with political parties friendly to the Soviet Union had made him more aware of the world at large than some of his other colleagues at the Central Committee. Zagladin was also well-known for drafting memos and speeches for Brezhnev. The promise of a meeting was given in early April. I got to see Zagladin toward the end of June 1989.

Since I enjoyed no diplomatic status, so important in Soviet officialdom, Zagladin chose to receive me at the Peoples' House of Friendship. This was a common venue for links with non-governmental, pro-Soviet organizations in Africa, Asia and Latin America. The House of Friendship was located in the handsome turn-of-the-century mansion of Sava Morozov, a pre-Revolutionary Russian millionaire, whose mistress had led him into the arms of the revolutionaries and kept him there long enough for him to become a devotee and contributor.

I knew Zagladin would come to the meeting well prepared. I had no idea of the extent to which he was influenced by the official dogma concerning Israel. From my experience in the Soviet Union, I had found many well-informed people reluctant to think for themselves on the questions of the Middle East. I had decided that at the risk of inflicting boredom, I would recapitulate the basic tenets of Israel's position, and touch on Soviet-Israel relations. Since it was such an important meeting, I thought I should also present a detailed summary of the obstacles hindering normal emigration procedures, in the hope that it would percolate to the top and help bring about a change.

Zagladin came in armed with a sheaf of white notepaper and well-sharpened pencils. He sat down facing me in the middle of a long dining table, meant to seat 36. After an assistant poured tea from an enormous blue teapot, we got down to business. Zagladin wrote down every word I said, occasionally interrupting me with short questions. He expressed surprise at the harsh treatment given Jewish emigrants by OVIR. Otherwise, his remarks were non-committal, rather in the spirit of 'everything will be all right in the end, don't you worry'. He thanked me for sharing my observations with him and promised to pass them on, evidently, to his mentor. He then asked me if I was happy with my situation in Moscow. I filled him in on our circumstances, and he said he would look into the matter and inform me.

I met Zagladin again in August 1990. By that time, things had moved along considerably but still there were no relations. I passed on a message from Foreign Minister Arens through Zagladin to Gorbachev, to the effect that there was no political wisdom in procrastinating on the renewal of relations. The Soviets would do well to follow the lead of the East European countries, which were renewing ties with Israel. A solution to the Middle East crisis could be advanced if the USSR had direct, official contacts with Israel. To Arens's message I added that there was no point in dragging out this process, best accomplished in one step. Zagladin replied that nothing could be more logical, but that in the interim, pressure groups had been formed against the renewal of ties; it would take time to overcome these negative influences. Later meetings with members of the Politburo taught me that these 'negative influences' were ignorance of the outside world, long-standing personal friendships with Arab leaders and, first and foremost, inherent anti-Semitism and distrust of Israel.

These meetings with Gorbachev's confidant gave me needed reassurance. It was not at all clear whether Gorbachev was being briefed on these subjects, and I knew Zagladin would loyally transmit my words. The basic theses I was intent on presenting to the Soviet leadership would finally get through: The Middle East peace process could be advanced through ties with Israel; the gross inhumanity in the procedures relating to Jewish emigration was unnecessary and counterproductive from the Soviet point of view. After talking to Zagladin, I could at least be certain that these arguments were not left to be examined by the professional departments alone. I felt reasonably certain Gorbachev himself would be apprised of them. This satisfied my need of getting a hearing.

I have reason to believe that my August 1990 conversation with Zagladin helped tip the scales in favour of the Politburo decision to re-establish relations at the consulate-general level. Soviet officialdom had been ripe for such a decision for quite some time, in spite of internal opposition. There had been several initiatives in that direction, including a Politburo directive in December 1989 to improve ties, but they were cut short for reasons discussed earlier. My second meeting with Zagladin turned out to be much warmer and more open than the initial one and he reacted positively to many of my arguments. When I visited Moscow in June 1994, I called on Anatoly Cherniaev, Gorbachev's private secretary. When I asked him what he thought Zagladin had done with his report, he said Zagladin had indeed been one of the most informed and loyal members of Gorbachev's entourage and there was no doubt that he transmitted my remarks word for word to Gorbachev.

MOSCOW: AN ISRAELI MECCA

Not everything in my life was as serious as the meetings I was having with Soviet officials. There were lighter moments — many of them connected with the Israeli VIP traffic to Moscow. Many members of the Israeli establishment were anxious to see 'the evil empire' for themselves. The Soviet authorities were aware of this growing interest of Israeli politicians, but their response was hardly encouraging: the granting of visas remained a long, drawn-out affair and had often to be accomplished outside of Israel, in Athens or Vienna. The Soviet Mission in Tel Aviv was not authorized to hand out any visas.

The desire of Israelis to visit the Soviet Union was commendable. A trip to Russia at that time was no picnic. Accommodations in the Soviet capital were difficult to find and lacked very much in comfort. These considerations did not daunt the many public figures who eventually made their way to Moscow and to Leningrad. Some ventured out as far as Kiev. There was usually some rationale behind these visits. Many came to see and get acquainted with what remained of the great Russian Jewish community — a centre of attention over the long dark years of communism. Some came expressly to encourage and promote immigration to Israel. Others proclaimed to have come to improve the economic links between Israel and the Soviet Union and promote trade; a number, simply to report back to the nation. Everyone was looking for a photo opportunity which could make the pages of the newspapers the following day. The preferred pose was arm in arm with an *oleh* (immigrant) or paternalistically smiling at the natives, who were standing in line for Israeli visas. These so-called *olim* were in fact mostly people going to the US, but that did not deter anyone. Another favourite spot to be photographed was in front of St Basil's cathedral — incontrovertible evidence that the visitor had been to the heart of Moscow.

Most VIP trips were harried: an inspection of the visa lines at the Dutch Consulate on Ordynka, a sortie to the synagogue, discussions with representative Jews, and a night at the opera. All wanted to meet with Soviet personalities, the more important the better. As I was the one who had to arrange these meetings, and the number of people who were allowed or prepared to meet with Israelis was limited, the reserves of goodwill we could count on would sometimes wear pretty thin. At least we had gotten the tickets-to-the-opera-purchase procedure down to perfection. Israel Mey-Ami, my devoted and efficient colleague (and a small-time operator), had all the theatre directors eating out of his hand and there were never any real problems in getting the best seats in the house.

These comings and goings increased the range of Soviet exposure to Israeli officials and personalities. I considered these contacts a positive impetus on the road to the renewal of official ties, since they helped dissipate myths and prejudiced opinions about Israel. With time, the concentric circles of contacts between Israeli visitors, Knesset members and Soviet personalities widened; government officials, scientists, journalists and professionals obtained growing access to their counterparts. At the same time, they created an increasing awareness in Israel of the Soviet scene. These frequent excursions of the Israeli political élite helped me to explain our problems to them and make them more tangible. Most visitors promised to help as much as they could. Some with international contacts really did put in a good word for us with Soviet personalities on visits abroad. But it did not help a great deal.

In September 1989 we were to be honoured by a surprise visit of the Israeli minister of agriculture, Avraham Katz-Oz. Because of its great achievements, agriculture was a showpiece in Israel's propaganda services (although the word propaganda was always strenuously eschewed). The minister, a close associate and friend of Shimon Peres, thought he could improve relations with the USSR if he came to Moscow and offered his services in modernizing proverbially backward Soviet agriculture. The Soviets wanted no part of this visit as an official act. Katz-Oz was due to come in on a flight from Helsinki, through Tallin in Estonia, where he was to visit a flower show. We had got word of this impending visit only at the very last moment and could do nothing to prevent it, although it was clear it would all end in a fiasco. The minister's assistants loudly proclaimed the coming of Katz-Oz even before he had received his visa. I frantically tried to discourage this unwarranted enthusiasm until I could procure the necessary permits. There were no visas available because Katz-Oz was not invited. Somehow, thanks to personal contacts and good relations, I set up meetings with the minister of agriculture of the Russian Federation, Gennady Kulik, and the mayor of Moscow, Gavril Popov. I had a member of the mission fly out to Tallin to help Katz-Oz with the necessary arrangements. However, the Soviet government and its consular services in Helsinki were unavailable because of the weekend and, as predicted, the whole visit fell through and caused great public embarrassment. The minister was not deterred. He returned to the idea with great gusto. I could not but admire his strength of will and perseverance. Only a few months later, toward the end of November, coming on an invitation from our good friend, the academician Yevgeny

Velikhov, Katz-Oz's assistants got a visa for him in Vienna and he arrived in Moscow.

Velikhov's official status was vice-president of the Academy of Sciences. Together with a few other outstanding scientists, like Roald Sagdeyev, the director of the Space Research Institute, Velikhov had set himself up in a special position in the Soviet *nomenklatura*, the roster of Soviet hierarchy, and he enjoyed relative independence. He was head of the Kurchatov Atomic Energy Institute, where he once invited me, to my disbelief, to meet and discuss his plans with him. Velikhov had contacts with some Israelis through the Global Forum and the World Lab, and having heard of the wonders of Israeli agriculture, formulated a scheme of introducing Israeli methods into Soviet dairy farming.

Velikhov's idea was to turn a Soviet kolkhoz at Istra, near the town of New Jerusalem, not far from Moscow, into a model farm. The intention was to provide dairy products to the atomic energy establishment around the capital and to the region itself. Apparently, the kolkhoz in question, which was on the payroll of the Kurchatov Institute, had fallen on hard times. The stainless-steel equipment for the new dairy farm was to have come out of the atomic energy establishment reserves. It was an excellent plan. We worked on it for many months, together with people from Agridev, an Israeli agricultural technology export group closely affiliated to the government and specializing in applied research in agriculture. Agridev had had great success in many parts of the world, in Africa, south-east Asia and Latin America. It had some excellent people in its ranks, such as Yitzhak Abt, an outstanding expert and devotee who had seen service in many parts of the world and was now often visiting Moscow and consulting with Velikhov. He and Amram Olmert, a director of Agridev, often came to spend their evenings with me at the Ukraina Hotel. I remember at least one occasion where we organized an impromptu supper of tomatoes, olive oil and feta cheese (a treat in Moscow), and swapped stories, confident that Velikhov's project would finally get off the ground.

Velikhov organized a series of meetings with Katz-Oz and people in the Russian Federation's Ministry of Agriculture and the Moscow Municipality, thinking that supplying the Soviet Union with fruit, vegetables and meat was a feasible proposition. Nothing could have been farther from the truth, and I already knew it from my previous contacts and activity. Israeli fruit was far too expensive for the Russian pocket, its transportation was problematic and the dumping policies that some eastern bloc countries or other countries practised (Hungary and Romania, e.g., unloaded apples and potatoes and Egypt dumped oranges against old arms debts), put us out of the market. Katz-Oz and his senior aides were terribly enthusiastic, however. Many promises were made, the only item left open being the money to be paid for goods and services. The Soviets, unfortunately, did not have any. There were similar results with Velikhov's pet dairy project, which was to be paid for by the Soviets, but could not be financed. Velikhov suggested we raise the money for him in the US. This turned out to be highly impractical. Katz-Oz promised to get the required million dollars from his friend Shimon Peres, minister of finance at that time, and the latter agreed. Katz-Oz then flew back to Israel, and we stayed behind to pick up the pieces. When the time arrived for making the investments, Peres was no longer minister of finance and his successor, Yitzhak Moda'i, had other priorities.

Objectively speaking, this exercise, as others like it, was pursued with great eagerness and goodwill on Israel's part. The Soviets reacted cautiously. At first they thought Israeli interest would be backed up by money — American, if not Israeli. Given the realities, any such notion soon evaporated. This was not the first time foreign organizations or governments had approached them with promises of advice and help. Somewhere down the line the Soviets knew they would have to produce the money. Soviet personalities who were more attuned to the realities outside their own borders knew the Israeli element in this formula to be relatively attractive. Israel was not a great power and its friendly intrusions and offers of technological aid were not as suspect as many others. I had the feeling that the people who met Katz-Oz and listened to his offers were quite receptive. In the end, no partner in this enterprise proved financially viable. The Soviet and the Israeli bureaucracy could not find a way to carry out the project, and Katz-Oz's visit ended where it began.

The New Jerusalem kolkhoz project, however, is still alive. In a meeting with Yitzhak Abt in summer 1994, I heard there were new

113

prospects for its realization. Israel's Ministry of Foreign Affairs is now about to help re-launch the project. On a trip to Moscow in 1995, I met with Ehud Gol, director of the international cooperation division, who came out to promote this interesting scheme. One hopes that this time luck will smile upon it.

New Jerusalem merits a digression. This small city not far from Moscow was built around a central cathedral in the eighteenth century, which is supposed to be an exact replica of the Holy Sepulchre in Jerusalem. The church was badly neglected in the Soviet period and is now slowly being repaired. The director, Vassily Nizhegorodov, asked me for the plans of the Holy Sepulchre, when I was on a visit there. He wanted to ascertain the extent to which the building adhered to the floor plan of its namesake in the Holy City. I sent him some material but unfortunately could not get funding for a visit I wanted him to make to see the place with his own eyes.

A VISIT BY PERES — PLANNED AND POSTPONED

A story of quite a different nature was the projected visit to the Soviet Union of Shimon Peres in 1989 when he was minister of finance. Always on the lookout for breakthroughs and political initiatives, Peres was convinced he could make a great impact on the Soviets and get our relations moving. I believe Peres also had it in mind to utilize Soviet lines of communication with the chairman of the PLO, Yasser Arafat, and Syrian President Hafez Assad. Peres had had continuous contacts with Moscow, through the many channels that he always kept at his disposal. He had had occasional meetings with Shevardnadze, but never an interview with the head of state, Gorbachev.

In order to test the waters, Peres suggested that he would come out with a large mission to see what could be done to establish a basis for economic and scientific cooperation. He had used this tactic often in the past. Leading figures in industry and the economy, as well as intellectuals, formed the vanguard of a Peres exploratory mission. The Soviet government must have had doubts on political grounds. They hesitated to invite Peres officially, in spite of the great esteem in which he was held. The Soviets wanted Peres in Moscow, but did not want to accord the visit the status it deserved. The hesitations arose due to the absence of diplomatic relations. Nevertheless, I soon started receiving messages from Nimrod Novik, Peres's able and devoted assistant, about the requirements of the visit: a series of high-level meetings, culminating in a coveted and prestigious summit with Mikhail Gorbachev.

We searched for possible venues to organize this visit on a non-governmental basis. My friend Radomir Bogdanov, the ex-KGB official, was now second-in-command of the Peace Committee, notorious for its past propaganda campaigns in the West and in the world at large. The Soviets thought the committee might be a convenient vehicle in this case. When I got back from the UN in New York in October 1989, where I had assisted Foreign Minister Arens in his meeting with Shevardnadze, I suddenly got a message from Bogdanov that Anatoly Dobrynin, the Soviet ambassador in Washington, had received instructions from Moscow regarding the Peres mission. Peres was to be invited as a guest of the Peace Committee, in his capacity as the head of the Israel Labour Party, rather than as minister of finance. I asked our Washington embassy to inform Peres accordingly, as soon as he arrived in the US on his official visit there. Novik then called me saying Peres wanted to make sure his arrival in Moscow would coincide with Simhat Torah, a festive event in the Jewish calendar when large crowds congregate at the synagogue. He wanted to be shown on television in the midst of celebrants and would be bringing an Israeli crew to film it. Peres also wanted to have a meeting with Gorbachev. This whole plan was to be carried out scarcely ten days hence. Nimrod informed me he would be coming in to oversee the preparations. This was forcing the pace as well as the events. I called Genrikh Borovik, the head of the Peace Committee. Borovik politely replied he would talk to Novik when he arrived. As to Gorbachev himself, no meeting could be promised beforehand and Peres, too, would get his reply after his arrival. Nimrod said he would not come unless the preparatory meetings were confirmed.

Several weeks later, after resorting to Bogdanov's services again, I was told Peres would be received by Alexander Yakovlev of the

Politburo, Prime Minister Nikolai Ryzhkov, and Minister of Foreign Affairs Eduard Shevardnadze. The Soviets also asked me to transmit to Peres their great interest in the proposed co-production of a new version of the Ilyushin passenger plane, together with the Americans (Pratt and Whitney were to contribute the engine and the Israel Aircraft Industry, the avionics). There would be other interesting projects to discuss. Peres, however, was playing only for high stakes: Gorbachev or nothing. I tried to reason with him. I felt Gorbachev did not want to be obligated and would meet Peres if there were a positive consensus among his aides regarding the nature of the other meetings in Moscow. Peres wanted to know if I could guarantee the meeting. There was no one save Gorbachev himself who could do that. So the trip was postponed.

Finally, Novik did arrive and even met with Valentin Falin, who sounded supportive. He set out a list of political desiderata: Israel should talk with the Palestinians and pacify Lebanon. Peres, for his part, was offering '80 per cent business and 20 per cent politics'. The latter portion would include discussions governing relations between the Socialist International and the Soviet Communist Party. Novik said Peres would come with a large group of bankers and financiers (Albert Reichman, Charles Bronfman, Nessim Gaon, and international barter authority Shaul Eisenberg — all well-known billionaires). The Gorbachev meeting was subsumed though not as a stipulation. But the plan was still very much in the air.

It was not difficult to understand this desire for a meeting with the head of state of the biggest country in the world. Still, I found it presumptuous. Israel's ministers, evidently, thought otherwise. They knew that in the minds of the Soviet leadership, a mere mention of Israel and the Jews conjured images of banks and credits which were supposedly available to Israel at a moment's notice. What the Israelis usually and conveniently ignored, however, was the fact that offers to bring in some of the biggest names in the financial world would be taken at their crudest face value by the Soviet leaders. They would think in terms of the Protocols of the Elders of Zion, a Russian invention; or the highly malicious characterizations of Jews by the high priest of communism, Karl Marx. Subsequently, it transpired that reactions of the Soviet leaders to such generous offers of help did indeed evoke unrealistic expectations of Israel's international financial influence. The sobering process did not do us great harm, though it led to a general, not necessarily favourable, reassessment of Israel's capabilities.

The mistaken Soviet notion that the greatest financiers were at Mr Peres's beck and call was leverage advisedly used by the Peres party. A meeting with Gorbachev, in the heady days of his greatest world popularity, could have been a feather in the cap of any politician. But the attitude smacked of provincialism, highly unexpected given Shimon Peres's statesmanship and political acumen. It was not only unrealistic to demand in those days that a meeting be arranged with Gorbachev in advance, it was unnecessary — a greater sin. This was precisely what I was trying to avoid, the perpetuation of Soviet myths, and the inevitable zero sum gains, to our own eventual detriment. I did not believe then in the magic wand of the billionaires in Russia and do not believe in it today, and events have entirely vindicated me.

While it was true that a meeting with Gorbachev would have made great copy, it was not Stalin that Peres would be meeting. Many of us had been mistakenly accustomed to thinking that the general secretary of the Communist Party had full power to cut Gordian knots. In reality, this view was an over-simplification of 'the System', as it was called by the Soviets. Gorbachev took no hasty decisions and in a meeting with Peres would probably not go beyond mouthing a few non-committal pleasantries (or demand the impossible, as he was to do in his meeting with the subsequent Israeli minister of finance, Yitzhak Moda'i). Indeed, the subject of Israel was psychologically more complex than we had at first imagined. Gorbachev would have to consult with his many influential Arabists on the Middle Eastern quandary. It was clear there would be no immediate results. Gorbachev's career up to and including 1989 had amply demonstrated that fact. We had a long way to travel in the USSR and we should have been giving a little more careful thought to the road ahead. Peres was right in expecting a more forthcoming attitude from the Soviets. Under the circumstances, however, I thought it would have been sagacious for Peres to go ahead and meet with Yakovlev, even if that were to be his only meeting. Peres, however, thought differently. For internal and international reasons, Peres was apparently of the opinion that he simply could not allow himself to go to Russia without meeting Gorbachev. While I did not share his feelings on this subject, I understood and respected them.

Eagerness for headlines and for 'PR' is universal and is, after all, part and parcel of political life. It would be the height of naïveté to try to fight it. Yet, Israel's renewed presence in Soviet Russia was a far more involved affair. It concerned relations with a world power whose proximity to our borders we had felt for 40 years. Our relations held great promise of reaching a strategic understanding, which would in no way impinge on our symbiotic relationship with the US. An understanding with the Soviets could have improved our chances for peace in the region, in view of the good relations between the USSR and the Arabs. Above all, we had to think of the USSR's three million Jews, who were the greatest reservoir in the world of potential immigration to Israel. It was mandatory to sit down and elaborate a sound policy to adopt over time *vis-à-vis* this colossus. In other words, we had to formulate a considered attitude and play the diplomatic game with care, transmitting signals appropriate to our tactical and strategic plans. A headlong rush, repeated requests for top-level meetings, unsolicited promises of help that we could not fulfil, seemed to me self-defeating. Henry Kissinger's affirmation that Israel had no foreign policy, only an internal one, was apt in this case as well. Peres's actions and reactions seemed too attuned to the undercurrents in Israel's internal politics.

The strategic dimension of our relations with the Soviet Union was ever present. Russia was, and is today, the superpower closest to our borders. The Soviet supply of weapons to the Arab countries in the early 1950s changed the relative strength of Israel and its Arab neighbours and created an arms race that lasted 40 years. The economic weakness of Russia, at the end of the era of perestroika, signalled possible advances to countries seeking rearmament, such as Iran. The loosening up of surveillance over the nuclear arsenal in the Soviet Union was already becoming apparent in late 1989. The fear was that Iran would gain access to Soviet nuclear secrets or lay its hands on nuclear weapons, although this dangerous development was not openly discussed at the time. The way our politicians related to Russia and still relate to it today, seems to me to lack sufficient perspicacity.

All this having been said, it remained true, nevertheless, that meetings with Soviet top officials held tremendous fascination for Israelis. If the climb to the Soviet political Everest was difficult, it made the challenge ever more attractive. And given the Byzantine characteristics of the Soviet regime, reaching the summit was feasible, even if one was motivated mainly by considerations of personal prestige.

Journalists and friends in Moscow, whom we were trying to canvass to help us make cultural contacts, at one point suggested we invite the great Kirgiz writer, Chingiz Aitmatov, to Israel. Aitmatov, a leading figure in the new era of glasnost and well-connected to the leading personalities of the Soviet Republic of Kirgizia (later Kyrgyzstan), became a member of the Supreme Soviet in the elections of 1989. Very soon afterwards, he was invited by Gorbachev to be his cultural adviser. Aitmatov's status as an important writer of Central Asian descent made him invaluable in the confused days of Gorbachev's first elected parliament and the creeping uncertainties over the future of the non-Russian republics.

The Ministry of Foreign Affairs in Jerusalem approved the invitation and I contacted the writer's entourage and finally the author himself in Frunze (later Bishkek), the capital of the Kirgiz Republic, to get his acceptance. We made the arrangements for his visit. On a periodic stay in Israel, I made sure every detail was in place for the forthcoming visit, but I had to return to my post in Moscow. We tried to get someone to escort Aitmatov full-time. Miron Gordon was cultural attaché in Rome, but in view of the importance of this visit, I talked the ministry into seconding him to Jerusalem through its duration. Everything seemed fine until the whole visit was nearly and unbelievably hijacked by a curious former Soviet citizen. This was Ilya Zemtsov.

Zemstov had been a lecturer in a sociological institute in Baku until 1971. He was forced to abandon his native city and seek other employment when the Communist Party in Baku discovered that he had been exploiting an invented close friendship with First Secretary Gaidar Aliyev in order to advance his own career. He found employment at a medical institute in Yaroslavl, as a temporary replacement for a professor of Marxism-Leninism. Zemtsov was later thrown out of the party for 'lying, misleading the faculty and students by calling himself a professor' and other such misdemeanors. His doctoral degree was revoked because of plagiarism. Soon after he arrived in Israel, presenting himself as a prisoner of Zion, he convinced Menahem Begin to help install him as head of a research institute in Jerusalem. He was also given a position as lecturer at the Hebrew University but was later dismissed because of incompetence. All this did not keep him from using the title 'Professor' in Israel, nor did it deter Ezer Weizmann from sending him to the USSR to establish connections with the Academy of Sciences.

Zemtsov saw an opening for a future career in the grey area of budding relations between Israel and Moscow. He began as a go-between with Soviet personalities, and had plans to go beyond that intermediary stage, to be appointed ambassador to the Soviet Union. He started using a tactic, soon to prove highly efficacious, of speaking in the name of Israeli authorities over the phone to the prospective objects of his attention. Uninvited and unsolicited, he called repeatedly on Aitmatov and, declaring himself to be the official sponsor of his visit, ingratiated himself with the important visitor. Immediately afterwards, Zemtsov started appearing in the ministry offering his help with the visit. He was turned down but would not desist, forcing his way into the Aitmatov schedule, appearing as a friend and confidant of the visitor at every gate he crashed. The ministry officials, eager to avoid public scenes and any hint of scandal, did not forcibly eject the intruder and he stayed on. He thus won his spurs and was a zealous instrument of attempts by various Israeli politicians to make their way into the Gorbachev court. Zemtsov gradually perfected this hitchhiking technique, by which he would try to exploit every visit of politicians as well as businessmen in Israel and in the Soviet Union. His efforts cost a lot of public money, were time-consuming and led nowhere through long, meandering byways. And they were detrimental to Israel's image, for the Soviets knew who Zemtsov was, but they became convinced that these were standard modes of operation for the Israeli government.

Unfortunately, this indeed was the way Israeli government operated. As I discovered, the mere promise of a meeting with a high official in Moscow was what middlemen thrived on. These suspect brokers not only sabotaged our efforts to establish ourselves as the future embassy of the State of Israel; in order to procure meetings for Israeli officials in Moscow, they raised the expectations of the Soviets, which ultimately undermined the trust and respect they had for the official Israeli mission.

The increasing appearance of visitors in our overburdened lives was a necessary by-product of our assignment. They contributed to the mission's exposure and to Israel's presence in the Soviet Union. Among them were journalists and researchers who came to see and take stock of the situation. I looked forward to these visits for they served as a lively and popular channel of information on the realities of life in Moscow. My reports were reaching only a select audience at the ministry.

A very real difficulty in Israel was the inaccessibility of information on the Soviet Union. The only Israeli paper that had an unofficial but active representative was *Yediot Aharonot*. The reports of their correspondent, Amnon Kapeliuk, figured prominently in the paper, although he was not given the privilege of in-depth reporting, as the newspaper apparently did not want to tax its readers' attention span. Other newspapermen were rarely permitted to pass the Soviet blockade against the Israeli media. The few who came, did so on tourist visas. Questions pertaining to Jewish emigration were always a priority, but the very few journalists who made their way to Moscow also observed and wrote about life and politics in the Soviet Union. They depicted their visits as though they were trips to the craters of the moon, so exotic and unusual were their first impressions of this 'enemy' territory.

One of the first organized visits to Russia was that of Akiva Eldar, at that time the political, and later Washington correspondent of *Ha'aretz*, the most respected Israeli daily. His trip was organized by Dmitri Zgerski of *New Times*, a Soviet political weekly more daring than most. Akiva wrote a few pieces, with his usual insight and discernment, but his trip was too limited in time for a broader picture, and he was in a hurry to get back to what really mattered, the political scene in Israel.

121

If normal access to the Soviet Union was denied to the Israeli media, the strategy of indirect approach was not to be counted out. Isabella Ginor, a practicing dentist and freelance journalist, who wrote largely for *Ha'aretz*, hit upon an extraordinary formula: if the Soviets were not allowing journalists into their country, then officials would be brought into Israel via telephone. With incredible perseverance and an intelligent use of her knowledge of Russian and Russians, Ginor established a strong link with prominent political personalities in Russia, the Ukraine and other republics of the Soviet Union. Ginor's contacts were more than ready to be interviewed and speak out, though they knew she was an Israeli journalist. The reason behind it, I thought, was their mythical belief in the powers of the 'Jewish media'. Gradually deciphering the hierarchical code of the Soviet establishment, and creating a directory of phone numbers, Ginor began presenting an accurate, up-to-date picture of the Soviet scene. She worked in tandem with Israel Radio's chief foreign news anchor, Gideon Remez, whose programmes became a star attraction of the state radio. This couple filled a great need for information. The only drawback was the inherent distrust of the Soviet Union and its politics that filtered through these reports. This was entirely understandable where the commonly accepted perceptions of the Soviet state were concerned.

BEARING GIFTS OF CULTURE

Aside from organized trade, which was still largely restricted, the surest and the safest way to build a bridge over the chasm that separated the two countries was through cultural contacts. They had completely dried up over time. One of the first tentative attempts to establish and develop such an exchange was the self-appointed mission of Israeli writers and poets, headed by the writer Bentzion Tomer. They came to visit in early spring 1989. Their first excursion was to Tbilisi in Georgia, where they were warmly received by the minister of culture and the Writers' Union, and promised full cooperation in publishing Israeli literature. Their next stop was Moscow. I had them over at the Ukraina Hotel many times as we discussed ways and means to establish links with the

Soviet literary world. Yevgeny Yevtushenko, a Soviet poet who had gained great renown in the days of Khruschev's Thaw, sponsored the visit to Russia. He also helped the Israeli writers make contacts with the Soviet Writers' Union. This was a controversial organization, already split along an establishment and non-establishment divide. But the union did sign an agreement with the Israelis to publish an anthology of modern Israeli literature.

Vladimir Karpov, the secretary of the Writers' Union was a member of the Communist Party Central Committee. He put on a big spread in honour of his Israeli colleagues at the House of Writers, which had survived the great fire of 1812 in Moscow and was the scene of the reception by the Rostov family in the opening of Tolstoy's *War and Peace*. Karpov raised a toast to the renewal of diplomatic relations. He was an obedient communist and party figure and not very popular among the more progressive writers, but in favour with Gorbachev. Karpov's enthusiasm, we hoped, was inspired from above and indicative of a tendency, stimulated by glasnost, to 'let a few flowers bloom' while the Soviets were biding their time.

Among the members of the writers' mission was David Markish, son of Perets Markish, a very important Yiddish writer of the war and the postwar years, killed by Stalin. David is an author in his own right in Israel. His reception in Moscow had special poignancy because of the trauma he suffered as a child. He was also a knowledgeable guide for his colleagues. The Russians knew his biography and there was a measure of respect for him because of his personal tragedy.

The enthusiasm with which this group of Israeli writers was received in the Ukraine, as well as in the Central Asian republics and in Azerbaijan, was far more sincere and open than in Russia proper. However, very little came of it all as the Russians did not find the money to publish the books they had promised, nor was funding provided for the parallel publications in Israel. I was interested in and supported this activity for its own merit, but also because it signalled a first important contact among intellectuals of the two countries. Eventually, this phase paved the way toward the awakening of a tremendous curiosity in the USSR regarding Israel. There was no burst of literary dialogue or a wealth of exchange in publications. On the other hand, the road was opened to visits to Israel by writers and members of the media, including some important opinion-makers. The scale and importance of these visits grew rapidly, in spite of official disapproval. Israel entered the public mind, albeit for reasons entirely different than those proclaimed by Soviet propaganda.

In connection with cultural activities, I recall the visits to the USSR of Becky Freistadt, Shimon Peres's adviser on women's affairs and the head of cultural activities of the Histadrut, the Israeli Workers' Union. Freistadt, an intelligent and attractive woman, came to Moscow with good introductions from friends in the West and in Israel and immediately established connections with people in the theatre, the cinema and the fine arts. She was received with benevolent curiosity by the Moscow beau monde.

Freistadt had a great number of plans and projects, including making a film on Solomon Mikhoels. Lack of funds, the usual impediment to cultural ambitions, blocked these good intentions. I kept warning her about the very limited amount of support she would receive at home, and tried to curb her enthusiasm, but she would not be discouraged. One of her fondest obsessions was to find the sum of 50,000 dollars to purchase an inscribed silver box that once belonged to Alexander Pushkin, the great and very venerated Russian poet. The box was supposed to have been a gift from Nicholas I. The Russian emperor was far from being an admirer and it is not clear why he presented the box in the first place. But Freistadt thought if we could somehow scrape the money together, purchase the object and then present it with a flourish to Russian writers at an appropriate reception, in the presence of television cameras, the effect might be electrifying. Well, impressive it would certainly have been, but in spite of all of Freistadt's good intentions and her contacts in the Histadrut and Israeli society, someone else finally bought the silver box and thought it more appropriate to keep it at home.

One of my first ventures out of the stultifying confines of the Ukraina Hotel back in December 1988 had been to visit the theatre. A Jewish group was playing *Benjamin the Third's Visit to the Holy Land* at the Hermitage Theatre in Moscow. This was a piece written at the turn of the century in Odessa by the great Yiddish and

Hebrew author, Mendele Moykher Sforim. Mendele, Eliezer Mapu and Yehuda Leib Gordon, the triumvirate of Russian Jewish writers, are considered to be among the founders of modern Hebrew literature. The many who followed in the rebirth of the Hebrew language drew on their works, including such talents as Haim Nachman Bialik, the Hebrew national poet, and Shalom Aleichem, who wrote mainly in Yiddish. Both openly admitted their indebtedness to Mendele. The theme of the play was taken from the well-known, probably the greatest, Hebrew poet of the Middle Ages, the Spanish Jew, Yehuda Halevi. In a widely quoted passage, Halevi wrote: 'My heart is in the east, though my body lies at the farthest reaches of the west.' The production was dedicated to the memory of Solomon Mikhoels.

As I had some difficulty getting tickets, I called the director, Michael Levitin, and was assured I would be received with all due respect, which indeed I was. The Hermitage Theatre was packed full and I could not help noticing the many typically Russian faces in the audience. The regime was already in its glasnost phase but the combination of a Jewish production and the implication of the Holy Land's attraction to Jews which Mendele had idealized was, at the end of 1988, explosive. When I went up to Levitin to congratulate him on his work after the performance, I saw several foreign theatrical agents who were interested in producing the play in Germany and in other European countries. There was nothing in the play from the theatrical point of view that merited such attraction or saleability; only the fact that it was being produced in Moscow. *Benjamin* was celebrated in the Soviet capital as marking an important stage in the life of Moscow Jews. This was a slight exaggeration, although it did give the overall impression that the regime was beginning to move away from its unofficial but widely practiced anti-Semitism.

I found Soviet theatre to be very heavy on the classical side and rather lacking in vivacity — far less experimental and venturesome than Soviet painting, for example. The dramatic innovations of Stanislavsky and Vakhtangov, the pace-setters of acting and theatre in the early 1920s, had endured, but their style, so revolutionary and captivating in its prime, had become dull. Nevertheless, the theatre, as an expression of political form, was beginning to blossom. Old plays were being resurrected, like Bulgakov's *Heart of a Dog* and other satire. When later into 1990 some theatres staged Babel's *Sunset* with its powerful depictions of a marginal group of Odessan Jews, so full of vitality and thirst for life, and of passages replete with ironic humour, it became a hit overnight. Moscow theatre was highly reminiscent of Habimah, the national Hebrew theatre, whose original actors had been students of Stanislavsky and Vakhtangov. The great tragic actor of Habimah, Aharon Meskin, playing in Eugene O'Neill's *Anna Christie*, was really portraying a Russian character, in heavily accented Hebrew, with his gesticulations, poses and comportment dictated by Vakhtangov. The combination was highly dramatic, but when one listened with an inner ear, it all could have been taking place in Moscow.

One day I received a call from Catherine, the wife of the well-known Russian theatre director Yuri Lyubimov. Lyubimov staged politically controversial, artistically innovative and thought-provoking productions at the Taganka Theatre, which he had created. Lyubimov is a man of great integrity and a director of remarkable breadth and theatrical sense. His independence was bound to lead him to quarrel with the ideologues of the Central Committee. The temperature of this dispute was constantly on the rise but Lyubimov would not give in. Finally, he was called in by culture and party officials. Lyubimov was informed his productions were being banned and he himself was ordered to travel to London to stage Dostoyevsky's *Crime and Punishment*. In 1983, Lyubimov received a highly coveted award from the British royal family. The Soviet Embassy curtly informed him that he was being divested of his Soviet citizenship. Thus, one of the greater interpreters of Soviet and Russian life was turned into a man without a country. Israel granted Lyubimov asylum and citizenship, and Teddy Kollek, the mayor of Jerusalem, offered him housing, as he did on a previous occasion to the Soviet ballet dancers Galina and Valery Panov.

The establishment of perestroika and glasnost put mounting pressure on the Soviet government to erase this shameful chapter in the cultural life of the country. Lyubimov was invited back in 1988. Anatoly Lukyanov, the president of the Supreme Soviet (and later one of the leaders of the 1991 putsch), summoned the director to the Kremlin and condescendingly reinstated his Soviet citizenship, although Lyubimov had never requested it. The Taganka Theatre was given back to its rightful owner and its director tried to carry on the tradition he had created. However, there was a great deal of resentment on the part of the party *apparatchiks* inside and outside the theatre and relations were strained. Lyubimov's Israeli connection left an anti-Semitic residue as well. Catherine had called to inform me of the theft of her Israeli passport and to request a new one. This served as my introduction to the inner life of the Russian theatre, a world that had been closed to me before and had now opened up a crack. I became a frequent visitor to the Taganka.

In the following years, I saw many of Lyubimov's productions, including *Alive*, a potent satire on the kolkhoz and party discipline in the Khrushchev period; *Vysotsky*, a piece based on the life of the famous bard who was a member of the Taganka theatre company; *Boris Godunov*, a collage of Pushkin's plays, and many others. Taganka was original, full-blooded, entertaining and thought-provoking. Some of my friends, who were close to the establishment, expressed the opinion that Lyubimov had lost his magic touch and was past his prime, after a long absence abroad. I did not know a great deal about Russian theatre and there was much experimentation going on in Moscow, but I did not see anything which came close to the Taganka productions. My wife and I became good friends with the Lyubimovs and shared the news of their subsequent trials and tribulations. Taganka was again taken away from Lyubimov in 1990 by Nikolai Gubenko, the minister of culture of the USSR until its collapse, and a former disciple. Gubenko decreed that Lyubimov could not hold on to the Taganka because of his many trips abroad, directing in many cities, from Paris to Tokyo. This attitude reflected on some of the social and political problems arising in Russia with the dissolution of the Soviet Union. The government was no more the sole supporter and guarantor of all art. The artists began fending for themselves, with the attendant tensions, jealousies and greed. There were ugly scenes, in a theatre that had contributed a great deal to the cultural life of Russia, and Lyubimov's pride was unjustly injured. Yuri Luzhkov, the mayor of Moscow, has restituted the theatre to Lyubimov again, but the regrettable tug-of-war still continues.

This chapter in mid-1989 cannot be completed without a few words about the most important visitors of the year, my wife Aliza and my daughter Yael, who came to stay with me at the Ukraina for a few weeks. Up to that time, the only permanent visitors to my rooms were two devoted friends, Misha and Grisha, who would come out to observe me each evening without fail and partake of the cheese that I had laid out for them. Amnon Kapeliuk of *Yediot Aharonot* once visited me in the evening, saw the two rodents with his own eyes, and put a story about them in one of the leading Israeli papers several days later. I did not inform on my friends to the hotel's exterminators, feeling that I needed their company to share the silent presence of the KGB.

I was still contemplating placing Yael, who was 13, at the international school run by the American Embassy and community. After Yael came to Moscow and saw where she would have to live, we came to a common accord on the undesirability of her leaving Jerusalem. She was released and I was condemned to continue of my enforced lonely existence, as Aliza would have to stay behind, see to Yael's schooling and tend to her own career as well, a status not provided for in the Israeli foreign service. However, we tried to make Yael's stay on this occasion as pleasant and interesting as possible. We all travelled to Kiev and to Leningrad and saw the sights. We introduced Yael to some Jewish girls of her age, we took her to the circus and tried to give her the opportunity to continue her piano lessons. To that end, we looked for a tuner for the upright in our suite. I asked the maids on our floor if they knew a tuner. Their answer was that the piano must certainly need fixing, since the rooms had been used by a group of Georgians, who poured champagne into the works and pounded the keys with their feet. We got another piano.

Yael was keen on learning the cello. As this new direction in her life had surfaced just before she came to Moscow, we started looking for a cello to buy for her. Everyone said buying a cello was the easiest thing in Russia, a musical country. It was easier said than done. Here is an excerpt from Yael's diary:

> We looked into every music store in Moscow. Unfortunately, the celli were made out of plywood and the sellers, oh God!,

were all from the same mold. A usual scene in a store visited by mother and myself:

The store looks completely deserted. Deep inside the huge recesses, a man, standing, staring into space.

We approach him. Nothing happens, the man continues to stare beyond us. A few minutes pass. Finally, mother, very bravely, says a few words, at first, in English. The man still stares. As we begin to realize we're wasting a lot of time, mother does the impossible and addresses the man in Russian:

'Could you show us a cello?'

The salesman continues to stare. Then, turning toward the person addressing him, says: 'Nyet'.

At this point, [we see] three celli proudly facing us on a stand nearby. We leave the store.

Word got out that I was looking for a cello for my daughter. There was a stringed instrument factory that we went to see. It had beautifully crafted instruments, but they wanted 12,000 dollars for a cello. Yael said: 'Leave it for Yo Yo Ma.'

There were many musicians emigrating from Russia. They were not allowed to take their instruments out of the country. We heard of a cellist who was willing to sell his. We called him. He was apprehensive, but finally said he would meet us at Pushkin Square. For identification, he told us he was red-haired and had a beard. I said I would be carrying a blue and white hat in my hand. His name was Maxim Steinberg. As we approached the statue of Pushkin, we saw no red-haired men. We went around the statue several times. Inadvertently, I hid my hat in my pocket. It was a hot day. People were beginning to stare at us. My driver was having a difficult time trying to stay close by in all that traffic. There was a man with a brown beard but he was wearing a hat and we could not discern the colour of his hair. Aliza, a musician, felt the vibrations of a colleague. She approached him. 'Are you Mr Nordau?' she said, in conversational tones. The man paled. We thought he would faint. Suddenly, I realized that we should have asked him if he was Steinberg, not Nordau, the name of the manager of the stringed instrument factory. The poor man said a weak 'yes' and tore the hat off his head. He was almost totally bald with a thin fringe of red hair at the back of his head. I produced my blue-and-white hat for confirmation. We all got into my car and in stultifying silence rode to one of the Moscow suburbs. After we got out of the elevator on the ninth floor where he resided, he turned to Aliza. 'How did you know my mother's maiden name?' he asked, still deeply suspicious. We explained. Steinberg was convinced we had checked him out thoroughly. It took us a while to persuade him we had no ill intentions. Only then did we get on to the business of the cello.

Aliza returned several times to visit me in Moscow and picked up enough Russian to carry on a conversation. She would sometimes turn to me in Russian and ask if I was Mr Nordau. But I would only laugh.

11 · A Turn of the Tide

The year 1989 seemed then, as it does today, to be a point of no return. There were important measures being taken by the Gorbachev government: elections to a fledgling parliament, promises of greater freedoms and unrestricted political activity, continued lifting of censorship and an open debate about the road ahead. There was a relaxation of international tensions. Yet, there was scepticism. Similar periods in the life of the Soviet regime, notably Khrushchev's Thaw, had ended in failure and in the reinstatement of a stagnating and corrupt regime. The tempo of Gorbachev's perestroika was reminiscent of the period of the New Economic Policy, introduced by Lenin after the end of the Civil War in 1921. The New Economic Policy had reinstated small- and medium-scale private enterprise. The economy forged ahead with surprising speed and, before being nipped in the bud by Stalin, created an environment of hope. Perestroika was, at least partially, modelled on NEP, but Gorbachev's version of economic reform was badly mismanaged. One of its byproducts was countrywide chaos, which sapped the very foundations of the communist establishment and caused ambivalence and vacillation at the top. The result was a mood of uncertainty and gloom.

The death of Lenin in 1924, Stalin's full takeover of the party in 1927 and the years of repression that followed, left a deep imprint upon the psyche of *homo soveticus*. The supremacy of centralized power, the institutionalization of falsehood and cynicism were the ground in which Gorbachev began planting the tender saplings of perestroika and glasnost. Few had faith in the good intentions of the new leaders. As changes began taking shape, the long-forgotten reflexes of open debate activated a bitter, long-winded dispute among intellectuals as to the goals of the regime and its intended reforms. The existence of a grave crisis was evident to all; it was clear there would be no panaceas. After an initial period of sloganeering about the need for change, it became apparent that Gorbachev and his government had no precise plan for how to improve the bleak prospects of Soviet life. The questions revolved around the introduction of a market economy. The implications of such an economic revolution in the life of the population at large, and especially the ruling class, would be grave. Over the years, the Soviet *nomenklatura* and its dependents had grown into a 60 million-strong monster, in a population of 300 million; they would not easily give up their privileged lifestyle.

The positive aspect of this difficult turning point was the realization that there could be no retreat to the horrors of the past or even to the stagnation of the Brezhnev period. The recurrent questions asked by foreigners and by Russians on the likelihood of a regression, were hesitatingly but persistently answered in the negative.

THE CHALLENGE OF PERESTROIKA

For me these questions were not merely of academic interest. The goals we Israelis had in mind, immigration and an improvement of relations with the USSR, were fully dependent on the direction of developments within the Soviet Union. I realized how little I knew about this immense country and its people, how much there was to observe and to learn and how very little time I had to do it. My advantage over some of my diplomatic colleagues in Moscow was my background and my ability to converse in Russian and establish an intimate dialogue. As the representative of Israel, I was the object of a great deal of curiosity, and this also helped me to make my way. I could, thus, get acquainted with many individuals who could help me understand the intricacies of Soviet life. Not everything I heard was the total truth nor always a revelation, but I often caught a good glimpse inside the enclosure that Bolshevism had built around the Russians, its 'chosen people'.

Among the many individuals I met, I especially recall my conversations with people like Roy Medvedev, the historian and proponent of democratization of the Soviet system, and Vitaly Korotich, the editor of the weekly magazine *Ogonek.*

Medvedev and his brother Zhores — the latter exiled abroad — were articulate and forceful dissidents and their sharp criticism of the Soviet system and its policies, coming from within, was highly revealing to western eyes and must have been particularly damaging to the Russians. Toward the end of the 1960s, creeping re-Stalinization under the influence of the conservative leadership of the party and the support of Leonid Brezhnev began overshadowing the more liberal tendencies introduced by Khrushchev. Roy Medvedev, who had written about the need to democratize the existing system and had critically appraised the history of the USSR, was severely attacked, expelled from the party, fired from his job and restricted to his home. All the while, however, he remained a convinced Marxist and never repudiated the communist system. Toward the end of the Gorbachev period, Medvedev made a comeback and was even elected to the Russian Parliament as a member of the new Communist Party.

When I first went to see Roy on a cold February day in 1989, I expected, in my imperfect appreciation of Soviet complexities, to find him in circumstances befitting a vocal opponent of the regime — dilapidated lodgings, cut off from the world. But there seemed to have been a tacit understanding with some of the regime's opponents, especially those who did not challenge the basic precepts of the system. The ferociousness of the Stalinist repression became muted after the death of the tyrant. After the Twentieth Party Congress and Khrushchev's revelations about Stalin, the regime began acting with greater restraint against its critics. After his expulsion from the party, Medvedev enjoyed a certain demonstrative tolerance, as a showcase opponent. In 1982 he wrote a biography of Nikita Khrushchev, for which he gained a great reputation abroad but which was strongly frowned upon by the propaganda establishment.

Although well on the outskirts of Moscow, Medvedev's apartment was warm, comfortable and neat. It housed a substantial library. His telephone was in working order and he had a long conversation during my visit with his editor in London. Medvedev seemed self-assured and relaxed. A likeness of Jesus and a silver cross on one of the shelves made me wonder at the depth of the atheism inculcated into people like him in the process of gaining a communist education. Religion and Russian tradition seemed to have great powers of regeneration. I suspect that the cross was an open proclamation of Medvedev's belief in the eternal values of Russia. I found this difficult to understand, but was highly interested to hear this man expound on his ideas and beliefs.

Vitaly Korotich, very much in vogue in 1989 as a centre of opposition to the right-wing revanchists, had also become a good friend, willing to offer his guidance on the Soviet enigma. I especially enjoyed meeting him at his office. He was surrounded at the time by the adulation of his staff, and very much the outstanding and authoritative editor in the country. *Ogonek* was always awaited with great expectancy and its circulation soared from several hundreds of thousands to five million. The magazine had been known for its staid and grey subject matter but became, under Korotich's guidance, an explosive literary weapon against backtracking conservative communists. The magazine was replete with revelations about the communist regime and articles criticizing the wrongdoings and stupidity of the administration. A copy of *Ogonek* was hard to come by. I once stood in line at the Ukraina Hotel and awaited, with many others, the arrival of the journal. Twentieth in line, my turn finally came up, but the last *Ogonek* went to the man who was ahead of me. The others sincerely commiserated with me on my tough luck.

Korotich was a medical doctor by profession but had gone through stormy times in his life before being appointed editor of *Ogonek*, which gave him entry into the corridors of power. As a sign of special favour he consented to set aside two copies of the magazine to be picked up by my driver a day before its appearance.

There were a good number of Muscovites with whom I became acquainted, some more famous than others, but all intimate with the texture of their country's life and mentality. I had the privilege of knowing a number of political and social scientists and economists. I had established a good working relationship with the academy's Social Sciences Institute and the Social Sciences Institute of the Central Committee. I had also made friends with people knowledgeable about agriculture and other important fields. Already toward the end of 1989, I had been introduced to the new class of politicians, such as the future mayor of Moscow, Gavril Popov, and others in the liberal and democratic movement; the minister of foreign affairs of the Russian Federation, Andrei Kozyrev, and his deputies; Arkady Volsky, the head of the Scientists' and Industrialists' Union and a number of others. Some I met fleetingly or for brief but revealing conversations, as with Boris Yeltsin. I also met right-wing thinkers and writers. A few of these new acquaintances had access to top officials and were willing to share their impressions with me. There were many disparate views within this group, but a surprising consensus on the nature of the problems and the personality of the leader.

Perestroika's challenge, all agreed, could not be fulfilled in the current generation. Recent years had not and could not have produced the professionals who could lead the country out of its doldrums. The early history of the USSR had caused a dwindling of the country's political and administrative talents. Lenin's conception of the communist state was based on a determination to clear the slate of everything that had preceded, and construct an entirely new system. But Lenin went to unnecessary extremes. He left no political or economic culture save that of coercion. The intellectual landscape was completely devastated. The tragic history of Russia, over a thousand years before the Revolution, had nevertheless created a stratum of intellectuals and administrators immersed in the country's traditions and capable of ruling and managing the vast country. They would have done alright under any well-defined policy. These administrators were largely gone after the Civil War, the period of War Communism and the liquidations and banishments that followed. The better-known intellectuals, the economists, philosophers and scientists fled to the West where they made quite a name for themselves.

Lenin and his companions presumed that the proletariat would produce a new crop of extraordinary people to revitalize the country and lead it into world revolution. This hope foundered as a result of the intellectual and physical oppression that became an integral component of the stifling totalitarian system. The new atmosphere of fear could only produce a banal and flat intellect, devoid of inspiration or self-criticism. All of this led to the destruction of the human reservoirs of the country and, consequently, of the rich culture that had developed over centuries. Any fresh attempts to raise a new generation of men and women capable of turning the country around were mercilessly subdued: Stalin liquidated the NEP entrepreneurs and the leadership of the Red Army; Khrushchev trampled down the first budding of new minds; Brezhnev's regime strangled the initiatives of economic and social reforms. Gorbachev, for his part, suffered from a loss of direction and clarity of purpose, bringing about a feeling of rejection among those who could truly contribute to the emerging, post-communist state.

These opinions were echoed and re-echoed in many of the conversations I had with my acquaintances. The predominant view was that the situation that had developed in 1989 manifested the economic, political and social disorientation of perestroika. The Gorbachev era was, in fact, ushered in by a group of élitists, products of the Soviet educational and managerial machine, who foresaw the coming disaster already in the late 1960s but were deprived of an opportunity to introduce the gradual changes necessary to redress the mistakes. It was widely known, for instance, that Alexei Kosygin, prime minister under Brezhnev in the mid-1960s, had intended to launch economic reforms that would limit the extent of the central planning system and seek to move into a moderately market-oriented one. At the time it was believed that Kosygin's ambitions were thwarted by an opposition which feared its own eventual obsolescence and which forced Brezhnev to curtail and cancel the reforms. The Prague Spring of 1968 provided an excellent excuse for the conservatives to squelch the ambitions of the reformers who saw the looming crisis. However, serious economists are of the opinion today that the Kosygin reforms fell through because of their intrinsic inadequacies.* There were

---

* See, for instance, Abel Aganbegyan, *The Economic Challenge of Perestroika* (Bloomington, IN: Indiana University Press, 1988); Georgy Arbatov, *The System: An Insider's Life in the Soviet Union* (New York: Random House, 1992).

renewed attempts in the early 1970s to tackle basic issues. They ended in a similar manner.

In the period preceding Gorbachev's appointment as general secretary, it had become amply evident that reforms were unavoidable. The coming of perestroika was thus ineluctable, for economic and consequently political reasons. Perestroika's first and most important message was that the time had come to take cognizance of the failure of Soviet economy — a state of affairs which was generally accepted but not officially acknowledged. The implication was that the political structures that had brought this about (mainly the Communist Party) had to be redesigned. There was little effective opposition to the tearing down process. It was the rebuilding that was problematic. Soviet methodology was outmoded and inefficient, and had to be rejuvenated. No one knew how. The shock winds of change were sweeping everything aside, including sensible alternatives. As a result, the perception of reality dimmed. The political leadership was perplexed and wavering and hardly in a position to direct or lead.

The Soviet economy had been hit very hard by the defence-oriented investments that had produced nothing for the benefit of the country at large. Some 52 per cent of all energy produced in the country was consumed by the defence establishment. Only six per cent of total production was allocated to the consumers; the rest went into grandiose schemes to excel in size and in importance, or into inflated agricultural and scientific projects, which ultimately did not feed or clothe the people. The fabulous natural wealth of the USSR was exported to pay for the economic foibles of the central economy. Resources were thoughtlessly squandered, much of the land was polluted for many generations to come by incessant testing of nuclear and chemical weapons. The country's efforts only served the paranoid compulsion of the rulers 'to stand up to the threats of the imperialists'. Anyone visiting the Soviet Union, flying its airlines, boarding and disembarking in airfields, shopping in its stores or seeing the quality of life of its cities, the living standards of its people, came to this inevitable conclusion.

There were a great many positive achievements, nevertheless. Heavy investments were made in basic scientific research and development, albeit largely security-oriented. As a result, very great discoveries were probably made in all scientific fields, but most were left in the government's secret files. The Israel Chamber of Commerce came out for a first round of talks with its Soviet counterpart, the All-Soviet Chamber of Commerce, at the beginning of 1990. After we had signed an agreement on cooperation, our Soviet hosts proposed that we choose for joint commercialization any one of some 2,000 new patents in industry and science. These patents had never been exploited, and had apparently been frozen for future use. It was a standard practice to declare any important discovery a state secret, in order to keep it from reaching the hands of the enemy, rather than publishing and using it for the good of the economy, to say nothing of the country or of mankind. When a certain Dr. Leizer Mekler, an outstanding Soviet biochemist, offered his discovery of a stereochemical genetic code to use in the folding of proteins in 1978, the first reaction of the Academy of Sciences was to declare the information 'classified'.

The waste of resources and of the country's treasures was carried out on an incredible scale. In the words of Roy Medvedev, over a hundred billion dollars were spent on building three defensive perimeters against China, from the Afghan border to the Kuril Islands. A hundred divisions were positioned in that area. An additional trans-Siberian railroad, BAM, was built at tremendous cost, in the extremely difficult conditions of the frozen north, in order to face the 'Chinese threat'. BAM is now considered a white elephant and has been all but abandoned.* The rivalry of the two communist powers probably could have been resolved at far more modest expense, if a less megalomaniacal policy had been used by the successive Moscow regimes and the fear of a new Mongol invasion had been less acute. A different, but no less typical delusion was evident in the dealings with Japan. It had already become clear to the Soviet leadership that the Kuril islands would have to be restored to the Japanese. The problem was finding a plausible pretext. For want of a better policy toward Japan, this economic giant, which could have become instrumental in the

---

* Nikolay Shmelev and Vladimir Popov, *The Turning Point* (New York: Doubleday, 1989) p. 105.

development of eastern Siberia, was kept completely out of the Soviet orbit. The nine million Russians east of Lake Baikal, a richly promising territory, have progressed little in the last half-century, largely because no substantial physical or economic links were established between European Russia and its far east. With recent internal political difficulties and embarrassments, the problem of the Soviet Far East remains unresolved.

Soviet policy towards the Middle East was a reflection of the situation inside the country. Everyone realized that the 1967 decision to sever relations with Israel had been a mistake, yet no one had the courage to reverse it. Soviet Arab policy was often incomprehensible — certainly in the eyes of Israel, but in the view of some leading Soviet experts as well.

The larger policy framework on the Middle East was the superpower contest over supremacy in Asia and Africa. It had started very soon after the Second World War and continued to the very last year of the Soviet regime in 1991. Much of the strategy of the USSR's Middle East policies was predicated on confrontation with the West. At the same time, the Soviet Union had ideologized its presence in the Middle East and had striven to install socialism in the Arab world, which ultimately rejected it. Algeria, the only country whose economy was consistently modelled on the Soviet socialist idea, became as wasteful and irrational as the Soviet mould into which it was cast. The other countries that toyed with socialism — Egypt, South Yemen, Syria — have all lived to regret Soviet interference in their affairs and have changed course. The Soviet Union did not gain anything from its intimate relations with the Arab world, forged only through an extremely generous export of arms and influence and financed by the export of Soviet oil during the world energy crisis. Glasnost brought increasing criticism of this wasteful Soviet policy, which was carried out with little consideration for the improvement of living standards in the USSR.

Despite its close relations with the Arab world, the Soviet Union had no accurate assessments of the true nature of Muslim fundamentalism, even within its own frontiers: in Central Asia, Azerbaijan and within European Russia itself. It was accepted that fundamentalism was a menace to the existing order as well as to the future of Russia. Yet, it is doubtful whether a thorough discussion of this crucial topic ever took place at the highest levels of policy making. Certainly, no far-reaching measures seem to have been taken. The authority for such a review nominally rested with the Central Committee. Already in 1989, the Central Committee and the Politburo were left with mere vestiges of their former preponderance. They were not replaced by another authority after the inaguration of the presidential system in March 1990.* On a matter so important for the Soviet state — the future of the Central Asian republics with their considerable Muslim populations — there was no organized thinking or decision making.

GORBACHEV, THE PRIME MOVER

Gorbachev was a new-style Soviet leader. He appeared more polished, more open and accessible than his predecessors. He had studied law at Moscow University and was considered to be an educated and modern person, in contrast to former leaders. Yet Russians were ambivalent about him. Perestroika aroused great curiosity and even hope. However, the public had little confidence in Gorbachev's personal courage and his ability to withstand attempts by the Communist Party to derail the reforms. For all his dexterity in managing the opposition, Gorbachev never inspired devotion. He seemed to have an extraordinary ability to manoeuvre in and out of reforms and confound his many critics. But he had no general concept of a plan of operations and had no political platform. Thus, his motives appeared suspect, and both the left and the right began seeing him as a turncoat to the interests of the Communist Party and the Russian state.

I once heard a noted anthropologist from Moscow University assert that Gorbachev, like many of his assistants or even members of the Politburo, was in reality, a country bumpkin. The anthropologist complained that those at the very top echelons of

---

* Aleksandr Yakovlev, *Predislovie, obval, posleslovie* (Preface, Landslide, Epilogue) (Moscow: Novosti, 1992) p. 135.

the communist machine were not in the habit of sitting down and thinking. When a crisis developed, the only thing they knew how to do was roll up their sleeves and 'fetch the spade'. This description was a trifle harsh, perhaps, but not very far from the truth. Those who spoke with Gorbachev or had the opportunity to observe him at close range, respected him. All agreed, however, that he had the tendency to rush into new projects and be as indecisive in their execution as the advisers he so often shifted around.

Later, more intimate portraits and stories about Gorbachev began appearing in the press. There was more information about his earlier years, about the difficulties his family, like millions of others in the rural areas of the country, had experienced. There was a documentary film made in 1990 on Gorbachev's life before his attainment of national prominence. I saw this film, shot by Gerd Rude of German Television, at a private showing in the home of the well-known journalist Elena Korenevskaia. The film included a long interview with Gorbachev's mother. Among other things she said that when he was young, Gorbachev had to walk eight kilometres to school every day. She also revealed that Gorbachev's father had been oppressed during collectivization.

Gorbachev was a man with provincial roots, who educated himself and made it to the top. This was not an unusual story in the Soviet Union. Most Soviet leaders had been through the same process. He was especially fortunate in having been appointed to a top Communist Party job in Stavropol, the administrative centre of a large resort area for the upper crust. Communist bosses taking their frequent rest cures in the region became acquainted with Gorbachev, a very active and communicative Soviet *apparatchik*, who knew how to impress the visiting dignitaries with his openness and charm. Raisa Gorbachev helped her husband considerably in advancing his career. She was an intelligent, educated and attractive woman, who knew how to keep her youthful figure, dress elegantly, and play a valuable supportive role. Raisa also made her mark among the politicians who came to Stavropol. Eventually, Gorbachev got an appointment to the Central Committee in Moscow, where he continued his swift ascent.

Perestroika came after many painful years. Both the leadership and the population lived with their memories of Stalinist times, of the Civil War, the famines, the collectivization, the liquidations, the forced labour camps and the Second World War. There had been much suffering and pain. For these reasons, and because of the nature of his personality, Gorbachev could not and did not become a tyrant or have a tendency toward drastic solutions, irrespective of the cost. There were no known cures for the incremental illnesses of the regime. On the other hand, the country was not ready to submit to another Stalin or Khrushchev. Times were different and there was no going back. Yet had it not been for the astuteness, the flexibility, of Gorbachev and of his intrinsically positive qualities, the way of perestroika could have been different. Had Andropov remained at the top of the Soviet pyramid, his powerful personality might have set events in an entirely different direction. The USSR probably would have been preserved, even at a high cost in lives. But Andropov's reign was brief, and Gorbachev's brand of leadership saved much blood and tragedy.

When the results of the March 1989 general elections came in and the initial 1,958 (out of a total 2,250) deputies were elected to the new Congress, and the two chambers, the Supreme Soviet and the Soviet of the Nationalities, were formed, the 70-year-old tradition of silence was shattered. No more rubber-stamped decisions, obsequious odes to the wisdom of the party or adulation of the leader. The new Parliament engaged in endless, acrimonious, long-winded speech-making. There were hardly any rules of procedure and there was a lot of static in the air. Gorbachev, who sat in on most of those first meetings, had a hard time keeping order and would himself speak out of turn. The proceedings at the new Parliament were shown in their entirety on state television and the devolving debates were watched with bated breath. At times, the Parliament resembled Gogol's description of the enormous Sorochin Fair in the Ukraine. I had a television installed in my office and found it difficult to tear myself away from the dramatic parliamentary broadcasts. The Russians had a great weakness for Mexican soap operas, and Moscow streets used to empty out when they were aired, but the 'ratings' of the parliamentary debates were unsurpassed.

On one memorable occasion, a group of so-called 'security loyalists' under Marshal Sergei Akhromeev, the former Chief of Staff of the army, and Colonel Alexis Alknis, organized a strong and insidious attack against Andrei Sakharov, the father of the Russian hydrogen bomb. Sakharov, who had become an opponent of the regime, had been banished by Brezhnev to the city of Gorky. Upon his accession to power, Gorbachev demonstratively recalled Sakharov back to Moscow. The military deputies said they wanted to clear the army of the calumny spread by Sakharov against the Soviet Expeditionary Force which had been supposedly shooting down its own men in Afghanistan, rather than see them fall into the hands of the *mujahedin*. Sakharov wanted to reply but was rudely blocked by Gorbachev. When Sakharov finally did get the floor, Gorbachev could not hide his anger. He kept making arrogant remarks, and finally turned off Sakharov's microphone. The fear of the military and of authority was still great enough to prevent any deputy from standing up for Sakharov. Only on the following day did the philosopher Yuri Kariagin get up to defend him, pointing out that Sakharov had been the only person who had protested against the Afghan war. Kariagin insisted that had it not been for Sakharov, the Soviet Union would still be entangled in Afghanistan, and the army would still be losing men.

Gorbachev's behaviour, to say nothing of the atmosphere that prevailed in the chamber that day, was humiliating. I later talked with Sakharov about this. He did not entirely acknowledge it, but he was offended and confused. Sakharov's wife Yelena Bonner said she was terribly upset about the incident in Parliament. I am certain this confrontation worsened Sakharov's heart condition, from which he passed away some months later. In early 1995 rumours surfaced about Sakharov having been poisoned.

The whole country was listening so intensely to these proceedings in Parliament, shown on television and broadcast on radio, that these open debates took on the character of a massive national catharsis. Everywhere we went, in government and municipal offices, in the streets, in cars and trams, at homes, ears were glued to the radio and eyes riveted to television. I remember seeing an army officer on duty at the entrance to the Ministry of Foreign Affairs, listening to a tiny radio while checking visitors, and loudly

143

arguing with his colleagues over statements being made in Parliament. The debates were taken up by the public at large. The whole country was paralysed, doing absolutely nothing but participating in this new, strange and mesmerizing pastime, compensating for the many years of suppression. The parliamentarians, thrown into an entirely new situation, were in reality verbalizing the confusion of the populace.

Who were they, these new parliamentarians? Korotich related to me how, in an unguarded moment before the elections, Gorbachev had confided in him that only 'dependable' people would be elected. He wanted pragmatic, visionary deputies, but good communists. They should not deviate right or left, but proceed straight toward the dismantling of the existing establishment, Gorbachev had said — and most of that work had already been done. During Gorbachev's tenure, two-thirds of the cadres were replaced. Many were retired, others moved to alternative jobs. To underline his words Gorbachev had paraphrased the well-known communist maxim, saying each would have to give according to his abilities, to receive according to his achievements. Korotich was impressed with Gorbachev's self-confidence when he said subjectivism and personal ambitions would have to be eliminated. On the other hand, Gorbachev had added that alternative paths, political speculation and abstract ideas, like the multi-party system, would not have a place in the new system either.

In the elections, many candidates were rejected by the voters, a situation unprecedented in the history of the Soviet Union: members of the Central Committee, including the head of the Moscow City Party Committee (the mayor), the head of the KGB in Estonia, the prime minister of Lithuania and many others failed to get themselves elected, where only a few years earlier they would have had guaranteed seats. Gorbachev seemed at peace with himself when interviewed during the elections. He said there would not be any great leaps forward. He was not geared to hasty reforms. And the Soviet public was beginning to realize that the heavy burden of the past could not be lifted in a day. It would take at least a generation. Gorbachev's problem, of course, was that he felt certain he would still be around when that bright day dawned.

Whatever Gorbachev may have said, his purpose was clear on

one point: to clip the wings of the Communist Party, its myriad organizations and millions-strong membership. Gorbachev did not want to destroy the party, only to mitigate its ambitions and powers. He did not aspire to the total democratization of the system. The election of Boris Yeltsin upset and angered him, as he saw in it the creation of a dangerous opposition that might challenge his status as the supreme leader of the country.

It was, on the other hand, precisely this election of Yeltsin that was seen as proof of deep and serious changes coming over the country. Igor Kliamkin, a well-known political analyst, wrote in the February 1989 edition of the widely read *Novy Mir* magazine that the communist principle of keeping people in the dark as a matter of policy, ought to be abolished. This was the first time a serious writer was asking the Communist Party to stop regulating people's lives without their consent. The election of Yeltsin, Kliamkin said, was the first important breakthrough because it was a truly democratic and open step into the future. The smokescreen descending on the elections, Kliamkin remarked, indicated the crisis had not been resolved. As events later showed, this was an understatement.

ISRAEL'S CONCERN

What could Israel expect from this new regime? Had it distanced itself from the old? Would the Jews have a respite from their painful experiences in the land of communism? Would Gorbachev's much-touted 'new thinking' bring about a change of heart and policy on human rights and free emigration? Would Soviet insistence on Israel's recognition of and negotiations with the PLO, as a quid pro quo for renewed relations and freer travel of immigrants, be abandoned? Would the continued amelioration of contacts with the West make the new Soviet Union change its subversive policies in the Middle East, its support for terrorists? Would it see the peace process in the Middle East as an intrinsic part of global détente and discontinue its fight for strategic advantages in the region in its rivalry with the West? I saw no such indication.

In my repeated meetings with Tarasov, my official correspondent at the Ministry of Foreign Affairs and the supposed spokesman for his government, it was still the old refrain. Public opinion in the USSR, Tarasov said, was very much against the renewal of relations with Israel. The Soviet public could not forego its opposition when faced with the constant scenes of popular Arab uprising in the occupied territories. I could not but reflect that at the time we were having these discussions the Soviet army had already caused the death of over a million Afghans in a cruel war which, according to Gorbachev's personal adviser Anatoly Cherniaev, was being perpetuated for virtually no intelligible reason, apart from the desire of a few obstinate old men in the Politburo to save their chums in the Communist Party in Kabul.

Tarasov's words were not a reflection of the ongoing reassessment of foreign affairs. He was still the defender of the official hard-line policy, a rather dwindling majority within the government, but still a majority. Tarasov declared himself and his colleagues to have been surprised at our reaction to the Shevardnadze speech in Cairo, which threatened us with sanctions. As Shevardnadze's special representative on the Middle East, Tarasov sought Israel's acceptance of the international conference framework, a precondition for the renewal of relations.

Every meeting with this official in his cubicle at the ministry would start out with an inquiry as to my choice of tea or coffee. After a short interlude, the cafeteria having been duly alerted, a waitress would roll in a small tray of hot drinks and the standard fingernail-sized granite biscuits. Tarasov would studiously avoid any talk of business while we were being served. He would then open with remarks about long-range missiles, chemical and other weapons of mass destruction which Israel possessed and would express the need for disarmament in the region. On the other hand, he described as purely defensive the Soviet supplies of sophisticated weapons to Iraq, Libya and Syria. He maintained a cynical and arrogant posture on the need to open a direct and candid political dialogue. Like some other Soviet officials, Tarasov kept implying that the US was acting in liaison with the USSR in favour of a large, all-encompassing international peace conference. Both of us knew these assertions to be false, yet he would not change his stance. He seemed to be the leading member or the mouthpiece of Shevardnadze's hard-line advisers who, for various reasons, thought this policy would secure political advantages. Perhaps the status quo could not be changed until decisions were taken by the Politburo.

'As regards relations, you ought to be informed', Tarasov once said, 'that in spite of anything you hear from your many contacts in Moscow', it is the government alone which takes the decisions. If Israel exhibits more flexibility and accepts what the whole world has already recognized, Soviet public opinion might also change. I had to remind him that Soviet public opinion was being fed by the government alone and that the media were far from free. Tarasov would then sharply change the subject and haughtily remind me that all contacts with Aeroflot on direct immigrant flights had to be made through the consular department. When I inquired why, in that case, we had not received any feedback from that department in over ten months, his answer was: 'Apparently, it didn't interest us'. When once I saw him glancing at his watch and asked if he could not spend more time with me, he replied: 'Oh, I am only looking at my wrist'.

Rumour in the Academy's Oriental Institute had it that in the past, young Tarasov and other colleagues had had a more positive disposition toward Israel and were supporters of the renewal of ties. That was before they became prominent in Arab affairs and had served in Arab countries. In Moscow in 1988 and 1989, Tarasov was showing great ardour for keeping Israel at bay. I could understand him. I was the embodiment of Israeli officialdom, with which the Soviet government was reluctant to deal.

There was another possible explanation for Tarasov's attitude. The Soviet government was misreading the internal situation in Israel. Tarasov was putting all his cards on Peres's return to premiership and more flexible attitude on the Palestinian problem. Tarasov was undoubtedly the leading specialist on the Middle East crisis, which meant that in those unsettled days in Moscow he was the only official who was entrusted with the baffling Arab-Israel conundrum. The other functionaries in the Middle East Department, though more senior and of higher rank, including Vladimir Poliakoff, the former ambassador to Cairo, usually stayed out of the picture. Tarasov had apparently persuaded his directorate that it was good policy to maintain contacts with the Peres group, and he thus lost no opportunities to meet with Nimrod Novik to discuss the Israeli internal scene and Israel's possible participation in an international conference. The procedure was simple: almost every time Tarasov went abroad on business, he would call Novik and set up a meeting, usually in Europe. On one of Tarasov's trips to the Middle East, I suggested he visit Israel and confer with us as well as with the Arabs. Tarasov refused. But he was prepared to meet with Novik in Cyprus. Word of this suggestion leaked out in Jerusalem and there was a lot of angry commentary in the Israeli press.

I would often point out to Tarasov that I found nothing wrong in his meetings with Peres's people, but not at the price of ignoring the appropriate agency in charge of foreign policy. Tarasov was paying exaggerated importance to loose commentary in the Israeli press on the politics of the coalition cabinet, and the prospects for the establishment of a Peres government. The Peres retinue did not discourage Tarasov; quite the contrary. So there was a strange reversal of roles. I was the emissary of the Israeli government to the Soviet Union; yet I was treated as a member of the opposition.

In a situation where so much in Soviet Russia was dependent on the improvement of contacts with officialdom, which could, at will, relax the existing constraints, I thought Peres would realize that he had to be very cautious about his use of 'unofficial' contacts. I wrote to him on this subject. He replied that if it was accepted practice in the West for a country to maintain a variety of contacts, including informal ones, on all levels with other countries, why should it not also be true of the East? The solution, he suggested, would be for me to be kept abreast, unofficially, of the conversations with the Russians and for us to exchange ideas during my subsequent visits home. I let the matter rest there. This was quintessential Peres: intellectually and politically resourceful, highly mindful of his own political interests, and keeping the bigger issues in view as well. I was satisfied Peres understood my dilemma. I knew I could rely on his support, as he realized how difficult a struggle it was to obtain recognition in the hostile environment of Moscow. I was sure he would do nothing to undermine the efforts invested toward the establishment of an official presence in USSR.

The irony of the matter is that in September 1993 Israel recognized the PLO and Rabin shook Arafat's hand. In September 1994, even the Likud Party, realizing the hopelessness of its insularity on the question of relations with the Palestinians, indicated that if brought to power, it would be willing to live with the PLO under certain political and territorial arrangements. A great deal of time and pain could have been spared if there had been a little less obstinacy over the years, both in the Soviet and the Israeli camps. This is true not only with regard to the PLO. If in April 1987 the then Prime Minister Yitzhak Shamir had shown greater statesmanship, swallowed his pride and personal frustration over Shimon Peres's understanding with King Hussein reached in London, perhaps Israel would not have had to deal with Yassir Arafat in 1993 at all. Peace would have arrived earlier and would have cost much less — in time, money, and above all, lives. However, this is fruitless speculation. In Moscow in 1988, 1989 and 1990, Israel was on an entirely different track and the Soviets simply refused to go along and accept facts as they were. It was the Soviets who wanted to have their own way, and paid little attention to the Israeli public's prevalent disposition. The Soviet government needlessly procrastinated on the renewal of relations and did not gain any advantages for itself or for its Arab friends.

Into the second half of 1989 the hostile attitude of the Soviet Ministry of Foreign Affairs began imperceptibly to change for the better. We were beginning to come to an understanding on an exchange of experts to explore more deeply our disagreements about the Arab-Israel crisis. There were more contacts with the Ministry of Foreign Affairs and conversations were less acerbic. Sergei Rogov of the USA and Canada Institute, one of the co-authors of the disarmament proposals in the Shevardnadze Cairo speech, was trying to persuade me that all we had to do was agree to set up a regulating defence agency. He said Shevardnadze was highly interested in the question of general disarmament. If only Israel would agree to open a dialogue on that question, all other demands (recognition of the PLO) would be overlooked. Shevardnadze would then find reason to promote the idea of a substantial improvement in relations. It was clear Rogov was pushing an idea which he cherished personally. To me, it meant there was an opening, but my suggestion to try this, even as an initial approach to a dialogue, did not find an echo in Jerusalem. It was clear that Jerusalem was wary of any suggestions for Soviet meddling in the fundamentals of the peace process as understood by Israel and the US. We also noticed that the references to the international conference were becoming less frequent. Evidently, that idea was losing its popularity. In October, Alexander Bovin, a senior political commentator in *Izvestiia*, who had had from a long association with the Central Committee and had been a speechwriter for Brezhnev, published an article recommending the renewal of diplomatic relations. I was certain Bovin was backed by highly placed individuals at the Central Committee. I thought we were on the verge of a breakthrough. I was not wrong.

HINTS OF RENEWED RELATIONS

The possibility of a visit by Shimon Peres, never off the agenda for the Russians or for us, surfaced again in the last week of November 1989. Radomir Bogdanov called me to his office at the Peace Committee. He said Peres could not possibly come to Moscow in the second half of December. Gorbachev and the other members of the political leadership would be busy with the renewed session of the Congress (both houses of the new Parliament), opening on 12 December. Gorbachev would then be going to Italy and Malta for the summit with Bush. He would be back only on Christmas Day. He then looked at me and said, 'I have just received word that a memo has been prepared by a member of the Politburo on an immediate restoration of relations. It was submitted to Gorbachev's office on the 21st. With everything he has on his mind these days, he will hardly have the time to read it before he goes off to Italy. But I am told he might be taking it with him. A decision will thus be taken very soon.'

A few days later, I was invited by Albert Reichman, the Canadian entrepreneur, to be on hand for the visit of Prime Minister Brian Mulroney and Foreign Minister Joe Clark at the

Steinsaltz Yeshiva. After I was introduced, Reichman took me aside. Alexander Yakovlev, number two at the Politburo, had told him relations with Israel were about to be renewed. Reichman asked me to transmit the message personally to Foreign Minister Arens and would he please keep this information to himself, since if it were leaked, the decision would be annulled before it was taken. Yakovlev was worried about opposition inside the Politburo.

I knew that Bogdanov's source was Yakovlev, either directly or through Nikolai Shishlin, a senior adviser on international affairs at the Central Committee. According to Bogdanov, the memo presented to Gorbachev was signed by one member of the Politburo, probably Yakovlev himself. Eduard Shevardnadze would have supported Yakovlev, I thought. This was good news but I was not breaking out the champagne yet. We did not hear anything else on this subject for a number of weeks. My conclusion was that the whole thing had been shelved, for internal reasons.

My friends in the institutes were telling me there was a growing confrontation between the Russian chauvinists and the 'patriots', on the one hand, and the neo-Marxists and the neo-socialists, on the other. The neo-socialists were promoting the reforms; the bureaucracy and parts of the *nomenklatura*, worried about their privileged place in society, were trying to subvert the progress of these reforms. There was another, smaller group, the intellectuals of the younger generation or those who had emerged with ideas more in line with market economy concepts. They favoured far-reaching reforms in property laws, political pluralism and parliamentarianism. There were growing signs of embarrassment both inside the Gorbachev government and in the Politburo, which did not know how to move forward without getting into a confrontation with wide segments of the power élite. There was also uncertainty about how the army would react.

A telling development was the large-scale demonstration in Leningrad on 22 November. The chairman of the Leningrad Soviet, Boris Gidaspov, and close friends in the Leningrad party organizations, brought out several hundred thousand party members into the streets, carrying banners against Gorbachev and criticizing the proposed economic and social reforms. Gidaspov was an energetic leader and enjoyed strong support. The daring manoeuvre in Leningrad underlined the growing rivalry and power struggle over the future of the Communist Party and its machine. Gorbachev had been too hesitant and had failed to maintain an active dialogue with the party as a power base. He was now facing a strong challenge from within.

The liberals and the democrats among Gorbachev's supporters were convinced that the newly elected Parliament and the proposed new presidential system would divide the ranks in the party organization and weaken its effectiveness. The Congress was to be convened in mid-December and municipal elections were to be held in the spring, all raising hopes for an organized resistance against the Communist Party. The conservative leaders of the party and the *nomenklatura* were aware of these possible developments and were striking back.

Gorbachev had, in fact, no personal power base. In promoting the presidential system of government, he was not overly active in assuring strong political support for himself. It appeared paradoxical that the only massive power he would have to rely on was the very force he was trying to dethrone, the party and its apparatus. Alexander Galkin, co-rector of the Communist Party Social Sciences Institute, the party's think-tank, thought the presidential system would have to lean heavily on the party cadres to survive. Galkin, one of the the foremost specialists in the party on the world social democratic movement, was convinced the party could rehabilitate itself and play a role in future politics, only if it shunned its past brutality and remodelled itself along more humane lines. He declared that under no circumstances should the party revert to its status of economic tsar of the USSR. The individual must become the party's first order of priorities in economic and social considerations, he insisted.

In this situation, there were recurrent allusions to the responsibility of highly placed persons for the protection they were according the Jews. Alexander Yakovlev himself, in spite of his position as number two in the administration of perestroika, was being accused of being a Jew-Mason. There was an ongoing discussion about the Middle East, Zionism and the Jews with anti-Semitic overtones. Soviet Jews were more than concerned, as all these symptoms are classic forerunners of anti-Jewish waves.

Undoubtedly, these phenomena made it difficult for Gorbachev to take a unilateral decision on Israel. In typical Gorbachev fashion, he chose to defer judgement on the issue and let it die down. This was also the wish of the majority of the Politburo, as I later found out. Thus, in spite of the many significant changes reshaping the destinies of the Soviet Union, in spite of the diplomatic drawbacks that continued aloofness from Israel had for Soviet policy in the Middle East, the Yakovlev memo (which I later discovered had been authored by three Politburo members) was ignored.

As the year 1990 dawned, we had to maintain the unsatisfactory status of a 'group of Israeli diplomats' at the Netherlands Embassy. However, for the Jews whose exodus had become a fact, for the growing numbers of Soviet agencies and private citizens who were in contact with us, for the Moscow diplomatic corps, the Israel Mission had long ago become an embassy.

12 · An Endemic Disease

At an Israel Bonds dinner in Baltimore in January 1986, the then under-secretary of state for human rights, Ambassador Richard Schifter, recounted that in a conversation he had had a few months earlier with a visiting Soviet delegation, a high Soviet official had said there were no more than 300 Jews in all of the Soviet Union who wanted to emigrate. The official added that there was absolutely no trace of anti-Semitism in the USSR. To prove his point, he said that although they constituted only seven-tenths of one per cent of the population, six per cent of all doctors, five per cent of lawyers, five per cent of students of higher institutions of learning and three per cent of teachers were Jewish. This, out of a total population of nearly 300 million. Another member of the Soviet delegation had then raised his hand and remarked: 'And none are workers!'

The facts were different. An estimate based on a study carried out in the Soviet Union by western embassies through contacts with Soviet Jews showed that no less than 400,000 would immediately apply for permission to leave the USSR, given the opportunity. Toward the end of 1985, however, the number of exit permits granted to Jews wishing to leave amounted to a mere 110.

The main reason for the desire to emigrate was the existence and the growth of anti-Semitism. There was anti-Jewish discrimination in education and in jobs. The strangulation of Jewish culture continued. This policy regarding the Jews was evident also in the propaganda practised by the USSR toward Israel. In a coordinated and sustained campaign, the USSR continued its barrage against Zionism, depicting Israelis as Nazis and publishing caricatures of Israelis which strongly resembled the portrayals of Jews in the Nazi period. These attacks against Zionism and Israel were a thinly veiled form of state anti-Semitism. There had been many examples of this attitude, and the generation that grew up after the Second World War had felt it and remembered it well into the 1980s.

The Jews were worried that the unsettled times of perestroika would lead to a deterioration of the economic and social order, to rioting and civil war, and as this would be accompanied by anti-Jewish violence — perhaps in the larger cities, certainly in the countryside. In the 70 years of communism the Jews of the Soviet Union had experienced many varieties of anti-Semitism. They had no desire to relive them. The future of the regime looked dim and inauspicious. Gorbachev had not delivered on his promises and could hardly do so in the future, in a system which was dying of heart failure and could not be resuscitated.

Many Jewish intellectuals, scientists and professionals whom I met had an additional reason to leave the USSR. There was growing preoccupation with the impoverishment of the scientific institutes and the resulting curtailment of their wide-scale activities, in which Jewish scientists had been playing a prominent role.

The Second World War had brought unexpected revelations about the West. Stalin had come to understand that Europe and America had far outdistanced his country in science and technology. It was clear that the Soviet Union was not prepared for the severe competition which would, inevitably, follow. Thus, Stalin concluded that the theoretical and technological infrastructure had to be laid down as soon as possible after the end of the conflict with Germany.

Lavrenty Beria was instructed by Stalin to set up scientific institutes which would provide the theoretical and practical basis to turn the USSR into an invincible military-industrial machine. Within a few years, huge institutes were established for scientific research. They were spread across the country and liberally subsidized to fulfil their assignments. Thousands of scientists were recruited into these organizations. No questions were asked, no limitations were set on nationality or Communist Party affiliation. Many Jews were recruited into the institutes and worked there for many years. The higher echelons were made up of Slavs, Russians, Ukrainians and others. Jews filled positions in theoretical science and advanced technology, but were not allowed to hold managerial positions. However, no restrictions were imposed on their scientific work.

The atmosphere inside many of these large establishments was liberal. As incredible as it may sound, the only requirement was apparently getting to work on time. The Jews suffered little or no discrimination. On the contrary, people guilty of anti-Semitic remarks or behaviour were ostracized. Complete academic freedom in thinking, working and discussion prevailed in an extremely collegial environment. The pay was average but people in these establishments were fully provided for in education, housing, medical care, transportation, entertainment, and retirement benefits. There was no coercion to fulfil 'norms', so common in other Soviet places of work.

The institutes served another important function: because of their permissiveness and the limited time demands which they made on their employees, the bulk of 'underground' literature was produced in their laboratories and offices. The KGB knew exactly what was going on but did not interfere. They apparently judged that the work done in the institutes was more important than prosecution of the culprits under Soviet law.

As perestroika got into full swing, budgetary considerations began to outweigh needs of government prestige and the relentless race to outdistance the West. The institutes began to want for money and started imposing restrictions. This was true even of the venerable Academy of Sciences. The growing difficulties awakened gross doubts about the stability of the institutes, a way of life for millions of people who lived a protected existence within their walls. The same was obviously true of Jews, as a bastion of liberal life, free of anti-Jewish pressures, was collapsing. Members of scientific institutes feared the way back into the world outside and the exposure to life's growing uncertainties.

Rumours of anti-Semitism, persecution of Jews and imminent pogroms began to spread toward the end of the 1980s simultaneously with the closure of the ivory towers which were the institutes. With no visible options inside the Soviet Union, Jewish scientists began to seek an escape in emigration, first to the West and then, in increasing numbers, to Israel. This phenomenon explains to a large degree the preponderance of scientists among the swelling ranks of immigrants seeking a haven from the coming storm in the Soviet Union. Many remembered the fate of the Jews in Germany, who would not listen to warnings about the intentions of the Nazis.

As the numbers of applications for exit visas kept growing at an increasing pace, it was said that Jews, as well as other ethnic groups — Volga Germans, Armenians, Tatars — wanted to leave for economic reasons. As we have seen, this was not entirely true. The Jews wanted to take advantage of the opportunity to exit the USSR. With the expected ruin and the degradation around them, they believed they could never become full-fledged citizens, could never enjoy equal rights, free of the harassment which they had known. They wanted to live in democratic countries, and enjoy civil and human rights.

The best example of Jewish continuity in a hostile Soviet Union is the way in which the Six-Day War revivified a flagging national spirit. Perhaps the clearest exponent of this innate force is the fervour with which young Jews in their teens took to studying Hebrew. There had not been any indication of such a strong interest before 1967. As soon as it became clear that Israel was under threat of destruction (and so it appeared at the time, even beyond the wall of silence and censorship imposed by the Soviet government), Soviet Jewry was gripped by a fear for its own survival. Israel's brilliant victory reawakened pride and a desire for identification. Thousands of young boys and girls began studying Hebrew, often to the dismay of their parents, who understood the dangers implicit in an enterprise frowned upon by the authorities. There were many cases when outstanding young scholars, on the verge of their entry into the university, threw away their future careers in favour of organizing clandestine, self-taught Hebrew classes. This enthusiasm lasted for a number of years, eventually leading to the exodus of 1972-79.

After 1980, the Soviet government prohibited emigration to Israel. The paradox was that Jews could leave the Soviet Union, irrespective of destination, only with an Israeli visa, handed out by the Dutch Embassy in Moscow. Between 1979 and 1988 some 320,000 *vizovs* were sent out to the Soviet Union; from these some

85,000 emigrants reached the US and other countries in the West and only 17,000 arrived in Israel. The emigration during the era of perestroika consisted of a different generation of people, with less knowledge about Israel and less attraction to it than the preceding wave of over 300,000 Jews who emigrated from 1972-80. Half of this earlier wave settled in Israel and is doing remarkably well.

At the beginning of 1987, there was a change of tactics: the Soviets decreed that Jews could apply to emigrate to any country, if they were invited by their close relatives. Where *vizovs* (invitations for Soviet Jews to emigrate) had previously been accepted only from Israel, they could now come from other countries, including the US. The fact of the matter was, however, that Israel remained the main source of *vizovs*. Procedures for immigration into other countries on the basis of invitations were severely restricted by national laws. The US maintained its open-door policy for Jews entering as political refugees on Israeli visas processed by US immigration personnel outside of the USSR (primarily in Rome and Vienna). The entry of Jews on invitations from the US was subject to the usual US immigration procedures carried out in Moscow, with its complicated paperwork and delays.

Nevertheless, the decision to widen the acceptance of *vizovs* from additional countries was considered by Israel to be an unwelcome precedent. We thought it would reduce even further the number of Jews coming to our country. Toward the end of 1988 in Moscow, when it was becoming quite clear Soviet Jews would use every opportunity to emigrate to the US as political refugees, I could not but wonder how long we would go on issuing visas under these circumstances. This was very much against the sanctified policy of striving for *aliyah* at all costs. Nativ's great concern was that if the emigration out of the Soviet Union, to countries other than Israel, went unchecked, the number of *olim* would remain extremely low, while the reservoir for *aliyah* would be exhausted within three to five years. Nevertheless, Nativ persisted in collecting requests for *vizovs* from Soviet Jews, starting the long and painful process of obtaining an exit permit. This was done primarily in the belief that all options should be kept open and Israel should maintain its unique position as a haven for Jews coming out of the Soviet Union.

The steeply rising number of emigrants was the immediate consequence of the declining rigidity of Soviet policy. If in 1986 only 900 Jews left the Soviet Union, in 1987 the figure rose eight-fold to over 8,000 and past 20,000 in 1988. At the same time, over 400,000 requests for *vizovs* were received by Nativ in Tel Aviv. This was an indication of the eagerness to take advantage of the new opportunities afforded by the internal changes. We had no idea how many of these applicants would arrive in Israel in the end.

There was an additional problem: Nativ took many months to process the *vizovs*. As the number of applications grew, so did the delay. This was a substantial stumbling block, as Israeli dallying compounded Soviet procrastination. Nativ maintained it lacked the means to process the growing requests for *vizovs*. This explana-tion seemed hardly adequate. The frustration over supplying *vizovs* for emigrants, who ended up going to the US rather than to Israel may have been the root cause of Nativ's heavy-handedness, but I had no means of turning the situation around. Whatever the reason, there was an ever-growing backlog. Requests for *vizovs* in the tens of thousands were coming in from all across the Soviet Union. These applications came in straightforward typed lists or, more usually, in small, handwritten, often illegible notes bearing the names and addresses of families. The pieces of paper would be stuck into our pockets often without our knowing it, to be dis-covered later at the hotel. Alternatively, they would be placed in newspapers or books or passed in a handshake. Any person who had the remotest chance of forwarding the messages to the mission or out of the Soviet Union to Israel, would become a vehicle for the lists. When the all-powerful document from Tel Aviv failed to reach the addressee in the promised two months, it caused growing irritation and bitterness. The request would be repeated and Nativ would be sent additional notes, unnecessarily creating confusion in the data for the *vizov*. Although the inadequacy in the distribution of *vizovs* was a temporary problem, it added a considerable burden to the work of the mission. A great deal of time was spent in correction of these documents, since OVIR would permit no changes in the document supplied from Israel, and insisted that the entire process be repeated.

As we have seen, toward the end of 1987 and in 1988 Soviet Jews were allowed to widen their contacts with Jews outside the country. These were signals directed mainly at the West and did not significantly carry over to the official attitude *vis-à-vis* the Jewish masses. Beset by continued concern over their future, the Jews continued to seek a way out.

A MEETING WITH PAMYAT

In 1989 there were new signs of rising anti-Semitism. It was still not blatant or widespread, but the press was already discussing 'Jewish responsibility' for the murder of the tsar in 1918 as well as for the Bolshevik Revolution and the terror and collectivization that followed it. Other well-known arguments from the anti-Semitic arsenal were also being reactivated. There was an open debate about the theories of the outstanding Soviet mathematician Igor Shafarevich. In a number of articles and essays which attracted attention among the intellectuals of the Russian right, Shafarevich took the position that the West had disparaged Russian culture and history and treated the Russian race as backward and deficient. The Jews, Shafarevich claimed, were prominent Russophobes, and appropriated leading roles in Russian culture because of the Russians' supposed inadequacy. In the years of perestroika, Shafarevich's writings and lectures, on television and radio and before the public, struck a sympathetic chord. The Jews made only a few attempts to counter these pseudo-intellectual outpourings. Although Shafarevich did not become a national leader, his ideas became widely known and gained legitimacy in the eyes of real anti-Semites.

One of the most talked about manifestations of glaring anti-Semitism in recent years was the emergence of the Pamyat (Remembrance) organization. Originally conceived as a group of Russian activists, eager to preserve monuments of the past such as architectural landmarks and art, Pamyat splintered in the early 1980s. A small group took on a chauvinistic tinge, mainly in support of a return to Russian traditions of monarchy and the Russian Orthodox Church. They also adopted an anti-Jewish stance. As the anti-Semitic aspect of Pamyat's activity was the most eye-catching, the group used it to promote its interests and to bolster its political power. The strength and efficacy of anti-Semitic movements in Russia traditionally depended on the support of the government. This had been the case during the days of the tsars. It was also true under Stalin and Brezhnev.

Gorbachev's administration did not part ways with these traditions. The Central Committee had a unit (under the head of the department for propaganda, Andrei Grachev, and his special assistant Vladimir Tumarkin) whose task was to monitor the Jewish problem. I eventually got to meet these people and even socialize with them. The Central Committee was well briefed about Jewish life, about the hopes and the aspirations of the community and the wish to emigrate because of anti-Semitism and the uncertain future. It was widely known that the KGB and the Ministry of the Interior were capable of controlling anti-Semitic movements and of throttling them if necessary. In the same way, they could enhance the importance of anti-Semitism if they thought it necessary for the regime.

Many Jewish leaders in Russia thought the frequent demonstrations by Pamyat and by other groups were an indication that the Central Committee and the KGB were wilfully negligent. The freedom of speech and assembly granted to the anti-Semites was considered to be symptomatic. Many foreign observers, for whom the Jewish question had for years been a barometer for the state of the Soviet Union, were not entirely convinced this assessment was justified. I tended to agree with them. There was a lot of talk in those days about the deterioration of discipline in various state agencies, including the Ministry of the Interior, whose charge it was, at least in theory, to prevent outbreaks of violence. Anti-Semitic activity, organized or not, never developed into violent attacks against Jews, nor to their property. Nevertheless, the developments were not reassuring.

The question of anti-Semitism was constantly in the spotlight of the glasnost era press. In the typically Slavic soul-searching that went on in this context, questions were asked as to what kind of people the Russians were, what communism had done to them, and to their human values, where the Russians were heading as a civilized nation. In autumn 1989, *Literaturnaia gazeta* (fondly referred to as 'Literaturka'), a literary journal with a circulation of six million, ran a series of articles on the Jewish question. Literaturka dealt with controversial themes, providing that they had the seal of approval of the CPSU. One of the questions widely discussed was the role of the Jews in the Revolution and the importance of their contribution to its success. It was claimed the Jews had played a dominant role in the Revolution and in the strengthening of the Bolsheviks. It was repeatedly noted that of the group of seven, which led the country after the death of Lenin, there were four Jews, two Russians and one Georgian. At the conclusion of the open debate, the editors called on their readers to decide for themselves, saying: 'We are incapable of resolving the pros and the cons'.

I thought a good place to inquire into this strange debate would be in the lair of some of the ideological bosses of Literaturka. With an introduction from Mikhail Agursky, a lecturer in Russian history at the Hebrew University of Jerusalem*, I called on Felix Kuznetsov, head of the Institute of World Literature, a well-known writer, publicist and promoter of foreign literature in the Soviet Union. It was after working hours. The institute looked deserted. November frost had already blanketed the street. I made my way into the building and found Kuznetsov's secretary, speaking into the phone. She showed me into Felix's dimly lit study, where he sat behind a large desk. He examined me through his glasses and asked if I wanted tea. He said he had a special brew. I said I was sure I would like it. The tea was brought in two large glasses in silver holders, and Kuznetsov offered me a saucer full of 'Mishkas', little chocolate-covered waffles, available only to the privileged. We delved into a long and frank discussion on anti-Semitism in Russia, going back to the publication of the Protocols of the Elders of Zion by the tsarist secret service, the Okhrana, at the beginning of the century.

As I had suspected, Kuznetsov was poorly informed about the

---

* Agursky and Shafarevich had cooperated with Aleksandr Solzhenitsyn in the publication of *Iz-pod glyb: sbornik statei* (From Under the Rubble) (Paris: YMCA, 1974). They engaged in a public debate at Moscow University in early 1989 on the question of the Jewish role in the Russian Revolution.

Jews, Israel and the reality of anti-Semitism, but I had the feeling he understood the problem. He agreed to write a condemnation against anti-Semitic writings and of anti-Semitism in general in *Literaturnaia gazeta*. The article appeared a few weeks later. It was widely discussed and I thought the impact to have been great.

My hope was that expressions condemning anti-Semitism, whether totally candid or not, might have an influence on a wide circle of people. I appealed to the government to make its position known on this subject. I did this through the office of Gorbachev and the Ministry of Foreign Affairs. The invariable reaction was that the situation did not demand it, and at the same time, that it would not do to condemn one racist attitude and not another, for instance against certain Asiatic ethnic groups. Gorbachev's officials did not want to admit to the existence of anti-Semitism on a wide scale; nor would they do anything to root it out.

I wanted to find out more about Pamyat by going to the source. I encouraged two friends, Dina Yablonskaia and Victor Karetski, the latter a member of the 'Friends of Israel Organization', to confront the heads of Pamyat. An attempt was made to meet with Sichev of the Fatherland Russia breakaway wing, but he refused to 'talk to Zionists'. Dmitri Vasilyev, the head of the main Pamyat group, accepted the challenge.

The meeting was at Vasilyev's headquarters — a large apartment in a run-down section of Moscow. The place was decorated with monarchic memorabilia, pictures of the Russian imperial family and other national heroes of the past. Vasilyev himself, like his assistants, was dressed in a black shirt and riding boots. His chest was decorated with tsarist military medals. My friends were received courteously. Both parties taped the conversation.

Dina started out by saying she was a Pharisee and a Zionist. Vasilyev said he did not mind that and then asked how things were, 'over there'. Dina told him Israelis lived very full lives because they were in their own country, which they loved and defended. At this point Vasilyev asked some young people, including his own son, all wearing black uniforms and boots, to join in, telling them there were persons from Israel with interesting things to say. The conversation lasted three hours.

Vasilyev asked a great many questions about Israel and

expressed his great admiration for the Israel Defence Forces, saying he well understood the need to fight Arab terrorism. Then he said he understood the Israelis well, they had to fight for their country. He added that the Russians had no country, as it had been taken over by International Zionism (as opposed to Zionism in Israel) and the Masons. He insisted that Pamyat had a deep understanding for Theodore Herzl (the founder of modern Zionism) and his ideology, but none for political Zionism, led by Jewish capital.

Vasilyev criticized those who accused him of anti-Semitism. He said he was against the war-cry of the Black Hundreds: 'Beat the Jews, Save Russia!' He added he had forcefully gone on record against anti-Semites and even saved Jews from a possible pogrom in Leningrad. He did not elaborate. Vasilyev had many accounts to settle: with Lenin, Trotsky, Marx, Kerensky, all Jews, as far as he was concerned. The Jews had destroyed Russian culture, in league with international Zionism and Masonry, as part of an anti-Slavonic conspiracy. He argued that Marx was an anti-Semite. Vasilyev was especially ferocious about the 'ritual murder' of the tsar, by a Jewish commissar. Then, for good measure, he added that the Jews had also crucified Christ.

Although Vasilyev has not been able to act on his ravings, he is probably the most quoted among his fellow anti-Semites. There are others, less prominent. One, Yevgeny Evseev, was a member of the Communist Party and vice-chairman of the Russian-Palestinian Union connected with the Soviet Academy of Sciences. This organization goes back at least a century. It was founded as an arm of Russian colonial and religious ambitions in the Middle East, in the waning days of the Ottoman Empire. It controls much church property in the Holy Land. Evseev was a philosopher and worked at the prestigious Institute of Philosophy. His racism led to his expulsion from the Communist Party shortly before his death. He was also highly vocal in his attacks against the Jews and Israel and an energetic organizer of demonstrations with an anti-Israel and anti-Zionist bent. He was killed in February 1990 in a car accident, an event which sparked large demonstrations against Israel, the Jews and the Masons. The government was cautioned against a 'conspiracy to renew diplomatic ties with Israel', but this disturbance soon died down.

There is a passage in Anatoly Cherniaev's memoirs of his years with Gorbachev that throws a great deal of light on the attitude of the Soviet leadership toward anti-Semitism. Gorbachev once talked with his assistant about revelations regarding Lenin's Jewish and other non-Russian antecedents ('Lenin is only one-quarter Russian'), which appeared in Alexander Solzhenitsyn's *Lenin in Zurich*. Gorbachev told Cherniaev that as soon as he heard this talk, he demanded 'all the facts' and then hid them away in the 'farthest safe'. 'These things', he said, 'could affect people terribly... It was revolting, foul... but there was nothing to be done.' Cherniaev claims it was then he understood Gorbachev's lenience toward the earthy and anti-Semitic group of writers which included Belov, Rasputin, Alexeev, Proskurin and even Bondarev. They felt for the Russian peasant, were horrified by the ravages the Russian people had gone through. It was these feelings that had brought about their search for the 'Jewish roots' of collectivization, civil war, mass terror, and of the entire October Revolution, which demeaned everything Russian in Russia and destroyed it as such.* Gorbachev continued to play up to this rightist Russian trend, hoping they would prop him up where others were deserting him, knowing full well that flirtations with this movement tended to be interpreted as indulgence toward the anti-Semites. There was no clear-cut indication of displeasure or disapprobation of the anti-Semites, which goes a long way to explain the relative freedom they enjoyed. I tried to meet with some of these writers, unsuccessfully, for they always had excuses. Rasputin lives in Irkutsk, Siberia. When I once visited the city, I phoned him, but he said he was indisposed.

Between 1988 and 1992 there were numerous outbreaks of anti-Semitic and anti-Israel sloganeering and demonstrations. In reality, few had much direct contact with either the Jews or Israel. Violent outbreaks of this social ailment are symptomatic of a general disease of the body politic of the country. But so long as the regime in power does not deem it necessary to use anti-Semitism to save itself, pogroms seem unlikely to occur.

* Anatoly Cherniaev, *Shest' let s Gorbachevym* (Six Years with Gorbachev) (Moscow: Kultura, 1993) p. 279.

The undeniable fact is that anti-Semitism is embedded deep inside the Russian psyche. One day when a group of colleagues and I went for a tour of the cities in the so-called Golden Ring surrounding Moscow, we stopped at Zagorsk, the seat of the Russian Orthodox Church. We were about to get into our Volvo, with its Dutch Embassy plates, when a Russian peasant woman approached and asked us to whom the car belonged. We said it belonged to the Israeli Mission. She asked 'who' Israel was and we said it was the Jewish state. She looked puzzled. 'You are Jews?' We said we were, but she said we could not have been Jews, as we looked like foreigners. When we insisted, she would not believe us. It was a Thursday, she added, and Jews send out destructive rays on Thursdays. She was told always to leave her house on this day. The rays can penetrate anything — doors, walls. She had been attacked only the week before and her whole body still ached. We all laughed. Of course we were not Jews, she concluded, we were Polish or something. And she was off. The poor woman did not look demented or retarded and, except for her abysmal primitiveness, did not behave in a strange manner.

It is not always the Jews who experience Russian prejudice. One evening my driver, Viktor, asked to be excused early. When I asked the reason, he said he had to go and help his neighbours. His wife had asked him to hurry home. A girl kidnapped the day before had been found and was to be taken urgently to the hospital. Viktor went on to explain that a few days back, in preparation for their yearly rites of child-sacrifice, the Baptists who lived in his apartment house had kidnapped a neighbour's eight-year-old daughter. Luckily for the girl, a psychic had divined her whereabouts. She was saved before they could cut off her head. When I asked what the neighbours intended to do, Viktor said they could not do anything as the Baptists were too well protected.

These two examples are not as far-fetched or atypical as they might seem. The Revolution did bring literacy to Russia, but it did not eradicate the biases that always existed against non-Russians. The years of institutional prejudice, from Stalin to Brezhnev, deepened the predisposition against the Jews. Thus, in the firm belief that nothing better could be expected from the Soviet Union in future, many Jews voted against perestroika with their feet.

13 · Emigration to Immigration

THE US CHANGES ITS POLICY

In autumn 1989 the United States changed its regulations: refugee status would not be automatically granted to Jews any longer. Requests for such status would be examined more stringently. Refugees were entitled to US government help and much more rapid processing of applications for citizenship. Not so regular immigrants, who had to make their own arrangements and go through the bureaucratic mill. From the date fixed at the end of October 1989, this process would be carried out by the US Consulate in Moscow, not in Italy or Austria, where previously applicants arriving on Israeli visas had near-certain assurance of being allowed into the US. With the closing down of the operation in Rome and Vienna, Jewish candidates for a US immigrant visa would have to wait for the papers in Moscow and it would now take nearly two years. This development rendered the new situation precarious in the eyes of the Jewish population interested in leaving the Soviet Union. The protracted waiting period could bring on anticipated pogroms or other unforeseeable crises. Information on the US decision had seeped through to the Jewish public in Russia in the summer months.

The US government considered that in view of the liberalization of exit regulations in the USSR and the overall improvement in human rights, a mandatory entitlement to refugee status was no longer justified. Furthermore, the Jewish community in the United States was not prepared to reimburse its government for the heavy outlays incurred during the processing, transportation and arrival of the refugees in the US. There were, perhaps, additional underlying reasons. The practical aspect was that although refugee status was to be accorded on a much narrower basis, it would not necessarily be refused. But the procedure would take a long time and a positive reply was not assured. It was clear that Israel would become the preferred destination for emigration out of the Soviet Union. The Israeli process took only a few months and there were the many privileges from which an immigrant in Israel could benefit.

The American Embassy in Moscow began beefing up its consular department in the summer months. The custom of accepting an Israeli visa issued by the Dutch Embassy in Moscow as the basis for an application for refugee status, when the person in question reached Italy or Austria, was to be discontinued. A circular issued by the American Embassy in Moscow on 1 November 1989 announced that henceforth any Soviet citizen seeking to emigrate to the US must apply to the American Embassy in Moscow and that applications for an American immigration visa would not be accepted anywhere else. The only exception to this requirement, according to the announcement, would be the bearer of a Soviet exit visa issued before 1 October 1989, and an Israeli visa issued before 6 November 1989. Such a person could proceed to Rome or Vienna as before.

As rumours about the new arrangements began filtering out already in October, all those who were eager to get to the US through the transit areas in Rome or Vienna with an Israeli visa issued in Moscow, rushed to get their visas at the Netherlands Consulate before 6 November. Following that date, the Israeli visa was no longer valid insofar as the US authorities were concerned. From then on, an Israeli visa would take the recipient 'only' to Israel. Forward intelligence of these developments brought an avalanche of people who wanted their papers stamped before the fatidic date of 6 November. We had been forewarned but did not foresee the extent of the onslaught. There were literally thousands of people a day, and they all had to be attended to.

As the tension mounted and developed into virtual hysteria over getting to the Dutch Consulate on time, a whole new bribery network was organized by the emigrants to get the Soviet officials to release the OVIR exit documents, for stamping with the desired Israeli visa. The payment for an antedated document got as high as the price of a Soviet-made Zhiguli car, or the car itself. As soon as the OVIR document was obtained, there would be a mad rush to the Dutch Consulate to get an Israeli visa. As only the Dutch consuls and members of Nativ dealt with Israeli visas, there was no fear of bribes being taken there, though there were plenty of offers. The months until the end of October were a real circus. I still cannot understand how we survived that assault. The week after 6 November, there was an unaccustomed hush over the grounds. Then, the number of Israeli visas handed out to prospective *olim* began rising with unequalled speed.

Another tidal wave began building up, this time for emigration to Israel. The numbers started climbing steadily into December. Toward the end of 1989 and into 1990, they finally reached the vicinity of 30,000 recipients a month. This statistic, its highs and lows varying but little, held well into 1991, bringing a total of over 400,000 *olim* to Israel by the end of 1992.

This was the great turning point of *aliyah* to Israel. We were witnessing a historic migration of peoples, a veritable evacuation. Not one of us had the time to reflect on the significance of the times we were living through. Nativ officials worked around the clock. The number of young Jewish volunteers helping Nativ grew proportionately. They stood at the gates, trying to contain the pressure, to prevent people climbing in over the walls, to settle the quarrels between the impatient and irritated callers standing in line in the snow, or in the heat of summer, to help the old and the very young and to keep an eye on the traffic in the street. The Soviet policemen at the gate shared the load with all the rest. They too struggled to keep order and let people in according to our instructions.

By the end of 1989 emigration had reached massive proportions. But there were still special cases of administrative problems resulting from lack of relevant political decisions. One such aberration was the power given to a spouse or a parent to veto a relative's emigration: the 'poor relatives' restriction, one of the most painful companions of the emigration process. This limitation caused great suffering and tragedy, broke up families, but seemed to make little impact on the Soviet administrators. Soviet Jews, by themselves and with the assistance of Jewish organizations abroad, fought this regulation for many years. There were numerous instances where we sought the intervention of international figures, including US presidents.

A case in point can illustrate the difficulty: Rimma Mushinsky, the wife of my local personal assistant, was prevented from leaving because her father was a military expert and was not allowed to give his consent to his daughter's departure. Rimma's mother had been divorced from her father for more than 20 years and lived with her daughter in Moscow. The father lived in Tashkent, 2,000 kilometres away. In 1991, with the new emigration law that was finally adopted by the Soviet Parliament, it was decided that 'poor relatives' could ask for court injunctions. Thus, the ignoble 'poor relatives' regulation was, to all intents and purposes, laid to rest. The refuseniks' quandary too was all but over, except for some very hard core cases involving security-related subjects, real or manufactured.

One of the constant problems we faced was in the human dimension of our work. Most people calling on us came from very far away. From Vilna to Vladivostok, there were no other consulates to process emigration papers. We were the only one among the foreign consulates in Moscow not retaining its callers for over a day. The others had them return repeatedly for completion of the paperwork.

Usually, the prospective emigrants would camp with their relatives, close or distant, in Moscow. Visa seekers who were not Moscow residents sometimes came straight from the railroad stations, to wait in front of the embassy. Many were accompanied by additional family members. Some had nowhere to go. They sat out the required hours in front of the gates, received their documents and then journeyed home. We were neither equipped, nor able to help them in any way, save by hastening the bureaucratic process. Only later, some accommodation began to be provided. A typical problem we ran into with the UPDK, officially the owners of our embassy building, was their reluctance to have us construct restrooms for the thousands of people who visited the compound. The neighbours constantly complained of the invasion of their front yards and stairwells. In desperation, I ordered the go-ahead without UPDK's sanction.

The crowds inside the compound were large. They lingered on, comparing notes with fellow emigrants. On one occasion, when I asked a woman to please leave so we could take care of others, she turned to me and complained bitterly: 'Jews were chased away from everywhere all their lives, from the universities, from jobs, from city to city and now, here on Israeli soil, they are being chased away again.' She appeared genuinely offended, and I suddenly felt a pang of remorse as well as shame, at my attempts to shoo her away.

The corridors and offices on the first floor of our building were constantly occupied by people going through various stages of the bureaucratic process. There was great difficulty apportioning the available space, as the number of rooms was totally inadequate. The Dutch Consulate, busy with the visa-stamping detail, had also to take care of its own non-Jewish clientele. We thus had lines of Africans and Asians, mingling with the Soviet Jews from Russia, the Ukraine and Central Asia. Surprisingly, for such large crowds, there was very little friction. The Dutch consular officials, who were busy with a work load far beyond what they had probably contracted for, applied themselves with the greatest devotion and perseverance. We worked together with them in perfect harmony. The Soviet women helping the Dutch officials were also overworked, but we all got along extremely well.

THE VIEW FROM MY WINDOW

When, by the end of April 1990, I had settled into the refurbished apartment on the top floors of the embassy building, my wife Aliza, on her many trips to Moscow, also became exposed to the throbbing life-cycle of the 18-hour work days. There was no separation on the open wooden staircase that led to our apartments from the ground floor. People would often wander into our private rooms looking for the Consul and begging to have their papers stamped: 'Please put a stamp here, little sister!' the Caucasian Jews often implored. Aliza would have to turn them away, not without regret at being unable to help them out.

Hours before dawn, Jews from all over the Soviet Union would begin congregating around the outside perimeter of the embassy compound: men, women and children, some of the older folk moving about with great difficulty, all patiently awaiting the opening of the gates. The crowd was never noisy. There was just a murmur, like wind passing through the leaves of a tree. Often, Aliza was unable to sleep. She would wake me to come to the window overlooking the gate and watch the silent, patient crowds, relentlessly swelling into a massive multitude, blocking the entrance and the street beyond. The people at the gate bunched together at the entrance, in order to be able to see the building and the people inside. The pressure at the gate slackened in the late evening hours. A lull would then intercede, before the next working day.

It was difficult not to visualize the hardships these people would endure, leaving behind their birthplaces, their friends and relatives and the culture in which they grew up, going to a country almost totally unknown to them. There were few Zionists among them. They were seeking a better life for themselves, some as Jews, most as human beings. Their main motivation was to get away from the drudgery and inequality of the Soviet state, the hopelessness and despondency that had characterized many of their lives. They had little idea of what lay ahead. Their convergence at the gates of the embassy, for what they hoped would be a better life, was a moving sight. We and the many guests who came to visit us at our apartment overlooking the Bolshaia Ordynka, could not tear ourselves away from that view, pondering the magnitude of the process and the lessons it taught us in human terms.

In the embassy compound, there were Jews from all the republics of the Soviet Union, people speaking many tongues, though all knew Russian. Understandably, all they wanted to talk about were the conditions of their future life in Israel. They wanted guidance and they needed help. They knew Israel was not one of the Soviet republics and that they would be going to a Jewish country, which was capitalist. Their image of Israel tended to be distorted. Having rarely been beyond the borders of Eastern Europe, Soviet Jews expected to find the same type of socialist state they were leaving, perhaps with the difference that a Jewish state would be more mindful of their needs. Although the bare facts about the immigrants' 'absorption' process in Israel were known, inwardly most emigrants were still convinced they would be welcomed by a state providing free education, housing, guaranteed employment and a fixed pension for veterans of the Second World War. Even if many suspected life would not be terribly easy in the new country, whose language they did not speak, they hoped life would eventually turn out better than in the homeland they were leaving behind.

We all constantly endeavoured to define the differences between the Soviet Union and Israel, but it was hard to predict the conditions that would prevail on the immigrants' arrival. Nativ officials, whose duties brought them face to face with the *olim* on a daily basis, never lied about the prospects. But they were not instructed to underline the difficulties ahead, either. They did their best to supply as much information as possible, even though there were constant complaints about the paucity of comprehensive information on Israel and its living conditions. There was a growing amount of written material distributed among the future *olim* before they reached the mission compound, in order to reduce the time spent on the premises. All to no avail. The whole gamut of questions would begin anew every time there was contact between an immigrant and a mission official. Very often people would seek a second opinion on the information they had already received, if it seemed unsatisfactory. All of which showed the degree of anxiety about the transfer to a new and unknown country, where the social and economic life was incomprehensible to a person brought up on the Soviet socialist diet.

There were many non-Jews as well, among the great mêlée in the embassy grounds. Members of families with Jewish husbands or wives, or parents and grandparents, were also allowed into Israel, under the umbrella of the Law of Return. There were non-Jews who had no eligibility under the law. Such people had forged documents, such as birth or marriage certificates. Most of these false documents were recognized as such and their owners sent away. Yet there was something extraordinary in these attempts of non-Jews to feign Jewish identities. In all the 3,000 years of Jewish history, there were probably few examples of a similar phenomenon.

NATIV: ZEAL AND INDEPENDENCE

Nativ was running a very large-scale and complex operation. Its officers in Moscow were a part of the mission, but acted independently and were answerable to their Tel Aviv headquarters. When it became clear in the early 1950s that the Soviet Union and Eastern Europe were countries with heavy anti-Jewish discrimination, Israel's government set up the Lishka/Nativ to maintain links with the Jewish population there, to support and encourage them insofar as possible, and arrange for their immigration. This was a very responsible task. It involved a great deal of undercover activity, though none of it spread beyond the assigned area of Jewish affairs. During the years preceding the Second World War there was no Jewish state and there was no Nativ, whose efforts might have made the difference to many in Nazi-occupied Europe. The work of Nativ was outstanding and the great amount of coverage this once secret organization has recently had in the Israeli media hardly does justice to its many achievements.

For many years, Nativ maintained representatives at diplomatic missions in various capital cities of the world. These officials never proclaimed their identity but were usually well-known to the local authorities. Their role was to step in and help the Jews out of communist countries or to line up diplomatic and public appeal for Jewish emigration from Eastern Europe. A special division bore responsibility for increasing Jewish and non-Jewish awareness of the Soviet stranglehold on the Jews. In the great 'Let My People Go' campaign that followed in the 1970s and 1980s, Nativ played an important, though not an exclusive, role.

Nativ's presence in the East European diplomatic missions before the break in relations in 1967, helped a great deal in observing and analysing the problems of Jews living there. Their services were invaluable. This was also the case during the harsh period of our relations with the Soviet Union. With the tragic memories of the Holocaust still fresh in everyone's mind, the destiny of Jews in these countries was deemed to be in the balance. Israel's government was determined not to lose any opportunity of extending aid and proclaiming its readiness to support fellow-Jews, even if the task was sometimes extremely complicated.

The director of Nativ, hierarchically responsible only to the prime minister, was almost entirely on his own. His people, spread over many countries, reported only to their chief, although they were expected to keep the head of the diplomatic mission fully briefed. In practice, this always depended on the relations between the ambassador and the Nativ representative. Very often there was friction, as the independence Nativ enjoyed was not always easy to handle, for either party.

Prior to my own departure for Moscow, fully aware of the potential for conflict, I decided to set the ground rules with the then director, David Bartov. I asked to be kept abreast of all their activities. My mission to the Soviet Union was extremely delicate and the actions of Nativ, if not kept within certain limits, might cause damage. The director said that of course, my conditions would be met.

Generally speaking, these rules were observed for as long as we were a mission working under the Dutch umbrella and our political status in Moscow was unclear. Relations between myself and the constantly changing personnel of Nativ were excellent. Paradoxically, difficulties began cropping up when our general situation improved. There was a great deal of excess zeal, and an exaggerated sense of self-importance on the part of the Nativ personnel which I found objectionable.

The greatest area of disagreement was Nativ's insubordination and its disregard for the diplomatic requirements of our relationship with the Russians and with our Dutch hosts. They also failed to acknowledge that there was a connection between the future of Soviet Jewry and the higher policy of emigration to Israel. Nativ refused to relate seriously to the fate of the Soviet Jewish community after the great wave of *aliyah* subsided. The present Nativ director has publicly asserted that there will not be a Russian Jewish community beyond the year 2000. In 1995, with the information that is at hand, such a public prediction is odd, self-serving and certainly uncalled for.

The number of Jews in Soviet Russia was officially declared to be just over 1,200,000 by the 1989 Soviet census, but it was known to be at least twice, if not three times, greater. Nativ had been saying in 1987 that Jewish *aliyah* would come to a halt in three to five years because of legal limitations and a massive drain to the US. In 1989 and 1990 Nativ had to cope with an unprecedented tide of immigration. They were certain most Jews would emigrate to Israel within two to five years. They were not far off the mark, except that immigration has subsided and there are one to two million Jews still living in the heartland of Russia and Ukraine.

The successful integration of hundreds of thousands of immigrants into a country the size of Israel is a task rarely accomplished in the history of immigration. All things considered, the Israeli government and society have performed an extra-ordinary feat absorbing this massive immigration, and in record time. Nevertheless, very great problems still remain to be solved. The arrival of a large number of highly professional and educated people of every description could have produced a greater economic boom had Israel possessed the scientific, technological and human infrastructure, and planned ahead. More could have been done if the national implications of this immigration were taken at their face value. If the political leadership of the country had really desired it and saw in it a historical mission, as it claimed, a bi-partisan and multi-party approach could have brought about a much wider recruitment of practical measures and of goodwill at the national level. More could be done to give these immigrants, for whom we waited so expectantly, a better welcome and greater means for integration into our lives. It gives many of us great pain to know that the word *nikayon* (house cleaning) has become an accepted term in Russian to describe the job most available to immigrants, not only immediately after their arrival but also two or four years hence. The sight of thousands of well-educated and talented professional people doing menial jobs, or going hungry, or homeless, should not sit well with a country's collective conscience. The official statistics say over 80 per cent of all immigrants have found employment, a remarkable fact in itself.

However, this figure does not indicate the field of employment. In fact, a much lower percentage have found jobs in their profession, which is understandably a source of great frustration for the new immigrants.

Nativ opposed the formation of centres of Jewish life in the USSR, claiming it would be an aberration and a waste of time and resources, a stumbling block for *aliyah*. The Jews had to be mobilized for transfer to Israel. When asked how they would live once they arrived, Nativ's director and his closest deputies, themselves Soviet immigrants, would shrug their shoulders and proclaim their responsibility lay only in organizing the move. For this reason, officials of Nativ denigrated the formation of the Jewish Vaad and the All-Soviet Jewish Congress at the end of 1989, and viewed its leaders and activities with disdain. It was true that the new organization had no experience and was blinded somewhat by the international spotlight. I thought Nativ's attitude was shortsighted and represented narrow sectarian interests, when great cause was at stake. Our mission did not consist only of getting as many Jews out of the Soviet Union as possible. It was also to help organize the lives of those who would perforce stay behind, and to render them able, and, we hoped, spiritually and ideologically determined to join us in a few years' time. Otherwise, we stood to lose future immigrants to the US, South Africa, Argentina, Australia, and even Austria and Germany, if Jews were allowed entry.

Unhappily, these things have come to pass. The 1989–91 *aliyah* will stand out as a great achievement. It was a feat, both for the people who braved the uncertainties and the great personal difficulties involved, and for Israel, which remained true to its national ideals. But the wave could not but subside. The bulk of the Jewish population inclined to exit the USSR departed over the years 1989–92. In addition, Jews in Russia have grown wise to the realities of Israel as far as immigrant welfare is concerned. If the State of Israel is not mindful of the situation toward the end of the century and does not set out a more rational policy of immigration and absorption, it might see the stream of immigration into Israel reduced further. Insofar as the goal of traditional Zionism is concerned, *aliyah* cannot be built on Ethiopian Jews alone. Jews from western lands have not made a great showing of their willingness to settle in Israel and there are simply no other Jewish populations left to count on.

As I never hid my opinions from anyone and felt a moral responsibility as head of the mission to the Soviet Union to make my position known, there was disagreement between myself and the heads of Nativ. The Ministry of Foreign Affairs, though fully cognizant of the merits of the case, shied away from taking a position. The Nativ tactic was to soothe ruffled feathers and to carry on as before. In late 1989 and 1990 these discordant views began interfering in our work in the form of sudden and unnecessary flare-ups in tempers. Nativ had but one goal in mind: 'Get the Jews out, that is the only thing that counts. Everything else is just a waste of time.' This totally single-minded approach, even if understandable in itself where Nativ was concerned, meant endless quarrels over turf, space, communications and coordination. This would not have been critical in itself, but Nativ was increasingly adopting an independent attitude, trying to stake out its territory in the soon-to-be embassy.

There was another topic that became highly controversial in my view. At a certain point, as exit permits from the Soviet Union were becoming less of a problem to obtain, the number of departures was being reduced by the limited number of flights. In their eagerness, people began leaving by any means available to them, buses and trains, private cars and even small yachts. Nativ was very much against these 'freelancers' and afraid of the possible leakages to other countries on the way to Israel. They wanted total control over every person who was getting a visa. They forbade railroad, bus and other means of transportation, allowing only airplane travel from Moscow to Israeli transit camps, first in Budapest, then in Bucharest and Warsaw.

On one occasion, I was present at a personal briefing given by the director of Nativ to Prime Minister Shamir. When Shamir heard how difficult it was to get the Jews out of the Soviet Union, there being no direct flights, he asked why trains were not being used. The director said there was not enough room on the very few trains. In fact, there were several trains going to the European border every day from Moscow with enough space to transport hundreds. Many Jews wanted to use the trains, but Nativ was demanding to see their air tickets, issued by the organization, before allowing Israeli visas to be stamped in passports. Bus transportation was also frowned upon, for the same reasons. The fear of losing immigrants was misplaced. No country on the way to Israel was willing to allow Jews in. Few immigrants wanted or could abscond. The overwhelming majority of the *olim* travelled with no protection, with hardly any funds and were eager to accomplish their journey as soon as possible. The restraints engineered by Nativ were not easy on the immigrants during the months preceding the normalization of travel to Israel.

The ticketing agreements with air companies, transportation of the immigrants' luggage and personal belongings and other ancillary activities finally became bones of contention between Nativ and the Jewish Agency. Nativ, for reasons of institutional prestige and for the sake of proving their indispensability, wanted to control these procedures, but had no budgetary funds to cover the costs. The expenses were to be covered by the Jewish Agency, which balked at Nativ's presumptuousness but did not have the sufficient presence in Moscow to carry out the actual tasks. One of the reasons for this shortcoming was the lack of Soviet registration for the agency, which made it unable to operate and have the necessary staff, whereas Nativ, under the umbrella of the Israeli Foreign Ministry and its Moscow mission, was free to do as it pleased. Later, the agency forced Nativ to limit its activities to the issuing of visas. The Nativ-Jewish Agency struggle expanded into other areas, such as the information centres, set up by both contending parties in some 12 cities in the Soviet Union. This struggle over prestige and positions between two Israeli institutions was not only shameful, but also a terrible waste of money and energy. It also pointed to structural weaknesses in the organization of immigration as practised by the government of Israel, a lacuna that could have been exploited by the Soviets at will.

This constant tug-of-war between the agency and Nativ, and the overzealousness of the Nativ directorate, totally transmuted Nativ's former status as a special clandestine agency. The brazen behaviour of Nativ representatives, their open and continuing telephone consultations between Moscow and Tel Aviv revealing details of personnel, methods, financing and other operational questions, left not even a fig leaf over Nativ's unmentionables, its secret techniques and practice.

In recent years, Nativ has become an open, well-known and much trumpeted institution, carrying on its business like any other organization. In case of a severe political deterioration in the Soviet Union and a renewed need for clandestine activity, there will be no secret service to operate the underground pathways. Nativ has completely blown its cover and lost any justification for the mandate handed to it in a different period. Times have changed but the logic of the Israeli government has not evolved accordingly. The reason is simple. Nativ is under the aegis of the prime minister and not really answerable to anyone else. There is almost no public access and therefore no critical assessment of its activity or inflated budget. No Israeli prime minister wanted to lose such an important agency, one that carried with it considerable prestige and authority. Today, however, the activities of Nativ do not differ from the duties of any consular service in handing out visas to the eligible. The logistics can and should be handled by the Jewish Agency, for which it was constituted. Recent structural and personnel difficulties of the agency have perhaps weakened its *raison d'être* and obscured the merits of its case. But if the State of Israel feels it cannot rely on the Jewish Agency in carrying out the immigration of Jews from the areas of the former Soviet Union and other countries, it should face the facts and take the Israeli public into its confidence. The influx of hundreds of thousands of new immigrants into a country the size of Israel is a matter far too important to leave even partially in the hands of a secret service which has become anachronistic with the passage of time. In 1994 and 1995 the competition between Nativ and the Jewish Agency has even broadened. Paradoxically, under Peres's foreign affairs administration Nativ gained greater weight, apparently because Peres preferred to 'join' Nativ rather than trying to 'beat' it. It is unclear whether now, at the end of 1995, the situation might change under Peres' premiership.

As in everything else connected with government, there is an additional, political leitmotif which issues from Nativ's longevity. Nativ remains one of the principal analysts of the political situation in the former Soviet regions. This tends to weight Israel's strategic assessment of the former Soviet countries, primarily Russia, with considerations of immigration. As a matter of general policy, this approach must be avoided. An analysis of the situation in Russia, Ukraine and other countries cannot be made predominantly from the perspective of the immigration factor, nor by officials who might confuse their own interests with the subject they are required to examine. Russia will probably return to its former status of superpower in a decade and will, as before, influence the future of the Middle East. Israel is duty-bound to develop the tools and methods which will enable it to ponder this question objectively.

Attempts have been made to discuss the future of Nativ both in the Israeli press and in government. Two high-level inquiries were instituted, in 1991 and in 1992, the latter by a former head of the Mossad, Yitzhak Chofi. Contrary to good sense and sound administration, but evidently in keeping with the desire of the Prime Minister's Office, the inquiries concluded that virtually nothing should be changed. There seems to be no hope that the necessary far-reaching reform will be undertaken soon.

When all is said and done, the year 1989 stands out as a compelling and promising point of departure. This was a different Soviet Union, the scenery had changed beyond recognition and for the better, insofar as we were concerned. The way to Israel was now completely open for Jews desiring to immigrate and many tens of thousands were taking that path. Despite the many frustrations and problems that still had to be solved, it had become clear that there was no going back. In a conversation with Prime Minister Shamir I was asked what the future of immigration would be. I answered unhesitatingly that there was not a shadow of doubt that immigration would continue and expand, and the decisions governing it would not be altered. 'Not a shadow of a doubt?' the prime minister asked. I repeated my assertion, for I was absolutely certain of its veracity.

II

From Consulate to Embassy

14 · High Stakes: Jewish Magnates and Middle East Peace

The year 1989 was truly epoch-making, but it left the Soviet system confused and breathless. In autumn 1989 the regimes of Poland, Hungary, Germany, Bulgaria and Czechoslovakia, all lost their moorings in the socialist port and started sailing away under their own steam. The Soviet Union could muster neither the will nor the motivation to do anything but watch. The Soviet system was collapsing.

The political, economic and constitutional cross-currents in the vast country were growing stronger by the day. There was increasing nostalgia for discipline and sound administration, in spite of their faulty performance in the past and an impending fear of famine prevailed. Yet, at times, trains of rotting food stood at railroad stations, their unloading sabotaged by anti-government politicians. At one of its sessions the Politburo debated the shortage of soap powder. It was helpless in greater crises as well: the Caucasus was in flames, Central Asian irredentism was growing and the Baltic republics were beginning to break away.

Gorbachev was an unbelievably captivating, charming and courageous leader in the eyes of the West. A January 1990 issue of *Time Magazine* declared him the Man of the Decade — *the* figure who had transformed the world. This was true enough and would turn out to be more prophetic yet. His success with the media was all that a western politician could hope for. He very soon became a television personality. Perfectly aware of his popularity with the media, he made use of it to his personal advantage in projecting the image of a new type of Soviet leader — open, charismatic and inspiring trust in his determination to reform his country. Gorbachev completely broke with the tradition of inaccessibility of his predecessors in favour of open and warm contacts with western leaders. Some General Secretaries, such as Brezhnev, did establish personal contact with their western colleagues, and even enjoyed their friendship, but Gorbachev's ties were on an entirely different plane. His growing interest in foreign affairs brought him important dividends in the form of foreign support. His relations with Reagan, Kohl, Mitterand and other Europeans brought him a level of international prestige unprecedented in Soviet history.

What is perhaps less widely known in the West is the impact his friendship with Margaret Thatcher had on the Russians. The British prime minister enjoyed extraordinary popularity in the USSR. I remember few discussions on international themes when she was not mentioned as a leader whom the Russians would have readily accepted as their own. This was no small compliment in Russia's strongly chauvinistic society, although Catherine the Great was also greatly admired. Yet it was not so much Thatcher's politics as her strength of character and bearing that people liked. To the Russians she was the consummate prime minister. Stalin and many of his countrymen believed in the mythical powers of British Intelligence. In the eyes of Kazakhs and Uzbeks, Estonians and Latvians and certainly many Russians, Great Britain is still the master of international conspiracies and plots. America is strong and the undisputed world power, but England, ah, England... And Margaret Thatcher was the British prime-minister-matriarch — the embodiment of all these qualities. I often heard friends express admiration for Mrs Thatcher's grace and good looks, her taste in clothing, and even her sex appeal. Margaret, or Margo, as she was affectionately called, stood in a class of her own. Surprisingly, this admiration was shared by many Russian women, who never had a kind word to say about Raisa Gorbachev — a woman they loved to hate and whom they criticized for damaging her husband's prestige. Jealousy of Raisa's clothes and elegance, and of her many trips abroad with her husband, go a long way towards explaining the popular grudge.

In his book *Six Years with Gorbachev*, Anatoly Cherniaev, Gorbachev's political consultant and companion, describes how he sat opposite Margaret Thatcher in one of the early meetings at 10 Downing Street, and how 'magnificent' she looked. Cherniaev claims she tried to 'bewitch' Gorbachev and although the Soviet leader played along, he was distant. On the plane back to Moscow, Gorbachev's advisers roundly criticized him for not having been sufficiently open with Thatcher, even if only as a measure of appreciation for the prime minister's extraordinary support, which increased Gorbachev's credibility in the West. 'Besides', Cherniaev added, in a typically Russian expression of unwitting chauvinism:

She is a woman. Not merely a guy in a skirt. Her whole character and political behaviour are feminine. It was remarkable for an Englishwoman to be so candid and if Gorbachev would not answer in kind, her pride might come into play and we could lose a great deal.

To his countrymen, Gorbachev was a loquacious, shrewd and artful politician. He possessed great dexterity in navigating through the reefs of opposition; his folly was his inability to ever cast anchor. He was a leader who lacked the presence of mind, or the will, to end a crisis or stabilize a situation. Gorbachev and his close associates were being accused of selling out to the Germans and the Americans. The Russians were losing patience with him. The non-Russian subjects of the empire were encouraged by this lack of resolve to seek independence from the colonial regime that had been oppressing them since the days of the tsars.

In this general chaos, with so many fires to extinguish and such demands being made on the Soviet establishment, it was not surprising that the question of the Middle East, and especially that of renewed diplomatic relations with Israel, was not on the list of immediate priorities. Nevertheless, as a quiet cure for the moroseness and despondency that occupied the public mind, the regime sought a way out of its predicament, or at least a momentary reprieve. Thus, in a typical delusion induced by Soviet myths, two courses of action were pursued regarding the Jews and the Middle East: to attract Jewish capital and seek a breakthrough in the peace process.

Soviet leaders had always been attracted by wealthy capitalists. Relations with people such as Armand Hammer had proved fruitful after the revolution, when Hammer helped supply food and built factories. Big industrialists who helped the Soviet government were always popular. In the perestroika years, there were a number of such magnates who sought to increase their fortunes in Russia. They were assiduously cultivated. Prominent among them was a group of Jewish financiers. Hammer, a man nearing his nineties when perestroika began, was still very much on the Moscow scene; Albert Reichman and Edgar Bronfman of Canada, Robert Maxwell of Britain, Marc Rich, Nessim Gaon, both of Switzerland, and later Shaul Eisenberg of Israel, all were busy with concrete projects and plans and were heeded attentively. They had entrées at the highest level of government and hobnobbed with men from the Politburo and the Central Committee. Their money and their international financial authority simply fascinated the Soviets, although there were few people in the Soviet administration who really knew how to exploit the connection. Poor business legislation in the Soviet Union did not make matters easy on investors. Private deals and special arrangements always had to be worked out with each one, individually.

Out of loyalty to Israel and in order to make a statement about their support for my position in the Soviet Union as the representative of Israel, I was sought out by some, though not all, of these Jewish financiers. Albert Reichman, who always made a point of meeting with me and inquiring about our activities, once invited me to a discussion about Israeli fruit and vegetable supplies to the USSR. The meeting took place at the Kremlin with Lev Voronin, first deputy prime minister in charge of the economy under Nikolai Ryzhkov. After a long conversation about ways and means of financing business deals, Voronin saw he was not getting anywhere. He had difficulty explaining how he would go about providing payment in foreign exchange for the goods he wanted to purchase. Then, he suddenly turned to Reichman and asked why western businessmen would not set up a fund of a few billion dollars to purchase food. Voronin said the government would pay it all back in time, in money or in goods. As he saw his visitors were staring at him incredulously, he repeated the question, emphasizing, 'You businessmen should set up a fund.' Reichman, a mild-mannered and thoughtful person, turned to me and said, in a rather loud voice, 'This man is crazy.' He added that Voronin had not the slightest notion of what he was saying. Reichman did not even bother to reply and Voronin's question hung in the air for a few additional minutes, before being superseded by another non-starter.

Toward the end of 1989, Al Schwimmer, an Israeli aviation specialist and one of the main founders of the Israel Aircraft Industries, conceptualized an imaginative and attractive project, to which I have already alluded, in connection with preparations for the Peres visit. The plan was to combine three air industries, Soviet (fuselage), American (engines) and Israeli (avionics), in order to build a new airliner to be sold in the West as well as in the East. The plane was first to be purchased by the aging Soviet Aeroflot airline, which needed new and modern airplanes but had no foreign exchange. This would establish a market. The idea went over very well and Gorbachev, in one of his public appearances in the Soviet Union, mentioned this project as an example of what positive and fruitful cooperation with the West could do to generate the large profits which the country needed to replenish its coffers. The potential financiers of this great and promising initiative were to be Hammer, Maxwell and Reichman. They agreed to cooperate on this grandiose programme to help out the USSR and Israel as well. With the death of Armand Hammer the partnership fell apart. Maxwell and Reichman left the group and Al Schwimmer, the moving spirit behind it, resigned. The main supporter of the deal was now Shaul Eisenberg, who demanded that Aeroflot agree beforehand to purchase a certain number of airplanes. Such a sale would assure eventual buyers. But the Russians refused. Because of this and other complications, the airliner project was abandoned, although it had engendered many hopes and expectations. This project is now being carried out on a reduced scale, without Israel's participation, although Israeli industries are involved in limited cooperation with Russian counterparts in producing small commercial and passenger airplanes.

What united these men, so outstanding yet so different one from the other, was their Jewish blood, a fact that did not go unnoticed by Soviet officials. Reichman and Bronfman were also extremely involved in attempts to promote Jewish life and culture in the USSR. Both are well-known philanthropists, the former contributing great efforts and funds to the establishment of Jewish theological seminaries (*yeshivot*) as well as the promotion of Hasidic tourism to the graves of famous Jewish rabbis of the seventeenth and eighteenth centuries, in the Ukraine and Belorus.

On one occasion, a large group of Hasidim from Brooklyn were invited by Reichman to witness the presentation of a new Torah Scroll to the main Moscow synagogue. The preliminary celebrations took place at the Hall of the Communist Youth League (Komsomol) in the heart of old Moscow — a theatre that certainly had never been used for similar purposes before that occasion. It was only thanks to Reichman's excellent connections that the hall could be rented in the first place. The festivities culminated in dancing, everyone linking hands and cavorting out into the street. As I joined the others, I saw the dumbfounded faces of the Muscovites, who were witnessing something highly unusual: tens of devout Jews, in their black silk caftans, wide-brimmed hats and side-curls, emerging from the Komsomol theatre. As the passersby stood completely transported, I approached them and asked what they thought of it all. An old man, his eyes popping, turned to me and said: 'What is this? Who are these people? Were the neighbourhood authorities warned? They should have posted a public announcement of this strange event. This is all very irregular! You see what the country is coming to?'

Dave Kimche, a former director-general of the Ministry of Foreign Affairs under Yitzhak Shamir, was employed by both Maxwell and Eisenberg, giving their contacts with the Soviet government an aura of diplomatic conspiracy. Kimche made wide use of his diplomatic passport and the title of special envoy, granted him by Shamir when he was minister of foreign affairs. His principals came to an agreement to cooperate in some of their projects in the USSR. Dave had me host a dinner for Soviet businessmen and officials to celebrate the event. Messrs Maxwell and Eisenberg sat to my right and left. It was an amusing occasion. Maxwell, a man of considerable girth, was pedantically going through some kind of ritual about his slimming diet, and was busy giving the waiter a piece of his mind about the food. Eisenberg was taciturn.

At one point Maxwell got up to make a speech on perestroika and the contribution that business could make to it. He was a strong speaker, though the guests lost most of his speech because of the peculiar version of the Russian language (his own), which he insisted on using. Eisenberg declined to speak and so I had to 'say a few words' as host. Mindful of the new Soviet predilection for joint ventures in business with any willing partner, I evoked the memory of the hippie movement, which proclaimed: 'Make Love, Not War'. In my adaptation of this idea to Soviet reality I appealed to 'Make Joint Ventures, not Love or War. JVs can be even more interesting than both, now that the houses of Maxwell and Eisenberg have joined hands.' The guests were nonplussed. I had the feeling that my eloquence had been wasted. Reflecting on it today, I suspect the Russians thought I was hinting at a Jewish conspiracy.

Manifestations of anti-Semitism often surfaced in the behaviour of Soviet government officials. They were convinced that Jews were all-powerful in the world and closely connected with Israeli interests in the Soviet Union. The fact was that most Jewish investors were conscious of Israel's interests, where immigration and the normalization of relations with the Soviet Union were concerned. They spoke about it often to ministers and members of the Politburo. Gorbachev himself willingly received them in his office, making a point of showing the meetings on prime-time television. This connection seemed to be politically convenient for the USSR. Soviet leaders were of the opinion that their initiatives in improving human rights, relaxing Jewish emigration and moving toward relations with Israel would encourage investments and improve the Soviet economy. From the point of view of priorities, however, money was a far more pressing matter than the renewal of relations with Israel. The restoration of diplomatic relations, on the other hand, carried the risk of raising a storm of protest both in the rightist Soviet camp and in the Arab world.

Nonetheless, the Russians thought, if properly exploited the Middle Eastern question could be prestige-building in the international arena. To that end, the Politburo discussed the Soviet Union's relations with Israel in December 1989*. I have already alluded to this event in a previous chapter. What I did not know at the time and found out only later were the important details. Relevant memoranda on the agenda were usually submitted by Politburo members prior to the discussions. On this occasion, Alexander Yakovlev, Eduard Shevardnadze, and the head of the KGB Victor Kryuchkov presented their joint recommendations. The upshot was a series of decisions: to upgrade the consular groups in Tel Aviv and Moscow to official consulates, develop relations with Israeli political parties, promote cultural relations and charge the Ministry of Foreign Affairs with the coordination of political contacts. Another recommendation was to 'activate' exchanges with inter-parliamentary and social organizations in Israel, primarily those opposed to the occupation of Arab land. Scientific and cultural exchanges were also mentioned. Israel's desire to re-establish diplomatic relations was interpreted as a wish to help end the isolation caused by the Intifada and improve Israel's contacts in the USSR with immigrating Jews. Supporting official consular relations, the document stated, could help the Soviet Union obtain modern technology. These decisions were seen as favouring Israel. Countersigned by Mikhail Gorbachev, they formed the basis of the USSR's policy for the three following years.

The substance of this new directive remained top-secret, although hints about its contents were leaked. In addition to opening consulates, the points in the Politburo document related to the establishment of trade relations with Israel at the level of chambers of commerce, and opening a Soviet media representation in Israel. This part of the directive was carried out in the new year. The decision to postpone any action on direct flights also became

---

* Extracts from Protocol 175 of the Politburo meeting of 29 Dec. 1989 and special addendum to the Protocol signed by E. Shevardnadze, A. Yakovlev, V. Kriuchkov and entitled 'On Future Relations with Israel', Tsentr khranenia sovremennoi dokumentatsii, fond 89, perechen' 9, papka 68, nomer 2577.

painfully clear to us. It was adhered to until the collapse of the Soviet Union.

The Politburo decision only called for an amelioration of the general atmosphere in relations with Israel. It did not modify the basic stance, which was strongly slanted toward the Arabs. In summarizing their memorandum to the Politburo, the authors stated that easing relations with Israel might arouse concern especially in Iran, Syria and Libya. It was feared Soviet-Arab relations might also suffer; such effects, it said, had to be neutralized. The memorandum also recommended the upgrading of the PLO office in Moscow to an embassy, to counterbalance the inauguration of a Soviet consulate in Tel Aviv.

EZER TAKES THE INITIATIVE

The Soviet administration knew these conditions were unacceptable to Shamir's cabinet. For this reason, they preferred to deal with Shimon Peres and personalities thought to be more accommodating to Yasser Arafat. Among the Israeli leaders who were on record as supporters of negotiating with the PLO, rather than solely with Jordan, was Ezer Weizmann.

Weizmann had joined the Begin government as minister of defence. A popular figure in Israeli public life, who later attained the post of president, he had been a member of the Israeli team in the Camp David peacemaking negotiations with Anwar Sadat and Jimmy Carter. Weizmann made an important contribution to the final, successful outcome of those historic first negotiations between Israel and its Arab neighbours. Subsequently, Weizmann changed his mildly hawkish views to dovish ones. His new convictions made him part ways with the Likud Party and join Labour. In the new coalition government, Ezer Weizmann received the portfolio of minister of science and technology.

I first met Weizmann when I was still in the army, many years ago. I had the pleasure of receiving and taking care of Ezer and his wife Reuma on their visit to Iran in 1974 and met Ezer many times afterwards. When visiting Israel from Moscow, I made a point of calling on him and reporting on our work, in which he, as others, expressed interest. Weizmann would speak of his deep frustration over the stagnating peace process and often assured me he would resign from the government if he saw no movement toward peace. He was very favourably inclined toward reaching an understanding with the PLO, though he was guarded about the idea of talking to Arafat — a daring and unpopular subject in 1989 among all but a small minority. Weizmann's position and beliefs were no secret. The Soviets probably became aware of them through their mission in Israel and the international press.

At one of the meetings I had with Weizmann toward the end of 1989, he said he was looking into a possible visit to the USSR, in his official capacity, in order to sign an agreement on cooperation with the Soviet Academy of Sciences. He added that he would very much like to meet with Gorbachev, or Foreign Minister Shevardnadze. Mindful of the fiasco we had had with our former minister of agriculture, I was reluctant to recommend such an attempt. Weizmann, however, assured me that he would not force the issue. In any case, his adviser, Ilya Zemtsov, was already contacting people in Moscow through the good offices of Chingiz Aitmatov, whom Weizmann had met when the writer visited Israel. In Moscow shortly afterwards, Zemtsov appeared on the scene declaring that members of the academy held the rank of ministers in the Soviet government, legitimizing the Weizmann trip from the point of view of protocol. Weizmann would not be embarrassed like the minister of agriculture Katz-Oz was when he was snubbed by Soviet officialdom, Zemtsov maintained.

Weizmann arrived in Moscow a short while later. He came with a group of journalists, including Nahum Barnea, a prominent analyst for *Yediot Aharonot*. The Academy of Sciences put them up at the Central Committee hotel, an unheard of privilege for non-party members or affiliates. On one of my visits to Weizmann there, I inadvertently walked in on a press conference being given by Lebanese Druse leader Kamal Jumblatt. Weizmann was delighted to hear of this, but his hope of 'accidentally' running into Jumblatt or any other prominent Arab or Palestinian figures came to naught. Before his departure for the Soviet Union, Shamir had advised Weizmann not to have any political meetings and to limit his visit to the business of contacts with the academy. On a trip to

Washington, a number of weeks prior to his departure, W had been invited by Anatoly Dobrynin, the Soviet ambassador, to meet and talk with him, but Shamir expressly forbade it and there was a lot of fiery commentary on this subject in the press. Following this incident, there was a political uproar when Premier Shamir accused Weizmann of having consorted with the PLO — at that time a punishable crime. Shamir fired Weizmann from his cabinet, but was countered by a Labour Party ultimatum and had to retreat. The compromise was to discontinue Weizmann's membership in the security cabinet meetings.

Weizmann was convinced he could generate Soviet participation in the peace process by talking to them. Frustrated over Shamir's objections to a meeting with Dobrynin in Washington (and over being fired from the security cabinet), he wanted to go one better in Moscow. The object of Weizmann's visit, it transpired soon enough, was to meet with Shevardnadze. I discovered that Weizmann's aide, the director-general of the Ministry of Science, Aryeh Shumer, who was accompanying him, was visiting the Ministry of Foreign Affairs without my knowledge.

When the appointment with Shevardnadze was finalized, Weizmann informed me I was not to be included in the Israeli party. The Soviets adamantly declined to have me, according to Zemtsov, who claimed there was room in Shevardnadze's office only for three: Weizmann, Shumer and himself. By that time (January 1990), I was well-known in Moscow as the official representative of Israel even if I had not been invested with the official title of ambassador. Snubbing me did not make any sense and could be harmful to the mission's prestige, which we had built up with great effort. When I objected, Weizmann looked ill at ease and said he would have to think it over. I suspected Weizmann did not want any witnesses to his conversation with the Soviet minister. I suggested he categorically state he would not attend the meeting unless the head of Israel's mission accompanied him. I was quite certain there would be no objections on the part of the Soviets. The next morning, Weizmann said he had not slept the whole night, but decided he could not forego meeting with the foreign minister of the Soviet Union just because the official

195

representative of Israel was not accompanying him. 'That would be stupid', he remarked.

The meeting lasted about an hour. Weizmann was pleased at having gained entrance to the Soviet High Command. In spite of the very poor communications in Moscow, the news spread immediately and was widely reported in Israel. There was a great deal of adverse commentary against Weizmann for not having me accompany him to this meeting. Everyone seemed to think that the Soviets had wilfully ignored the mission. Subsequently, it became clear that this had not been their intention.

At the meeting itself, Shevardnadze said the usual things about the 'dangers of Israel's policy', about Israel being isolated, and so on. Surprisingly, Shevardnadze repeated much of what Weizmann had said in his interview to Moscow's *Izvestiia* newspaper just the day before: the Intifada was a popular Palestinian uprising, negotiations should be held with the Palestinians and the PLO, and other statements to the same effect. The Soviet minister praised Arafat, whose position, he said, had undergone a complete turnabout under Soviet influence. Shevardnadze implied that the Soviets had applied a lot of pressure, but did not elaborate. In fact, the Soviet Union armed, trained and supported the most extreme Palestinian terrorist organizations until virtually the last day of its existence. Documents were published after the collapse of the Soviet Union which indicated Gorbachev's personal approval had been given to this activity. In answer to Weizmann's inquiries, Shevardnadze promised to renew relations with Israel. He did not say when. He also responded positively to Weizmann's request for direct flights, but I knew the Politburo's recommendation was to postpone this question, and so it did.

The Weizmann-Shevardnadze interview ended on a sour note. It was difficult to believe that the Foreign Ministry in Moscow was simply trying to embarrass the Shamir government, but it looked very much that way. In fact, they even embarrassed Weizmann. No sooner was he out of the ministry, when Shevardnadze called in the press and announced the elevation of the Palestinian representative to the status of ambassador, according him the right to open the Embassy of Palestine in Moscow. This was strictly in keeping with Politburo recommendations.

The Soviets appeared to be apprehensive about the Weizmann-Shevardnadze *tête-à-tête*. That same evening, Yuri Vorontsov, first deputy minister of foreign affairs and erstwhile ambassador to Afghanistan, called in all the Arab heads of missions resident in Moscow to announce that the Soviet Union had elevated the status of the Palestinian representative in Moscow and would itself send an ambassador to the PLO in Tunis. It was a clumsy exercise bringing neither improvement in the peace process, nor an incentive to Israel to work with the Soviets on the PLO track. There was no basis to expect such a decision or initiative in Israel. The Soviets ignored all this in their eagerness to smooth over the meeting with an Israeli minister.

A week or two after Weizmann's visit, Zevulun Hammer, the minister of religions, came to Moscow. I took him to visit a number of officials, including Alexander Belonogov, a deputy to Shevardnadze in charge of Middle Eastern Affairs. When we were leaving, Mikhail Bogdanov, the official in charge of Israeli affairs at the Foreign Ministry who sat in on the meeting, asked me why there had been such a commotion in the Israeli press about supposed Soviet objections to my participation in the Weizmann meeting. 'There was no objection at all on our part', he revealed. On the contrary, they had fully expected me to show up. It was Weizmann's people who excluded me, for reasons unknown to them, he added. I translated for Hammer, but refrained from commenting.

The Moscow scene greatly intrigued and interested President Haim Herzog. He was always very well briefed. Herzog's long career in intelligence and high diplomacy served him well. He showed keen interest in the most minute details of developments in the Soviet Union. He was always encouraging and supportive in the difficult times that I went through in the USSR, both as head of mission and on a personal level. Whether in his study at the presidential residence (with the white Isfahan carpet underfoot), or lunching with him in his private dining room, I always had the feeling he was genuinely interested in what I had to say.

When I was first leaving for Moscow, I was impressed with one of the stories President Herzog recounted from his discussions with President François Mitterand. Gorbachev told the French president that he had once asked the top Soviet army command what it was the Soviets had against Israel. Not one general could answer. I found that an indication of a positive attitude toward us and it heartened me. Later, I wondered whether there really had been such a good disposition and where it had gone. Gorbachev's favourable intentions toward Israel, as toward many other subjects, did not seem to translate into policy. Not unlike many of his western colleagues, Gorbachev was a politician first and foremost, and his priorities were strongly tied to the perception of his momentary needs.

The Soviet machine failed completely in its attempts to attract 'Jewish' money and to lead the Middle East into a new and more Soviet-oriented phase of peacemaking. The misconceptions that governed Soviet policy were the product of closed minds and faulty education. Yet inside the Soviet system there were people who could and did advise the Soviet government and party to act more openly and to be more involved in events. A great deal of time was lost on stubborn refusals to modify policies established in the preceding 20 years. As a result, aside from seconding the motion on the Madrid Conference of 1992, the Soviet government was completely left out of the Middle East peace process, which has since been led solely by the Americans.

15 · *Aunt Sonya*

One day in my office, while digging into the ever-increasing mountain of letters from all and sundry, I came across an unusual missive. It inquired whether I was Lev Levin, son of Olga and Boris, in which case the writer was a cousin on my mother's side and would I please contact a number in Leningrad to get acquainted. If this were not the case, would I please overlook the imposition.

Of all the Israeli mission members in Moscow, I was probably the only one who had no contacts with his immediate Russian family and no notion as to their whereabouts. My mother had passed away in Tehran when I was only three months old. My father was so affected with his loss that he never spoke about her and I never dared ask. Consequently, I did not even know the names or the details of the family connections of my mother's four sisters. Somehow, in all the turmoil of the many months I had spent in Moscow, I never went out of my way to look for my parents' relatives and I had, in any case, almost nothing to go on. I only knew that the whole family, as many others, survived the Nazi occupation by being evacuated to Siberia, just before the Germans reached central Ukraine. My cousin's letter was totally unexpected.

I felt a close affinity to the extended Russian Jewish Diaspora, to its history, its cultural fabric, its concerns and hopes. I was in the midst of these people every day and thought about them a great deal, but discovering my own roots was something new. I had never experienced this type of contact before, anywhere, as we were completely cut off from our family in the years after the

Second World War and we had no known relatives in any part of
the world except in Russia. Only vaguely did I remember stories
from my early childhood about these Russian aunts, uncles and
cousins.

I was aware of the bitterness of my father's generation: the years
of the First World War, the Revolution, the Civil War, the New
Economic Policy, the Stalinist years, the 'Great Patriotic War'
against the Germans, the adversities of the postwar period and the
beginning of a new era. After the war my father had given up hope
of seeing the members of his family. Suddenly, I was about to establish a link with the days of my parents' youth in the Ukraine, and
with the great Russian-Jewish saga unfolding under my very eyes.

I sat back in my chair and wondered what it would be like. I
picked up the telephone. The voice from Leningrad was like any
other; however, it was that of my first cousin, my aunt's daughter.
It was hard to believe.

The night train to Leningrad brought me to the address of my
cousin Galia — an apartment block in a grey and dusty neighbourhood. Galia opened the door. She had the fair hair and the green
eyes I remembered from the old portrait of my mother's family:
young sisters standing behind their Orthodox parents, slim and
proud and smiling benignly at the photographer.

I was introduced to the other members of Galia's family. We all
brought each other up-to-date. The luncheon was laid out and the
conversation went into the late afternoon. Galia was a physician,
head of an internal medicine department in a Leningrad hospital.
She was in her fifties. She took me aside, to a room lined with
books. 'We have asked for a *vizov*', she confided. Did I think they
should go through with it?

I looked around me. Galia was living in a comfortable, well-
appointed three-room apartment, a great luxury and privilege in
the land of socialism. She had a good job, was held in esteem by her
colleagues in spite of being Jewish, she said. Her grown children
were all employed, although kept from studying the professions
they preferred because of anti-Semitic constraints. They did not
want for anything, Galia said, but they were worried about the
future of their children. I knew the story.

Galia gave me a present: a large and beautiful album of

Leningrad, with photographs of its gardens, canals and imposing public buildings, erected under the tsars. She cared about her city, about its opera, its ballet, and about the Hermitage — the world-famous museum housed in the former Winter Palace. She had her friends. There were also the hardships she and her family had gone through in the evacuation, in her first years as a medical student in a city destroyed by war, and her own personal losses and struggles in an anti-Jewish environment. She spoke of her fears and of her hopes for a new life.

In my mind's eye, I saw Galia and her family going to Israel, to them a strange and different country where Russian culture was respected but not essential, where there was a need to learn an entirely new language, to speak it, to negotiate in it with the administration. Her first years would be tough. She would not find employment in her profession. The climate was a great deal warmer and more difficult to withstand than the long winters and springs of the north that she was used to.

I asked her what she wanted me to say beyond what she already knew. 'We are aware of the problems. But I want your honest opinion.' Did they feel they wanted to go on living in this country? Would they regret leaving it? Were they prepared to face a possible repetition of the hardships they all had gone through in those long and painful years? Their son had decided to leave, come what may. Would she stay behind with her grandchildren if he left? Was there an alternative? I told her she would have to begin a new life, but that I thought she would not regret it in the end. She was thoughtful as she looked out of the window. It was a sunny and warm autumn day. The trees in the yard below were tinged with gold. Galia said she would have to think about it. But I knew her decision had been made.

My mother's sister Sonya, Galia said, was alive and well and would be eager to meet me. She was living in Voronezh with her family. Before I left, Galia and I decided to get together in Voronezh, a few weeks hence. I was extremely busy and time went by quickly. Arrangements were made with the UPDK, the official Foreign Ministry diplomats' travel bureau, and a few weeks later I took the flight to Voronezh, some 400 miles south of Moscow; a short hop in an Aeroflot plane.

On the flight, I sat next to a former pilot of the Soviet Air Force, who had served in Egypt during the War of Attrition against Israel in 1970. I told him who I was, but he told me his story without reservations. He was a fighter pilot and flew one of the planes in the Soviet squadron based near the Suez Canal. The Israeli Air Force had been penetrating deep into Egyptian airspace and bombing military and industrial targets at will, making daring raids into the heartland of enemy territory. At some point, the Brezhnev regime, responding to Egyptian pleas for help, sent down a Soviet Air Force unit that became operational when the air war reached a critical stage for the Egyptians. Soviet pilots appeared in the skies. Our intelligence picked up Russian speech on the radio waves and our fighters knew they were up against Soviet competition. In a dogfight over the Suez Canal, the Soviets flew out against us. On 30 July 1970 five Soviet planes and pilots were shot down, causing consternation among the Russians (but a certain satisfaction among the Egyptians, whom the Soviets had been berating for their incompetence). The Soviet-Israeli confrontations continued for some time, but were not publicized, and this episode did not become prominent in the public eye.

My travelling companion made a claim that I had not heard before: Soviet pilots had downed Israeli aircraft in dogfights over Egypt. This may or may not be true; Israeli losses in air battles were rather rare. Some Israeli planes were in fact shot down — not in dogfights — but by Soviet-controlled electronic warfare and ground-to-air missiles. The Soviet airman also told me about talk of Soviet pilots at the military air force bases in Egypt and the high regard they had for their Israeli 'colleagues'. Nothing at all was published in the Soviet military or civilian press about these incidents, but the image of the Israeli pilots' superior fighting ability endured for a long time to come, reinforced once again after the great air battles with the Syrian Air Force over Lebanese skies in 1982, when the Syrians lost over 60 planes in a series of encounters lasting about two days.

This conversation, so interesting in itself, could certainly not have taken place a few years before. Talking to a stranger, a foreign diplomat at that, about secret military operations (even if they had taken place almost two decades back) was unimaginable and would have carried a severe penalty. It seemed that perestroika had made a big dent.

In Voronezh, family members were waiting for me, roses-in-hand, at the airport exit. Tamara, another cousin, and her husband Mark piled me into a taxi and brought me to their apartment. Galia was already there. I had brought a case full of goodies that I had picked up in the dollar store in Moscow. Times were difficult; there were no matches, no candles, and not much of anything else. I was careful about the food since I did not know if the family observed kashrut. 'Oh, put it in the kitchen', said Galia. I noticed there was no great enthusiasm about the gifts. Aunt Sonya, my mother's sister, appeared a few moments later. She was a spry, diminutive woman of 89, with clear blue eyes and an inquisitive manner. She said she was overjoyed at finally meeting me. She had lost her own son when he was a young boy and if it had not been for the great distance between us, she certainly would have brought me up after my own mother's death. She was thus adopting me now as her own child.

We all entered the dining room. A large table occupied the centre of the room. It was piled high with every known Jewish food and delicacy. I could not believe my eyes and understood why my case full of foreign goods did not cause any excitement. Some 20 family members were seated around the table. There were cousins from Leningrad, Voronezh and Kursk, their spouses and children, all entirely unknown to me. They were doctors and engineers; the young were all into mathematics, physics and chess. Every one introduced himself and in a few words described the ties that bound us together. I was urged to taste everything that was laid out in my honour, and I thought to myself that at a good, brisk pace, it would take us a week of eating to clear the table. There were accounts and stories galore about the other members of the family who were unable to make it to Voronezh. Photographs were produced. In one, I saw myself standing among cousins or in-laws I did not recognize and could not understand how such a recent photograph was unknown to me. Only after a second look did I realize that it was a woman, an aunt (who had been dead for ten years), whose age in the photo was similar to mine and who bore an amazing resemblance to me.

As the day merged with the night, the samovar was brought out and we drank tea with jam and cakes freshly baked the day before. I was tired and begged leave to sleep off all the excitement. They wanted me to stay with them but I was afraid it would implicate them in some unknown Soviet transgression, for which they might have to answer to the security services. In fact, I discovered much later that Mark, who had a 'responsible position' in a 'closed' scientific institute, had been photographed by the KGB whilst meeting me at the airport, taking me to the hotel and talking with me. Fortunately, there were no consequences. I could not bear the idea of any harm befalling my new family. So I went to the best hotel in Voronezh, provided for me by the UPDK — a run-down rat hole creeping with drunks and prostitutes — and tried, unsuccessfully, to fall asleep.

The next morning, Mark came to collect me and take me 'home' for breakfast. Aunt Sonya said she wanted to speak to me in private. She was living in a one-room apartment in the same building and had spent the early hours of the morning going over old photographs. She produced a handful of me, aged one and three, with my father, which I had never seen before. She showed me the back of the photos, where my father had written a few words in Yiddish when he sent them to the Ukraine. The handwriting was crossed out in black ink. Aunt Sonya explained that they had to block out any mention of family living abroad, as any person with relatives outside the USSR was automatically suspect and could be arrested for no other reason than the possession of a photograph proving it.

Aunt Sonya then said there was one very special thing she had kept for me, always hoping she might see me some day. She handed me a small white card. It was the invitation to my parents' wedding, on 13 July 1919, at the home of the Kaplunovs, in Krolevets, Ukraine. 'We would be honoured to see you among our guests', said the card. I was being invited to my parents' marriage ceremony. Aunt Sonya said my father had only briefly courted my mother; it seemed they were predestined for each other. I wondered what the wedding was like, who the guests were and what the circumstances had been. It took place, after all, just a year and a half after the Bolshevik Revolution of October 1917.

Fate had not been kind to my parents. They had married in a period of great upheavals. The Germans had occupied parts of the Ukraine in the First World War, then came the revolution. The Civil War broke out in 1918, with its dire consequences: the revolutionary but anti-Bolshevik government of Petlyura; the Anarchists under 'Little Father' Makhno, fighting Petlyura; the Red Army, the White forces, each fighting the other and ravaging the countryside; bands of brigands and guerrillas, taking turns occupying, retreating and reoccupying the towns and villages of the Ukraine, with intermittent pogroms, pillaging, marauding and famine following each other at regular, short intervals. A little-known but important statistic: nearly 300,000 Jews were killed in these disturbances. The great emigration to the US and western Europe had already followed the tsarist-organized pogroms at the turn of the century.

The New Economic Policy was declared by Lenin in 1921 and my father's family fortunes prospered again. In 1926, however, my father received a warning that he was to be arrested by the GPU (the forerunner of the KGB). He dropped everything he was doing and fled to Palestine. As the GPU was hot on his trail, he did not take the normal route through Poland, but was advised to go through Persia. Eventually, he reached Persia and remained there for many years. My mother arrived in Persia with my two older brothers in 1928 and perished from typhoid in 1930. My brothers died from disease before my birth.

This story, known to me in its general outline, has been filled in with many details by Aunt Sonya in the many long conversations we have had since. As the sisters closest in age among the five, my mother and Sonya were together much of the time and went to the same primary and secondary schools. They would both eagerly await the end of the Sabbath to compete getting to the piano, as music was not to be played on the day of rest. Sonya told me of the days when she started meeting young men, whom she liked and whom she did not, who was the most handsome, what my paternal grandmother looked like, how she dressed, the great deeds of charity that she performed, the authority that she enjoyed in the community, and many other details of which I had been deprived all my life.

Thus I heard how the family hid away the silver from the Makhno gangs behind a double partition in the dining room, which had been turned into the headquarters of a local band of marauders; how, at the height of a period of famine, a friendly peasant rode into their yard on a cart with a number of sacks of pea-flour hidden under a load of hay, an act for which he could have paid with his life; and of another occasion, when Aunt Sonya herself was dragged out of the house by a bunch of drunken bandits, who were at the last moment surprised by a Red Army patrol and abandoned her. These and many other stories filled out the image I had formed from history books and the little I had heard from my father, who would only rarely indulge in recounting the experiences of his turbulent life.

For my own relatives, as for thousands of other Jews in the USSR, the die was cast. As soon as the road was opened and the difficulties overcome, their destination became Israel and no other. True, not all of them came at once, nor did all take the decision easily. There are some who have stayed behind, unable to confront the known and the presumed challenges. For the most part, however, there was no great hesitation. One after another, the members of this large family, to me a faithful indication of what Russia and what Israel meant in their lives, began making their way to the mission to get their visas. First Galia and her children, then Mark and Tamara, followed by Aunt Sonya, then my other cousin Fanyura and her children too, crossed the Rubicon and landed at Ben-Gurion airport, the gateway to a new life, in a country where they would not suffer merely for being Jews.

Aunt Sonya and her family now live in Jerusalem, in an apartment which they own. Most of the members of the family are gainfully employed or studying. At first, they were preoccupied mostly with Russian television and debating the course of recent Russian history from the departure of Gorbachev to the arrival of Yeltsin. Their bookshelves are still filled with the Russian classics, but they read them less. These days, the image of Russia is becoming hazier. Interest in its fortunes is flagging, as new life takes root in the soil of Israel. The children refuse to talk about Russia. Life is not an uninterrupted holiday, but the refrain is *'vse normal'no'* (everything's OK). It is only Aunt Sonya who complains that she is not contributing anything, and is not being kept abreast. Having been a callisthenics instructor for many years, she is also dissatisfied that members of her family and her grandchildren do not do their morning workouts. It is indeed difficult for her. In Voronezh, in her apartment block, she was well respected by the neighbours, who would often stop by to chat, to ask for advice, to listen to her stories. Now, she lives with her family, but is not the centre of anyone's attention. She can only read the Russian-language newspapers, mostly sensationalist. She is upset by almost everything in them: the politics and the politicians of this new country, the crime rate. 'I always knew Jews to be honourable people', she laments, 'speaking the truth and never hurting anyone. I can't understand where all these criminals came from.'

16 · The Curtain Falls – Halfway

The beginning of the year 1990 augured well for the mission. My 14-month stay in Moscow was showing positive results: there was a Politburo decision to restore relations, the emigration to Israel was rapidly surpassing all of our expectations, and initial trade and cultural exchanges had been established. On 29 January, I was suddenly called to meet with the first deputy minister of foreign affairs, Yuri Vorontsov. No explanation was furnished for this unexpected summons.

Vorontsov was considered to be (and still is, as Russian ambassador to Washington) one of the foremost Soviet diplomats. He has served as adviser to the leaders of his country on foreign affairs. Vorontsov was also the last Soviet ambassador to Afghanistan before the Soviet withdrawal and can thus be considered to be one of the chief architects of the retreat, although he is also reported by Cherniaev to have addressed recommendations for massive air strikes against the *mujahedin*, which might have resulted in thousands of victims among the civilian population. Vorontsov held several important posts before his promotion to first deputy foreign minister. He served in India, and some of the officials in the Near and Middle East departments of the Ministry of Foreign Affairs who assisted him there still owe him allegiance. He has been a perennial candidate for foreign minister, but has been unable thus far to achieve that post.

Vorontsov was one of the first harbingers of the new opening in

Israel's contacts with the Soviet Union. In July 1985, as Soviet ambassador in Paris, Vorontsov met his Israeli counterpart, Ovadiah Sofer, and proposed a 'package deal': the USSR would raise the number of emigrants to Israel in return for Israel ending the anti-Soviet propaganda which, it was alleged, was being directed world-wide. The large-scale and embarrassing demonstrations in favour of an open-door policy on the emigration of Soviet Jews had become a permanent fixture in international life. Vorontsov told Sofer that his country much preferred the Jews to go directly to Israel, rather than to the West. The Jewish immigrants' potential, Vorontsov said, might strengthen the West. He intimated that a renewal of diplomatic relations was possible. However, the USSR first wanted Israel to come to terms with Syria on a general formula concerning the Golan Heights and agree in principle to convene an international peace conference on the Middle East. The Soviet Union would figure as a co-partner with the US in the conference. No mention at all was made of the PLO. This was an intriguing detail in itself, since all we ever heard from the Soviets before and after usually zeroed in on that organization.

In the tense and suspicion-laden relationship that Israel had had with the USSR since 1967, there had been a number of meetings between ambassadors and ministers of foreign affairs. The themes had not varied much. Vorontsov's words had the virtue of novelty regarding the possibilities of a bargain. Vorontsov asked Sofer to treat his proposal as top secret and transmit it as such. Unfortunately, no sooner was the meeting over, than its central theme was splashed all over the front pages of the Israeli press and broadcast on five continents. The news was denied by the Soviets. Vorontsov soon left his post in Paris, hardly as a result of this diplomatic mishap, but he has probably harboured a feeling of strong dislike toward the Israeli establishment and its diplomats ever since.

When I sat down in Vorontsov's office he warned that while my first meeting with Minister Shevardnadze had been a pleasant one, my meeting with him would not be. He then read out a protest to the effect that Israel's prime minister had been urging the new immigrants from the USSR to settle in the occupied territories. This had to stop as it was causing misunderstandings with the

USSR's Arab friends. The tone of the diplomatic note was dry and arrogant.

Vorontsov handed me a copy of the statement. It had no heading and no signature or stamp as there were no relations between the countries. In the course of our conversation Vorontsov told me we should 'stop digging in', in the occupied territories, since they did not belong to us; we should not expect direct flights of immigrants to Israel, for 'political reasons'. He asked me why we were not using trains to send immigrants to East European capitals and flying them to Israel from there. I could hardly answer that question since I had heard the director of Nativ tell Prime Minister Shamir there was not enough space on the trains (which was not true). Vorontsov also confirmed that the new emigration law, much more liberal than the preceding one, would be adopted soon by the Parliament. He summed up the relations between the two countries by saying that everything was proceeding normally, including the emigration of Jews. Vorontsov then strongly hinted we should let it go at that for the present as the Soviet Union had a great many problems of its own, and we ought to be aware of them.

Yuri Vorontsov's words were harsh at the beginning, during the purely official part of the meeting, but he sounded more open and approachable when he spoke off the cuff. The message was clear: the Soviet Union has to make this *démarche* because of domestic and external pressures, but basically there is no great need to worry. As the man was a seasoned diplomat and in perfect control of his words, I transmitted this impression to the ministry in Jerusalem.

There was neither a response of any kind from Jerusalem, nor any intimation of what I was supposed to do. I had the impression that the Ministry of Foreign Affairs in Jerusalem wanted to take Vorontsov's advice at face value and ignore the official declaration. I was not entirely certain this was the intention of the Soviet government, but I was especially concerned over what might follow. Vorontsov's words appeared to be an opening salvo to cover the retreat from former promising positions.

In March, I was again called in for an additional 'dressing-down', on the settlement of immigrants in the occupied territories. This time, I was invited to the Near East Department, whose deputy, Filev, voiced an implicit threat, saying his government did not know if it could withstand pressures from the Arab countries. There was, in any case, nothing we were going to do about it, as the emigration was taking on a life of its own. Soviet threats were becoming less severe. We were being assured everywhere that there was no intention at all to renege, since emigration did not only concern Jews but also Germans, Armenians, Tatars and Russians.

The feeling was quite widespread that the regime was unwilling and unable to backtrack. The emigration joke current at that time was that Shevardnadze looked out of his office one day and could not find a soul in the corridors or the offices of his ministry. The telephone rang and as he picked up the receiver, he recognized Gorbachev's voice. Shevardnadze told him of his distress, but Gorbachev assured him all was fine, the Supreme Soviet had already approved the problematic emigration laws. Shevardnadze insisted on discussing the problem with the general secretary right away and asked him where he was. 'Oh, I'm calling from London', Gorbachev replied.

This was the broad picture of emigration. The finer details were still worrisome: Soviet citizenship was still stripped from Jewish immigrants to Israel; Soviet bureaucrats were still dragging their feet on procedural questions; Jews were still harassed and fired from their jobs as soon as they announced their impending emigration. In spite of the many signs to the contrary, all of us were pursued by a nagging doomsday paranoia of waking up one day and finding the whole set of rules concerning emigration changed. This fear never left us, even well into the crest of the great wave of emigration in 1990–91.

The Soviet government was busy mending its fences with the Arab world. A show of force was undertaken in March by sending emissaries to the Near East: Vladimir Poliakov went to Saudi Arabia, Vitaly Naumkin to South Yemen and Yuri Vorontsov was dispatched to Morocco, all to ward off the evil eye — the possible effects of the Jewish emigration to Israel on Soviet relations with the Arab countries. In the meantime, Prime Minister Shamir and the new Foreign Minister David Levy made statements in the Knesset denying Soviet allegations that Israel had a policy of settling Soviet immigrants in the occupied territories. Even Ariel

Sharon, the housing minister, made a statement to the effect that the government was not encouraging the immigrants to settle outside the so-called 'green line', which demarcated Israel's undisputed pre-1967 territory. This did not interest the Russians. In a closed party caucus, Shamir had said the immigration from the USSR was going to help the creation of a 'Greater Israel'. The smoke signals from Vorontsov and from others referred to this particular 'secret' declaration.

In Jerusalem, the Soviet representative, Grigory Martirosov, met with the head of our East European division, Yosef Govrin. In the course of his conversation, he too complained about the prime minister's words and added that Vorontsov had to countermand growing Arab displeasure with the Soviets for letting such a large number of immigrants settle in the occupied territories. Martirosov was basically repeating what was being implied to me in Moscow: 'the immigration will continue, but can't you please keep your mouths shut?'. What Martirosov also said was that the Israeli press was sending up such fireworks about the two non-scheduled Aeroflot flights to Israel that the government had to close the chapter again. Martirosov's displeasure about the publicity on the flights was justified, perhaps, but there was nothing we could do. In any case, it would not have had any effect, as the Politburo had expressly postponed the decision on direct air connections.

Martirosov, like Vorontsov before him, complained we were not using the half-empty trains going to East Europe, from where the immigrants could be flown by El Al. As we kept hearing this suggestion over and over again, it appeared the Soviets were genuinely perplexed over our insistence on using direct flights, which they believed would have caused embarrassment with the Arabs. We all knew that trains could not cope with the large number of people involved, but they could have helped a great deal. Nativ, ever expanding its activities for the promotion of immigration, was preventing Jews from getting out. The price of the possible defection of a few families from the approved route seemed small if it meant that many thousands would reach their destination sooner. I very much doubted this was the approach sanctioned by the government. The cabinet was very far removed from the day-to-day administration of the immigration problems in the USSR, and Shamir was leaving the matter entirely in the hands of Nativ. It was a machoist initiative, typical of the Nativ administration.

I discussed this matter on many occasions with Nativ colleagues in Moscow, some of whom were very well-positioned to change this practice. They would not admit to it, nor did they wish to discuss it. There was no point talking to Prime Minister Shamir. He was an excellent listener, and that was about where it stopped. I failed to draw out Foreign Minister Arens either. Usually of an extremely open, no-nonsense manner in his politics, he was diplomatically overcautious on this particular subject and did not want to get into a scrap over immigration or its Nativ administrators, as he was evidently fully aware of the prime minister's attitude.

My discussions in the ministry concerning policy and administration of immigration would usually begin at the East European division, and move upstairs into a meeting with Director-General Reuven Merhav, who loved well-organized staff meetings with extensive participation of officials, follow-up notes and reminders. The issue would then reach the table of the foreign minister in the presence of Nativ officials. The latter would always react with the 'Who, me?' innocence of courtiers well-practiced in fighting encroachments on their territory. Every attempt to beat some sense into the system would quickly run aground. As I did not easily give up, this charade was usually repeated at bi-monthly intervals, with everyone around the foreign minister's table clucking his tongue but slinking back from unseemly exposure. The issues that I raised did not concern the question of trains alone. Nativ's self-appointed tasks were getting out of hand and impinging on the functions of other agencies. Moreover, their superfluous and grandiose involvement in the business of transportation, forwarding and contacts with the political élite were hampering the pace of their regular work.

One of the more difficult aspects of the emigration process was the question of flights. Aeroflot had to sanction every flight and get paid a commission, which was their right under international agreements. The other East European companies were asked to leave the reservations to the mission, which they did readily. As a consequence, hundreds of people were being called in daily for the process of making reservations. A computerized system was installed and a number of additional local staff were hired for the purpose. The East European companies were not always terribly efficient and there were many flights cancelled without prior notice, leaving emigrants stranded and helpless, often far away from their homes, which they had had to relinquish or abandon. Nativ dealt with all these on a day-to-day basis and did wonders in getting the emigrants out. However, visas would be refused to persons unwilling to take the sanctioned trajectory. The Dutch consuls who were issuing the visas did not interfere. Nativ verified the eligibility of the emigrant for a visa and gave the green light to the Netherlands Consul for its issuance, or refused if the person did not conform to the restrictions.

The problem of baggage was more intractable still. Understandably, the emigrants were emotionally attached to their belongings and wanted to ship every item, large or small. As only 40 kilograms were allowed on flights, the rest had to be forwarded. This created an unbelievable backlog at the Soviet customs, which was completely unprepared and unable to respond. I held a number of meetings with customs and was told their throughput capability was sufficient for only three families a day. They complained to me that every family usually came down to customs with one, two or three very large trucks laden with every imaginable object belonging to the family, as well as to friends, who were planning to emigrate later. The customs officials had to check out every sock, book and frying pan. After this painful process, they packed everything in large customized and padlocked pineboard boxes and sent them along by rail to the port. From there the boxes would make their way to Israel, to be stored in a warehouse and await their owners.

I imagined this had been standard procedure in the days of Ivan the Terrible and could not be altered because of some mysterious reason known only to the Soviet administration. But the inspection was only a part of the difficulty. Customs simply did not possess the hardware to move great quantities of goods. They asked me to help them by purchasing modern equipment and building the proper warehousing, to increase their efficiency. I passed this suggestion on to my government. The response was to ask friendly forwarding agencies to come up with solutions, but the main obstacle was the investment involved. There were few takers and the action went no further. As the number of emigrants rose and prospective newcomers to Israel got wise to the logistics involved, the volume of baggage was considerably reduced. Another solution the emigrants themselves discovered was getting the luggage to other cities with less encumbered customs for checking. The Jewish Agency had to pay for the transportation and the storage in Israel of the belongings until such time as the family arrived and rented an apartment — a good year or two down the line.

Insofar as relations with Israel were concerned, the Soviets were again lowering the curtain on our contacts, out of internal weakness and unwillingness to devote greater attention to the subject. There was clearly impatience with the Arabs as well. *Pravda* came out with an important, no doubt officially inspired article on emigration, saying that the Arabs should not forget that they themselves had let over 800,000 Jews into Israel in 1948–50. Jewish and other emigration, the article concluded, was an internal affair of the Soviet Union.

It was as difficult for us to understand the ups and downs of Soviet policy as it may have been for the Soviets themselves to adopt a clear-cut attitude. The minimal understandings reached at the meeting between the two foreign ministers in Cairo were not acted upon. Foreign Minister Moshe Arens's letter to Shevardnadze on political and diplomatic questions was held up for five months without any response. Soviet propaganda and diplomatic language grew harsher; plans that had begun firming up at the end of the year were postponed; the political and diplomatic agendas were held up. There was nothing left to do but wait.

17 · Agony and Death of the Regime

The increasing convulsions of the Soviet system were influencing our life at the mission. The taboos surrounding Israel began to erode with the lessening of fears and the de-ideologization of the political and social life in the country. A sign of the changing times was the big Passover Seder which I organized at our refurbished apartments in April 1990. This was the first Seder held at the Israeli mission in 23 years. There had been Seders organized by the ambassadors of Israel before 1967, but they could include only a closed circle of privileged individuals allowed to venture into the embassy compound. US ambassador in Moscow, Jack Matlock, had invited prominent Jewish activists to a series of Seders at his residence, with kosher food flown in from the US. On one occasion the guest of honour was Secretary of State George Shultz. With Israel's mission securely ensconced in its own home in the Soviet capital, it was only fitting that we celebrate the Passover with Soviet Jews and other friends on territory officially recognized as Israeli.

So it was that Yevgeny Velikhov of the Academy of Sciences, Radomir Bogdanov and Vladimir and Tatiana Nosenko of the Institute for World Economics and International Relations graced our Passover table in the spring of 1990. Also present were our Dutch 'hosts' and another ambassador, whose story was highly typical of Jewish postwar life in Eastern Europe: Rudolf Slansky, the ambassador of Czechoslovakia. He had been appointed by President Václav Havel in an apparent effort to remind the Russians of their crimes against Czechoslovakia. In 1952, Stalin ordered a public trial of Czech leaders, who included the ambassador's father, Rudolf Slansky, a communist of Jewish origin. They were accused of taking part in a 'Zionist-imperialist conspiracy' and executed. In the process, all of the East European press and media carried poisonous anti-Zionist propaganda with very strong anti-Semitic overtones. A number of similar trials had already been held: in Hungary in 1949 against Laszlo Reyk, and in Moscow against Jewish writers who were secretly executed in 1952. The murder of actor Solomon Mikhoels in 1948 opened an anti-Semitic campaign a mere three years after the end of the war. One of the cruelest aspects of these Soviet excesses was the involvement of the victims' families in the persecution. When Rudolf Slansky was standing trial in Prague and was being tortured in order to get him to confess his alleged crimes as a 'Zionist', which he never was, the Soviet media approached his son Rudolf, then studying in Moscow. The younger Slansky had been raised in the spirit of Pavlik Morozov, a mythic young 'pioneer' (the Soviet version of the boy scouts), who informed on his parents' 'anti-Soviet' activities and became a Stalinist role model for Soviet children. Rudolf told the press he was angry about his father's betrayal. When I asked him if he would accept the invitation to the Seder, he said he knew next to nothing about Jewish traditions but was curious about them and would come with his wife, a non-Jew.

The Passover dinner is always imbued with feelings of renewal, but on that April night in Moscow it had special meaning. We had dug out the porcelain that was used by Golda Meir in 1949 and felt her spirit was with us. We were once more among Russian Jews as we celebrated the Exodus out of Egypt and spoke of the miracles that had brought us together again under that roof. I distributed the Haggadah in different languages to guide the guests in the ritual and the story of the Exodus. The guests read portions in their own language with lively interest. Soviet Jews and our foreign guests sat around the table discussing the meaning and the implications of the Exodus, the 40-year march in the desert, the progression from slavery to freedom under the lawgiver Moses. We also spoke about the wondrous rebirth of nature after winter's slumber, about new hopes and new beginnings, all relevant to the transmutations of Soviet life. The country was indeed beginning to change in front of our eyes.

YELTSIN, A NEW FORCE ON THE HORIZON

Some observers in Moscow saw the first significant steps toward the collapse of the communist establishment in Boris Yeltsin's 'mutiny' in October 1987. Yeltsin was brought to Moscow from Sverdlovsk, where he had been first secretary of the party, by Yegor Ligachev, a fellow Siberian. Ligachev, already a member of the Politburo, was an arch-conservative. He wanted to keep communism alive at all costs and intended perestroika to be a communist reform from the top. He believed Yeltsin to be a kindred spirit and thought he could be a useful ally in Moscow. Yeltsin was made a secretary in the Central Committee and later appointed first secretary of the Moscow City Party Committee — the city party boss, who always enjoyed a privileged position *vis-à-vis* the Politburo.

Yeltsin was an interesting new personality on the Soviet horizon. When he began making his way in Moscow, some of my friends who had known him in Svedlovsk spoke disparagingly of him. He was an ordinary *apparatchik*, they said, wise in the ways of the communist establishment, but hardly a man who could challenge Gorbachev. Yeltsin, however, turned out to have a mind of his own. He declared his dissatisfaction with the pace of perestroika and with the indecisiveness of the Politburo. As a candidate for full membership in the Politburo, Yeltsin boldly used his power to propel himself to the top. Eventually, he ran afoul of his ally Yegor Ligachev. In the tug-of-war that ensued, Gorbachev, true to his practice, sided with the establishment. Yeltsin was ousted from his position as first secretary of the Moscow Party Committee in November 1987, and was demoted from his candidacy to the Politburo in February 1988.

In September 1989, *Pravda* reprinted from the Italian paper *Reppublica*, a vilifying article concerning Yeltsin's behaviour on a trip to the US. Viktor Afanasyev, the editor of *Pravda* at the time, recounts how this article affected Yeltsin's career: Yeltsin was depicted as a hopeless drunk, a clumsy Russian bear. The article backfired. 'He's one of us', most people said. 'The party simply wants to bury him.' Another article described Yeltsin's romantic escapades. He became the public's darling. Quickly awakening to the effect derogatory articles on Yeltsin were having on his image, Gorbachev dismissed Afanasyev.* The lesson was not lost on the politicians.

Yeltsin became a central figure of the opposition, rallying liberal members of the party and a nucleus of political outsiders around him. Subsequently, Gorbachev made heavy-handed use of the Communist Party to try and sabotage Yeltsin's election to the presidency of the Russian Republic, thus deepening the personal hatred between them. Yeltsin won the elections in the Russian Parliament in May 1990 and became the first president of the Russian Republic. This development closely followed the election by the Supreme Soviet of Gorbachev as the first president of the USSR.

Gorbachev's newly instituted presidential system broke with the long-standing traditions of the communist regime, disorienting the administration and creating eddies of strong internal opposition. Yeltsin's election, on the other hand, put Russia on the map as an independent entity within the USSR, a political precedent of great significance to the future of the country and the Communist Party. In June 1990, Russia declared its sovereignty. Yeltsin's election to the Russian presidency took on an unexpectedly important turn in the attempted coup of summer 1991. He fully exploited his position as president to foil the coup, thereby gaining much prestige and public support.

Earlier, in June 1990, the Russian Parliament had abolished the one-party system, leaving the Communist Party adrift. Yeltsin saw the opportunity afforded by the failure of the August 1991 coup, and declared the suspension of the Communist Party. A day later, on 24 August, general-secretary of the Soviet Communist Party

---

* Viktor Afanasyev, *Chetvertaia vlast' i chetyre Genseka* (The Fourth Force and Four General Secretaries) (Moscow: Kedr, 1994) p. 7.

Mikhail Gorbachev decreed the 'self-dissolution' of this once all-powerful organization. Yet these two extraordinary developments were not unexpected. In the preceding year, the party had been exposed and weakened, and was later strongly affected by the coup, which it was seen to have supported. The rapidity with which these developments took place somewhat deadened their effect. Nonetheless, the demise of the Communist Party in the Soviet Union, almost unopposed and without firing a shot, bordered on the miraculous.

In the confusion that ensued, the Russian government began to aggressively expropriate movable and immovable party property, including the Central Committee headquarters building on Staraya Ploshchad. Muscovites were dumbfounded at this development. Alexander Yakovlev said that even a cat had to ask for permission to cross Staraya Ploshchad in the old days. Another concomitant of these surprising transformations was the tearing down of monuments to old Bolsheviks all over Moscow: first among these was the statue of 'Iron Felix' Dzerzhinsky, the founder of the Cheka, forerunner of the KGB. The massive ten-foot likeness was taken down in a night raid organized by the Moscow Municipality. There was no attempt made by the KGB to interfere, in spite of its ability to do so with the military forces at its disposal. The statue's pedestal was left standing, and was immediately covered with graffiti. One of the messages was in Hebrew, strangely enough. It said *'Il'an abouk, ya maniac!'*, a half-Arabic half-Hebrew curse which, literally translated, means 'Damn your Father, you maniac!'. There was a mad rush to acquire bits of the stone pedestal for souvenirs. I obtained some myself and sent them to the heads of the intelligence community in Israel. When I next visited one of them, he proudly showed me the red bit of granite set on a clear plastic support, to remind all in his office of the monster an intelligence organization could become if left unchecked.

DISTURBANCES IN CENTRAL ASIA

Free elections burst the dam of internal nationalistic tendencies and unshackled the individual republics' ambitions for independence.

220

The trauma of the early April 1989 bloody demonstrations in the Georgian capital, Tbilisi, and the tragic pogroms against Armenians in Baku, Azerbaijan, had marked the beginning of new waves of discontent. The Soviet government was clearly incapable of controlling these events. Within a very brief period of time, the Baltics, the Ukraine, the Caucasian and Central Asian republics all declared their sovereignty, plucking the Soviet bird of many of its fine feathers. News of these events and their repercussions was disseminated the world over, shattering the image of the Soviet superpower.

The Israeli mission was acutely aware of this growing turmoil. As soon as the pogroms broke out in Baku, I got through to the heads of the Jewish community, deeply concerned about their relations with the authorities and the behaviour of the populace. However, we were reassured. Jewish-Azeri intercommunal relations remained excellent. There had always been an intermingling of cultures and peoples, which now created a protective cordon around the Jewish community in a difficult and dangerous period. At times, Jewish women or men were stopped by troublemakers in the city and asked if they were Armenian, but upon being shown the Star of David on amulets they wore, they were allowed to proceed unharmed. This was a surprising commentary on the Azeri Jews' position in Baku but a very sad one on that of the Armenians, who had also been part of the historical, social and cultural fabric of Baku, an international city for many generations.

Even if Jews were not molested, they felt threatened. Burgeoning Azerbaijani nationalism was followed by Muslim fundamentalism seeping in through the Iranian border, which had been left open as the result of the unsettled times. As the mission could not extend help right away to those who might be needing it if a further deterioration suddenly affected the Jews, it began making preparations for the possible evacuation of those who would make their way to Moscow. A growing stream of Jews from Baku began arriving at the mission, asking for the immediate processing of their papers. A strong contingent of Russian troops finally entered Baku and restored order, in the course of which three Jews were inadvertently killed. The Jewish population of Baku, however, began to decrease. Thousands left the city they had

221

lived in for many years only because of the potential dangers involved.

The deepening political and military crisis between Azerbaijan and Armenia left few prospects for an early resolution. The ethnic ferment in Uzbekistan and Tajikistan in Central Asia took on ugly forms of persecution of smaller minorities. Jews were not involved, but thousands nevertheless sought a way out, even at the expense of leaving behind their ancestral homes and extended families. In May 1990, there was a pogrom against the Jewish, Armenian and Russian quarter in the city of Andijan in Uzbekistan's Fergana Valley. The pogrom resulted from a rampage of disillusioned football fans. A Jewish woman was raped and some 15 houses were burned down. This abhorrent incident was not publicized, and the Ministries of the Interior and Foreign Affairs, which I contacted, feigned total ignorance. The whole Jewish community in Andijan, however, decided to move out as quickly as possible. There were additional outbreaks of violence, though not widespread, in Moldavia, Dagestan and elsewhere, which served to deepen the prevailing pessimism about the future of Jewish life in the Soviet Union.

In spite of the very heavy workload that mounted in this period of spring and summer 1990, the mission coped with its tasks rather well. Each new wave of frightened emigrants required that special arrangements and quick decisions be made, usually in connection with evacuation plans from Moscow and flights to neighbouring East European countries, from where emigrants were transported directly to Israel. The laboriously negotiated agreements on direct flights out of Moscow had been shelved. The Soviet government was immune to signs of urgency, and the bureaucratic work involved sometimes held people up for many weeks. The offices of OVIR in Moscow and the republics were overwhelmed with the large numbers of refugees from troubled zones.

The growing number of people requiring the mission's services amplified our logistical difficulties. I finally persuaded my ministry and Nativ to build a separate pavilion on the grounds to house the larger volume of emigration work, but the plan was difficult to carry out because of continued Soviet obstructionism. I requested Soviet permission to bring in more diplomats to help us. There were still only six of us, only three directly dealing with the thousands of emigrants who appeared daily at our gates. The Foreign Ministry would not accede to our request. It was not due to ill-will but to the fact that there was no possibility of getting clearance from the ministry's directorate, plagued by its own internal problems. Toward the end of the summer the ministry's attitude softened up, the pavilion was built and the pressure on our offices decreased.

GERMAN REUNIFICATION AND FEARS OF REVANCHISM

As the internal crisis steadily deepened within the country in the spring and summer of 1990, so did the frustration and helplessness of the military and security establishments. There was talk of the betrayal of the *gosudarstvo* (the Russian state), laboriously built over a thousand painful years. From contacts in the Central Committee I heard of accusations being levelled against Shevardnadze and Gorbachev, who had 'sold out' to the West, particularly to Germany. Shevardnadze was being called 'that Georgian traitor'. The generals were upset over Russia's being denuded of defences on its western approaches. Others were concerned over the fact that two élite Soviet armies would have to evacuate Germany and return to the Soviet Union, where they had no housing, no provisions for their families, and would soon find themselves unemployed. There was dark talk of the army's growing displeasure with the government. On the other hand, some generals and a part of the public were pinning their hopes on the large sums of money the Germans would inject into the Russian economy as compensation for the withdrawal from German soil.

At the same time, Germany's economic might was inspiring other fears. The unification of Germany appeared to threaten Russia's security. Middle-aged men recalled the lesson they taught Germany in the Second World War. I was once witness to these deeply ingrained fears at a dinner with a group of leading Israeli, Russian and German industrialists. After many toasts, a German, who had been speaking about plans to reactivate East German industry referred to the negative economic impact of the Soviet occupation. The Russian guest of honour, a former minister of heavy industry and a senior officer in the reserves, warned that Germans should beware of provocation. The Soviet Union, he said, would not tolerate attempts to take over Soviet industry, even if it were in temporary difficulties. 'Don't ever forget', he told the German, 'the Russians have enough weapons to destroy Germany with one single blow.' The German paled and said he must have been misunderstood, but the Russian repeated his threat. For additional emphasis, he said he knew very well who the Germans were. As Hitler's armies invaded Russia, his family had had to flee the border area where they lived. His mother piled what she could on a cart, hitched it to their horse and fled with his older brother and himself along the routes, crowded with refugees. Suddenly, a German Stuka fighter dived out of the sky and started strafing the refugees. People were killed and wounded all around them. His mother ran into a field, pulling her children after her. The field had no cover and the Stuka pilot came after them again and again until he ran out of ammunition. The Russian said he would never forget the rage he felt that day and he would never forgive the Germans. There were a number of Jews sitting around the table, he added. Millions of their relatives were slaughtered for no other reason than for being Jewish. The Germans would never be forgiven. If Germany dares once again to use its might, he said, 'We shall destroy it. Don't ever forget that.'

A year later, already in the position of consul-general, I was approached by General V. I. Filatov, the editor of the *Journal of Military History*, a vehicle for radically conservative views. The General told me that he believed Israel could be a very useful ally to the Soviet Union in helping project the dangers of German ambitions and revanchism. He showed me the manuscript he was preparing on this subject and said he wanted also to publish a book on Nazi atrocities which were still unknown to the general public. Filatov produced a sheaf of photographs to prove his point. One showed a two-metre high pyramid of guillotined heads, said to be those of Jews. I had never seen this sadistic spectacle before. When I reported this incident to friends in the Yad VaShem Holocaust Memorial in Jerusalem, I was told this photograph was well-known to specialists. But General Filatov's plans came to nought:

he was fired from his job soon after the August 1991 crisis for his support of militant communists and army ultras.

RELATIONS CONTINUE TO SEESAW

In this difficult period Israel must have been quite low in Soviet international priorities. The Kremlin wanted to avoid sudden changes in relationships with what they considered to be their remaining loyal friends, including the Arabs. Changing its course on Israel was considered untimely, and so the Politburo procrastinated. Yuri Vorontsov, who had the run of Middle Eastern affairs in the Foreign Ministry, was one of the proponents of this approach and provided the proper apologetics. Maestro Zubin Mehta, on a working visit to Moscow in the autumn of 1989, reported a typical Vorontsov line: 'The Israelis are deporting Arab villagers from the West Bank to Jordan', he had said, and settling Russian immigrants in their place. Mehta, an old and loyal friend of Israel, was shocked, and I had to reassure him it was not true. I thought Vorontsov, about to be appointed as the permanent Soviet representative to the UN, was trying to plant this false information on the disbelieving east coast élite through the permanent conductor of the New York Philharmonic. Vorontsov promised Mehta he would 'twist the arms of the Americans' to allow more Jews in, implying that the 40,000 immigrant US quota should be raised to diminish the number of Jews going to Israel. Vorontsov was thus contradicting what he had told Ambassador Sofer in Paris in 1985, regarding Soviet preferences that the Jews settle in Israel, rather than in the US.

The American Embassy in Moscow took issue with Vorontsov's claims on this subject, made in an interview to the *Moscow News* on 18 February 1990. The *Moscow News* correspondent had asked Vorontsov to substantiate his claim that the US had purposefully closed the immigration doors to Soviet Jews to direct the torrent of emigration to the occupied Arab territories. Vorontsov had replied that for many years the Soviets were being accused of restricting Jewish emigration. When the Soviets did lift the limitations, the US closed the immigration doors. The US deputy chief of mission,

John Joyce, wrote to the Moscow weekly (on 4 March) to point out that the US was granting an increasing number of visas to Soviet immigrants to the US, but with the changes brought about in the work of the US Consulate in Moscow, immigrants were being processed in the Soviet capital instead of in the western European capitals (Rome and Vienna). Ironically, Joyce continued, the Soviet deputy-minister of foreign affairs was complaining about the fact that the Jews were now emigrating to the country (Israel), for which the Russians had been issuing exit visas all along.

Vorontsov, an able and thoughtful official, was looking ahead to his move to New York. He had had a strong presence in the Ministry of Foreign Affairs, but after his return from Afghanistan, his relationship with Eduard Shevardnadze, never too friendly, deteriorated even further. Vorontsov was asked to concentrate his attention on his post of permanent representative at the UN in New York and stay put. His job as the overseer of Near and Middle Eastern affairs was taken over by Alexander Belonogov, a much milder and less authoritative person.

The departure of Vorontsov was soon followed by that of Tarasov, appointed chargé d'affaires in Saudi Arabia, with the opening of the new Soviet diplomatic mission in Riyadh. Still in the department among the visceral anti-Semites was Turdeev, who had on one occasion told me it was the Zionists themselves who had caused the bloody Kishinev pogroms at the turn of the century (presumably to attract world attention and gain political influence). To our relief, we did not have to meet with him ever again. With the appointment of Belonogov in May 1990, there seemed to be a change of heart as well as personnel. The arrogance of the Near Eastern department appreciably lessened. The new officials, Oleg Derkovsky, formerly counsellor on the Middle East at the Washington embassy, and Mikhail Bogdanov, transferred from Damascus, Syria, seemed to have been instructed to improve the department's image. This new policy facilitated the political dialogue.

The climate of Soviet-Israel relations began to improve again. The new signals emanating from the Near East department were that our requests for the improvement of day-to-day relations would soon be filled. Valentin Falin's Central Committee

International Department invited me in for a chat. This was important as this department had a highly influential position with the Politburo. Even Yuri Reshetov, chairman of the prestigious Human Rights Committee of the Foreign Ministry, finally condescended to meet me, although he had a pompous remark: 'I am receiving you even though I was advised otherwise, due to your lack of status'. But anyone legally residing in the USSR could ask to meet him, he added, so he was not risking anything. I reminded Reshetov of the humiliating treatment Jewish emigrants were still receiving. He assured me these wrongs would soon be put right by the new legislation being prepared in Parliament.

This turn for the better in relations accompanied the rapidly changing political scene. Russia was beginning to function as a new and independent republic, which it had not been under the Soviet regime. Yeltsin wanted to impress this fact on the minds of Russians. He emphasized it symbolically by returning to the pre-revolutionary double-headed eagle as a replacement for the communist hammer and sickle; and Alexis II, the head of the Russian Orthodox Church, officiated at Yeltsin's inauguration as president, to the stirring enthronement music from Glinka's opera *A Life for the Tsar*, probably the first performance on such an occasion.

Yeltsin's election in the summer of 1990 appeared to be, even then, a decisive turning point. In June, I cabled Jerusalem that Yeltsin's election was a historic event, likely to change the whole Soviet-Russian perspective within the year. This turned out to be close enough to the truth, for in less than 14 months' time, Yeltsin would not only help quell the rebellion against Gorbachev, but would supercede him as well.

The overall feeling in Moscow, however, was that of loss of self-confidence and perspective. A deep pessimism was beginning to grip the Soviet establishment. This was the feeling conveyed to me by sources close to Valery Boldin, Gorbachev's chief of staff. The Gorbachev administration was powerless to fight the growing irredentist tendencies in the republics. The need to make painful decisions to limit the damage was heading toward a consensus. Unexpectedly, the Soviet government seemed resigned to cede independence to the Baltic states and to the Caucasian republics.

Strategically, they were considered expendable and did not justify the effort needed to maintain them within the Union. The Central Asian republics, on the other hand, were seen as too enmeshed economically to break away. This was the assessment of several specialists at the time, including Alexander Galkin, the co-rector of the Central Committee's Social and Economic Research Institute. Arkady Volsky, chairman of the Entrepreneurs and Scientists Union, formerly of the Central Committee and a close Gorbachev adviser, was worried about the rapid decrease in industrial production. He told me it would decrease by 40 per cent in a year's time, an indicator of catastrophic economic failure.

Professor Seweryn Bialer of Columbia University, a widely respected specialist on the Soviet economy, disputed Volsky's figures but not their overall significance. On a visit to Moscow, he told me that the Soviet economists were confused and the government was maladroit and bungling. Professor Marshall Shulman, the renowned scholar from Columbia University, whom I also met in Moscow, expressed his doubts that the Soviet state could survive intact with such large-scale economic and organizational mismanagement.

APPEALS TO ISRAEL

The continued deterioration of the Soviet economy brought cumbersome and unwieldy attempts to obtain large credits for the purchase of food abroad and to relieve monetary pressures. There was a great casting about for possible sources of immediate aid. One of the initiatives taken by President Gorbachev's office was again to seek the support of Jewish financiers. In this respect, it was thought Israel could be of significant help. An informal five-man committee, formed from among presidential advisers to seek urgent international aid, was asked to tend to the Jewish-Israeli angle as well. Its members were Yuri Osipyan, an outstanding physicist well known in Israeli scientific circles, Stepan Sitaryan, an economist and deputy to Prime Minister Nikolai Ryzhkov, Arkady Volsky, Yevgeny Velikhov and Igor Malkevich, president of the All-Soviet Chambers of Commerce. By force of circumstance, this group became a reference point for Soviet-Israeli relations. It considered the co-production of a Soviet-US-Israeli airliner and other key projects.

This select committee operated under the December 1989 directives of the Politburo, which had set out parameters for relations with Israel. The far-reaching developments which had occurred since, did not seem to have substantially broadened the scope of the Politburo's decisions. Malkevich was permitted to develop an initiative of his own in line with the chambers of commerce. Danny Gillerman, president of the United Israeli Chambers of Commerce was invited to Moscow. The visit took place in January 1990. Gillerman was accompanied by Moshe Sanbar, chairman of the Leumi Bank Corporation, and Yaacov Cohen, the Israel Foreign Ministry's assistant director-general for economic relations. At the end of a two-day visit, Malkevich declared that justice had been done in signing the protocol of cooperation reached between the parties. It was seen to be an important step ahead in relations. Several months later, Malkevich returned Gillerman's visit. In Israel he met with Finance Minister Yitzhak Moda'i, whom he invited to Moscow. Moda'i agreed, on condition he would meet with Gorbachev. Upon Malkevich's return to Moscow, he consulted with Yakovlev, Volsky and Osipyan, as well as with Ivan Petrakov, a close Gorbachev economics adviser. Petrakov warmly recommended the meeting. An invitation was forwarded to Moda'i, but the timing of his visit was to be decided at the very last minute.

At this point, Moda'i was approached by Ilya Zemtsov, who had heard about the invitation, but wanted to appear to have pulled off the arrangements all on his own. He got himself an assignment to Moscow by Science Minister Yuval Ne'eman, whose ministry was providing the budget for Zemtsov's Sociological Institute in Jerusalem. Zemtsov arrived in Moscow 'on behalf of the government of Israel', and asked the Academy of Sciences to arrange a meeting with Gorbachev for Moda'i and Ne'eman. The Russians did not ask any questions and promised to help, which must not have been difficult as the decision had already been taken on Malkevich's initiative. Zemtsov came to see me but did not report on his activities. The first intimation of the coming meeting

the evening before Moda'i's arrival, when his office
of his expected meeting with the Soviet president. I
n a little taken aback, but went down to the airport
next day to receive the ministers. Igor Malkevich, the president
of the Academy of Sciences, Guri Marchuk, and a number of others
were at the airport.

Zemtsov made sure I was excluded. Cherniaev, Volsky and
Malkevich later told me that Zemtsov had presented himself as an
Israeli government representative and had stipulated that only he
and the two ministers should be present. When Moda'i weakly
insisted I should accompany the group as the official representative
of Israel in Moscow, Zemtsov told Ne'eman that if the ministers
refused 'the conditions laid down by Gorbachev', they would be
asked to leave the USSR right away. They were cowed into
obeying.

The meeting with the Soviet leader was relaxed and friendly,
but the Israelis did not quite realize its implications. No minutes
were taken at this unprecedented interview, the first ever between
the Soviet leader and Israeli ministers. This was of course a serious
mistake, as it later turned out. When the two ministers emerged
from that meeting, each of them had a different version of what had
transpired, and they had difficulty tallying their reports. Both
agreed, however, that the only subject on the Soviet leader's mind
seemed to be the abject state of Soviet finances and the looming
food shortages. He talked at length about the USSR's difficulties.
Moda'i asked when he would renew diplomatic relations, and he
replied that there was no fundamental problem but that the time
was not yet ripe for it. Relations would have to be reached step by
step. Gorbachev then got to the heart of the matter, for which he
had consented to receive Israel's minister of finance.

Gorbachev and at least some of his advisers were convinced that
Moda'i held the reins of international finances in his hands. This
impressionistic view of Israel and its relationship with the world of
Jewish financiers was confirmed every time Maxwell, Hammer,
Reichman, Bronfman and others appeared in Moscow. Did they not
repeatedly inquire about cultural freedom for the Jews and
diplomatic relations for Israel? Was not the world of finances
controlled by the Jews? Were not the world press, the

230

entertainment industry, science and other centres of international power all controlled by the Jews? The corollary was that Israel's finance minister was an exceptionally influential man. If the USSR did not receive urgent aid of 50 billion dollars in the next six months, Gorbachev announced, the country's economy would collapse. To which he added: 'I know Israel is limited in its resources, but I am sure it could help us in getting at least ten billion dollars.' Moda'i, an extremely intelligent man, must have been aware of the implications of this postulation, but he was not sufficiently briefed to respond in the categorical terms required. Moda'i's reaction did not relate to the enormity of Gorbachev's ignorance and naïveté: while he should have stated in no uncertain terms that Israel was incapable of procuring such large sums of money, he left the impression that he would try his best. Gorbachev and his advisers came away confident that help was on its way — including the purchase of fruit and vegetables from Israel for hungry Russia, bankrolled with the help of Israeli ministers who were interested in the export of agricultural produce.

Following Moda'i's visit I started getting requests from various agencies in Moscow for finalization of credits for the promised supplies. Gavril Popov, the mayor of Moscow, and Gennady Kulik, the minister of agriculture of Russia, called me to discuss the arrangements for the supply of fruit and vegetables. My requests for clarifications from Jerusalem went unanswered. Moda'i's additional meetings with Soviet officials the day after his meeting with the president, produced similar misunderstandings and added grist to the mill of accusations against Israel for 'not keeping its word'.

Additional proof of the misconceptions that arose in high places were two conversations I had in October, a month after the conclusion of Moda'i's precipitous visit. The first was with Professor Yuri Osipyan, who insisted that the Kremlin protocol of Gorbachev's meeting with the Israeli finance minister recorded an undertaking by Israel to provide a monthly 35 million dollar credit to cover the purchase of food for Russia. At the same time, Shaul Eisenberg, the Israeli financier, was negotiating an 800 million to one-billion dollar loan to the USSR. Osipyan inquired whether, perhaps, Eisenberg could use this money to finance the food purchase. The Ministry of Foreign Affairs in Jerusalem could supply neither explanations, nor instructions on how to meet the barrage of demands and criticism I was facing. Finally, I appealed to Moda'i, whereupon he strongly denied that he had made any promises to Gorbachev.

At that time, Valentin Pavlov was the Soviet minister of finance. In his memoirs *Has the Opportunity Been* Missed?*, in the context of what he calls the 'super-secret financial underground of international affairs', Pavlov says he was not at all surprised that one of the first Israeli political leaders to visit the USSR on an unofficial visit was the minister of finance. His main interest in his meeting with Moda'i in Moscow was to get the latter's promise to help the USSR regulate its relations with private European and world banks. Pavlov goes on to describe his visit to Robert Maxwell in Luxembourg, for the same purpose. He says he chose to negotiate with Jewish magnates (of whom he considered Moda'i to be one) because of the high regard he had for their ability to influence international financial circles.

The Gorbachev-Moda'i talks were discussed again in a meeting I had with Arkady Volsky. He described the fears of famine in the approaching winter and added that the USSR needed urgent financial aid for the purchase of foodstuffs for its population. The USSR's leaders knew Israel had no money of its own, but they felt Israel could assist in the provision of the credits. They were expecting a show of goodwill and would I please try to persuade Shaul Eisenberg, Edgar Bronfman and Albert Reichman to get together and organize a fund to help rescue the situation over the next two to three years. The Soviet people would be forever grateful.

The most incredible aspect of this affair was the absolute, mutual misreading of abilities and expectations. There was an absence of preparation in Israel. In the light of the importance of our relations with the Soviet Union, it must have been self-evident that a meeting at this level should not be carried out haphazardly.

---

* See excerpt in 'Tainaia diplomatiia finansistov' (The Secret Diplomacy of Financiers), *Rossiiskaia gazeta*, 8 Oct. 1994.

The laborious arrangements that went into the projected Peres visit to Moscow could have served as an example of the preliminary steps which needed to be taken. Yet Shimon Peres, too, went to Moscow as minister of finance with a basic misconception about the workings of the Soviet mind. In many ways, Peres's declarations of intent, his projected arrival with a retinue of top financiers, Israelis and others, conditioned the Soviets to expect miracles from Moda'i. Likewise, it was difficult to understand the confusion of the Russians. Lack of rudimentary intelligence information on Israel, on its real financial position in the world, was demonstrated by the abysmal ignorance of officials, whose duty it was to brief their leader before the meeting with the Israeli ministers. The blame must be apportioned partly to the brokers who acted to bring this meeting about, but who did not show great concern beyond their ambition to be recognized and applauded for the results. The Israeli press went overboard on the subject of the Gorbachev-Moda'i meeting. Ilya Zemtsov was said to have 'delivered the goods', but it was not clear what had been delivered to whom.

One way or another, the Kremlin was preparing to renew its relations with the tiny country whose help it was seeking. After the many hints and whispers I had been hearing toward the end of summer, Yuri Osipyan told me sometime after the Moda'i visit that relations were soon going to be re-established — but not yet at embassy level, only consulates-general in both countries. The Politburo just could not dare to take that step.

18 · For Purely
Humanitarian Reasons

On my first furlough home from Moscow at the end of 1988 I came across an advertisement: a concert was being given by Yosif Kobzon, the popular Soviet singer at the main Tel Aviv concert hall, the Heichal Hatarbut. I was intrigued: guest artists from the Soviet Union were not an everyday occurrence in those days and they certainly did not appear before large audiences. I decided to see for myself. Kobzon was a big man with a warm voice and a professional glitter. He appeared with his own orchestra and had a repertoire of old Soviet favourites, some dating from the Second World War, when this music was carried all over Eastern Europe by the Red Army. These songs were widely sung in Israel, in Hebrew translation, and became the backbone of Israel's musical tradition. Kobzon directed his performance at the émigrés who had left in the 1970s. Representatives of the more recent wave of immigrants, who were beginning to filter through to Israel, were in the hall as well. The audience loved him.

I went backstage to get acquainted. Kobzon was very friendly and invited me to come to hear him in Moscow. I did not see the singer, however, until one morning in the spring of 1989 when he called on me at my Ukraina Hotel suite. Kobzon had asked me for an appointment on a 'very important matter' and I felt unable to cancel, in spite of the fact that I had a bad case of food poisoning and was certain I was about to die. When Kobzon saw the state I was in, he offered to send for an ambulance to take me to the

1. An official portrait taken by the Russian Foreign Ministry photographer, for the record

2. Waiting in line at the Israeli mission, May 1990 *(photo by Doron Bacher, courtesy of Beth HaTefutsoth Photo Archive)*

3. With Mikhail Gorbachev and
   David Levy during Levy's
   visit to Moscow

4. With Foreign Minister Andrei
   Kozyrev

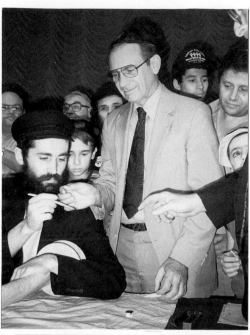

5. Signing a Torah scroll

6. *Below:* In the Moscow synagogue

7. *Opposite:* With a Jewish activist in Leningrad

8. With Ezer Weizmann
in St. Petersburg

9. With Maestro Zubin
Mehta during the
Russian tour of the
Israel Philharmonic

10. Reception for Israeli Transportation Minister Moshe Katsav (front row, second from right); Levin in conversation with Russian Civil Aviation Minister Boris Paniukov

11. First meeting with Foreign Minister Eduard Shevardnadze

12. Arrival of Foreign Minister Boris Pankin at Ben Gurion airport *(photo – Dan Nataf)*
13. *Opposite top:* Affixing the Israeli Embassy plaque after a 24 year hiatus
14. *Opposite bottom:* Meeting with President Boris Yeltsin

15. Official photo of the Israeli embassy staff at the presentation of credentials; from right to left, Garry Koren, Avi Idan, Yossi Bendor, Israel Mey-Ami; Director of the Russian Foreign Ministry's Near East and North Africa Department, Vassily Kolotusha (third from left)

16. With Prime Minister Rabin and Russian Vice-President Alexander
Rutskoi (opposite) at Labour Party Headquarters *(photo – Dan Nataf)*

17. Press conference with Shimon Peres; Yossi Bendor (right) *(photo – Scoop 80)*

18. With Soviet Ambassador to Israel, Alexander Bovin (right) and head of the Parliamentary Foreign Affairs and Economics Committee, Vladimir Lukin (centre)

19. Seeing Gorbachev off on his visit to Israel

20. Shimon Peres searches for the graves of family members in Belorus *(photo – Scoop 80)*

21. At Babi Yar

22. Standing before the statue of Felix Dzerzhinsky, founder of the Cheka, removed to a public park after it was toppled by angry demonstrators

23. *Below:* Aryeh and Aliza Levin at Izmailovsky market in Moscow
24. *Opposite:* At Novodevichii Monastery

25. Aliza and Aryeh Levin with the Armenian Patriach in Echmiadzin

26. On a visit to Tbilisi

hospital. I declined. A hospital was no place for an Israeli 'unofficial' diplomat. We were sternly warned against going to hospitals in Russia by our vigilant security services, very knowledgeable about Soviet methods of extracting information. Pale and trembling, I motioned the singer to a seat.

Kobzon told me of his very close friend, who had emigrated to Israel a number of years before, had had an extremely successful business career and become very wealthy, but 'had run into difficulties with Israeli security'. Kobzon added that it must have all been a very great misunderstanding. His friend was in reality a great Israeli patriot and had done a great deal for the country. Kobzon said he could vouch for him and wanted very much to arrange for his release, for 'purely humanitarian reasons', as his friend was very ill and could not get the proper medical treatment in prison.

As soon as Kobzon's story began unfolding, I knew whose name would emerge. Shabtai Kalmanovich had been very prominent in economic and social circles in Israel, knew almost everybody and had his finger in many pies. He had risen meteorically from the status of an ordinary immigrant, who arrived in Israel in the early 1970s, to that of a leading businessman. The discovery of his real profession came as no small surprise to his many friends. He was so gentle and kind, volunteered for good causes, was always ready to lend a helping hand. Together with his wife Nellie, they held open house in Savyon, the poshest Tel Aviv suburb. No run-of-the mill spy for the USSR, Shabtai showed great resourcefulness and imagination, but was apprehended, tried and sentenced to nine years. He was in the second year of his jail term when Kobzon came to see me. I told my visitor I doubted very much we would release this person because of the nature of his crime, but that I would pass this request on to appropriate officials.

There was no cipher and virtually no communications with Jerusalem, and so, several weeks later I still had no reply from home. The Russians, however, were impatient. I was called to an urgent and very important meeting with a certain Luzinovich, the head of OVIR services in Moscow, who was accompanied by Ivan Pogrebnoy, the deputy of the Foreign Ministry's consular department, officially in charge of relations with the Israeli mission. At first I thought this would be a genuine consular matter and I took along Maya Gal, my assistant in Moscow at the time, who was a professional and very able consular worker.

After a few introductory remarks, Luzinovich said his office had been getting many hundreds of letters from Israel and from all over the Soviet Union, protesting the inhuman treatment our government was giving Shabtai Kalmanovich, a Soviet citizen in Israel, unjustly condemned to a prison sentence. Luzinovich added, in what appeared to be a veiled threat, that prospective immigrants who were coming to the OVIR offices were indignantly complaining about Israeli violations of basic human rights and asking the OVIR offices to forward all their written complaints to the Israeli Mission in Moscow, to show how strongly Soviet society felt about these violations. He offered to transmit these 'vast' amounts of mail to me, so I could judge for myself. He thought I could surely find a solution. I told Luzinovich he could keep the letters as a souvenir, that Kalmanovich had been convicted for spying (had he not heard?), and would be released only at the end of his term. Whereupon Luzinovich asked me to pass on the request that Kalmanovich be released for humanitarian reasons, because of the medical problems involved. I told Luzinovich that my enquiries had shown Kalmanovich was getting the best medical treatment available but that, certainly, I would transmit his request.

Undercover Soviet activity in Israel had always been fairly extensive, and spying was not unknown. There were several abortive attempts to recruit our Moscow diplomats. The late Yosef Tekoa, one of our last ambassadors to the USSR before the rupture of relations in 1967, related to me on a visit to Moscow how the KGB had planted an attractive maid in his household. Her task was to seduce the ambassador and, having compromised him, force him to cooperate. Tekoa was not all that gullible, however. Suspecting the fly in the ointment, he asked his family to be extremely outgoing and kind to the maid. At some point the maid broke down and revealed the nature of her assignment, at great risk to herself. A day or two before his final departure from the Soviet Union, Tekoa said, he threw open the large window of his apartment on the third floor, and in full view, passionately kissed the maid. He knew that the large building across the street had a KGB observation post constantly watching his residence. After the kissing was over, Tekoa thumbed his nose at the KGB post and although there was no response from the other side, he knew the little demonstration must have been noticed.

There were other cases, less amusing, of attempted infiltration into the embassy. In the summer of 1965, after we had just moved into our new building on Bolshaia Ordynka Street, a thorough inspection by our security revealed the building to have been set up and fine-tuned for eavesdropping by the KGB. The parquet floor in the ambassador's office had a well camouflaged opening into a passageway underneath, which led to the adjacent building. The trap door could be easily lifted, allowing entry from the tunnel, along which ran a thick cable. Listening devices were discovered in the garden of the embassy as well. As the tunnel had a steel door at the point where the territory of the embassy crossed that of the red KGB building, our security barred the door to prevent further entry. This precaution was immediately discovered by the KGB and the tunnel was flooded. David Bartov, the chargé d'affaires of our embassy, was called by the municipal services and told a pipe had burst and workers had to come in to urgently repair the damage. Since the embassy was considered to be Israeli territory, entrance was not allowed. In the diplomatic tussle that ensued we offered to withhold publicity about their antics on condition that the Soviets refrain from further intrusion and harassment. They accepted, and after a crew came down and blocked the tunnel with concrete, the incident was considered closed .

The neighbouring red building of the KGB seemed to be empty before we moved into the embassy in June 1989. As soon as we were back, the building sprang to life and I was certain the KGB was again attempting to reanimate its listening devices, although in the daily mêlée on the embassy grounds, with thousands of people constantly on the move, it was probably not an easy task. In fact, we had no secrets from the Russians, and as our telephones were constantly in use, a tremendous amount of information on our activities probably engulfed the KGB eavesdroppers.

One afternoon, as I was showing Radomir Bogdanov out of my embassy apartment, I brought his attention to the KGB building next door, with all its protruding electronic devices. I said it was difficult to understand what all this listening activity could be worth. After all, a whole regiment of specialists had to be working, listening, registering, translating, summarizing and transmitting material that ought to be quite worthless to the KGB. Was all the effort and expense really necessary? Bogdanov thought a while, looked at me and said: 'Aryeh, inertia, inertia'. What he really meant was that the KGB was probably well aware of the dispensability of that operation, but could not simply discharge the crews involved, for fear of unemployment in the ranks of the agency. In fact, the problem of millions of people possibly being thrown out of work in Russia's passage to a market economy was on everyone's mind. Even so, intelligence work against Israel, as against other countries, probably never stopped, even if the KGB was cosmetically reorganizing to appear less sinister. The persistent effort to free one of their agents in Israel is proof of the continuity of the agency's life and traditions.

Kalmanovich's handlers maintained their pressure on the Israeli government in Jerusalem. Kobzon's great loyalty to 'his friend' was as remarkable as his unflagging persistence. I greatly admired Kobzon's ability to recruit the support of many influential personalities in Moscow. He had been the favourite singer of the top Soviet bureaucracy for many years — ever since the prosperous and pleasant *nomenklatura* days of Leonid Brezhnev, the secretary-general of the party, who held unflurried permanence to be the highest achievement of his regime. As the fortunes of the Soviet Union waned, Kobzon maintained and providentially widened his close connections with Soviet politicians and personalities. His many appearances before the Soviet fighting forces in Afghanistan, when few other entertainers ventured into those dangerous areas, added to his popularity in the defence establishment.

Kobzon was elected a member of Parliament in 1989 and used his position to arrange meetings with top Israeli politicians, to plead for the release of his friend Kalmanovich. Kobzon met several ministers, including Roni Milo, the then minister of police, and Dan Meridor, the minister of justice. Even Yitzhak Shamir was approached to free the Soviet spy, for purely humanitarian reasons. All we were asked for was Kalmanovich's release from prison, so he could get proper treatment. He would be prepared to remain at his home and report to the police twice a day. The Israeli security services were not forthcoming. I personally spoke to Yitzhak Shamir several times and asked for a straight yes or no answer. The prime minister, a veteran of the Mossad, was hardly a man to encourage Soviet spies. It did not seem likely that he would pressure the internal security agency for the release of Shabtai Kalmanovich.

Kobzon employed several lawyers, who all pleaded for leniency on medical grounds. Kalmanovich had circulatory problems in his legs and his friends were warning us that there was a threat of amputation. In the meantime, the spy's wife gave up on her husband and obtained a divorce. It turned out that Kalmanovich had been leading a life of leisure in prison. He had been receiving visits from female friends and getting special food rations, even though Kobzon always told me that his meetings with Kalmanovich greatly upset him because of the state he found him in.

Kobzon's explanation of his special interest was that the two wives, Shabtai's and his, had been very close friends and that when Kalmanovich became wealthy he never missed a single Kobzon concert, wherever it took place. Kobzon repeatedly told me that the KGB had absolutely no more interest in Kalmanovich. I was quite surprised when I was approached on that subject by none other than Arkady Volsky. He essentially told me the same sad story. Emphatically nodding in the direction of the KGB building, he said: 'They have absolutely no interest in Kalmanovich and don't care what happens to him.' I was even more tantalized when, on another occasion, Volsky told me that Yevgeny Primakov, now on Gorbachev's Security Council team, would be pleased to maintain a regular dialogue with me, 'beginning next week', and would discuss direct flights to Israel. Volsky added that Primakov was also requesting my help in releasing Kalmanovich, for purely humanitarian reasons.

This sustained attack never let up. After I had already become consul-general and the Russians were still dragging their feet on diplomatic relations, I obtained an interview with the new Russian vice-president, Alexander Rutskoi. When I arrived in Rutskoi's office, I found Kobzon sitting in on the meeting. In the long conversation about the future of relations and the possibilities of economic cooperation, Rutskoi said full diplomatic relations would be restored if Kalmanovich were released. Prior to the meeting with Rutskoi I had seen the then chairman of the foreign and security affairs committee of the Knesset, Eli Ben-Elissar, in Jerusalem, and talked to him about the limpet-like Russian insistence on Kalmanovich's release. I told him of the prime minister's unwillingness to override the security services and asked Ben-Elissar if he would consider talking to the prime minister about this. Ben-Elissar said he would get the man released if the Russians renewed relations. Without naming Ben-Elissar, I told Rutskoi I had an important personality's promise that we would release Shabtai if relations were restored.

Full diplomatic relations between Russia and Israel were in fact restored shortly afterwards, but the Israeli authorities still refused to release Kalmanovich. Ben-Elissar could not deliver on his promise, which put me in an unpleasant position with the vice-president. Kobzon's lawyers tried smearing me, for 'making false promises'. It did not help them. Up to the end of his term, Shamir did not want to overrule the security services and Kalmanovich stayed put in his cell. Only after the 1992 elections and the ascendancy of Yitzhak Rabin as prime minister was Kalmanovich paroled, following many additional appeals. Rabin stipulated, however, that the Soviet spy never return to the country he had betrayed.

At the time of writing, Shabtai Kalmanovich was living prosperously in Russia, doing a roaring business with his friend Kobzon and the rest of the old boys' network, left over from the happy days of the communist regime. In a far-ranging interview granted to the Israeli paper *Yediot Aharonot*, he was shown in a large photograph, a well-groomed and self-assertive man of the world, staring confidently into the future with attentive, cold and calculating eyes. As he has gone into entertainment and sports, among other fields of honest endeavour, he organized a very plush reception for the Israeli national basketball team when they played in Moscow in February 1995.

The closely-knit group of former Central Committee, government, party and large industrial enterprise officials were not left homeless after the collapse of the Soviet Union. With salutary foresight, they acted vigorously to ensure that the vast properties belonging to the old establishment would be privatized, at least in part, under the control of the influential and privileged few who had banded together to protect their mutual interests. Shabtai Kalmanovich numbers among this group of intelligent survivors. Kobzon, although he still astonishes his audiences with the length and breadth of his repertoire of old favourites, is blossoming as a successful businessman and toting up more mileage in his business travels than in his concert tours. He always told me that he would have to think of his future when his voice started failing him, but he seems to have kept his timbre as well as developed his business acumen, for which he must be congratulated. At the end of 1994 Kobzon became the business adviser to Moscow mayor Yuri Luzhkov and still remains a good and loyal friend to his old pals. All for purely humanitarian reasons.

19 · *We Raise the Flag*

A NEW GOVERNMENT, A NEW MINISTER

The Likud Party formed a new government in Israel in the summer of 1990. The new minister of foreign affairs was David Levy, a politician who was a complete stranger to the field, but whose strong position in Israel's internal politics allowed him a considerable margin of manoeuvre, even if his ideas did not always tally with those of Prime Minister Shamir. This was a new experience for the ministry, up to then led by chiefs with a wide knowledge of the outside world, though not always familiar with practical diplomacy. We all felt uneasy, wondering who the man behind the pompous politician really was and how he would function as minister of foreign affairs.

I was in Jerusalem when David Levy held his first meeting with the ministry's political directorate. He was recuperating from a heart attack. We were pleasantly surprised to hear of his determination to get the peace process moving ahead as quickly as possible. He wanted our suggestions for concrete initiatives but held us to the strictest secrecy. He did not want to reveal his hand, and preferred the ministry to remain in the shadows and leave centre stage for him. Levy was more positive and forward-looking than some of his colleagues in the cabinet but wary of compromising himself in his rightist milieu by unseemly moderation toward the Arabs. As he lacked the political support to become prime minister, he wanted to make a name for himself as a mover and shaker, at least in foreign affairs. In his two years in the ministry Levy gave sufficient proof, not only of his genuine interest in hastening the peace process, but also of basic common sense — a welcome trait in any politician.

David Levy was inaccessible to the ministry's officials and left the running of his bureau to a former journalist, Uri Oren, who attempted to ride the Foreign Ministry rough-shod, with questionable results. At the same time, Levy's lack of English (he is French-speaking) and inexperience in contacts with the Americans made him overly dependent on the advice of the ministry's North American department. I discovered Levy had almost no interest in the Soviet Union or Eastern Europe, beyond accepting the hard and fast principle that Israel ought to maintain the rhythm of Soviet emigration and strive for the renewal of diplomatic relations. He made it painfully clear that he could not be bothered with the administration of his ministry or its diplomatic work. Insofar as I was concerned, this defensive attitude of the minister created an additional and superfluous obstacle in my work. The two ministers who preceded David Levy had been personally involved in the whole complex of questions dealing with the Soviet Union. Levy was not. I had great difficulty in getting a hearing. Levy had no time for my colleagues in the East European department either, and the subject was orphaned. Uri Oren would not let anyone near the minister, demanding to be fully briefed but hogging the information for himself. He insisted on being present at all private meetings with David Levy, which later strengthened his position as sole arbiter of requests for the minister's time. Nevertheless, on questions that I found to be vital, I did get through to Levy and his decisions were swift, logical and supportive.

Levy's appearance at the ministry was propitious for him on the Soviet front. The Politburo was running out of steam in its stubborn opposition to renewing ties with Israel. I had got word from the Soviets that our 'unofficial' mission in Moscow was about to be elevated to a consulate-general. The Arabists were still too powerful and I fully expected more waiting was in the works before we would become a full-fledged embassy. Nevertheless, this change of status could also be presented as a positive development and be attributed to the new Israeli minister's personal powers of persuasion.

Levy's arrival in New York for the General Assembly meeting of

September 1990 would thus be crowned with much welcome success for the Moscow mission and positive exposure for him. After I got through Uri Oren's defensive perimeter around the minister in his suite at the hotel, I imparted to him the ideas I thought he would find useful to discuss with Eduard Shevardnadze, who would be getting acquainted with his third Israeli foreign minister in as many years. When the meeting did materialize, it was held in the chambers of the president of the Security Council and was attended by Yuri Vorontsov, the Soviet UN permanent representative, and Vladimir Petrovsky, a deputy foreign minister, well-known for his liberal views. Gennady Tarasov was also there, prepared as always to marshal his negative opinions. Another member of the delegation was the talented and agreeable Vitaly Churkin, who, after the fall of the USSR, climbed the ladder of the newly formed Russian ministry unimpeded, unlike some of his colleagues. He made a swift career, becoming, in rapid succession, spokesman of the Foreign Ministry, the special Russian envoy to Bosnia and ambassador to Belgium.

When we were preparing to sit down for the meeting with Shevardnadze, I was approached by Tarasov. Would I translate for them? David Levy did not speak English or Russian. The Soviets were forewarned but could not provide a suitable translator. Ordinarily, they were very strict on such matters and made a point of having their own translator for every language in meetings of state importance. This time they seemed to relent, in view of the unavailability of a Soviet Hebrew speaker.

David Levy and Eduard Shevardnadze, both warm-hearted and full-blooded politicians, seemed to hit it off from the start. Levy said he hoped their strong handshake symbolized the future warm relationship between the two countries. He had listened to Shevardnadze's speech at the General Assembly and found it of importance to the whole of mankind. The road the USSR had recently adopted would have tremendous repercussions. The USSR's position now made international blackmail in the wake of Saddam's invasion of Kuwait impossible. 'The developments in the USSR could not have been foreseen by any professor.' The USSR's daring decisions had changed Europe and the world. Israel wished it success. Every birth is painful, yet a great event in itself. To all of which Shevardnadze replied that, yes, indeed, he had trouble recognizing his own people, a new and different nation, which, as a result of recent transformations, had reached a higher plane. A complex and painful metamorphosis, but there were no inner doubts. Levy chimed in here, saying his hopes for the USSR were very great. The Soviets were represented in Israel not only by their mission but by all the Russian Jews, who had 'tremendous influence in every field'. Levy added he had many Georgian friends (Shevardnadze is Georgian), they were all as plain-speaking as the rest of the Israelis, and he, Levy, wanted to talk to Shevardnadze like the Georgians themselves, as directly as he could. The existing state of relations was anachronistic. There was no point developing relations step by step. Everybody was renewing relations with everyone else, even the Americans with the Vietnamese. There had been no quarrel between Israel and the USSR, but while the USSR, a great power, appeared to be punishing Israel, its behaviour inspired Israel's neighbours to follow suit. The time had come to do away with the anomaly and establish diplomatic relations.

Shevardnadze said he agreed in principle, but that the USSR carried the burden of its inheritance. He, Shevardnadze, firmly believed relations had to be maintained with all nations. However, the need to pass the required stages was unavoidable. He remembered the difficulties he had had (with the Politburo) even in meeting Shimon Peres, but these problems had been overcome. He proposed to take an additional forward step and declare the opening of the consulate-general, 'to be followed by a discussion of the Gulf crisis'. Shevardnadze then added that Iraq must be shorn of its weapons of mass destruction, indirectly implying that questions pertaining to the Middle East should involve a discussion of unconventional weapons. What Shevardnadze really had in mind were Israel's long-range missile and nuclear capabilities.

The Soviet minister also broached the long-standing difficulty of direct flights to Israel from Moscow. He said 'tens of thousands of people' were pressuring the USSR government to take a positive decision on the subject. President Gorbachev first wanted assurances from Israel that Soviet citizens would not be settled in the occupied territories, as this would surely cause an 'explosion' among the Arabs. Levy surprised us all at this juncture, by saying that if the USSR wanted such a declaration, he was giving it right then and there, and that it was quotable. However, no Israeli government would dare prevent its citizens from settling wherever they wished. Shevardnadze retorted that he was taking due notice of Levy's declaration and would bring it up in Moscow.

The conversation went on for an hour and a half, ending with the adoption of a joint statement, drafted by the Soviets, that said the USSR and the State of Israel, in order to facilitate the solution of humanitarian issues and to assist in the development of mutually beneficial contacts between them, had reached on 30 September 1990, an agreement to reorganize the consular groups of the ministries of foreign affairs of both countries, respectively in Moscow and Tel Aviv, into official consulates-general. The decision would be carried out immediately.

The two ministers came out to an impromptu joint press conference. Shevardnadze seemed to have a somewhat pained expression. Levy was beaming, as he talked to the newsmen who crowded around us. He spoke of the great friendship and understanding achieved with his colleague. Shevardnadze grimaced, as he strained to hear the translation.

The announcement of the opening of consulates disappointed a great many people, who were hoping for more, but had to be satisfied with less. For me, a long and arduous journey seemed to be coming to an end. The journalists huddled around me, asking for my plans. I said I was off to Moscow to raise the flag. This long-awaited act, however, took longer than I thought to materialize. I took the first available direct flight back to Moscow and started to prepare the transformation of our mission into the long-awaited diplomatic representation. The Politburo's decision not to open embassies appeared to be more in the nature of discomfort in owning up to the stupidity of severing relations in 1967. Whatever the reason, our many friends in Moscow greeted the announce-ment with relief. Our official status improved even before we put out the consular shingle on our gates. I was being greeted as consul-general before I received the so-called exequator from the host government, empowering a consul-general to fulfil his duties.

In any case, our unofficial position and our popularity had already given us many of the entrées we needed in the Soviet capital.

A consulate-general has its own proper status under the Vienna Convention governing consular and diplomatic relations between nations. There is little difference of substance between consular and diplomatic missions. This was especially true of the Israeli and the Soviet consulates-general about to be set up. But there was no other example of a consular establishment independent of an embassy in the Soviet capital, all consular work being carried out as part of a diplomatic mission. The Soviets had not overlooked this detail, but a consulate seemed less of a shocking change than an embassy to the sclerotic members of the Politburo and the Central Committee. The Soviet Ministry of Foreign Affairs was hard put to make special arrangements for us as a separate and independent consular entity and the procedure dragged on for many months; all of which did not prevent me from renewing my demands to increase our six-man team in order to ease the heavy immigration and political work we were doing. Up to that time, the Soviets had been uncompromising in this regard, but they now changed their position. Soon, additional Israeli diplomats began arriving, in expectation of the opening of the consulate-general.

THE FATE OF WALLENBERG

Just as my duties included an interest in the life and fate of Jews in the Soviet Union, it also encompassed people who had helped Jews. One such person who assisted Jews under Nazi occupation in Hungary had got caught up in the intricacies of the Soviet machine. His name was Raoul Wallenberg, a man whose courage and dedication saved many thousands of Jewish lives. In October 1990, my attention was again attracted to the mysterious disappearance of Raoul Wallenberg. He had been taken by Lavrenty Beria's NKVD* people and disappeared from sight following the Second World War.

---

* People's Commissariat for Internal Affairs; a precursor of the KGB

On an evening at the 'Central House of Cinema' I attended the showing of a film on the life of the Swedish diplomat. The Soviet government maintained that Wallenberg had died of a heart attack, but reports of prisoners meeting him, which persisted for years after the war, reawakened hopes that he might still be alive — even if quite advanced in age. A few weeks before the showing of the film, Wallenberg's personal possessions, kept in his KGB headquarters file, had been handed over to members of his family. The film documented the great effort made since 1945 to discover his whereabouts. It showed members of Wallenberg's family wandering through Soviet prisons in the perestroika years, hearing recurrent rumours of his having been seen by Russian or foreign prisoners.

I found the film intriguing. Over the years, I had discussed the fate of this benefactor of Hungarian Jews with many Swedish colleagues. In recognition of the extraordinary service he had rendered, Israel had kept Wallenberg's memory alive. The day after this film showing, I was having lunch with Radomir Bogdanov and asked him if he had any notion from his KGB years of what had become of Raoul Wallenberg. Bogdanov said he had and told me the following story.

Wallenberg was an enigma to the Soviets, who had known of his existence from his contacts with the NKVD before the Red Army captured Budapest from the retreating Germans. The Swede also had excellent connections with the Wehrmacht and the SS as well as with British Intelligence and the American OSS wartime secret service. In fact, his successes in gaining the freedom of thousands of Jews was seen by the Soviets not as the miraculous achievement of a single man working in an extremely hostile environment but as a western conspiracy. Bogdanov said the NKVD had had a plan they thought they could carry out with Wallenberg's help. Lavrenty Beria, head of the NKVD at the time, had already begun laying the groundwork for the 'Zionist-imperialist plot against the Soviet Union', to be launched after the Second World War. This project would help rid the East European countries of their Jewish leaders. Indeed, the Reyk and Slansky trials, the anti-Semitic campaign in the USSR, the 'Jewish Doctors' Plot' and much else followed.

For these reasons, Beria made the arrest of Wallenberg his personal concern and had his own private interrogator 'work him over'. The process lasted two years. Joseph Stalin was kept abreast of the Wallenberg interrogation, but as there were no sensational discoveries, Stalin began getting suspicious and Beria, to avoid Stalin's displeasure, had Wallenberg 'liquidated'. The file was destroyed and no traces were left. The fact that some personal belongings were handed over to the family did not signify anything, Bogdanov added. The KGB did not want to admit to the truth, Bogdanov said, because it was busy preparing similar plots against the Jews — even though on a far smaller scale. Pamyat and other anti-Semitic organizations were supposed to take pressure off the government and give the masses 'something to do'.

Bogdanov said it was some of the family members who, in order to remain in the public eye, perpetuated the myth that Wallenberg was still alive. Bogdanov's variation on the Wallenberg theme appeared strange. In communicating it to Jerusalem I said I had no way of double-checking it and asked for additional information, but received no reply. Swedish Ambassador Orjan Berner, with whom I shared the Bogdanov version, checked into it but told me he could not confirm it.

Bogdanov's account was partially confirmed to me some months later during the visit of a Swedish rabbi to my office in Moscow. He said he had written on the subject. The rabbi's history touched on the very wealthy Wallenberg family, who refused to bring Raoul into the family business because he was a poor relative. Raoul joined the Swedish foreign service, but with limited means, could not advance in the hierarchy and was sent to a third-rate posting to Budapest. He began saving wealthy Jews, who gave him most of the liquid money and jewels they possessed in return for helping them. In this way, Raoul thought he could end the war as a rich man and continue his career on another footing. I never saw the rabbi's book nor did I look into the nature of these 'revelations'. It was sad that the rescue of thousands of Jews under the impossible conditions of the war by this extraordinary man should have trailed off on a sad note of sometimes ugly, unsubstantiated rumours. The Wallenberg story did not resurface again before my departure from Moscow.

There was, however, no end to the stories about the KGB and its long and bloody history. As more and more of its activities were being brought into the open, a great many questions were arising on the fate of well-known Jewish leaders, writers, rabbis, and intelligentsia in general. Aryeh Naor, Menahem Begin's cabinet secretary, appeared one day in Moscow and spoke with me for half the night. Naor said he was working on a book about the late prime minister of Israel and wanted me to procure Menahem Begin's file from the KGB. Begin had been arrested in Vilnius, Lithuania, in 1940, and the KGB had kept him in prison for nearly a year, releasing him into the newly formed Polish Army of General Anders in 1941. He wrote an autobiographical book about this period, which he called *White Nights*. I did try to accommodate Naor, but could not, at that time, lay my hands on the file. It was eventually unearthed and received in Israel.

HOLDING ON TO JEWISH BOOKS

Another strange, though typically Soviet story, was the tale of the Lubavitcher Rabbi's private library. The Habad movement was perhaps one of the strongest popular religious Jewish groups in Russia, and later in the Soviet Union. It maintained its faith and integrity even in the most difficult years of the Soviet regime, when atheistic propaganda and the unofficial but very effective anti-Jewish policy was destroying the infrastructure of Jewish culture. My own family belonged to this movement and my grandfather, a wealthy owner of sawmills in northern Ukraine, supported the Habad.

The Lubavitcher Rabbi Shalom Dov Schneersohn, head of this branch of the Hasidic movement, had lived in a town by the name of Lubavi in Belorussia, from where the group drew its name. The venerable rabbi's library, a collection of rare volumes of law, commentary and manuscripts, was transferred to the town of Rostov where the Rabbi moved in March 1920. Rabbi Schneersohn passed away in Rostov and with the coming of the Civil War, the unsettled times and the famine, the library was packed and placed for safekeeping at the Rumiantsev Library in Moscow, which eventually became the Lenin Library, and is now the Russian State Library. A decision was taken by the new Soviet government in 1921 to restitute the collection to the Lubavitcher movement, but it was not carried out for bureaucratic reasons. Subsequently, the books seemed to have disappeared, but with the coming of perestroika there was renewed hope that they could be found and returned to the Lubavitcher Rabbi in Brooklyn, who set great store by it.

When representatives of the Habad movement arrived in Moscow in 1988 to claim the rabbi's library, the initial Soviet reaction was not discouraging. The Habad movement recruited the help of Armand Hammer, the American industrialist and financier, who had access to top Soviet officials, and he actively supported the request. The Soviet minister of culture, Zakharov, promised help. The Lenin Library did not seem to have an exact inventory of the books and manuscripts in question. There were rumours that the common practice of pilfering books had also affected the Lubavitcher collection. Water was seeping into the basement of the Lenin Library, where books were in danger of being damaged. The rabbi's representatives were allowed to inspect some of the volumes in the rare books section of the Lenin Library and to their amazement found most of the 10,000 volumes were kept there. Zakharov was soon dismissed, however, and was replaced in 1988 by Nikolai Gubenko, a former actor at the Taganka Theatre. The new minister was at first willing to release the Lubavitcher library. Shortly after, Gubenko demanded that the Habad movement rebuild the Lubavitcher village in Belorussia, set up a Lubavitcher Fund, create another cultural fund in Moscow and build a hospital for children affected by the Chernobyl nuclear power station disaster in 1986. This smacked of crude blackmail.

The Habad movement appealed against this decision, gradually climbing the ladder of influential individuals in the USSR and in the West. Appeals were made to the Russians at the highest level, through Presidents Ronald Reagan and George Bush, through Margaret Thatcher and President François Mitterand and others, all to no avail. I also tried to appeal to various personalities and leaders, asking for the library to be released. Soviet bureaucrats, for no clearly understandable reason, remained obdurate and proved impervious to persuasion or criticism from Russian scholars, who brought irrefutable proof that the library was absolutely private, and would not serve Soviet ambitions of a Jewish cultural revival. People like Dmitri Likhachev, an old and highly respected historian and member of the Soviet Academy, declared it to be of no value to Soviet culture per se and pronounced himself in support of reinstating the library to its original owner. Even Alexander Yakovlev and Raisa Gorbachev stepped in, but were powerless to dissuade the chauvinistically inclined hard-liners.

Eventually, the atmospherics of this cultural tug-of-war got out of hand. There were demonstrations tinged with anti-Semitism near the Lenin Library in Moscow, and wide-ranging arguments pro and con splashed across the pages of the press. The whole question became so distinctly etched into Russian politics that it was only the faith and perseverance of the Lubavitcher community that maintained hope for the collection's retrieval.

The Lubavitcher collection was not the only archival problem I had to deal with. In the 1920s, there had been an oral agreement with representatives of the Hebrew University National Library and the Soviet government about the purchase of the Baron Horace Ginsburg collection. This was a uniquely rich and important collection of Judaica. It too had reached the Lenin Library. The agreement was not finalized, although it was never cancelled by the Soviets, either. We unsuccessfully tried to revive the agreement in 1990. One of the promoters of this project was Eli Rubinstein, at the time secretary of the Israeli cabinet. The Soviet government was not prepared to budge on this subject.

Important and perhaps unequalled collections of Judaica are available in many libraries of the former Soviet Union, including the Saltykov-Shchedrin Library in St Petersburg. Even before the fall of the Soviet Union, but certainly after it, these repositories became accessible. The only difficulty seemed to be the pecuniary shortcomings of Israeli institutions. Competition from far wealthier universities and collectors in the US and in Europe has often been insurmountable for the Israeli centres of research. After the collapse of the USSR, even secret archives of the Communist Party and government agencies were opened, at least for a time, before limitations were reimposed. Individual documents can now be inspected and photographed, opening doors to the study of Jewish history, which has been highly restricted since the Revolution. Thus, the story of the Bund; of the *evsektsii* — special Jewish sections of the Communist Party established in 1918 to spread communist propaganda among Jews; the liquidation of the Anti-fascist Committee by Stalin after the Second World War and many other fascinating and sometimes tragic chapters of Soviet Jewish history are now coming to light.

In spite of the many budgetary difficulties, a number of Israeli institutions did take advantage of the opportunities. In summer 1992 we discussed a project with the Russian Foreign Ministry to publish joint volumes of documents on Israeli-Russian relations over the years. This plan was finalized at a meeting Professor Gaby Gorodetsky of Tel Aviv University's Cummings Center and I had with the Foreign Ministry archives director, Igor Lebedev. Volumes containing such documents are being prepared — an initiative that probably has few parallels.

VISITORS FROM JERUSALEM

For many years trade between the USSR and Israel had been non-existent, even though some commerce was taking place through third countries. Now the Soviet Union was opening up for business and a basic agreement between the chambers of commerce was signed, all of which promised broader trade relations. Dan Gillerman, the president of the United Chambers of Commerce of Israel brought over an important delegation representing big business interests: Victor Medina, head of the Chemical Industries, Mattie Morgenstern, chairman of ZIM shipping lines, Aharon Fogel and Shimon Ragiv, chairmen, respectively, of the very large Israeli Leumi and Poalim banks and a number of others. I took them to see the Minister of Finance Valentin Pavlov and Deputy Prime Minister for Economic Affairs Stepan Sitaryan. The latter was a well-known figure in the economic movement that had attempted reform years before perestroika. Pavlov made a very poor impression. His high-handed 'command and administer' style (a Russian expression describing unchecked authoritarianism

253

in government administration), looked like backtracking on the proclaimed intentions of economic reform. It was not clear why Gorbachev had agreed to appoint him, unless he was of two minds about rapidly going into a market economy. The subsequent promotion of Pavlov to prime minister and his heavy-handed authoritarianism strengthened doubts about Gorbachev's resolve to unloose the economy from its Bolshevik moorings.

The rapidly rising inflation in the USSR led me to suggest that Medina and Fogel offer their expert advice. They had been at the head of our Ministry of Finance when Israel's inflation was brought down from 500 to under 20 per cent per annum, a considerable achievement. Pavlov did not want to adopt the method of strict indexation and market economy controls and showed only slight interest in the ideas tentatively offered by the members of our delegation. I knew there would be no point in trying to transplant our experience: the difficulty was not in grasping the concepts but in their application. Sitaryan was interested in trade with Israel and gaining access to western markets through Israel's privileged relations with them, but on a scale far grander than Israel could deliver. We also discussed, with little success, direct flights and shipping, excellent sources of cash flow for the Soviet economy. This was a visit I was counting on to help establish good working relationships with the Soviet government, but it was clear the timing was not auspicious. The outstanding specialists we brought to Moscow still had some hope for the future of the Soviet economy. Israel had actually gone through similar stages on a smaller scale, transforming its directed, socialist-oriented economy into a freer market system and privatizing its state and trade union-owned enterprises. But the Politburo was behind the times, still fearful of Arab reactions; the opportunities for a go-ahead with Israel were overshadowed by the deepening Gulf crisis, which was placing the Arab-Israel conflict in a new light.

LAST DELAYS

As November came around, the Soviet Foreign Ministry was still procrastinating in making its decisions on opening the new consulates. However, in a meeting I held with the new director of the Near East and North African department, Vassily Kolotusha, his deputy Oleg Derkovsky, and Mikhail Bogdanov, who was in charge of Israel affairs, I sensed the change that had come over that hitherto hostile department. Gone were the condescending tones and the arrogant manner. Conversation was conducted in a normal spirit of give and take, even if positions did not coincide any more than in the past. Kolotusha told us, in essence, that the ministry was trying to work out the legal aspects of establishing a consulate such as ours, which would be independent of an embassy. They said they had their own problems in that respect: finding the necessary budget to run their consulate in Tel Aviv and staffing the new positions — all of which sounded plausible enough. They promised to expedite the process.

In mid-December, Prime Minister Shamir's path crossed that of Eduard Shevardnadze in Washington and they met for an hour. David Levy's assurances about Israel's non-coercive policy of settling immigrants and the absence of official urging to settle in the occupied territories had not satisfied the Soviet leadership. Shevardnadze again complained about Arab protests and said an official Israeli statement was needed to sanction immigrants' direct flights from Moscow to Israel. Shamir did not oblige; he pointed to the numerous statements already made to that effect, but Shevardnadze seemed to be in a bind. He said diplomatic relations would still have to wait.

The Shamir-Shevardnadze meeting took place against a background of deepening tension over the Iraqi invasion of Kuwait and the anticipation of a military conflict in the Persian Gulf between a former ally of the USSR — Iraq — and the US. Shevardnadze referred to this situation only obliquely in his conversation with Shamir. The Soviet government was still trying to use its waning influence to prevent the war, and persuade Saddam Hussein to relent, but to no avail, as it turned out.

What must have worried Shevardnadze much more, however, was the dislocation of power inside the Soviet Union. He was appalled at the course of developments as the rightists were swiftly regaining their influence, without any opposition from President Gorbachev. Shevardnadze seems to have been particularly sensitive to the personal attacks against him in the government and by the right-wing of the party over the massacre in Tbilisi and questions concerning the reunification of Germany. He felt Gorbachev was not supporting him and was trying to evade his own responsibility for these decisions. Shevardnadze's thoughts must have been far removed from the hotel where he had called on the Israeli prime minister.

TWENTY-FOUR YEARS

I was invited by protocol to be invested as consul-general by Foreign Minister Shevardnadze only five days after his dramatic resignation from the government and the Politburo on 20 December. Shevardnadze was withdrawn and distant and looked paler than usual. This was the last act of official business at the Foreign Ministry over which he would preside, and the conversation was desultory. I contained my curiosity and made no reference to the dramatic events of the week. But if it was Shevardnadze's farewell, it was my own beginning. With the many-layered meaning of this official act, I was opening a new page in Israel's presence in the Soviet state.

The promotion of our mission to its official status as a full-fledged consulate-general brought with it the need for the Dutch Consulate to vacate our building and move to its own chancellery. However, they had no space left there, as a new military attaché had arrived and taken over the two rooms that had originally been the seat of the consulate-general. They asked if we could let them stay on in our building until they found a proper location for their office. With the long-awaited additions of Israeli personnel about to arrive in Moscow, it was not easy to oblige, but we could not turn the Dutch down. So they stayed on, in a curious reversal of roles: enjoying our hospitality, where we had been privileged with theirs for so many years.

We ran up the blue and white flag of Israel on the tall pole in front of the embassy building on 3 January 1991: just over 24 years after it had been taken down. I invoked the ancient biblical phrase: 'God grant courage to his people and bless them with peace'. The

Israeli community, 50-strong, was all present and accounted for. In addition, there were many Jewish and Dutch friends who had seen us through the thick and thin of our pioneering days in rejectionist Moscow. Vilma and Petrus Buwalda were there, as well as Colonel Yuri Sokol, a Jewish hero of the Second World War, who stood at attention, deeply moved, in his imposing Red Army greatcoat with its gold shoulder-boards. It was cold. Tiny pellets of snow, borne on the light wind, were dusting our dark official clothes with minute specks of white. There was a moment of silence as the flag was unfurled and taken up by a slight breeze. And then, spontaneously, Hatikva burst out, the strains of the national hymn growing stronger and surer until all joined hands and broke into a joyous hora, dancing around the flagpole, relieved to have finally arrived at this moment, the long road left behind. We had closed down the compound for the ceremony but the crowd of *olim* was thick at the gates, watching through the fence, sensing that this moment was also theirs. The Soviet policemen looked on, smiling benignly. After their many months of helping us with the multitudes of visa-seekers, they were now sharing in the excitement.

We celebrated our new status at an official reception a few days later in the newly refurbished embassy building, decorated with paintings by Israeli artists and lit with the antique chandeliers that we had discovered in the cellar and repaired. I invited two Moscow veterans to join us on this occasion: David Bartov, chargé d'affaires, and Yosef Govrin, first secretary at the embassy's closure in 1967. Both remembered well the day when the Soviet government sent down a rowdy mob of demonstrators who blocked the street and shouted invectives and slogans at the gates of the embassy. We re-enacted the flag-raising to give them a feeling of closing the circle, compensating a little for the humiliation they had endured over two decades back.

There was a very large crowd of Soviet officials, academicians, artists, musicians, journalists and writers at the reception. For the first time, the Soviet Foreign Ministry sent down a representative, albeit junior, to show its official recognition. Archbishop Kyrill, the head of the foreign relations office of the Russian Orthodox Church, was there too, adding substance to the significance of the event. The front yard filled with diplomatic cars, bearing the flags of the many nations whose representatives came to mark the occasion with us.

After all the guests had arrived, I invited them down to the entrance of the building to unveil the consulate-general plaque. The four representatives of the Habad community from the US, who were in Moscow to 'liberate' the Lubavitcher collection from the Lenin Library, led the procession, dancing and singing. In their enthusiasm they collared Gavril Popov, the mayor of Moscow, who, lumbered awkwardly after the hatted and bearded gentlemen, trying his best to humour them.

When we finally got back into the building to raise a few toasts, Valentin Pavlov, the minister of finance, arrived to join us. He raised his glass to me and said: 'To your promotion, expected soon'. This was welcome news, coming from a member of the Gorbachev cabinet. That very morning I had got word of Gorbachev's intention to replace Nikolai Ryzhkov, his faltering prime minister, with my guest Pavlov. So, after thanking the minister of finance for his good wishes, I said I wanted to raise my glass to his own promotion, which I was sure would precede mine. Pavlov stared at me through his thick glasses, obviously surprised at my being privy to the information which had reached only a few people in Moscow that day. He did not say anything, but drank his vodka, I thought with greater relish than one would expect. In a few weeks' time, Pavlov was indeed appointed to the premiership, a promotion which did not augur well for him or for the Communist Party.

Later that evening, after all the guests had gone, Aliza and I retired, exhausted but satisfied that we had done everything we could to make this a memorable occasion for our guests. It was very late. Bolshaia Ordynka was deserted and an unusual calm had settled on the house and its vicinity, but we knew that in only a few hours, in freezing and dark pre-dawn Moscow, the lines would start forming again for visas to Israel.

20 · *Still No Ordinary Days*

I had been looking forward to the raising of our national flag in the embassy compound ever since the first day I arrived in Moscow. Now it was done. This objective having been achieved, its importance seemed to diminish. The next plateau would be the restoration of full diplomatic relations, an expression of complete normalization of relations between Israel and the USSR. But the singularity of Soviet conduct and the complications of perestroika seemed to put that end beyond our reach for the moment.

The Soviet position in the Middle East was changing perceptibly. Toward the end of 1990 the Gulf crisis had made it obvious that even Arab states like Syria and Iraq, erstwhile allies of the Soviet superpower, were concerned far more with the US and the West than with the interests of the formerly dependable Russians. There was, in any case, little encouragement or material support for the Arabs. Under these circumstances, the Soviet government could have been more forthcoming and decisive on the renewal of relations with Israel. It was not clear why the fig leaf of consulates-general was so expedient. Eduard Shevardnadze had an interesting comment on this subject when he said in the memoirs he published in 1992 that the USSR's position in the Middle East peace process had initially weakened because of the break with Israel in 1967 and that 'everyone' had concluded relations had to be re-established. Cautious people, however, said the right moment would have to be found. Finally, Shevardnadze noted, when the USSR established relations with all the countries in the region, the only thing it could manage was to exchange consulates-general with Israel and he quite regretted not having brought about an exchange of ambassadors.*

Many inside and outside of government in the Soviet Union appeared to be of the same mind. Yet I found few people at the top affected by the minor limitations that consular, rather than diplomatic, relations imposed. People were aware of our emergence 'from the trenches', as the writer Chingiz Aitmatov once described it to me. The flag-raising ceremony was broadcast on television and viewed by a very large audience. In the popular mind, there were no more problems with the Israeli diplomatic mission, whatever its name or formal status may have been.

The immediate result of this new freedom was a vastly increased exposure to the Soviet public through the media. The biggest break for us came right after we raised the flag, on 3 January 1991. As I retreated into my office, tens of journalists, cameramen, television crews from the USSR and other countries of the world stationed in Moscow, surged in. Some sat on the floor. I made sure to talk to all of them, the British, American, Canadian, French, Italian, Spanish, German, Mexican, and others. In a few days' time I got voluminous feedback from home on the material published in those countries. It really seemed like a global event, at least to all of us in Moscow.

Soviet propaganda had inculcated a very negative view of Israel and the public had become used to the stereotypical images. A series of films shot in Israel by Yevgeny Kiselev toward the end of 1989 and screened at prime time on the first channel, produced an effective break with this tradition. Kiselev offered live and objective reporting which showed how spurious previous presentations had been. In one scene, he showed a western television crew busily provoking an incident in East Jerusalem, to enable them to present a 'topical' story. The impact of these reports was so great that the bosses of Ostankino (the state television) had them discontinued. A similar situation developed when a Leningrad television pro-gramme called 'The Fifth Wheel' wanted to run a series on Israel,

---

* Eduard Shevardnadze, *Moi vybor* (My Choice) (Moscow: Novosti Publishers, 1991) p. 188.

which they had shot during a week-long visit to the country. The programme was censored and allowed to be shown only a year later. The essence of both productions was that Israel was a 'normal' country; that the Arab terrorist organizations, including the PLO, were making life exceedingly difficult; and the Israelis had to defend themselves. In view of rising political instability and crime, the need for self-defence against terrorism evoked a feeling of identification with Israel.

The winter of 1990 was also a period of widening liberalization and diversification of the press, radio and even television all over the changing Soviet Union, now into its fifth year of glasnost. The consulate began receiving endless requests for interviews and appearances. Israel Mey-Ami was all but overwhelmed as Soviet journalists lined up at his door trying to get personal meetings and statements. Mey-Ami did a superb job of managing the journalists, and I saw my picture and remarks splashed all over the Soviet Union. The Jewish press had a head start on us in Riga and Vilnius, as well as other major Jewish centres. To them, the presence of an official Israeli representation was more than just news. It was a point of reference in their lives as well, and they were eager to share this feeling with their readers.

Israel became attractive for the non-Jewish media as well. In addition to press and radio coverage, a film on Israel was made and shown in theatres in Moscow and other large cities. *Izvestiia* correspondent Alexander Bovin wrote and spoke authoritatively and positively about Israel and the Middle East (and ultimately became Russia's ambassador in Tel Aviv). Nikolai Shishlin, a member of the Central Committee General Department, ran the weekly television programme 'Panorama' — a review of foreign affairs. He invited me to appear on his programme to discuss the question of 'settling immigrants from the USSR in the occupied territories'. No form of denial, at any level of government in Israel, seemed to satisfy the Russians, who worked on the assumption that nagging Israel with this question would somehow pacify Arab criticism against free Jewish immigration. On television, Shishlin also posed questions regarding Israel's position on the Gulf crisis, which was building up to the Allies' military intervention in January and worrying the Soviet establishment about the future of its relations with the Arab world. The Soviet leadership, as that of the West, wanted Israel to keep out of the crisis and not rock the boat of East-West consensus regarding Saddam Hussein.

In December 1990 I received an invitation to the dacha of Victor Lewis and his wife Jennifer Steisam-Lewis. The dacha was in Peredelkino, an area where many of the well-known Russian literati had their homes, including the late Nobel laureate Boris Pasternak. I was driven there by the former editor of *Sovetskaia Kultura* (a weekly cultural magazine), Elena Korenevskaia, and her husband, science fiction writer, Zinovy Yurev. Elena had known Victor Lewis for many years and admired his achievements: his survival in Stalin's Gulag camps and his subsequent successful career. He was knowledgeable about the world and exploited the keen curiosity in the West about Soviet affairs. He lived well in the West, and in Moscow, and had an aura of impenetrable mystery about him. Lewis was known in Israel from several visits, beginning in 1971, when he came for medical consultations. He once told me he liked the city of Eilat on the Red Sea and wanted to settle there, but his health had not permitted it.

Lewis was a charming host and a very interesting man. His dacha was large and comfortable, with an indoor heated swimming pool, uncommon in Russia. He proudly showed me a collection of art nouveau and Russian bourgeois furniture. He had garnered these pieces in Moscow by simply going from house to house and carting them away, as they were thrown out when small buildings were torn down during the Khrushchev apartment building craze in the early 1960s. But the jewels in his crown were in the garage. He showed me an early Rolls Royce, a later model Bentley, a modern Cadillac and a Mercedes. The only question I asked was if he ever used those cars, to which he replied affirmatively. The provenance of those automobiles was unclear, but I guessed they were purchased from the heirs of Brezhnev, who had a soft spot for western models.

Officially, Victor Lewis was the Moscow correspondent of the *Sunday Express* and Jennifer wrote for the *London Times Education Supplement*. However, there was no doubt that Lewis had a good number of other western contacts. He knew about our mission from the very first day of its appearance and put our name on the roster of foreign missions in his Moscow guidebook — a novelty in those days. The Russian press found Lewis to be enigmatic. Most requests for personal interviews were turned down. In the West, Lewis was recognized as a harbinger of the many twists and turns of Soviet policy. It was he who broke the news of Khrushchev's ouster in October 1964, and later obtained the Khrushchev memoirs from the KGB for publication in the West. He also managed to transmit Solzhenitsyn's manuscript of *Cancer Ward* and the memoirs of Svetlana Alliluyeva, Stalin's daughter. The beginning of the mass emigration of Jews was announced to the world by Lewis quite early in 1987, when few people thought it possible. Lewis steadfastly denied being an agent of the KGB and maintained he was a freelance journalist in the USSR, with open access to the West.

I last met Lewis at the Queen's birthday garden party at the British ambassador's residence in June 1992. He knew I was due to wind up my assignment in the autumn and he asked for my assessment of the changes my four years had brought to Russia. I told him I marvelled at the Russians' will to survive in spite of their thousand-year history, fraught with bloodshed and disregard for human life. Lewis remarked that he had believed in the Soviet system but since he had had to suffer through it, he hoped the Russians would finally find a better way to live. A few months later, I heard of his death in London.

Soviet radio broadcast interviews with me on a whole variety of questions ranging from the influence of Russian literature in Israel, to public opinion regarding Jewish immigration. On one occasion, at the Central House of Radio and Television at Ostankino, my interview was slated to follow a talk with Boris Yeltsin. This was before his election to the post of president of the Russian Supreme Soviet, and he was under constant attack. I had the interviewer play a few minutes of music in order to avoid a sense of continuity and not give the impression that I was appearing together with Yeltsin. It was just as well, for the programme was heard all the way from Riga to Vladivostok, as I discovered later from the substantial number of comments that I received.

When we were allowed to increase our personnel in early 1991, a new associate, Yosef Bendor, was sent out to take charge of the press. Yossi was born in Moscow and finished his secondary education there. Communicative and possessed of a talent for interaction with the Russians, he wound his way into numerous editorial offices and made himself a welcome guest. We thus had access to an array of target audiences, poles apart on ideology and on their attitude toward Israel. Private radio broadcasters, often working on a shoestring budget, sought us out and got us acquainted with their public. There were some extraordinary breakthroughs in this and later phases. Almost single-handedly, Yossi organized trips to Israel for a number of leading Soviet journalists, publicists and writers, and in large majority they came back with positive reports, quite at variance with the picture painted by adverse Soviet propaganda.

Eventually, we broadcast two extremely important series on the main channels of Soviet state television: 'Pillar of Fire', a documentary presentation of Israel's history, and former Israeli Foreign Minister Abba Eban's 'Heritage' series on Jewish culture, which has had a great impact in the Western world. Both would have been impossible to screen only a year earlier. These series helped to place Jewish history and the interrelationship of Jews with the non-Jewish environment in perspective. The large number of press and radio interviews that I gave over this period of approximately two years, as well as the steadily growing volume of information on television and in the press reports by journalists back from trips to Israel, helped change the jaundiced perceptions in the minds of the intelligentsia and the 'thinking population'. Two interesting conclusions could be drawn: that the 'Soviet people', having become immunized to their country's political propaganda, never really believed the lies they were force-fed; and that they were receptive to fresh information. The surprising thirst for knowledge about Israel was genuine, for it continues, almost unabated, to this day. There was negative reporting as well, mainly from sources close to the military and security establishment or from rightist power centres. Overall, the prevailing mood about Israel, as projected by the media, decidedly improved.

Our unqualified success in the USSR did not please everyone at home. The East European division of the Foreign Ministry, formally in charge of the interests in the Soviet Union, was immersed in the developments in Eastern Europe and not particularly responsive to our activity. At one point, however, Yosef Govrin, who headed the division, transmitted a complaint he had received from Prime Minister Shamir's bureau chief Yossi Achimeir. The latter had handed over an anonymous letter that claimed I had been speaking inadvisedly about the difficulties Jewish immigrants would face in Israel and discouraging them from emigrating. There was also a reference to my supposedly politically incorrect usage of the term 'occupied territories' instead of Judea, Samaria and the Gaza Strip, which was the geographical appellation (to which I always adhered), sanctioned by the Likud government. There were a few other points of a similar nature, all quoting me entirely out of context and giving a twisted political interpretation of my interviews, with innuendoes about my 'disloyalty' to the cause of immigration. Achimeir's accompanying letter said the matter had been brought to the prime minister's attention and he had expressed his displeasure. Govrin, without consulting me, wrote to Achimeir that I had been misquoted and that my intentions were good. This was a bureaucratic and subservient way of shrugging shoulders. Knowing who the slanderer was, I lost no time in exposing him. I sent a personal note to David Bartov, head of Nativ, asking him to check with his assistants. He denied it had emanated from his office. When I next saw Prime Minister Shamir, I told him about this story and asked him if he thought it right for me to be exposed to KGB-like denunciations. He asked Achimeir to step in. Evidently, Shamir had not known anything about the matter, or he would have remembered it. Achimeir mumbled something unclear. When I sat down with him in his office, Achimeir asked me outright why I had not gone to David Bartov and denied the accusations in the first place. Achimeir was inadvertently, but unmistakably, corroborating my suspicions. I never mentioned the subject again, but these unpleasant digressions did not make my life any easier.

One of the few in-depth and far-ranging reports on the emigration of the Jews of the Soviet Union to Israel, was prepared by Israel's first channel anchorman Haim Yavin. The report was filmed in Russia and in the Ukraine and made into a series called 'The Smouldering Embers', an account of emigrant farewells to their home country. One of the instalments showed leave-taking from the city of Odessa, which had been the sight of a Russian-Jewish renaissance at the end of the last century, and home to writers such as Bialik, Sholom Aleichem, Mendele Moycher Seforim, Babel and others. The series portrayed the Jewish exodus as a massive movement of a people resolved to part with a country which held no promise of a future. It also brought home to the Israeli viewer the immigrants' uneasiness over resettling in a virtually unknown country, whose social and political system was difficult to fathom and whose language was still to be learned.

The growing volume of immigration, its problems, and the Soviet political scene, with its turbulence and unpredictability, were of undying interest to the Israeli public and media and I was very much in demand on my frequent trips home. There was a great need for information on subjects related to the future of our relations with the USSR. It was important that our public get better acquainted with an assessment from our vantage point in Moscow, as Israeli journalists still had difficulties in reporting from there. My repeated appearances and interviews on prime-time television and on the front pages of the papers did not sit well with Reuven Merhav, the Foreign Ministry's director-general. He complained I was 'getting too much exposure'. Yet I was working for the Ministry of Foreign Affairs, not for the Mossad, and my experience and knowledge were of great interest to the Israeli public. In any case, I made sure the foreign minister had no objections to my appearances.

In Moscow our new contacts gave us access to two important institutions, which offered me a platform to explain Israel's position and policy. These were the International Relations Institute of the Foreign Ministry (MGIMO, where Radomir Bogdanov was a professor, teaching courses on disarmament), and the Diplomatic Academy. When I arrived at MGIMO, the director, Timurid Stepanov, told me he had a surprise for me: the question and answer period would be conducted in Hebrew. The large lecture hall was packed with students and professors, who evinced a heightened interest in Israel and in its problems. I gave some unadorned references to the Soviet positions over the years, as I knew the material that was being studied at the institute was largely drawn from textbooks written by the professionals of the Oriental Institute and the Ministry of Foreign Affairs, all highly inaccurate and unfair.

The questions, put by some of the students in modern Hebrew, revealed sparse knowledge about Israel and the Middle East, but gave proof of genuine interest in our problems. I came away encouraged, only to discover, a while later, that my frankness had not paid off in at least one quarter. Stepanov told me he had reported on my lecture to Yevgeny Primakov, who was displeased.

At that time, in the summer of 1991, Primakov was a close adviser to Gorbachev, and still the authority on the Middle East. He had twice visited Israel in the 1970s on unsuccessful missions of bridging the gap between the two countries. Menahem Begin met him on his first visit and haughtily lectured him on Soviet behaviour. Perhaps Primakov had been offended and held a grudge.

In my lecture, I expressed Israel's views on Soviet policies and the disservice to the cause of peace by the indiscriminate Soviet support of Arab militarism. By that time, these views were not mine alone, but were widely accepted by important Soviet political observers, including some highly placed in the government. But I thought Primakov's real concern was different: in spite of objections by other experts, Primakov had promoted an initiative for solving the Gulf crisis which was based on his personal relationship with Saddam Hussein. The initiative had failed and embarassed Gorbachev. I had the feeling Primakov wanted to avoid any association with the representative of Israel, so as not to generate any possible misinterpretation of acting in collusion with us. In fact, in spite of the messages I got through Arkady Volsky and others of an imminent meeting with the Soviet *éminence grise* on the Middle East, it never took place. Soon, Primakov became head of counter-intelligence for the Federal Security Services, putting me definitively outside of his orbit.

At the Diplomatic Academy in late 1991, I met a group of professors and students with a noticeably more pointed interest in the Middle East. Their questions were up-to-date and revealed a wide knowledge of the Middle Eastern scene. The Academy is closely connected to the Foreign Ministry and supplies part of its cadres. The rector, Oleg Peresypkin, appeared one day in early 1993 in Jerusalem, in the retinue of Ruslan Khasbulatov, then speaker of the Russian Parliament. Khasbulatov had come on an official visit to the Knesset together with the chairmen of the Supreme Soviets of Tatarstan and Bashkortostan, Farid Mukhametshin and Murtaza Rachimov. The non-Russian members of the parliamentary mission underlined Khasbulatov's intention to promote his status in the Muslim republics. Peresypkin, on the other hand, was granted the excursion to the Middle East as a result of his personal standing and in recognition of the academy's position in Foreign Affairs.

LOOKING TO THE JEWISH AGENCY

One of the strange consequences of the growing wave of immigration into Israel was the birth of the idea in the Russian mind that the Israeli experience could be put to use in helping Russian refugees. The fear was growing that millions of Russians might see themselves uprooted in the course of the widening political crises. Some Russians had already had to flee Azerbaijan and Uzbekistan and thousands of Russian and Armenian refugees had arrived in Moscow, with nowhere to go and no means of support. Nikolai Melnikov, chairman of the Refugees Committee of the Moscow City Soviet, contacted me with the request to assist him in studying the technique used by Israel, to suggest ways and means of tackling this problem once it arose in greater magnitude. Melnikov told me the situation in the Baltics was especially precarious. Millions of Russians had settled there with never a thought to their future status under a different regime. They now feared the threat of expulsion. He warned that a similar development might also come about in the Central Asian republics such as Kazakhstan and Uzbekistan — home to many Russians in the 70 years of communism.

The Refugees Committee expected up to 25 million Russians to eventually be in need of relocation and assistance. The Russians were evidently planning for the worst-case scenario. I wondered what catastrophic visions prompted these estimates. It was doubtful they could do much even in the likelihood that there would be far less refugees. At the time of our first meeting with Melnikov in July 1990, there were already 50,000 refugees, some who had fled the Azerbaijan riots in 1988 and 1989, including 800 Armenians. Their prospects in Russia were not terribly bright. I had the occasion to meet some of them. I asked them why they had not received help from their fellow Armenians. They said no Armenian institution or personality was sufficiently interested to help them. The Moscow municipality was trying to make the necessary provisions ahead of time. Taking organized care of refugees requires careful planning and organization as well as extensive funds. It also requires motivation. I wondered if all those elements would be available if and when the time came.

There were many dissimilarities between Israel and Russia on the question of refugees. Israel's very *raison d'être* was the ingathering of Jews from many lands, out of need or idealism, united by tradition, religion and suffering. Russia's problem was to deal with people who would be forced to flee from former Soviet territories, but would never seriously be encouraged to return or be made welcome at home. Zionism had brought about the largest transplantation of people from many lands into one since the Second World War. The Russians feared they might outdistance us.

With the deepening of the political, social and ethnic crises, and the creation of a civilian refugee problem, there was a need to absorb hundreds of thousands of military refugees, armies that were about to leave Eastern Europe with no provisions for lodging, work or care for their families. This was a task on a grand scale. Melnikov and his committee, observing the activity of the Jewish Agency and other welcoming bodies in Israel, thought at first that Israeli methods could be adapted to face similar situations in Russia. After the initial visit of the committee to Israel, I heard of no serious follow-up. Perhaps the Russians decided they could solve their problems without further need of assistance from us. The refugees issue has in fact become serious, with the critical developments beyond the border of the Russian Federation, now called the 'near abroad', where large Russian populations have settled in the last 50 years.

Attempts also were made to attract the interest of the Russian diaspora, mainly with a view to gaining financial and political support for specific projects of economic and cultural development. In August 1991, an expatriates congress sent out invitations to prominent personalities of Russian background, but there was criticism about invitations sent out to Russian Jews. In any case, the results were not terribly encouraging. It seems the political instability and the strong traces of the communist regime still apparent in the texture of Russian society dampened the initial enthusiasm.

Nostalgia for Russia among first and second-generation Russians abroad still remains strong. The imperial family of Romanovs has never withdrawn its claim to the Russian throne. A monarchist movement appeared already in 1989, and in 1990 and 1991 there was even talk of a return to the old pre-revolutionary tsarist system, without its accompanying absolutism but as a unifying symbol of the country. The portraits of Tsar Nicholas II and of the royal family proliferated and some men began wearing the trim Nicholas II beard. Heated arguments on the subject of royalty and the Russian Orthodox Church were often sparked in street 'parliaments'. Even if the concept of monarchy did seem to attract a few nationalists, it did not get far. One of the highlights of monarchist activity was the burial of the 75-year-old scion of the Romanov family and 'head of the imperial household', Grand Duke Vladimir, in the Peter and Paul Cathedral in St Petersburg, where many members of the Romanov dynasty have found their final resting place. The burial chamber had to be repaired after the damage inflicted by the communist regime in the first years of the revolution. The decision on this act of reuniting the past with the post-communist present was taken by Russia's President Yeltsin himself and the ceremony was conducted by the head of the Russian Orthodox Church, Alexis II.

IN SEARCH OF A HOUSE

The growing anarchy in the Soviet Union in 1990 and 1991 was beginning to be felt even in our day-to-day relations with the authorities. The opening of the consulate-general necessitated the location of a proper chancellery and a residence for the future ambassador. The house on Bolshaia Ordynka, on which we had a lease, was getting to be too small for the volume of work we were doing. The government agencies that dealt with these problems in normal times were incapable of providing any solution. There had been no private brokers in Moscow for 70 years, but as soon as the limitations on private initiative were relaxed, a new contingent of energetic and manipulative businessmen appeared with good contacts at the highest echelons, and a realty market was created overnight. A typical figure was Jan Menukhin, an entrepreneur introduced to me by Albert Reichman, the Canadian developer from Toronto who had business interests in the Soviet Union. I was looking for a new building or plot of land for the embassy and was in need of advice and help, which Menukhin was presumably capable of providing. When I approached him, Menukhin said there would be no problem at all; what size of a building and in what area did I want it? I told him. When I met him again, after many weeks, he said he was in a position to help me rebuild and expand the existing embassy, as he had purchased the building and grounds. This seemed to be a lucky break, but Menukhin disappeared again. When he finally reappeared, he could not produce proof of ownership. I asked the UPDK, the Foreign Ministry agency for property and supplies to the diplomatic corps, if the embassy building had been sold. They professed total ignorance of any such transaction.

Months later, when we were looking for a number of apartments to house our expanding staff, I again happened to come across Menukhin. He said that there was no problem and took me a few days later to a large apartment building in the final stages of construction in the best new residential area of Moscow. That was in February. By June, the apartments would be ready for occupancy, Menukhin said. In June, Mr. Menukhin was nowhere to be found. The subject of the apartments was never mentioned again.

In July 1991, when he next appeared, Menukhin wanted to discuss an official invitation for the Israeli minister of transport, Moshe Katsav, to come to Moscow to negotiate an airlines agreement. Forewarned, I challenged Menukhin to get an official invitation, for which we had struggled, unsuccessfully, at government level. Surprisingly, Menukhin returned a few days later with an invitation from the minister of civil aviation, Boris Panyukov. The visit did indeed materialize and coincided with the August 1991 coup. Later, Menukhin got involved with Yaacov Nimrodi, a wealthy Israeli businessman and my personal friend of 40 years. Nimrodi, for commercial reasons and reasons of prestige, wanted to operate immigrant flights to Israel and share in this activity with El Al, the Israel national airline, and Aeroflot. After many frustrating negotiation sessions and mutual recriminations, the matter was dropped. Jan Menukhin seemed to have been a typical representative of the new class of entrepreneurs that had risen in Russia: unscrupulous and opportunistic to the core, with few if any compunctions and virtually no loyalty to anyone. These new businessmen rode on a rapidly rising wave of opportunities toward the final days of the Soviet Union. Many made tremendous fortunes; most contributed to the questionable reputation that Russian business practices have today in the West.

A MUSICAL SANCTUARY

The tension, the frustration and the excitement of running the mission usually could be relieved only by travelling, either home, to Jerusalem, or to other cities in the Soviet Union — in the line of duty and under the stress of unreliable logistics. There was another possibility, however, that offered a briefer but greater diversion — that of musical performances. To a certain extent, and due allowance being made, it reminded me of a story I had heard in Tehran. Ludmilla Petrovna, my Russian music teacher, was a student at the Leningrad Conservatory when the war broke out in 1941. The inhabitants of that city were under siege and relentless German bombardment. They suffered hunger so intense that it even led, on occasion, to cannibalism. Over a million people were killed before the blockade of Leningrad was broken in the spring of 1943. Throughout those terrible days, the authorities maintained Sunday concerts, in fair weather and foul, under fire or in the rare periods of calm. Ludmilla Petrovna told me that these musical events served as a massive catharsis, and were enormously uplifting to the tortured minds of the inhabitants, giving them the hope that the next day might be better than the preceding one.

Music and theatre were the balm of the communist regime. Culture was within the reach of the masses. The higher rungs of musical and theatrical achievement were, however, reserved for a select and well-connected few, who obtained their tickets through a highly ordered system. Ordinary mortals had to stand in long queues, though it was not seen as an imposition because of the great respect for culture, ingrained since kindergarten.

The month of December will always be associated in my mind with remarkable concerts for a relatively narrow circle of Moscow's musical connoisseurs. Instituted in the mid-1960s, the 'December Nights' at the Pushkin Museum of Fine Arts had become the centrepiece of the yearly musical season. This was opium on a silver platter.

Through my connections in the musical underground, I obtained a ticket to almost every performance for myself, and for Aliza when she was in Moscow with me. Together with the cream of Moscow's music lovers, we heard the greatest performers, Russian and non-Russian as well. We heard the Beaux-Arts and the Schubert trios, Vladimir Spivakov's Virtuoso Chamber Orchestra, new and very fresh orchestral performances of operas by Yevgeny Kolobov, and others. There was the master of the viola Yuri Beshmet, the violinist Gideon Kremer, and Natalia Guttman, whose brilliant performance of the Rudolf Schnittke cello concerto I still vividly recall. There were many other extraordinary talents, young and old. The high point for us came on a December evening in 1991, in a rare event — the appearance of an aging Svyatoslav Richter, playing Bach, Mozart and Beethoven. There was always a very distinguished crowd of people, among whom I could already recognize the habitués from previous concerts and seasons. A few of our colleagues from the diplomatic corps were also there. I was always pleased to see the Egyptian Ambassador Ahmed Maher among them. Maher was former legal adviser to the Egyptian Foreign Ministry and a disciple of Egyptian Foreign Minister Ismail Fahmi, who had demonstratively resigned his post rather than identify with Anwar Sadat's peace with Israel. Maher was a hard-liner and felt uneasy about having to greet an Israeli diplomat in public. He never answered my calls and ignored me even after I attained the rank of ambassador, so steadfast was he in his uncompromising attitude to peace with Israel. At the time of writing Maher was serving as Egyptian ambassador to the US.

There was an aura of a different Russia in those evenings, an air of other-worldliness, beyond the hue and cry in the streets outside, the demonstrations and the counter-demonstrations, the talk of famine, of the collapsing state, the growing crime rate. The Russians in the audience knew each other well and remembered the details of concerts from previous years. They greeted the performers as heroes, and, as dictated by custom, ran forward to present flowers at each interval. (Richter asked for the flowers not to be wrapped as the noisy cellophane distracted his concentration. His assistant laid out the ground rules at the beginning of the performance.) There was a communal atmosphere among the audience as they welcomed the players and rushed to each other in the intervals, exchanging gossip and comments. As always in concerts and theatre in Russia, everyone came dressed in his best clothes and there was always the feeling of a gala event. Whenever we arrived at the Pushkin on those nights and stood in line to hand in our winter coats, Aliza and I felt we were depositing our vexations outside the door. I always regretted having to leave and ride home through the dimly lit and badly policed streets of midnight Moscow.

It was ironic that although the majority of the musical virtuosos we met were Russian, most of them lived abroad. Freed from the tutelage of the state, which expropriated their earnings for its coffers, many chose the advantages the West so readily offered. Aliza and I met a good number of these musicians and formed friendships with a few of them. We first met cellist Daniel Shafran in Tehran in 1976, when he came on tour. I found it very difficult to arrange a meeting with Shafran outside the concert hall, as he was deathly afraid of KGB surveillance. We finally managed to have dinner with him at a mutual friend's house. Another musician we enjoyed meeting was Maestro Pavel Kogan, conductor of the Russian Academy State Orchestra. Pavel is the son of the violinist Leonid Kogan and Elisabeth Gilels, daughter of the pianist and a violinist in her own right. Leonid Kogan came to play in Israel only once. A reticent man, he was overwhelmed by the feeling of identification with everything that surrounded him. He was not allowed any more visits. From the accounts we heard of this appearance, and from stories related to us by other musician friends, we could easily understand the inhibition and the regimentation even an artist of Kogan's calibre experienced on his trips abroad. David Oistrakh was never allowed to play in Israel. Even though he never identified with Israel and was obedient and loyal to the regime, the KGB feared the associations that could be awakened in his bosom, coming to an independent Jewish state, seeing his people living free of constant mental persecution. Besides, it was inappropriate to send the USSR's greatest violinist to an 'enemy state'. The pressures these virtuosos were subjected to are no secret any more, and in fact never were, neither for the inhabitants of the Soviet Union nor for those who lived in the West and saw these outstandingly talented performers appearing on the stage — never far from their KGB chaperons.

Another musician we met in Moscow was Avet Terteryan, the Armenian composer. An extremely erudite and interesting man, Terteryan has written a number of works in a modern, very original style sustained by echoes of ancient Armenian culture and a highly theatrical production of sound. Aliza and I went to visit Avet and his wife Irina in their apartment in Erevan when we were in Armenia and were very much impressed by this courageous couple, living, like all their countrymen, under extremely trying circumstances.

THE CHIEF RABBI AND THE PATRIARCH

In the spring of 1991, we were still living in our apartment on Bolshaia Ordynka. The UPDK had promised in autumn 1990 to refurbish it within three weeks, but it took seven months to repaint the walls and polish the hardwood floors (and probably to reactivate the electronic bugs). We had to keep a steady influx of vodka, beer and victuals for the workers as well as supply the sanitary installations; but finally the place was cleared and we could move in, which we did in April 1990. We could now live normal, if unprotected, lives: after our late working hours the place would become totally deserted, with only the Soviet policemen at the gates. My government did not consider me at risk, which was all for the best, since there were no guards quartered with us or following us around, as became the custom after my departure from Moscow.

Among our first guests were our children Michal and Ishai, with their fiancés Shimmy and Aviva. They enjoyed visiting us and reacted perceptively to the Russian scene. The *olim* from the 15 Soviet republics would form at least ten per cent of the population of Israel and Michal and Ishai would be living with them and among them in their future lives.

Passover and Russian Easter came almost simultaneously in 1991. We held a large Passover Seder with almost a hundred participants, and the Passover Haggadah was again read and explained in three languages. On this occasion we had a number of visitors from the US, including Esther Coopersmith from Washington and our Moscow friends Chana and Marc Winer, the latter an old hand in the USSR and head of the McDonald's operation which brought the hamburger to Moscow.

At the midnight mass service of Orthodox Easter, 1991, at the main Moscow cathedral, we were rather astonished at the appearance of two outstanding representatives of the Soviet state, atheists perforce by education if not by inner conviction. The newly elected Metropolitan Alexis II officiating, Valentin Pavlov, who had by now become prime minister, and Boris Yeltsin, about to be elected president of the RSFSR a few months hence, stood at attention, visibly at a loss in following the ritual. At one point each lit a wax candle, taking the cue from the many worshippers around them. The ceremony was shown live on state television — the first time ever in the USSR.

In the course of my duties, I had been maintaining contact with the Russian Orthodox Church through the head of its foreign relations department, Archbishop Kliment. In the spring of 1991 I had the opportunity to meet the Orthodox Primate at close quarters, in his residence. The occasion was the visit to Moscow of Mordechai Eliahu, the Chief Sephardi Rabbi of Israel, known as the Rishon LeTsion (First in Zion). He wanted to see the miracle of the emigration with his own eyes and ascertain whether we were determining the Jewish origin of the *olim* in good faith and in accordance with the Jewish halachic laws. It so happened that Alexis II was on the verge of visiting the Holy Land and my suggestion for the two to meet was accepted, although the Chief Rabbi seemed reluctant at first. The Russian Orthodox Metropolitan was very impressive in his white headgear with a diamond-studded cross rising out of the crown of his head. He was anxious to know if his church could repossess the considerable property that was in the Israeli government's trust and wanted the rabbi's support in reclaiming it. The Rishon LeTsion thought for a while and replied that the Metropolitan should put his trust in God, who would solve this problem in the best way for all. Alexis could hardly object to that. The visit to the Holy Land was a success, although decisions on church property have remained in abeyance.

Patriarch Alexis II made a remarkable speech during a meeting organized with rabbis on his New York visit in November 1991. He greeted the rabbis with the word 'shalom', and said: 'Your laws are our laws, your prophets, our prophets.' He said he regretted the frequent expressions of anti-Semitism, widespread among right-wing chauvinists. The task of the Russian Church is to help overcome narrow egotism and national chauvinism, he added. Among the many Russians whom Alexis II mentioned as having brought about greater understanding betweeen Russians and Jews was Mikhail Agursky, the Hebrew University scholar, well-known before his departure to Israel for his connections with Russian thinkers and writers, and for his research into the role of Jewish intellectuals in the post-revolutionary years. Alexis II concluded his address by quoting the psalmist: 'Pray for peace in Jerusalem'. On his return to Moscow, the Patriarch was criticized for this statement among the rightist anti-Semites within the Russian Orthodox Church, but did not recant.

An interesting and somewhat unusual request was made in connection with Alexis II's journey to Israel, during the visit of the director-general of the Foreign Ministry to Moscow, in March 1991. I took Reuven Merhav to meet Alexander Yakovlev, who had already left his official post as number two in the Gorbachev cabinet, but was still in his Kremlin office. The Gulf War had already been fought, Iraq evicted from Kuwait and the conversation centred around what Yakovlev called 'the end of the Iraqi military cancer'. However, Yakovlev opened the meeting with a reference to the impending pilgrimage of Alexis II to the holy sites, because, Yakovlev remarked, it could have possible repercussions on the internal scene in the USSR. One should not overlook the fact, Yakovlev said, that Russian anti-Semitism was somehow related to the Orthodox Church. The impending visit did not sit well with the church establishment, but on the other hand, the publicity that such a visit would generate should help suppress the anti-Semites. For that reason, Yakovlev added, he wanted us to consider giving every support we could to the requests for the transfer of ownership rights on the church property. Yakovlev related this point to his own experience, saying his opponents were spreading the rumour that he was Jewish. Some obscure group in the Central Committee had sent agents to his native village, on three different occasions, to find out if he had Jewish roots in his family. Yakovlev then produced a newspaper published by the Soviet naval forces, where he was referred to as a member of the 'Judeo-Masonic conspiracy'. He looked outraged.

A SOVIET FOREIGN MINISTER VENTURES INTO ISRAEL

Throughout the 42 years following Israel's independence, the USSR was extremely active in the Near and Middle East, which had become an important theatre of confrontation between West and East. Hundreds of Soviet leaders visited the countries neighbouring Israel; the Soviet government was deeply involved in the military and economic life of the Arab states and helped their international campaigns against Israel at the UN and in other parts of the world. In all the years of Israel-USSR relations, from the recognition of Israel to the severance of relations in 1967 and their resumption 24 years later, never had a Soviet minister of foreign affairs made the trip to Israel.

In May 1991 the newly appointed Soviet foreign minister, Alexander Bessmertnykh, was to make an extended tour of Arab countries. The relations these countries had with the USSR had been diminishing in importance for a good number of years. It was difficult for the Russians to maintain the military and financial aid which formed the basis of Soviet influence. After the Gulf War, they began lagging behind even more, having lost a great deal of their initiative and presence in the region as a superpower. The attempt Bessmertnykh made to recapture some of the privileged place reserved for his country was a repetition of Shevardnadze's effort a year earlier. Bessmertnykh, however, went one step beyond Shevardnadze and decided to visit Jerusalem.

If the visit to Israel represented a new and unprecedented departure for the Soviet government, there was nothing new in the bag of goods Bessmertnykh had to offer. Its contents included the idea of an international conference and Israel's recognition of the PLO — suggestions that received very short shrift from the Likud government. The visit lasted only one day, brought no movement in contacts with Israel, and certainly did nothing for the peace process. Israeli Minister David Levy took the exercise in his stride. Bessmertnykh was making his entrée as the minister of foreign affairs. He was an experienced diplomat and did not appear to have any illusions about the possible outcome of his first visit to the region. There was no feeling of obligation in the meetings between the foreign ministers or with Prime Minister Shamir. Both sides sensed that this was purely protocol.

Expectations were higher among Israeli citizens. They watched television that morning with bated breath as the Soviet airplane landed and came to a standstill. The Soviet minister emerged and walked down the stairs to the group of officials waiting below. What was he going to say? Nothing much new, it turned out. The flags were there, the speeches, too, the ride to Jerusalem in the government limousines, the first view of the road from the plain through the hills into Jerusalem. Bessmertnykh was not too cold and not too warm, and that reflected the general tenor of his visit.

The added value of the visit was the presence of the director and deputy of the Near East and African department, Vassily Kolotusha and Oleg Derkovsky, in the Soviet group. Both had been dealing with the Near East for many years. Kolotusha had been an active Soviet ambassador to Lebanon during the difficult postwar days in the mid-1980s, and I often saw his name in the Lebanese press. He had also served Sadat and other Arab leaders as interpreter on their trips to the Soviet Union. He knew the Arab countries well. Derkovsky had been dealing with the Middle East conflict at the Soviet Embassy in Washington and knew the American pespective on the story. Neither had ever been to Israel. It was a beautiful Friday, early in May, the road to Jerusalem was still green, the fields covered with young plants just breaking through the soil. The Soviet diplomats looked a bit surprised at the colours of the landscape, in an area they knew to be predominantly barren. In spite of their knowledge of the region, I hoped they would be impressed enough to gain a new and unexpectedly fresh insight into Israel and that they would take it with them when they returned.

21 · A General, Then a Coup

Rafael Eitan (Raful), a former Chief of Staff of the Israel Defence Forces (IDF), is a soldier-farmer. He comes from a Russian family of Subbotniks, purportedly the personal bodyguards of Emperor Alexander II, who settled in the north of Palestine at the turn of the century and took up agriculture. Raful was brought up in an agricultural community, joined the Palmach pre-state commando units in his early years and went on to become a legendary commander, one of the most audacious soldiers in the annals of Israel's wars. In his many years in the IDF, Raful never abandoned his cooperative family farm at Tel-Adashim. A member of the Knesset and head of the Tsomet rightist political party, he produces some of the best olive oil in the country and is an amateur carpenter. In 1991 Raful was minister of agriculture in the Shamir coalition government. Like many others, he too wanted to see the Soviet Union and search for his roots. We arranged his visit through the courtesy of the Soviet Academy of Agricultural Sciences, whose president, Professor Alexander Nikonov, had visited Israel with a delegation in 1990 and had come away deeply impressed with Israel's advances in agriculture, as well as with the warmth of his reception. The Soviet academy organized a week's tour for Raful: Leningrad, Ukraine, Russia and Kyrgyzstan, on the Chinese border in Central Asia. The professional and private aspects of this tour became indelibly imprinted on my mind.

Raful's arrival in Moscow in the pre-coup days of August 1991 took place in an atmosphere of great political tension. A few weeks earlier, troops had entered the city, ostensibly as a fulfilment of

Gorbachev's promise to deal with the increasing crime rate. In reality it looked more like an attempt by the KGB and the Ministry of Interior to impress the new liberal political parties with the authority of the state and the resoluteness of its security forces. The new prime minister, Valentin Pavlov, had just demanded full powers to carry out economic reforms, after he had plunged the country into a deep crisis, by allotting three days for a mandatory exchange of ruble bank notes. This move pauperized many millions of ordinary people, who could not get to the banks in time, and made millionaires of individuals who had access to inside information.

TWO PRIME MINISTERS; TWO POINTS OF VIEW

Relations with the Soviet government were still in an embryonic stage. In mid-April Prime Minister Shamir asked me to arrange a meeting between himself and his Soviet counterpart Pavlov, on the occasion of the opening of the European Bank of Reconstruction and Development (EBRD). Established in London and headed by Jacques Attali, the bank is an international vehicle of financial aid to Eastern Europe. What I recall from this meeting is the sterility of the conversation between the two prime ministers. Pavlov kept harping on the need to cooperate in the economic field. Shamir wanted Pavlov to get his government to support Israel's peace initiative of May 1989. Pavlov, who had only very hazy notions about the Middle East and its problems, thought Israel did not wish to have superpower participation but wanted their guarantees. Israel should sit down with the Arabs, he said, until white smoke came out of the chimney. 'But how should we supply you with food and water while you're there?' he asked, implying it would not be realistic to avoid great power interference, as Shamir desired. Shamir countered that if the Soviet Union could coordinate its positions with the US, Israel would have no objections to its participation in the peace process, but it could not agree to the involvement of other powers.

Shamir was suggesting the USSR's role in the peace process be contained because of its incriminating involvement with the Arabs.

Pavlov was seeking the financial assistance and know-how of Israel and world Jewry, especially in the US. He also asked for Israel's guidance in advancing the USSR's public relations in the US. Pavlov said outright that if Israel were supportive on these points, the Soviet government would have something to show for its decision to improve Israeli-Soviet relations in the future. The Soviet prime minister added that while Gorbachev had no problems with the Muslims in the USSR, a sudden change in policy toward Israel could create ferment in the Caucasus and Central Asia. He insisted that Yeltsin's anti-government initiatives did not in the least trouble him, but that the 600,000-strong demonstrations in Moscow gave the government much food for thought. They wanted no additional causes of tension. Shamir was asked to understand that Pavlov needed financial support and did not want unwittingly to sink his own ship by changing policy toward Israel. As to Shamir's questions about direct flights for immigrants to Israel, Pavlov answered that he had thought a joint airline could be created, but the idea had appeared awkward to the members of the Politburo.

The meeting took place in the Soviet Embassy in London and the small table before the two prime ministers was laden with *pirozhky* (small Russian meat pies), and other snacks. Pavlov was liberally helping himself to the pies. Suddenly, he stopped and asked how he was supposed to persuade his countrymen that he was doing business with the Israeli prime minister, when he had not even tasted a single *pirozhok*. 'You're talking like a capitalist!' retorted Shamir.

This meeting typified relations between Israel and the USSR at that stage. The growing atmosphere of openness did not result in a strategic reassessment of mutual positions, only the continuation of traditional attitudes. Yet, the time was propitious for an in-depth study of possible political cooperation, at least in the foreseeable future. The USSR's exposure to the upsurge of nationalism and fundamentalist Islam in Central Asia and the Caucasus and in Russia itself was widely known. These developments were bringing a strong gravitation toward irredentism in their wake. Israel's encounters with terrorism (largely inspired and engineered by Iranian-supported Muslim fundamentalism) in South Lebanon, in the Gaza Strip and in the West Bank, was a fact of political life there. Another very important subject that could have been placed on the agenda was the rationalization of Russian involvement in the Middle East, through its special connections with the Arab leaders. The Soviet Union could support the complex peace initiatives developing in conjunction with the US. Israel preferred the simple expedient of rejection, rather than the alternative of discussion with a superpower that had shown its animosity in the past and that was regarded as unreliable.

Even if it might have been just the right time to clarify mutual positions and seek an understanding, the two prime ministers were simply unprepared, psychologically and politically, to coordinate policies. Unfortunately, too, this important meeting was not prepared ahead of time, and both sides were unrealistically seeking to gain concessions and help in a brief encounter. The end result was that important opportunities were missed by both parties to gain an understanding on their relations and to identify the strategic problems in the region that separated them geographically and needed further discussion. A similar opportunity would not arise again until the collapse of the Soviet Union. All that Shamir desired at the London meeting was to seek reassurances on the question of continued immigration from the new Soviet prime minister. On the other hand, Pavlov probably thought that in initiating this meeting, Shamir was signalling that he had concrete propositions up his sleeve and was prepared to cooperate with the Soviet Union in suggesting the means that might help Russia with its finances.

RAFUL TO THE RESCUE

If the political and financial problems were still unlikely to be addressed, the subject of agriculture was very much on the mind of the Soviet government. The supply of food was the foremost problem. Talk of famine was on everyone's lips in the winter of 1991. Could Israel help? Both Raful and Nikonov had no illusions and knew well the enormous differences in scale, climate and needs, but they thought Israel could bring its experience to bear in the growing of vegetables, the production of turkeys (rich in protein that was lacking in the Soviet diet), and in drip irrigation, which could save a great deal of water in the dry areas of Central Asia, where traditional flooding of cotton fields had already caused an environmental disaster to the Aral Sea. There was additional know-how that Israel had developed, which could be put to good use in the USSR: the genetic improvement of meat and dairy cattle, and of seeds, and the treatment, canning and marketing of products, in which Soviet farming was sorely lagging behind.

The Russians were not unaware of the possibilities. Raful's adviser, Professor Samuel Pohoryles, a leading Israeli specialist in agriculture and international cooperation, had already discussed fields of common interest with the Soviet academy and selected a few for decisions to be taken in Moscow. But there were difficulties. First, the Israelis had no ready cash to invest in the grand Soviet schemes; and Israel was still a country with which official agreements could not be signed because of political limitations.

The first wide-ranging discussions were held with the Soviet Deputy Prime Minister Senko, who was responsible for over-all agricultural policy. He told us Israel was at the forefront of world agriculture, and the USSR wished to gain its technological know-how, especially with regard to marketing agricultural products. The many Soviet immigrants in Israel who knew the climate and working conditions of their former country could be of great help. He also wanted to know more about life and work in Israel's kibbutzim, with their achievements in socialist and cooperative agriculture, an area in which the Soviets, ironically, had failed.

Raful expressed Israel's readiness to accept payment for services and investments in raw materials or finished products. He believed agricultural cooperation should develop along the lines of private enterprise. Pohoryles, chairman of the Euroconsortium Council in Warsaw, which reviews projects for the EBRD, volunteered to take care of the necessary paperwork for obtaining financing, which the Soviets had difficulty in managing. Senko was pleased with Pohoryles's offer of help with the EBRD. He even promised to talk to Gorbachev about speeding up the re-establishment of diplomatic ties. Raful's visit thus got off to an excellent start. The welcome was made even rosier by Soviet Agriculture Minister

Viacheslav Chernoivanov's invitation to a caviar and vodka lunch at the Writers' Union, where many toasts were raised to cooperation and understanding.

In the summer of 1956, Raful had participated in an international meet of military parachutists in Moscow, an occasion quite out of the ordinary for an Israeli military person in those days. In 1991 we spent a number of hours revisiting the old sights and then took the night train to Belgorod, in the Russian black-earth belt, legendary for the wealth of its agriculture. Alexander Ponomarev, the first secretary of the regional committee of the party, a man of great influence in the area, proudly showed us the kolkhozes and the main dairy farm. We admired the new brick houses Ponomarev had built for the kolkhoz, though a discreet inspection revealed no running water inside. Raful's wife, Mrs. Miriam, as we all called her, a practising nurse, wanted to see the dispensary. She inspected it and commented very positively on the devotion of its staff but shook her head sadly at the inadequacy of the medical equipment and services. On the whole, the place looked attractive and neat. The cows looked plump and seemed proud of their ability to produce 4,000 litres of milk a year, a high average for Russia, low for Israel and the West. The corn stood high. The wheat, the alfalfa and the sugar beets looked good. This was Russian agriculture at its best. But Ponomarev, a devoted communist and an elected member of the Supreme Soviet, was displeased and ill-humoured. It was not meeting officials from Israel that fazed him, as I had thought. He was angry at Gorbachev: perestroika was getting out of hand in its race toward a market economy, which the country was unprepared for. All of the efforts that had gone into the organization of agriculture in the Belgorod area, as well as in the country as a whole, would be ruined. Did Gorbachev really expect him, Ponomarev, to divide all this property among the members of the kolkhoz? Gorbachev did not know where he was leading the country; it would surely fall apart. Ponomarev was also angered at the proclivity for endless talk in the Soviet Parliament and broadcasts on television confusing the minds of Soviet citizens. Ponomarev looked authoritative and tough and fearlessly expressed his opinion of the country's leadership, in tones rare even in those heady days of perestroika.

RAFUL FINDS HIS ROOTS

After visiting Ukraine's Agriculture Academy in Kharkov, we went due south to be near Kamenka, the Ukrainian hamlet of Raful's mother. The academy scouts, sent down to find the right village in accordance with Raful's description, had difficulty determining which of the three local Kamenkas it was. Finally, one was found with a street named Orlov, Raful's maternal grandparents' name, and the academy decided it was probably the right one. We all accompanied the former Chief of Staff as he approached Orlov Street, knocked on a door and tried to strike up a conversation. No one had any recollection of the Orlovs. The Second World War had reduced the area to ashes and the original inhabitants had fled or were killed. The houses looked new and different from the other villages in Russia and Ukraine. They had been built by German prisoners of war, kept in the Soviet Union for many years and used as labourers, to make up for the devastation to which the Wehrmacht had subjected Soviet Russia.

As we were walking past a row of houses a man ran out. Now that the government had finally sent down its inspectors, they must know the truth, he shouted. Villagers were suffering, and the government was ignoring their plight. He was a worker at the Donetsk steel mill, many hours of travel away. Whenever he arrived home at the end of his shift, there was no water to wash off the grime, no stores to buy bread or vodka in. A crowd formed, haranguing us until we drove off.

Our next stop was to be Leningrad. On the long flight I had an interesting discussion about perestroika with Victor Shevelukha, the secretary of the Soviet Academy of Agriculture and Raful's official escort. Shevelukha did not totally share Ponomarev's negative posture toward Gorbachev's reforms but said he could well understand his anger and frustration. Shevelukha, a widely read scientist, poet and accomplished sportsman, thought the march towards the market economy must be disciplined and administered in the proper doses, if it was not to drag the country down into a maelstrom of mismanagement and destruction. Shevelukha stayed loyal to his version of communism and joined the new post-perestroika Communist Party, became a member of Parliament and in 1995 was active in parliamentary wheeling and dealing.

Quartered in the Leningrad suburb of Pushkino, at the aristocratic Kochubei Palace, where the master of the tsar's horses resided before the revolution, we shuttled to the Leningrad Agricultural Academy and the historical sights of the city. We visited the rooms of world-famous academician Nikolai Vavilov, a biologist and geneticist, who fell out of favour with Stalin during the rise of Trofim Lysenko. The latter ruled Soviet biology and agriculture with an iron hand, as Andrei Zhdanov ruled the arts and letters. Lysenko believed genes could be influenced by the socialist environment and their acquired qualities inherited, a thesis that highly appealed to communists but set Soviet biology back by at least one generation. Vavilov was an embarrassment to Lysenko; Stalin had Vavilov imprisoned in Saratov, where he died.

At an experimental dairy farm near Leningrad we were shown a large herd of beautiful Holsteins, with yields of up to and beyond 7,000 litres. Raful was told the government did not have enough funds to propagate this particular breed nor the wherewithal to provide an organized distribution of dairy products. There was, however, interest in joint-ventures. When we inquired about the terms, we were told Israeli companies would have to invest the money and provide the equipment. As legislation on foreign investments was hardly adequate for such initiatives, we could not get any Israeli companies to take the risks.

At the many dinners held in his honour, Raful would always end the evening by forcing everyone to sing the old Russian war songs, popularized in Israel during its War of Independence in 1948. Not everyone remembered them but those who did, supported Raful's 'la, la, la' with the Russian lyrics. Raful could not carry a tune but insisted anyone who did not sing was not a true fighting soldier. We never dared protest, even if this exercise usually went on into the wee hours of the night. Raful's qualities of soldierly forthrightness, his martial bearing and his knowledge of the minute details of the war against the Germans endeared him to his Russian hosts, and he made friends everywhere he went.

ON THE BORDER WITH CHINA

Raful's visit to the Kyrgyz Republic was probably designed merely to be a relaxing diversion and a means to take him off the hands of the academy in Moscow. The Kyrgyz were unaware of this line of thinking. In Bishkek, the Kyrgyz capital, which reminded me of Tehran in the 1940s, we were whisked off to the presidential palace, the former Communist Party headquarters. Before we entered the president's office, Levitin, a close adviser, took Raful and myself to an adjoining room and said we could get to see President Akaev only if we agreed to present concrete offers of help and cooperation and invited the president for a visit to Israel. Taken aback, Raful said he could not promise anything but would be willing to listen.

I found Askar Akaev a very thoughtful and cultivated man. A scientist and member of the Soviet academy, he was a highly respected Soviet personality. We talked about possibilities of cooperation between Israel and Kyrgyzstan, but the conversation was not very conclusive. However, the green light was given for a tour, and hospitality which none of us shall forget.

From the moment we left the presence of the Kyrgyz president, we never stopped eating and drinking until we were out of the republic. However, there did not seem to be any protocol requirement for lengthy toasts. A few brief words sufficed. As our party included the ministers of agriculture and health and the head of the Kyrgyz Academy of Sciences, we were never short of attention. This meant early morning drinking bouts: champagne, cognac and vodka, the drill repeated at every stop for inspection and at every visit on the tour, seven to ten times a day. We had all the horse meat we wanted to chase the alcohol with, and if we felt parched between meals, we could slake our thirst with *kumiss*, fermented mare's milk, the favourite drink of the steppes.

Our hosts catered not only to our appetites; they also tended to our spiritual needs. After we arrived in Przhevalsk, at the far end of deep and beautiful lake Issyk Kul, we took off in Jeeps, climbing into mountains where, on a wide meadow covered with wild flowers, our patrons had organized a picnic, with Kyrgyz singers in national costumes. We watched the sun go down in a blazing orange cloud into the fir trees of the meandering valley below, climbed back into the Jeeps and arrived at a large white felt yurt, richly decorated inside with tribal rugs. The entertainment went on into the night and included a steady stream of rich nourishment piled on trays and bowls placed before us. There was a sudden lull, as a toothy smiling sheep's head was brought in and ceremoniously placed before Raful. He was asked to cut it up and pass it around. After a moment's hesitation, Raful dutifully cut off the ears and handed them to the Kyrgyz ministers. I was offered a morsel, pleaded abstinence on medical grounds, and was pardoned. Otherwise, the laws of hospitality would have been painfully broken and I could never have returned to Kyrgyzstan. Raful, however, stood firm. He embodied the honourable guest and the noble warrior. We seemed to have genuinely found favour in the eyes of our hosts. The head of the Kyrgyz Academy of Sciences took a *kumiz*, a pear-wood stringed instrument and composed a poem dedicated to General Raful, his very honourable wife Mrs. Miriam, the most venerable Consul-General Levin, Raful's secretary Rivka and the talented writer Yosef Galili (the frail, unassuming correspondent of *Al-Hamishmar*, who kept body and soul together at this feast through sheer power of will).

While we were so engaged, I realized that our loyal companion, the Academician Shevelukha, had given us the slip, in a most uncomradely fashion. When I had a chance to leave the yurt for a breath of fresh mountain air, I inquired as to his whereabouts and discovered he was bathing, stark naked, in the swift waters of the ice-cold stream nearby. The idea of joining him, though attractive, seemed too wild, so I loyally returned to my post.

RAFUL IN THE KREMLIN

Back in Moscow, I took Raful to see Vice-President Gennady Yanaev, who was filling in for Gorbachev. The president had agreed to receive Rafael Eitan but had to leave on a visit to Mrs. Margaret Thatcher in London. The commandant of the Kremlin, in uniform, received our group, which included Samuel Pohoryles and Yossi Bendor. We were escorted into the office of Vice-President Yanaev, who, in a number of weeks, would officially head the attempted rebellion against Gorbachev. The office formerly had been occupied by Lavrenty Beria, Stalin's notorious chief of internal security. Yanaev politely inquired about the situation in the Middle East. Raful took to this question with great ardour. He produced a map of the Soviet Union, with a small yellow spot in the middle. The yellow represented Israel, Raful said. He wondered if the Soviets realized the dimensions of the Middle East problems, when they carried out their policy of supplying Israel's mortal enemies with sophisticated weaponry. Raful then spoke about the unwillingness of the Arabs to accept Israel's existence, about the terrorist PLO, promoted by the USSR, and about our struggle against heavy odds. It was a monologue of forty-five minutes. At first Yanaev attempted to insert an objection or ask for a clarification, but he gave up. When he saw Raful had ended his exposé, he said: 'I have understood you, general'.

At the final meeting with Minister of Agriculture Chernoivanov, six open bottles of champagne were brought out on a silver tray to mark the agreement on cooperation. When Raful saw he was to sign the document as representing his government, he demurred. He could only initial it, he said, as international agreements had to be discussed in the cabinet and signed by the minister of foreign affairs. Back went the champagne, unceremoniously on its tray, to the regretful clinking of crystal glasses. The cooperation agreement on agriculture was signed only three years later.

AN AGREEMENT ON FLIGHTS

Raful's departure from Moscow was soon followed by the arrival of Moshe Katsav, the minister of transport, on 13 August 1991, six days before the coup. Jan Menukhin had kept his word. The taboo on official invitations was broken. Katsav received his from the minister of civil aviation, Boris Panyukov. The Soviet airline, Aeroflot, owned by the government, was finally given the go-ahead to negotiate an airlines agreement with El Al. The presidential system of government, installed with the swearing-in of Gorbachev in March 1990, had done away with the arbitrary rule of the Politburo. The economic interest in direct flights to Israel, well understood for

291

a number of years, now took precedence over conservative views. One important aspect of the projected agreement was the feeling, already spreading in the Aeroflot directorate, that the largest airline in the world, with its tens of thousands of airplanes, thousands of airfields and related infrastructure, could not hold together any longer. A strong demand to parcel out Communist Party and government property among the republics had already surfaced, as well as moves to privatize segments of Aeroflot. There was a great deal of Russian and foreign interest in buying or leasing airplanes or creating joint ventures for organizing international flights. The civil servants in the Aviation Ministry were thinking of their futures and lining up potential business connections. The biggest catch at this time was the Jewish emigration to Israel, with its captive clientele and assured payments by the Israeli government.

Yet, even at this juncture, when every difficulty ought to have been swept aside, the Soviet government was still queasy over putting its name to an agreement with the State of Israel on air connections, landing rights and overflight concessions. El Al was already flying occasional flights to Moscow, but the Soviet government was refusing to allow regular ones and did not want emigrants to board our planes going directly from Moscow to Tel Aviv. Katsav did manage to sign a letter of intent, however, about commercial flights, and opening offices and airport services. Israel was highly interested in extending El Al lines into Moscow but also continuing on to Beijing and Tokyo, a dream which materialized two years later.

THE COUP

Very early in the morning on Monday, 19 August, a Russian friend phoned and inquired if I had heard of the takeover of power. I answered in the negative and he gave me a very brief account of what had happened during the night: the creation of an extraordinary committee headed by Yanaev, Kryuchkov, Yazov and others, to rule in place of Gorbachev, who was declared ill and incapable of performing his duties. I switched on the television and saw the long face of a Russian announcer reading the committee's proclamation. The body language of the man spoke more than any words could say. It was the face of a Soviet Union rolled back many years. Were perestroika and glasnost gone? Would unrestricted Jewish emigration be repealed? And what of the high hopes for the beginning of a brighter new world?

I called Nikolai Shishlin. He was still in the general department of the Central Committee. 'Is everything over?' I asked. Shishlin said, 'It isn't evening yet', quoting the bard Vyssotsky, to the effect that hope dies last, even in the sad reality of his country. Shishlin had an excellent feel for the political situation and though he was far from being voluble, I always gained insights from his measured words. He must also have had access to inside information, being the next door neighbour of Alexander Yakovlev, even though it was doubtful whether there was a great deal to be known at that early stage. From my conversation with Shishlin and others I could at least tell that the coup was news even to members of the Central Committee.

The telephones were working as always and all of Moscow was busy comparing notes on the day's sudden developments. I stayed close to my phone and tried to make sure that Israeli citizens were out of harm's way. When the ministry in Jerusalem anxiously called me a few hours later, I told them the situation had not played itself out as yet and there was a chance the coup would fail. I shared the same assessment in an interview with Israel radio. From the voices on the international telephone lines, it was clear the tension was as great in Jerusalem as in Moscow.

From late spring 1990, developments in Moscow had begun to take an ugly turn. There were recurrent coalminers' strikes in Siberia and in the Donbass, ethnic confrontations and riots in many areas of the Soviet Union, problems with the supply of oil, a steady fall in industrial production and a sustained rise in inflation. The grain harvest in the summer of 1991 was low and was not being brought in because of the usual logistical difficulties and the farmers' quarrel with the government over price. Famine was expected in the winter. The fear of massive unemployment and social unrest was being widely discussed. The conservatives in the country, including the army high command and members of the Central Committee were angry and frustrated over Gorbachev's peace with Germany, the coming withdrawal of Soviet forces from Eastern Europe and the mad rush into the market economy. The Communist Party's fall from grace and power was being greeted with bitter resentment. The power struggle between the establishment and the so-called democrats, headed by Boris Yeltsin, was growing daily. There was no solution in sight to any of these blows. A clash was becoming unavoidable. Everyone spoke about a takeover by conservative forces, yet no one really believed it would come about.

In Iran just before the Khomeini revolution, I had seen the gathering storm: the growing social and political tension, the army's demands for resolute action, and the vacillation of the Shah and his reliance on external advice. The Soviet scene strongly reminded me of those days. I spoke to many friends about the Iranian example, that of a regime, with a strong army and secret service, overthrown and destroyed. Gorbachev was acting pretty much like the Shah. At turns hesitant and unscrupulous, changing advisers and directions with growing rapidity, basking in the adulation of the West, ignoring the need for difficult decisions, Gorbachev, like the Shah, appeared to want his dirty work done by others.

When the coup came, everyone around me and I myself were at first incredulous. Muscovites adopted an 'I told you so' attitude. Many believed they were witnessing a grand theatrical production. Gorbachev had been asking for extraordinary powers and had presided over a nation-wide referendum in March 1991 about the desirability of preserving the unity of the 15 republics in one federal state. The outcome of the referendum having been positive, Gorbachev set the date of 20 August for the signing of the agreement on the creation of a new state within the boundaries of the Soviet Union. He would need much resoluteness to carry this plan through. The Russian Federation under Yeltsin was actively resisting this decision and taking unilateral measures to establish its own independence, an act followed by a number of other republics.

When the news broke and it transpired that Gorbachev was to all intents and purposes banished from the political scene, it fell to the Russian president to lead the anti-putschist forces. Yeltsin and his supporters began barricading themselves in at the White

House, the Russian Federation building. The Russian president proceeded to issue proclamations counter to those published by the coup leaders, declaring them null and void. Toward the end of that first day, tension began to grow and there was rising fear of a military clash between the forces of the committee and those loyal to Yeltsin.

That same afternoon I was due to give a private cocktail party for the send-off of Transport Minister Moshe Katsav. I asked the minister's party to make their way early to my hotel, which was out of the central area of Moscow and on the road to the airport. I was hoping the committee would not cancel flights in and out of the country. The city's traffic was heavily congested but Katsav made his way to the hotel and stayed with us late into the night before he took off for his early morning El Al flight. Prime Minister Shamir called to inquire if his minister of transport was safe. We all were. But I breathed a sigh of relief when the minister took off.

At the Russian White House, Yeltsin, Rutskoi, Popov and the other anti-putschist leaders were awaiting the next moves of the extraordinary committee's forces. Yeltsin's group was receiving a great deal of support and publicity by the local and international media. Hesitantly at first, statements of support started coming in from the US and Europe. Alexander Yakovlev, Eduard Shevardnadze and many others appeared on the White House balcony and made declarations against tyranny. Yeltsin climbed on a friendly tank and made a fiery speech. He waved a large, pre-revolutionary tricolour, thus demoting the red banner with its sickle and hammer. It was an event in itself. At several points during the siege of the White House, we thought Kryuchkov's KGB special forces would attack the Russian bastion and a blood-letting would result, but the face-off ended only in minor clashes on the street below. Three young men were killed and immediately promoted to the national pantheon. One of them was a 23-year-old Jewish boy, Ilya Krichevsky.

There was a swarm of onlookers and volunteer defenders around the White House. I also went out there and into the streets to observe, entirely alone. We moved about and saw the crowds milling around the tanks and armoured cars, talking with the bored soldiers who assured everyone that they had not been issued ammunition and consequently would not start shooting. The traffic was tied up but people got to work or went shopping in spite of the delays. The foreign restaurants were busy with their usual clientele. I had lunch with some people at the Delhi, in the middle of the crisis.

There was a good deal of anguish regarding the future. It would have seemed that Minister of Defence Yazov, head of the KGB Kryuchkov, and Minister of the Interior Pugo were an indomitable force that could easily have taken possession of the country's nerve centres and solidified their power within days. However, the appearance of the putschist group at a televised first evening press conference, their apologetic manner and totally inept responses to the Soviet press broke the spell. In the two days that followed, the insurrectionists did not act decisively and seemed to have lost their nerve early on, but at the time these facts were unknown and there was much anxious hand-wringing regarding the possible outcome.

Regardless of the general perturbation caused by the unusual turn of events, a very small percentage of the total population really participated in active resistance to the putsch. It was this minority that carried the day and wrote the obituary to Soviet power. The effect of the coup was more diluted in Leningrad and the other cities across the country. The censorship and strict control of the media, instituted with the announcement of the takeover, soon dissipated. There was an upsurge of informal media activity, and the public was kept abreast of the events.

When Gorbachev returned from his dacha in the Crimea, it was clear the coup had been no more than an unwieldy attempt of conservative forces to turn back the clock. The full story has not yet been told, although a whole literature has now sprung up in Russia, with accusations and counter-accusations in every direction about the three days of 19–22 August. To me, the role of Gorbachev is not entirely clear. I am not referring to the story of his communications being cut off, although I heard people in the Civil Aviation Ministry saying, a week after the coup, that Gorbachev was endowed with such a variety of systems at his dacha that he simply could not have been isolated and could have put himself in touch with anyone he liked, had he wanted to. The question, rather, has to do with the moral responsibility of the head of state.

Gorbachev must have known a great deal, and could have suspected even more, before he left on his vacation on 6 August; and he was not in isolation until 18 August. There is no doubt at all that he knew what his close collaborators wanted, what their state of mind was and what they were capable of. On the other hand, the men who attempted to take over the reins of power seemed to think they were doing a good turn to Gorbachev and that he surely would be grateful if they succeeded.

Yet Gorbachev must not be judged harshly. It was precisely his personality and disposition that created an atmosphere which countervailed the attempted coup. The population of the Soviet Union at large was no longer the muzzled multitude of the Khrushchev days. Under Gorbachev, the environmental impact of glasnost had become too great to be ignored. Finally, Gorbachev could not and would not support the heads of the coup: it was not in his temperament to lead a move against his own state and presidency and risk the possible consequences. For indeterminate reasons the heads of the KGB, the army and the Ministry of the Interior made too many wrong assumptions in believing that Gorbachev would readily follow them. The attempt to turn the country back to its pre-perestroika days was doomed before it began in earnest.

I went to pay a visit of condolence to the parents of Ilya Krichevsky and one of the other two young men, Vladimir Usov, the son of a retired admiral of the fleet. Krichevsky's parents were good and loyal communists and had almost no connections to the Jewish world. They had no notion of Jewish history, even in the USSR, knew not a word of Yiddish and had only vague recollections of their own parents, who were also communists. Krichevsky's sister Olga, however, had been studying Hebrew and was interested in visiting Israel, which was rather surprising, given the remoteness of the family from everything Jewish.

The Usovs, who seemed to be a typical Russian military family, were dignified and reserved and saw the loss of their son as an important event in the struggle for democracy in Russia. They showed no sign of surprise at my official visit, although I did not hear of any other diplomat who took such an inititative at the time. A few days later, both families were present in the central synagogue, where a service was held in memory of the three young men who fell defending the Russian White House against the attempted coup.

Krichevsky's death turned out to be an important landmark in the population's attitude toward the Jews. Ilya Zaslavsky, an intelligent and active politician and a member of the democratic movement, was at the time a senior official of the Sebastopol administrative region in Moscow. He told me several weeks after the coup that Krichevsky's death had acted as a strong unifying force between Jews and non-Jews, in the general post-coup euphoria. Suddenly, people understood that Jews, as much as many Russians, were defenders of the new freedoms and had shared the same concern in the tense days of the coup. The state funeral for the three victims had shown to millions of Russians, via television, the solemn and dignified Jewish rites, and that too made a strong impact. A pervasive sense of shame developed among much of the intelligentsia because of the previous distrust and animosity toward the Jews.

Visceral anti-Semitism, as we know it, has not died in Russia. But it has become less acceptable, at least among the intelligentsia, a stratum of society which was not entirely immune to it before. The establishment too is changing its attitude. The Jews are no more the pariahs that Soviet practice had rendered them. Jobs and opportunities have become more available, universities and special schools have opened up. A great deal of this new attitude can be traced to the events of August 1991. The longevity of this changing inter-ethnic texture in Russia is not guaranteed to last. But so far, it appears positive.

A week after the August upheaval, it became clear that Foreign Minister Alexander Bessmertnykh, having failed to unambiguously support his president, would have to go. The Soviet Union was visibly coming apart at its seams and with it the status of its foreign service. Was it to remain a Soviet ministry or would it too be divided up between the future, as yet non-existent, unified federal states; or would it be taken over by the Russian Federation, now rapidly coming into its own? The personnel of the ministry were agonizing over its future and I could feel for my colleagues in their uncertainty.

After a short time, I was invited to call on Oleg Derkovsky and Mikhail Bogdanov at the Near East department. They would resume where they had left off, they told me. Israel had already suggested before the August events that the time seemed appropriate to start discussing a Soviet pullback from the UN 'Zionism equals racism' resolution. The USSR had engineered this shameful UN decision in the early 1970s and maliciously hung on to it at the UN and throughout the world, in their sustained campaign against Israel. After the attempted coup, the Soviet Ministry of Foreign Affairs appeared more open to our request to strike the resolution from the UN roster. Eventually, this act of historical justice was indeed accomplished with the support of the Soviet UN delegation.

The perpetrators of the August coup wanted to preserve the empire. It turned out they hastened its demise. There was a certain wisdom in their being released from prison. Keeping them locked up and conducting a prolonged trial may have had strong repercussions and adversely influenced political life, beyond the uncertainty and the instability already present. The process that took Europe centuries cannot be completed in post-communist Russia overnight. Will Russia change its thousand-year course? Will it work out a more humane and democratic concept of governing its 17 million square kilometres, with its conglomerate of nations and ethnic groups, and the variety in its cultures and tongues?

22 · The Death of Friends

Moscow is a city of ten million inhabitants. I did not know a single soul when I arrived in November 1988, except one member of our mission who was on his way out. In the time I spent in the Soviet capital, I made many friends and got acquainted with hundreds, perhaps thousands of people. Unlike any other embassy or diplomatic office, the Moscow mission was, at its inception, primordial. I had to make my way to the top from the very bottom, to operate personally at every level of political or human contact in organizing our work, recruiting local staff, opening doors, getting the cold wind of Soviet receptions full blast in the face. There were no authoritative or influential persons that I could turn to for guidance and no support from Jerusalem, since communication was infrequent and unreliable in the extreme. I had found myself in a comparable situation in the Israeli diplomatic service only in Rwanda, Africa. Whereas in every other country difficulties of adaptation, language and custom are usually short-lived, I found the environment in Moscow inhospitable over a long period of time. I had never been to a communist country before and had to decipher the behavioural code of Soviet officials. The vigilance toward me evoked my own unflagging alertness. Perhaps these psychological constraints were not absolutely necessary, but they were inculcated into me by Soviet conduct toward Israel and other countries, as observed over the years preceding my arrival in Moscow.

This uninviting atmosphere, however, was gradually penetrated by the force of mutual curiosity. There were a number of individuals who helped me get oriented in the Soviet maze: in the workings of the government machine and in human subtleties. I valued this help in the initial period of my life in Moscow and much regretted having to leave these friends at the end of my term. I have tried to maintain contact with them since. But there were some who departed before I was prepared to let them go. Such was the case with three men, all very different, who were in some ways my mentors, even if not all a priori friends and admirers of the State of Israel, in whose name I appeared on the Moscow scene.

Radomir Georgievich Bogdanov was one such person. I saw him for the first time at the USA and Canada Institute. I have already described what I knew about Bogdanov some time after meeting him, having looked up his name in the pages of Barron's encyclopaedic books about the KGB. Evidently, Bogdanov was not employed at the institute as an expert on the US. Soviet Jews knew him from his interference in the visits of American and Canadian Jews. From his persistent interest in business deals with Israel I guessed he was charged with finding western investments in the USSR, through Israel. In the first meetings I had with Bogdanov he displayed great irritability during our conversations, to the point that I suspected I had fallen in with a person best to avoid. Shumikhin, a Middle East specialist who worked with him, seemed to be apprehensive of Bogdanov. I took it to mean that the gentleman was the KGB resident at the institute.

Bogdanov mellowed after his trip to Israel. For unexplained reasons, he soon moved from the USA and Canada Institute to the Soviet Peace Committee, where he got installed as deputy director. The committee was considered an important Soviet organization in propaganda operations abroad and in gaining friends and sympathizers for the USSR. It was very well connected with the Central Committee and other influential organs of the Soviet system. In his new assignment, Bogdanov continued to drum up business with Israel and the West. He kept telling me of his contacts with Bronfman and Reichman and other Jewish businessmen and of their projects. Bogdanov participated in the organization of an Orthodox Jewish pilgrimage to Ouman in Western Ukraine, to the tomb of Rabbi Nachman of Bratslav, a much venerated eighteenth-century Jewish mystic. When Shimon Peres was invited to visit the USSR in his capacity as head of the Labour Party, it was Bogdanov who set up the projected economic meetings with senior government officials. Bogdanov was very upset about the

301

incompetence and lethargy with which these preparations were being made and twice called off Peres's visit. Eventually, Bogdanov quarrelled with Genrikh Borovik, the director of the Peace Committee, and resurfaced at Arkady Volsky's Scientists' and Industrialists' Union, where he was again put in charge of contacts with the Jewish world. I suspected, throughout, that it was Bogdanov who was promoting himself as an expert on Jewish business, and not some secret Soviet department that was using his connections.

Bogdanov and I often lunched together, at times with other friends, such as Nikolai Shishlin. Radomir loved the most expensive spots, such as the Sakura, a Japanese restaurant at the Hammer Centre, or the Savoy Hotel. At times, he asked for the Delhi, an Indian restaurant, where he usually ordered whatever the waiter recommended. Once, I asked him why, after all his years in India as the KGB resident, he always asked for the waiter's choice. Bogdanov said, 'Oh well, order Tandoori'. Occasionally, he would invite me and my guests to the Kropotkinskaya, where the owner, Anatoly Fedorov, would personally wait on Bogdanov's guests. On such occasions, Bogdanov never failed to remind me that Fedorov had a two million dollar turnover, a remarkable fact in those days, when the market economy had still not gripped the imaginations of Russian entrepreneurs.

When he got established at the Peace Committee, Bogdanov began looking for likely clients on whom to exercise his consultation capacities. Among the first he lent a helping hand to was Dave Kimche, a frequent visitor to Moscow in his assignments for Maxwell or, later, Shaul Eisenberg. Bogdanov was a central broker in at least one of the projects Kimche's principals were involved in: the joint US-Soviet-Israel airliner. For two years, talk of this very ambitious plan nurtured the dreams of Israelis and Russians alike. The scheme itself did not materialize for purely economic reasons, but it gave Israel Aircraft Industries a presence and leverage in the Soviet air industry it would not have otherwise had. Subsequently, it contributed to cooperation in the construction of smaller aircraft. Bogdanov was not an altruist, and in the realities of the perestroika era, it was only natural for him to be remunerated for his advice and connections by the business people he was assisting. He often asked me to remind Jewish businessmen of his involvement in the airliner project and would express the hope that his contribution would not be forgotten. Beyond the fact that he might have found my support of importance in his own operations, I thought he was well disposed toward me and showed a certain understanding for my task. When I had difficulties in transmitting messages, I talked to Bogdanov, knowing that my words would reach the ears of at least one addressee I needed. When I told him there were certain persons I could not reach, he would often say: 'He has to be given a good bribe.' He also often complained about the western businessmen he was dealing with, saying the 'fat cats' would not help him or would not follow his advice. He never asked me for any compensation, nor did I ever offer him any.

Bogdanov proved of value in reading the political map and interpreting the moods of the governors and the governed. He often preceded others in describing the preoccupations of the security establishment with the perestroika policies toward the West. He talked to me about their anger and dismay over the 'ignominious retreat from Eastern Europe'. But most of all, Bogdanov spoke about the future of the *gosudarstvo* (the state) built up through the long and painful history of Russia, from the defeat of the Mongols to its unification and expansion into Central Asia and the Caucasus. To Bogdanov, the past and the present were indivisible, and Russian imperial tradition was to be continued come what may. These sentiments were not those of Bogdanov alone. I heard them from dozens of people, from high officials to academicians, from writers to cooks and drivers. For a time, when the future began looking dim, Bogdanov would conspiratorially whisper about a possible compromise: the Russians would be ready to give up the Baltic republics and the Transcaucasian territories, but would never give up their inherited right of ownership to the land mass from the Polish border to the Pacific. That was self-evident.

We all knew Bogdanov was ill with a number of serious ailments. He was forever toying with little brown bottles of medicine and packets of East European pills and asking for western prescriptions for his complaints. He knew he had to have open heart surgery but was constantly putting it off because of the inadequacy of Soviet hospitals. Finally, he had it in Germany in late 1990. The operation was paid for by a rich western patron. I thought he would sufficiently recover to lead a normal life, since he was only 65 years old. I heard nothing more of his difficulties for a good many months but a few days after Israel's independence reception, in April 1991, Boris Nefedov, Volsky's secretary, called me to say Bogdanov had suddenly died. Nefedov informed me of the arrangements for the funeral. I was stunned.

The official funeral service took place at the USA and Canada Institute. There was a small crowd of mourners, including Radomir's wife, his daughter and son. His granddaughter, whom he adored and incessantly talked about, was too young to attend. Arbatov and Volsky were glaringly absent, as were other important people whom Bogdanov must have served over the years, in and out of the KGB. As I watched from the railing on the second floor, Bogdanov's body was brought up the staircase, smiling widely in the open bier, and placed in the hall. It was not clear to me if the smile was Bogdanov's natural expression in death or was thoughtfully arranged by the morticians. It looked like a typically cynical Bogdanov comment on the proceedings.

Bogdanov's family members were seated to one side of the coffin as a number of former colleagues from the institute eulogized him. A few moments later, an attractive young woman in black approached and, unexpectedly breaking out into loud sobs, planted a kiss on Bogdanov's forehead. This caused a stir, and generated a wave of whispers around the hall. I did not know who the lady in black was, but her appearance suddenly cast an entirely new light on Radomir Georgievich. Only later, when I found out how devoted Bogdanov had been to his younger consort, did I understand the significance of the advice he often shared with me, to wit, that women were in their prime between the ages of 32 to 42.

As Dave Kimche happened to be in town at the time and attended the farewells at the institute, he and I joined the procession to the crematorium. I had been to crematoria in France but found the Soviet practice more spartan. There was no theatre in which the mourners listened to the funereal music, waiting for the body to be consumed. Bogdanov's coffin was lowered from the black hearse onto a moving platform and slowly disappeared from view into the maw of what presumably was the cremating machine. I paid my condolences to the family and went back to a meeting at the Ministry of Foreign Affairs where another Bogdanov, Mikhail, was expecting me to compare notes on the Middle East. My professional preoccupations, however, were far removed from my thoughts, as I made my way back through the busy streets of Moscow.

I regretted Bogdanov's passing. He was a dependable friend and a convenient channel of communication with the various personalities of the regime who had carefully avoided me until I ascended to my official status of consul-general. A colourful personality, he was also endowed with an analytical mind and knew well the workings of the Soviet machine. Often, when I complained to him of the inaccessibility of higher officials for an open dialogue, he would tell me I should organize a lobby in promoting my interests, a suggestion that I was unable to act upon. He was also a person who, for all his petulance and irascibility, was kind to his assistants and associates and thoughtfully provided them with financial help and jobs, to the best of his ability. He loved going on vacations abroad with his small retinue, and sometimes with his granddaughter. But above all he had a sense of humour, which I appreciated, as it put the oddness of Soviet behaviour in its proper perspective.

When the attempted coup interrupted our lives in the Soviet capital, I immediately thought of Bogdanov, who certainly would have had interesting commentary on the events, which he had in many ways predicted. I had another analyst at my side, however, with an encyclopaedic knowledge of Russia and its history and a mind just as incisive.

Mikhail Agursky was a man of many accomplishments. Son of American Jewish communists who came to participate in the building of socialism in the days of Stalin, Agursky was an expert in cybernetics and a scientific adviser to the Soviet military. Agursky became a political dissident. Together with Alexander Solzhenitsyn and a number of other intellectuals, he participated in the early 1970s in writing a compendium of articles called *From Under the Rubble*, essays that gave an explosive impetus to a new political consciousness and activity in the USSR.

In 'The Third Rome', his doctoral thesis for the Ecole des Hautes Etudes in Paris, Agursky discussed national Bolshevism as an ideology that legitimized the Russian étatist, rather than the Marxist, point of view. Therein lay, in his opinion, the drive for a universal Russian empire cemented by communist ideology. 'Lenin's grand design', Agursky argued, was to become the absolute world political leader, who would open up a new era in human history; Russia was the 'electoral constituency' that would aid him in achieving this objective. This description of Lenin, unthinkable in the Soviet Union in pre-perestroika days, gained ground later on. Among the many newfound critics who appeared after 1989 was Dmitri Volkogonov, the former official historian of the Soviet army, who wrote about Lenin in terms similar to Agursky's, in the last part of a trilogy on Soviet leaders, published in 1994.

Agursky eventually settled in Israel, becoming a senior lecturer at the Hebrew University and a distinguished political writer and commentator on the Soviet Union and communism. Not everyone accepted his ideas, but most admitted to the freshness and provocativeness of his approach.

Agursky had a wide circle of friends among philosophers, writers, sociologists and political analysts, to whom he introduced me when I arrived in Moscow. I made wide use of these contacts and kept up my relations with Agursky himself, from whom I gained enormous insights into the Russian mind. When greater relaxation set in and Agursky did not feel himself threatened any more, he reappeared on the Moscow scene and re-established his connections among his many former friends. It was Agursky who, as early as 1989, organized an open debate with the well-known Russian chauvinist and anti-Semite, the mathematician Igor Shafarevich, ·at Moscow University, on so-called Jewish responsibility for the revolution and adverse influence on Russian culture. He had known Shafarevich well and had worked with him in the publication of *From Under the Rubble*. The debate at Moscow University was well attended and widely publicized.

In Israel, Agursky and a few other Russian intellectuals constantly clashed with 'Professor' Ilya Zemtsov, whom Agursky considered to be a charlatan and an agent of western and eastern intelligence organizations. Agursky's feelings were shared by many. Ezer Weizmann once said of Zemtsov that one of his steel teeth was signalling to the CIA, the other to the KGB. The Israeli newspapers, always on the lookout for scandals, helped fan the quarrel between these two men, so different in their background and at such variance in their intellectual achievements. Agursky was very emotional about this private war and had his friends in Moscow uncover Zemtsov's personal file at the Communist Party, from which he was reportedly expelled in disgrace for unbecoming behaviour. But Agursky never got around to using this material against his long-time enemy. Zemtsov, however, had far greater capabilities in worming himself into the political establishment in Israel and proffering his services as a go-between with Soviet officials, using the tricks of the trade he seemed to know so well.

Soon after my arrival in Moscow, Agursky became a frequent visitor and renewed his contacts with the intellectual community in the Russian capital. He was used as a consultant by the Jewish Agency, and began staying for longer stints, sending his comments on the political scene to the *Jerusalem Post* or working with former Soviet colleagues on an interpretation of the political events and preparing a book on perestroika.

Agursky's son, Benny, a young man of 20, was an alpinist, practising this sport in the mountains of the Judean desert and participating in alpine ascents abroad. In the summer of 1990 Benny came out with a group of fellow alpinists to scale the Pamirs, a challenging mountain range in Tajikistan. This was his second venture into the mountains of the Soviet Union, closed to Israeli climbers before relations had started improving. I invited the group to stay at the consulate for a few days, before their departure to Tajikistan. Shortly after they left, news reached us of an earthquake in the Pamirs and the disappearance of Benny and other, non-Israeli climbers. In a few days' time a group of rescuers arrived from Israel, headed by Eli Raz, the head of the Judean Desert Rescue Team. They brought equipment and embarked on the search, with the active help of the Soviet Alpinists' Association of Leningrad and others. Agursky arrived with the group and in spite of being past 60 and not in the best of health, set out to look for his son. He stayed on at the foot of the mountain for over two weeks after the active search had been abandoned, hoping news would reach him, from somewhere, somehow, that his son was safe or at least alive. The Soviet sports organizations did all they could. They had little access, communications or equipment, and only a marginal presence in the Pamir area, although it was a favourite climbing spot. When the rescue team arrived back in Moscow, I invited them for a debriefing, to see what could be done to prevent such tragedies in the future. Agursky attended as well, outwardly calm and collected, although I could imagine what he had been through.

In Moscow, by chance, during the August events in 1991, Agursky was consumed by curiosity regarding the participants in the coup, which he had anticipated. I met him on the river boat Leo Tolstoy, just a day after the coup attempt was thwarted. He and I appeared as speakers at a Jewish Agency conference, which was to continue as the boat sailed along the Volga. Not being participants, we left the boat and I dropped Agursky off at the Rossiya Hotel, where he was staying, and made a dinner appointment with him for one of the following days.

The next evening, an unfamiliar voice called me at my hotel. Identifying himself as a police agent, he asked if I could help him locate the Israeli consul. When I asked what I could do to help, he said he wanted me to come down to the Rossiya Hotel to identify the corpse of an Israeli citizen, who had died early in the morning, but whose body was not discovered until much later in the day. I asked for the name and was told it was Agursky. I was shocked and could not bring myself to believe there had not been some mistake in identification. I tried very hard to get someone else to go down to the Rossiya but could not find anyone available. I was obliged to do the job myself. To my dismay, I found Agursky lying on the floor of his tiny hotel room, with his notes and books spread all around him. The police assured me they had no reason to suspect foul play and the physician on duty told me Agursky had probably suffered a fatal stroke. It was a difficult moment. Agursky's friends told me later he had never recovered from the death of his son Benny and had been in poor health since his watch at the foot of the Pamirs the previous year.

Nikolai Shishlin was my closest and most intimate contact with the Central Committee, even though I met people higher up in the hierarchy before and after I got acquainted with him, such as Zagladin, Dzasokhov, chairman of the foreign affairs committee of the Supreme Soviet, Yanaev and others. Shishlin, however, had many contacts with western intellectuals and politicians and had often been abroad. I enjoyed discussing current affairs with him. Shishlin had worked for many years together with a group of consultants at the Central Committee which included Georgy Arbatov, Alexander Bovin, Georgy Shakhnazarov, who later became a close confidant of Gorbachev, Fedor Burlatsky, whom I had met early in my Moscow days, and others. Shishlin cooperated in writing projects and position papers for Yuri Andropov's Central Committee General Department, beginning with Khrushchev's last year in power in 1964, and he retained his status as consultant for many years afterwards. A well-known publicist, Shishlin wrote widely and authoritatively in the international political literature on Soviet positions. He was well-known in Israeli academe. The Hebrew University in Jerusalem invited him to participate in a symposium on the Soviet Union in October 1991. He subsequently wrote an objective and informed analysis about Israel in the Moscow weekly *Novoe Vremia*, which contributed a positive point of view on our problems.

Shishlin was not a very talkative man and was not easy to draw out, but he was a good listener. This trait was important to me at several points in my career in Moscow, when I felt we were not getting through on the Soviet role in the Middle East and its relation to the peace process. I knew that the points I made in my discussions with Shishlin were transmitted to Alexander Yakovlev and also may have been included in papers that Shishlin often wrote on international subjects for the Central Committee. I also received replies or reactions, by word of mouth, through Shishlin. He did not have a position of great influence, perhaps, but he offered a dependable means of communicating the Israeli point of view.

Toward the end of my stay in Russia, Shishlin suggested much broader cooperation. He proposed that we set up a lobby and offered to head it. He said the idea had become quite feasible and that we could extend our activity into many areas, including trying to reach understanding on conceptual matters regarding future common strategic goals, giving assistance where needed to the promotion of economic contacts, and deepening understanding with Russian public figures, political scientists and publicists.

These ideas were extraordinarily important and helpful, I thought. Russia would not long remain the third-class power it had become after the collapse of the Soviet Union. In one generation its status in world affairs might change entirely. Given the vastness of its territory, its immense riches and the undoubted talents of its population, it stood to reason that the Russia of the next generation would not resemble the one we were seeing now. Israel, which had suffered plenty as a result of Soviet Middle East policy — itself a reflection of the Cold War, might still look forward to close and fruitful cooperation with the emerging Russian state. There were and are many elements of shared concern, including the threat of fundamentalist Islam in the Caucasus and in Central Asia. In addition, a good 700,000 of Israel's inhabitants have arrived from Russia and adjacent lands in the last quarter of a century and could help build a strong and lasting bridge of cultural and economic interests.

For this reason, Nikolai Shishlin's offer of setting up an Israeli lobby in Russia was timely and viable. However, I wanted to make sure it would not run counter to Russian considerations and requested an objective and authoritative reply. I asked Shishlin to consult with Alexander Yakovlev and anyone else he thought necessary. I also asked him to think of possibilities for gaining support for this idea among the Russian rightist bloc. After a time, he came back and affirmed that not only did Yakovlev express his support, but he was willing to lend his name to such an organization, once it was set up. This was the position of several other, including rightist personalities, and I was satisfied that even if we ran into some chauvinistic or anti-Semitic reactions, we would be able to withstand possible opposition.

I transmitted these thoughts to the head of the East European division of our ministry, Yosef Govrin. Weeks passed and I engaged in considerable prodding, but there was no reply either accepting or rejecting the idea. My days in Russia were drawing to a close. I was busy setting up diplomatic relations with 13 of the new republics that had emerged from the Soviet Union and tying up the many loose ends that were still left over from the four years of our intense activity in Russia. I did not have the patience and the persistence to push hard enough for a definitive answer or even a reaction from the Foreign Ministry. After several additional attempts, I let the matter drop. There was a great deal of indecisiveness in Israel's foreign affairs establishment, I felt, perhaps born of fear of initiative and innovation, nostalgia for the past and unwillingness to face the future. This was indeed not the first time I had encountered these deficiencies.

I had to part with Shishlin without the courtesy of an answer to his offer which, even if motivated by personal ambition, could have brought Israel considerable dividends. Toward my last days in Moscow Shishlin was in bad health and at one point he asked me for help, but I could do nothing for him, since my own ministry had no machinery for providing the necessary budgets. Shishlin turned to other people in other ministries in Israel and obtained medical and financial assistance for himself and his daughter who had contracted cancer. I said my goodbyes and left Shishlin with a great deal of regret at not having accomplished more with him.

In the intervening year, after my retirement from the Ministry of Foreign Affairs, I heard very little about Nikolai but in the summer of 1994, in a conversation with Ambassador Alexander Bovin, I heard the following story.

At one of the appearances of Ilya Zemtsov in Moscow, when he was staying at the Rossiya Hotel, he invited Shishlin to his room. The evening before, Shishlin had not been well but thought he had gotten over it. In the course of their conversation at the hotel, Shishlin asked for a glass of whisky. After he had drunk it he went pale and seemed to sink deeper into his chair. When asked if he was not feeling well, Shishlin replied it would soon pass but a few moments later he seemed to lose consciousness. An ambulance was called, but Shishlin had already died, apparently of a massive heart attack.

I left Russia still largely ignorant about the complexities of its life and reality. I remain grateful to the many people who helped me understand what motivates the Russians and their rulers. I shall not forget Bogdanov and Shishlin, who helped me get oriented in the Soviet maze, heard me out and helped me with their counsel when I required it. Agursky was in a different category: he was a man who understood both the world from which I came and the one I had stepped into. After his many years in the West, he saw the Russian scene with Western eyes. He knew Russian history and mentality and helped me interpret them in terms which were relevant to me and to those whom I represented. But most of all, I found in these three men, each so different, friends I could openly converse with and depend on, a rare gift — not only in Moscow.

23 · *The Embassy Opens*

At the end of August 1991 I flew to Jerusalem to give away my daughter Michal in marriage. The continued postponement of diplomatic relations was the last thing on my mind at this time as Aliza and I were preparing ourselves for the event. Michal was born in Kigali, in the African republic of Rwanda. After her peregrinations as part of an Israeli diplomatic family, in France, Iran, and the US, and after her two years in the Israeli army, Michal was settling down, not too far from our home in Jerusalem. It took me a few days to get back to the state of mind I was in before the wedding, to report to the ministry and to Prime Minister Yitzhak Shamir. The latter, as always, was eager to hear about the latest developments in 'Soviet Russia'.

The prime minister's eyes were riveted to mine as I gave him a blow-by-blow description of the three extraordinary days of the August coup. Yossi Ben-Aharon, the director general of the prime minister's office, asked as many questions, but there was no doubt as to who was the better listener and who related more personally to the earth-shaking events. The lemon tea and the dry poppy-seeded biscuits were consumed faster than usual as I talked about Boris Yeltsin waving the old imperial Russian flag from the White House balcony in Moscow and described the skirmish with the tanks, in which Ilya Krichevsky shed his blood for Russian freedom.

But what about Gorbachev, and who were the leaders of the new political parties? Who was this new Foreign Minister Boris Pankin? I tried to answer as best I could, thinking the events had finally broken down the barrier of the prime minister's passive curiosity. Shamir's eyes had a special twinkle when I talked to him about the Soviet Union, a vestige of his long-standing interest in communism. Would the *aliyah* continue? Yes, I assured him, now more than ever. But, alas, beyond this statutory expression of the prime minister's desire there was no statement of intent, no suggestion of policy. Nevertheless, I used the opportunity to brief Shamir on the political confusion in the Kremlin, the widening gap between Gorbachev and Yeltsin, the political uncertainties, the Foreign Ministry's struggle to survive as a ministry, the resultant indolence and the readiness to follow the American lead, at least temporarily, on the Middle East.

Since I expected little guidance from my own ministry, I thought it justified to ask for the prime minister's opinion on our possible attitude toward the evolving situation: should we not hurry with the recognition of the emerging republics and set up diplomatic relations with them; open consulates, invite the new heads of state on official visits and attempt to interest them in direct economic and political ties? The prime minister had evidently not had much time to think about these matters and although there were no objections to anything I said, he would not impart his views on our future relations with a whole group of new states emerging out of the USSR.

I talked to the prime minister about the growing rivalry and the confrontation between Nativ and the Jewish Agency; their competitive efforts to widen their operational territory; the resulting waste of effort and money as well as the negative effect on potential immigrants and the Soviet authorities in the field. I asked for the prime minister's decisions regarding this acute problem. Nativ was working under the mission's roof and under its diplomatic protection. Its officials were classified as 'consuls' in the diplomatic list and carried diplomatic passports — yet they worked entirely independently of the head of mission. The Russians knew their every move. The attempts I made to coordinate Nativ's activities in Moscow with my own, both before and after raising the flag and becoming the head of an officially recognized consular office, ended in failure. There was an increasing gap between Nativ's expanding initiatives and the briefings I was receiving. Yitzhak Shamir did not react, beyond the usual generalizations on the need for cooperation among all the agencies working in the field.

One of the projects Nativ was devising at this time was the selection of 5,000 Jewish youths per year to be brought to Israel to complete their high school education. The hope was that the freedom young people enjoy in Israel would prove attractive enough to persuade the youths to settle in there and urge their parents to come as well. The details of this plan were not publicized until January 1995*, but its essence came to my attention in the summer of 1991, along with Nativ's many other operations. This was an excellent plan, but it required continued and rapid expansion of Nativ activities in the Soviet Union, which would result in an even stronger tug-of-war with the Jewish Agency. There was already rivalry between the two services regarding the establishment of 'information centres', as well as in many other fields.

Finally, I suggested to the prime minister that great economic possibilities could be opening up for Israeli industrialists and businessmen. Markets and technological cooperation were awaiting us if we could learn how to reach them. The new Russian immigrants could presumably broker the contacts. The prime minister promised he would look into the matter and talk to Israeli business leaders.

The East European division organized an inter-departmental meeting on developments in the Soviet Union and the assessment of results following the attempted coup. This important discussion was chaired by the Minister of Foreign Affairs David Levy. He looked shocked when I recounted the information I had received about the probable availability of communications to Gorbachev during the days of his isolation on Foros, in the Crimea. Levy wanted to have this information suppressed. On the other hand, the minister urged us all to be highly attentive to the changes in the USSR, to intensify our research and to report our findings, for

---

* Rali Saar, 'Az lama be'etsem hatse'irim lo baim?' (Why Aren't the Young People Coming Then), *Haaretz*, 1 Jan. 1995.

which he promised his undivided attention. When I requested an appointment, however, the minister's alter ego, Uri Oren, told me David Levy avoided meetings with his emissaries abroad: he feared the inevitable headache setting on, when they asked him about their future appointments. There was no point in even trying to get decisions from the East European division, which had no access to the minister and would decide nothing on its own.

At the ministry, there was a change of directors general. Reuven Merhav had had a falling out with Minister David Levy, who hastened to accept his resignation. Levy appointed Joseph Hadass, with whom I had crossed assignments in the past. Hadass called a meeting with Yosef Govrin and Yaacov Cohen, the head of the economics division, and Moshe Ben-Yaacov, the head of the ministry's administration. We discussed current affairs and the problems in Moscow, but the brief get-together did not set any political parameters or goals for the coming months. I enjoyed sitting down with the top brass of the ministry, but the problems that I raised stayed as starkly bereft of solutions as they had been before. Perhaps it was too much to expect of a new director-general to make such difficult decisions (including settling ongoing disputes between immigration agencies), when these irksome matters had never been disposed of before, even at the level of foreign ministers.

After meeting with the chairman of the Knesset's foreign relations and defence committee, Eliahu Ben-Elissar, with whom I raised the subject of Kalmanovich, I took the flight back to Moscow. I found myself in the company of the Knesset immigration committee, which was off to the Soviet capital to see the future citizens of Israel getting their visas at the consulate-general.

A number of meetings were organized for this parliamentary committee, headed by Micha Kleiner and including Yossi Beilin, with whom I had worked closely in 1986–88 during his days as political director-general of the ministry under Shimon Peres. Among the people they met was the head of the Human Rights Committee of the Soviet Parliament, Sergei Kovalev, an exceptional and outstanding personality in Moscow's political life. A biologist by profession, Kovalev joined Andrei Sakharov in 1967 in his struggle for human rights in the Soviet Union. He was arrested and sent to the Urals in 1974 but eventually returned to Moscow and became one of the leading human rights activists. In spring 1995 Kovalev led the movement against the war in Chechnya, communicating with Moscow from the cellars of the besieged presidential palace in Grozny. The immigration committee was also received by Alexander Belonogov and Deputy Foreign Minister Boris Kolokolov, who willingly and openly discussed questions relating to emigration — an indication that Jewish emigration was not at all in jeopardy nor an impediment to improving Israeli-Soviet relations.

Soon after my return from home leave in mid-September 1991, Yosef Govrin called me from Jerusalem to complain that the chairman of the Soviet Prliament's foreign affairs committee, Vladimir Lukin (later, ambassador to the United States), on a parliamentarians' visit to Israel, publicly reiterated the Soviet creed: first a government declaration on not settling immigrants in the occupied territories, then diplomatic relations. I remarked that Lukin was pulling this battered statement out of his hat as a matter of form. In the conversations I had had with him he had shown a great deal of understanding and was positive on the need for the renewal of relations, more so than his deputy Yevgeny Ambartsumov, who, with his knowledge of the Arab Middle East and his many contacts in the Arab world, had a conservative bias, I thought. In fact, Lukin's statement did signal a change in the significant predisposition, current in Moscow, toward reinstating full-fledged embassies. Everybody was saying it would only be a matter of weeks. Nikolai Shishlin, who had left the Central Committee and had joined the new editors of *Pravda*, asserted to the Israel television correspondent in Moscow, Michael Karpin, that had it not been for the confusion in government, the step would have already been taken.

At the end of September, there was a brief encounter between David Levy and Boris Pankin at the UN in New York. Politically, it was not of great significance, but I thought it radiated assuredness that we were on the verge of a Soviet decision on diplomatic relations. David Levy felt he had established a personal relationship with Pankin. This self-confidence was to prove of importance later on in Jerusalem, when Pankin would arrive for an official visit.

317

UKRAINE MEMORIALIZES BABI YAR

Diplomatic relations receded into the background in the first days of October 1991, as Ukraine commemorated the 50th anniversary of the tragic events at Babi Yar.

I had been approached at the planning stage of the ceremony by Jewish activists in Ukraine, prominent among whom was Alexander Shlaen, himself a victim of anti-Semitism in Kiev under the communists. They wanted our assurances that the event would be well-received and publicized in Israel and that President Haim Herzog would attend. The preparations were carried out by the Ukrainian government with the help of Jewish lobbyists and international Jewish organizations. I could not promise to persuade President Herzog to come to Kiev, although I knew he was eager to do so. The problems relating to the movements of the Israeli head of state entail special protocol and security arrangements. These were difficult to execute in a city that was not sufficiently organized for international meetings and had no satisfactory contacts with the Israeli authorities. I informed President Herzog of the invitation, but he preferred to take a decision at the last minute. The event aroused considerable interest in Israel.

This was the first time that the government of Ukraine had decided to mark the date of the massacre by the German occupying forces. The series of killings began on 29 September 1941. It continued for two years in a ravine called Babi Yar, where Jews were forcibly marched out, shot and buried in mass graves. In 1946, after the war had come to an end, Stalin ordered that Babi Yar's victims be mentioned only as 'Soviet citizens', thus forbidding the association of Jews with this atrocity. No memorial was allowed to be raised on the site. The old Jewish cemetery nearby was also obliterated and built over, in a blatant attempt to stamp out the memory of Kiev's murdered Jews. Throughout the years, Soviet authorities thwarted repeated efforts to publish the story of Babi Yar. During Khrushchev's Thaw (1956–64), the massacre received wider international publicity through Yevgeny Yevtushenko's poem, 'Babi Yar'. The poet was shocked into writing the poem after his visit to the ravine in 1961. He first read it publicly the next evening, on the stage of the October Theatre in Kiev. According to information which I received years later from Yevtushenko himself, the very stage from which he declaimed his poem was built over secret cells, where thousands of victims were tortured and killed by the KGB over the years. Yevtushenko was punished for his 'defiance'. His poem was not to be reprinted for 21 years, and he was forbidden to appear in Kiev for 28 years. A similar fate awaited Dmitri Shostakovich's 13th Symphony, also devoted to the Babi Yar massacres. After its first performance in 1962 in Kiev, it took 27 years for the authorities to allow the piece to be performed once again in Ukraine. Yevtushenko read his poem and Shostakovich's symphony was performed at the close of the main event on 6 October near Babi Yar.

Leonid Kravchuk had been the hand-picked representative of Moscow as the first secretary of the Ukrainian Communist Party and a recognized ideological leader of Soviet communism. With the proclamation of Ukraine's independence on 24 August 1991, he had become the chairman of the Ukrainian Supreme Soviet, striving to lead Ukraine to complete separation from the USSR. Kravchuk's organization of the Babi Yar anniversary ran counter to the Ukrainian and Russian practice of suppressing the memory of the Holocaust, and attracted great attention in the West. The city of Kiev was decked out in slogans against anti-Semitism and condemnations of the Babi Yar massacre. A special exhibit of Judaic art was organized at the Kiev Museum and there were other signs of reconciliation with the Jews, who had for centuries suffered persecution in the Ukraine. Kiev was full of guests from abroad. I was pleased to see Shoshana Cardin, chairwoman of the US National Committee for Soviet Jews, who was invited as an official guest of the government; Dr Joseph Burg, former Israeli minister and peace negotiator; and the famous Israeli actor Haim Topol, who had been the most attractive and successful Tevye in productions of *Fiddler on the Roof* — itself a piece of Jewish Ukrainian folklore. There were many others as well.

Notwithstanding the fact that the Babi Yar commemoration was probably undertaken at the suggestion of Kravchuk's Jewish advisers, none could remain unimpressed by this unprecedented act, which must have required a good deal of personal courage on the part of the chairman. I expressed these sentiments to him and to Prime Minister Fokin when we spoke at Kravchuk's reception at the Mariinsky Palace, built in honour of Empress Catherine the Great (paradoxically, the Russian sovereign who had annexed the Ukraine).

When I was received by President Haim Herzog a few days before I left for Moscow, he said that in spite of his desire to do so, he would be unable to attend the memorial in Kiev, since it was not clear whether the Ukrainian organizers would be able to cope with the complicated logistics. President Herzog commissioned me to read out his message at the solemn main event near Babi Yar. At the ceremony, President Herzog's words were followed by those of the Israeli Minister of Education, Zevulun Hammer, who represented the government of Israel. President Bush's communication was read out by his brother. The other guests included Alexander Yakovlev, who spoke on behalf of Mikhail Gorbachev in a statement that owned up to the anti-Semitism of the past in the USSR and expressed regret at the departure of the Jews. Perhaps the most remarkable of all was the speech delivered by Chairman Leonid Kravchuk himself at the opening of the ceremony. He asked forgiveness for the many years of persecution perpetrated at the hands of the Ukrainians, including during the days of the Second World War, and solemnly promised Ukraine would never revert to anti-Semitism.

The Jews had settled in and around Kiev in the ninth century and historians note that the first pogrom took place already in the tenth. The history of the Jews in the Ukraine continued to be sombre. Tens of thousands of Jews — and Poles — were slain by the Cossacks of Ukrainian hero Bohdan Khmelnitsky, in the seventeenth-century insurrection against the Polish overlords. The notorious Beilis case, a blood libel against the Jews, came before the courts in Kiev in 1911, and was resolved in Beilis's favour, but not before it had aroused an additional wave of anti-Semitism in the Ukraine, and in Russia as well.* Hundreds of thousands of Jews were killed during the pogroms at the turn of the century by the

---

* Tsar Nicholas II distributed honours, orders of promotion and gifts of money to those who had participated in the prosecution of Mendel Beilis, after he was acquitted of ritual child murder.

Black Hundreds hooligans and others and also at the time of the Civil War. This record has not made the Ukraine a happy country for the Jews, many of whom emigrated to America before the First World War. Perhaps as a result of this fact, the thousands of communities that lived for centuries on the soil of the Ukraine and neighbouring Belorussia, developed a culture which played a leading role in the Jewish renaissance of the twentieth century. This rebirth brought many Jews to Zionism and others to the revolutionary movement. Throughout that time, no Ukrainian leader ever came forward to express regret, plead for forgiveness or try to turn over a new leaf between the Ukrainian and the Jewish people. Shoshana Cardin and I spoke of this sad record to the large crowd of Jews which had gathered at the edge of the Babi Yar ravine, the morning after Kravchuk's proclamation.

RUTSKOI PROMISES RELATIONS, FOR A PRICE

A few days after my return to Moscow from Kiev I had a long conversation with Alexander Rutskoi. A fighter pilot who had been shot down twice over Afghanistan and escaped from the hands of his captors, Rutskoi was a popular hero and had shown himself to be a loyal supporter of Yeltsin in the defence of the White House against the attempted *coup d'état* of August 1991. Yeltsin promoted him to the rank of brigadier general and gave him the star of the Hero of the Soviet Union, which was still in fashion, and chose him as his vice-president in May 1992.

I have already described the conversation with Rutskoi in the context of the Kalmanovich affair, but the projected purpose of the meeting was to discuss possible Israeli assistance to Russian agriculture, of which Rutskoi had become the policy maker and overseer in the Russian administration. Rutskoi insisted Israel had first to show the economic importance of cooperation for the critics to change their opposition to the renewal of diplomatic relations. He added that his position was rather delicate in the matter, as he had already been attacked by the reactionaries in the Russian government for the best wishes he had offered to the Jewish community on the occasion of the Jewish New Year. I pointed out to Rutskoi the advantages that would accrue from closer contacts with Israel, especially as regarded Russia's diminishing role in the Middle East.

Later that evening, I got a call from Yosif Kobzon, who had participated in the Rutskoi meeting. Kobzon said Boris Pankin, the new foreign minister, was about to set out on a Middle East tour, in the course of which he would visit Israel. Kobzon had spoken to Pankin about my point of view on the Soviet Union's role in the Middle East. Pankin agreed with my opinion, Kobzon said, except for the fact that relations had been put off so long as to become encrusted with embarrassments, which were difficult to shed.

Alerted by Kobzon, I requested that Jerusalem set up a tentative programme for receiving the new Soviet minister, on the assumption that the agenda would include discussions on the Middle East peace process and the renewal of diplomatic relations. A week later, I was called in by Vassily Kolotusha, head of the Foreign Ministry's Near East Department, to inform me of the minister's intended visit to the Middle East, which would include Israel. Pankin would possibly meet with US Secretary of State James Baker, who would be in the country at the same time. The Soviet Union, as the co-sponsor of the coming Middle East peace conference in Madrid, would then coordinate the timing and the distribution of the invitations.

ISRAELI INDUSTRIALISTS LIVE IT UP IN MOSCOW

There was an important piece of unfinished business that I had to attend to before I left for Israel to sit in on the talks with the Soviet foreign minister. For a number of months, I had been in contact with Dov Lautman, chairman of the Israeli Industrialists' Association, and its director-general, Yoram Belizovsky, in an effort to generate interest in cooperating with Soviet industries. I believed such contacts could be fruitful and might widen the scope of industrial and business partnerships. Lautman arrived in mid-October with a number of important businessmen. I had arranged for them to be officially hosted by Volsky's Union of Industrialists and Scientists. The meetings took place just outside

Moscow, in a country house that used to be Nikita Khrushchev's official dacha.

In the course of a four-day visit, the Lautman group met and discussed possible joint ventures with businessmen, visited plants and enterprises and met with Rutskoi and the Russian Prime Minister Ivan Silaev. The upshot of the trip was that Israeli industrialists found the Russian market of very great potential interest but were not eager to invest money in the Soviet Union, for lack of proper legislation and political stability. The Russian scene was still a mystery. I requested Marc Winer, McDonald's manager in the Soviet Union, to share some of the insights he had gained in his 19-year career in that country, and he was gracious enough to do so at a dinner Hanna and he gave at their home. The picture did not brighten up sufficiently, however, for the Israelis to change their basic assessments. Their additional difficulty at the time was that the government of Israel was not prepared to insure large-scale business against risks in the Soviet Union. This was not the only economic initiative of the mission but it was a very important one. My good intentions on this topic were thus thwarted for the time being. Economic relations began in earnest only two years later, when contacts with Russia had grown sufficiently to provide a better psychological atmosphere for trade and investments.

The grand finale of the Israeli industrialists' trip was an amusing one. They absolutely insisted on celebrating the end of their visit 'Tel Aviv style': a solid, well-lubricated dinner, with a lot of singing and dancing on the dinner tables. It was at the end of the Sabbath and Moscow usually closed down at ten o'clock in those days. There was no restaurant or hotel we could possibly have recourse to for such entertainment, unusual in the Soviet capital. I was saved by Andrei Fedorov, who agreed to have his Casino Royale restaurant completely cleared and a table laid just for the Israeli businessmen. The establishment was part of the casino at the Moscow hippodrome, a popular track where Muscovites went to bet and spend time on Sundays and holidays, even in the most socialist of times in the USSR. The food, the vodka, and the dancing on the tables, amid the fragile crystal glasses, were all unforgettable, as was the bill, which was disputed, but paid in full.

One other detail that has stuck in my mind in this connection is a remark made to me by Arkady Volsky when we had a free minute away from the industrialists. He told me of his great concern over the events in Chechnya-Ingushetia where, in his words, the 'slaughter' had begun again and the events, cruel and unpredictable, could lead to most serious consequences. Volsky's words were prophetic. As I write these lines, over three years later, repeated Russian attacks against the Chechen capital, Grozny, have been repulsed, a crisis situation has developed in Moscow and a possibly severe constitutional crisis is again looming ahead for Boris Yeltsin.

PANKIN IN ISRAEL

Soon after the Lautman group's departure from Moscow, Boris Pankin arrived in Israel, together with Kolotusha and Derkovsky, and we went into a long meeting at the Foreign Ministry on the future of the peace process, repeating the well-known positions on the PLO and the demand for an Israeli declaration on non-settlement of immigrants in occupied territories. When the subject of a joint communiqué came up, we demanded that the Soviets announce the renewal of relations, but this they would not do, pleading Pankin's lack of authority. All the same, we had the impression that it was the Near East department team reining in their minister. Resigned, we went to the King David Hotel for an official dinner. At the end of the meal David Levy made a speech in which he declared that there had been an agreement to renew relations. Pankin seemed stunned, but in his reply to Levy's words, to the visible dismay of his Russian staff, he did not deny the declaration.

The next morning, Pankin continued the discussions he had begun the previous evening with the Palestinians and then went into conference with the secretary of state. In the afternoon, with the beginning of the Sabbath closing in on us and the work stoppage approaching just before sundown, as Jewish law requires, Pankin reappeared at the Ministry of Foreign Affairs to announce that the USSR had taken the decision to renew full diplomatic relations. This decision, he cautiously added, was not meant to harm anyone, meaning the Palestinians. Pankin wanted to invite the press in, but Levy produced a prepared joint statement out of his coat pocket and asked Pankin to sign it, which threw the Soviet delegation into a dither. The two parties then went into consultations, adding many minutes to the wasted 24 years and three months which preceded the official renewal of diplomatic relations between Israel and the Union of Soviet Socialist Republics on 18 October 1991.

Photographers stormed into the conference room to register the exciting event, as champagne glasses were raised and the signatures affixed to the bilingual document that was at last produced by the nail-biting diplomats. There was little time to savour this moment as everyone soon decamped into the waiting cars to rush to the prime minister's office. Pankin sat down across the table from Shamir, expecting to launch into a diplomatic discussion, but as soon as the tea had arrived, Shamir rose to his feet, wished Pankin godspeed and rushed out to the microphones to make a statement. Pankin, not be outdone, did not wait for Shamir's declarations. Hurriedly shaking the prime minister's hand, he got into his car and scrambled to the King David Hotel to a joint press conference with Baker. The two co-sponsors then announced their agreement to send out invitations to the participants of the peace conference in Madrid. Everyone then rushed about in a mad mêlée to leave the hotel and dash to the airport, as the sun came down, and the Day of Rest settled over the land of Israel.

At its next meeting the government approved my candidacy as ambassador to the Soviet Union. That evening, before my departure to Moscow, Aliza and I celebrated the event at dinner with our long-time friends Ilana and Zefaniah Cohen at the King David Hotel. The wine waiter inquired whether I was indeed Ishai Levin's father. When I confirmed that this was the case, we were offered an excellent bottle of Cabernet on the house, in appreciation not of my new appointment, but of Ishai's short stint as barman at the King David before his induction into the army.

At the end of October, the Madrid conference opened with speeches by the co-sponsors, the US and the Soviet Union. Shamir rust David Levy with representing Israel, preferring this historic role for himself. This snub caused great friction ...e two men, who were far from close friends in any event. The Israeli Ministry of Foreign Affairs was left out of the picture. Shamir had a first meeting with Gorbachev, who spoke to him about the outdated Soviet positions on the Middle East but did not mention the fact that he had instructed Pankin to avoid, as far as possible, the re-establishment of relations with Israel, as I soon found out from my contacts. What Gorbachev also told Shamir was that he had viewed my appearance in the 'Beau Monde' programme on Moscow television, with two highly inquisitive and disrespectful interviewers, where I had decidedly held my own. I was pleased at this compliment, in spite of the fact that the complicated internal politics surrounding the Madrid conference prevented me from hearing it directly.

The embassy flag was raised on 24 October, to the renewed singing of 'Hatikva' and a hora around the flagpole. Golda Meir's embassy plaque had miraculously survived and been on display in my office for three years. On one occasion, Moshe Ben-Yaacov, the ministry's head of administration, jocularly remarked on a visit to Moscow, that it was bad luck to exhibit the plaque, which explained the long dalliance with the renewal of relations; if I really wanted diplomatic relations to be renewed and the brass plate attached at the gate, I should hide it from view. And so I did, just to make sure. Now I personally bolted the plaque to the embassy gate, as Nativ's representative in Moscow, Gershon Gorev, assisted me to symbolize the importance of our shared mission. Our friends and acquaintances met the re-establishment of diplomatic relations with a series of celebrations that started out with an impromptu concert organized by Yuri Sokol, the Jewish Red Army veteran. Mikhail Gluz brought out his Tum-Balalaika Jewish folklore troupe and the ubiquitous Yosif Kobzon sang the 'Yiddishe Mame'. Vladimir Panchenko, director of Goskontsert and other impresarios organized a performance at the Tchaikovsky Hall to celebrate the restoration of relations in May. Pavel Kogan led his academy orchestra and Maxim Vengerov, a talented young ex-Soviet, Israeli violinist, whom I invited for the occasion, gave a virtuoso performance of the Mendelssohn violin concerto. I never in my life dreamed that I would one day mount the stage of Tchaikovsky Hall, so renowned in the world of music, but on that occasion I had to address the overflowing audience that packed the house, which I did with more than a little trepidation.

It now seemed that the road toward the completion of my assignment had been thoroughly travelled: emigration was going ahead full speed, diplomatic relations had been re-established and contacts were being widened at every level in the political, economic and cultural fields. Our public image was at an unprecedented high, and options were opening up for greater understanding with the emerging Russian state, since the Soviet Union as we had known it, was crumbling before our eyes. Many Israeli friends and colleagues urged me to begin anew and stay on for another few years as ambassador. Nonetheless, I decided the time had come for me to draw the line. One additional year should be sufficient, I thought, to prove to myself that I had done enough and could do no more to introduce a strategic perspective to our view of Russia.

Did Israel really have too narrow an orientation towards the United States and Western Europe? Should we change this exclusive approach to our strategic interests? I knew it would not be easy to restructure the 'politically correct' division between the western and eastern lobes of the Israeli mind, to fuse them together into one conceptual whole. Over three or four generations we Israelis had grown up, as most people in the West, to fear and distrust the Soviet system — and were probably right in doing so. Indeed, I had discovered in my four years in the Soviet Union that the 'system' was as devoid of trust and respect inside the country, as it was outside. The issue was not one of Russian patriotism, abundant as always. Now, deep changes were on the doorstep of a new Russia. Would it be different from the old? Could Israel find better pathways to the Russian mind, persuade it to share a different view of the Middle East? 'Could the leopard change its spots?' Should any close association with Russia be avoided on the strength of its past and recent history? These thoughts were not a reflection on Israel's ties with the West. Relations with the West should not and could not be easily modified, although the feeling had spread that Israel must decrease its total reliance on America. On the other hand, why should we not attempt to increase our stability, fortify our national security and international standing, as compared to the situation that obtained during the Cold War?

The Cold War was over. Russia's energies and ambitions would have to be turned inward, at least for a time. The March 1991 referendum on maintaining the Union had been overwhelmingly adopted, but Gorbachev's concept of a new Union was nebulous. Even though the Novo-Ogarevo Union Agreement on internal economic and political cooperation was accepted in principle (its signature was deferred to 20 August) by nine republics, it was rejected by the others who opted for sovereignty and independence. The September suggestion of creating a Union of Sovereign States, too, died a quick and natural death. The map of the USSR was being redrawn. Russia would have to contend with nationalist forces which would oppose its centrality. One of the mainsprings of this opposition to Russia was nationalist, militant Islam in Central Asia and inside Russia itself: in Chechnya, Tatarstan and other areas. With the end of the Cold War, Russia would be spending far less on confrontation with the West and could invest in a policy of containment, one of the pillars of which could be opposition to Muslim fundamentalism, rapidly penetrating Central Asia and the Arab Middle East and North Africa. This could bring Russia closer to Israel. There were economic and cultural justifications, too, for a comprehensive review of mutual interests and strategies with Israel. Even if the scale of joint activity with Israel might be small, its intrinsic worth could be considerable. I know Russian expectations to have been great.

From the beginning of Jewish migration out of the Soviet Union in the years 1972–80 and 1989–91, almost 700,000 former USSR inhabitants arrived in Israel. Israel was becoming inundated with a substantial Russian-speaking and Russian-educated population, which if properly integrated into the economic and political life of the country, could both add to its strength and serve as a solid link to a new Russia, rising out of the ashes of its communist past. I had been trying out these ideas on a number of my Russian contacts, including military strategists and politicians, and was not meeting resistance or doubts as to their validity. There was a lack of clarity on Russia's future course and there were no directives from above. A whole new concept of Russia's place in the changing world order had to be worked out, and the field was wide open for discussion, suggestions and ideas. Jerusalem, however, was slumbering. I addressed these thoughts to the East European division but either received no response or was informed that the subject ought to be treated at the academic level, which was nonsense. This was material for policy-making organs of the government. But I knew that these too could not be easily persuaded to devote enough time and effort to redesign their mould.

During the one year that followed the August 1991 coup, strategic thinking and planning became dislocated both in the Soviet and the Russian Parliaments, in the Soviet Ministry of Defence and in the General Staff. There was a great deal of soul-searching, and contacts and discussions were possible. A number of Soviet generals arrived in Israel to participate in academic symposia at Tel Aviv University. There were no contacts outside the university with these important visitors. They were approached only by Nativ, which has no capability or responsibility to formulate strategic thinking, save on immigration. The Foreign Ministry found out about the existence of these visits only after the departure of the visitors. This was symptomatic of the official Israeli attitude towards the future of our relations with Russia. We were simply not built to think of Russia in strategic terms. When the time comes to face a new and different superpower in Eurasia, it will be too late. The train will have left without us.

24 · Heirs of the Empire

Deep woods, the underbrush overgrown with succulent, red, wild strawberries, the beauty of majestic firs and a pleasant, light breeze in the treetops met us in Pineray. This was the killing ground of tens of thousands of innocent Jewish children, men and women; Aliza and I were visiting the memorial, near Vilnius, to lay a wreath of flowers. The victims had been killed and burned by the Germans in the deep pits dug by the Soviets before the war for an oil dump. From the time of its takeover of the Baltic lands, the Soviet government refused to mark the site of the atrocities. When a monument was put up by local Jews, Mikhail Suslov, the cold ideologue of the Communist Party, ordered its destruction. What did the Russians fear? The memory of the victims, buried in these woods, could hardly threaten the Soviet state or feed a nationalist revanchist movement.

I had made an unofficial visit to Estonia in March 1989 to gain a first impression of these Baltic countries. The national Estonian flag already flew from the top of the eleventh-century Toompea Tower on Castle Hill in Revala, symbol of ancient Estonian independence. The Soviets had agreed to this concession provided it would be the only national flag publicly displayed. The confrontations with the Soviet government and the bloodshed were yet to come. My arrival evoked some curiosity in the press, radio and local television, hungry for any sign of international acceptance of Estonian sovereignty. I did not refuse interviews but spoke sparingly, deflecting attempts to read political significance into my impromptu visit.

In the summer of 1991, when I first visited Lithuania and Latvia, I made the acquaintance of the Jewish survivors of the Holocaust who had returned there after the war. The small, 30,000-odd Jewish population was but a pale reflection of the thriving communities of the pre-war years. At that time, before all of Europe went up in the smoke of world war, the Baltic Jews enjoyed a rich cultural life, were proud of their many Hebrew schools, their seminaries, theatres and press. From the turn of the century, their highly educated and active community leadership had a remarkable influence on Jewish life beyond their own borders, including active support for the creation of a national home in Palestine.

In the years after the Second World War, diligent attempts were made to reconstruct at least some of the landmarks of the past. This work gained greater official backing after the move toward Lithuanian sovereignty. Grigorijus Fainsteinas, a Lithuanian Jewish leader, showed us the small Jewish museum of Vilnius and a number of other areas of historical interest, all woeful reminders of a legendary past.

With the arrival of independence, the Baltic governments set into motion a process of liberating and rehabilitating individuals, considered national heroes, from Soviet jails. The years of the war and Nazi occupation left bitter memories. There were many Lithuanians who saved Jewish lives, but there had been considerable collusion between segments of the Lithuanian and Latvian population with the German Nazis in the atrocities committed against the Jews.

Some Lithuanians (and Latvians and Estonians as well) have been convicted of war crimes, including the persecution and killing of Jews. The subject of pardoning war criminals and finding those still at large was raised by the Israeli government in repeated representations but has not been satisfactorily resolved and leaves an area of friction between the countries. The Baltic governments have agreed to an examination of individual records. During my later visits I discussed the possibility of sending a commission to work with the corresponding organizations. The arrival of this commission was delayed but it did finally materialize in the winter of 1995, and a partial record of the crimes was examined. Among the 50,000 people who had been pardoned by the Lithuanian government, some 10,000 were suspected of having been involved in crimes against Jews. Dov Shilansky, at the time the Speaker of the Knesset, discussed the release of collaborators on his visit to Lithuania in December 1990. He also touched upon the absence of public memorials to the mass murder of Baltic Jews in the many spots where this had occurred.

Worsening relations with the USSR from 1989 onward made the Baltic states seek assistance abroad. Neighbouring Finland and Sweden, and other western countries as well, were supportive of Baltic independence from the Soviet Union. But they proceeded with caution for fear of offending Mikhail Gorbachev and their expanding ties with the Soviet Union. For historical reasons, Lithuania and Latvia, and to a lesser extent Estonia, gave high priority to receiving Israel's recognition of their national independence. For Israel it was an extremely delicate question: the Soviet government was watchful of any connections with these countries and we were concerned lest any overt manifestations of political ties affect the continued liberalization of the emigration process.

As the internal crisis in the USSR deepened and the separatist movement spread, I recommended establishing diplomatic ties with the independence-seeking Soviet republics, extending from the Baltic Sea to the Chinese border, which were expected to break away from the USSR. The Foreign Ministry was unnecessarily cautious, even after many western countries began to overtly declare their intention to set up official links. I had to intervene personally with Foreign Minister David Levy, who immediately understood the advantages of a swift decision and gave his blessing to the initiative. It was understood that first among these would be the Baltic countries. Still, our initial move was to establish diplomatic relations with Ukraine, in view of its size, its political and economic importance and above all its large Jewish population.

RELATIONS WITH UKRAINE

In Kiev, on 25 December 1991, we exchanged official notes establishing diplomatic relations — an exercise that would become familiar to me in the coming year. Israel was the fourth country establishing diplomatic relations with Ukraine. The Ukrainian Ministry of Foreign Affairs was just being set up (it had by the time of our arrival a nine-man staff), and was not sufficiently prepared yet to perform this simple act. I remembered our many debates at the United Nations in New York with the Ukrainian delegation, which the Soviet government insisted on treating as an independent republic. Foreign Minister Andrei Zlenko showed great interest in economic ties with Israel and suggested we help attract Jewish investors into his country. For my part, I warned against the sale of arms to the Middle East but came away with the feeling that Ukraine might be forced into it. Zlenko said the Russians were threatening to cut off oil supplies that had become the mainstay of Ukraine's energy supply, in retaliation for the Ukrainian claims on the Black Sea fleet, and their taking possession of the Crimean peninsula. Ukraine needed 50 million tons of oil a year and produced a mere five million. They were planning to buy oil from the Arabs. I knew of active contacts with Iran. This country was looking for arms and would be prepared to barter for oil. The other interesting thing we were told by the Foreign Ministry officials was that Ukraine intended to get rid of its nuclear arms arsenal and reduce its army from 1.5 million men to 150,000, a plan that has not been implemented in its totality.

Since Ukraine had as large a Jewish population as Russia, I also raised the problem of emigration, and was assured that the process would not be interfered with. Ukraine was one of the countries that actively cooperated with us in cancelling the 'Zionism equals racism' resolution at the UN. The Ukrainians were very eager to have as many foreign representations in Kiev as possible. We promised the Ukrainian government to set up an embassy in Kiev as soon as we could. We maintained close ties with the Ukrainians from our mission in Moscow until such time as we overcame the logistical problems involved and opened our chancellery in the Ukrainian capital. In 1995, the Ukrainian government reversed its policy on non-interference in the business of Jewish emigration and began to actively encourage Jews to remain in the country. Emigration had been reduced already as compared to its 1991–92 levels, but the Ukrainian government's policy did not seem to have any effect on those who had set their sites on leaving the country.

It would have been a moving event for me, a child of Jews who had lived and suffered persecution in the Ukraine for many generations, to be received as the head of a delegation to an independent Ukraine. But the commemoration of Babi Yar, only several weeks prior to my arrival in Kiev, had drained me of any emotion I could have mustered for the setting up of diplomatic relations. I therefore limited this visit as much as possible to official business and skipped the tourism. On previous occasions I had already seen the beautiful setting of this city, the grandeur of its monuments, its ancient Greek Orthodox churches and monasteries, the fountainhead of Christianity throughout the Russian lands, after Prince Vladimir's baptism in 988.

We flew back to Moscow in the last days of 1991, to the rising tension of Gorbachev's final acts in his capacity as president. Protocol could not persuade Gorbachev to receive credentials of new ambassadors. There were 23 new ambassadors, including those of China, Nepal, Bahrain, Saudi Arabia, waiting in line before me. Anatoly Cherniaev, Gorbachev's closest political adviser, later told me that Gorbachev feared going through with such formalities which would make him appear to be hanging on to his presidential powers, instead of transferring them to Boris Yeltsin. The Soviet Ministry of Foreign Affairs was also in near-disarray: its officials were highly nervous about their fate, with the end of the Soviet Union closing in on them and their ministry severely reducing personnel. Eduard Shevardnadze had given up his post of foreign minister a second time, having served only 26 days. He did not seem to have formulated any views on his future activity and was unhappy about the only prospects that appeared realistic at the time: responding to the advances of his Georgian countrymen, who wanted him in Tbilisi, to stem the tide of civil war. He resisted for a time, but eventually responded to their appeals and began what became probably the most difficult part of his career.

THE HAMMER AND SICKLE DESCENDS

As Gorbachev made his dramatic resignation speech in the last hours before the end of the year, Aliza and I rushed to Red Square to witness the lowering of the Soviet flag. A very large and boisterous crowd of young people swept into the area in front of the Lenin Mausoleum and the Spassky Gates, drinking champagne and smashing the bottles onto the granite pavement. To our great surprise, they were singing 'Auld Lang Syne' and other, rowdier songs, in English, German and French. There were no Russians to be seen save a small, forlorn group of old-timers, bunching together and holding up communist flags, trying to preserve their dignity. American, Canadian, French and other non-Russian flags took over the square where massive parades of Soviet tanks and missiles had instilled terror in the hearts of millions in the West just a few years earlier.

One of the interesting commentaries on the final days of the Soviet Union was the personal story of Lazar Kaganovich, a close companion of Stalin and a totally devoted, uncompromising executive of the tyrant's will. Kaganovich came from a small Jewish family but fiercely abnegated his identity. He was the last survivor of Stalin's circle, living well into his nineties in a grand apartment on the banks of the Moscow River. Kaganovich did not give the impression of being burdened with a guilty conscience for the lives of the millions he helped to despatch in the collectivization of agriculture, the forced building of the canals across Russia or the Moscow metro. His death anticipated the last days of the Soviet Union by only a few weeks. He refused to meet with the Soviet or international press or anyone who wanted his opinion on various developments. The only exception was a single interview he granted to an Italian newspaper, an occasion for him to deny all of his past wrongdoings. Inaccessible even to the members of his closest family, he did, however, meet with his grandniece. It was rumoured that when she asked him for advice on what to do with her future, he told her to go to Israel. This was an eloquent statement on what had become of the socialist paradise.

Moscow was now shorn of its communism, the Central Committee officials were forced out of their offices and droves of people were hunting the cellars for the records of the Communist Party. Sundry souvenir seekers were stalking the once unapproachable party premises, and the awesome guards had now totally disappeared from view.

THE BALTIC STATES

With the excitement of the final days of the year behind us, we flew out to Riga to begin our Baltic tour. The capital city of Latvia, with its Hanseatic* past, looked very European. In the years of Latvia's independence between the two world wars, Riga developed rapidly, the architecture of the city evidently influenced by art deco and other modern styles in its public buildings and the layout of the city's avenues and squares. The Latvian government gave our delegation a royal welcome and so did the Jewish community, one of whose leaders, Mavrik Wolfsohn, was also an adviser to the government on foreign affairs. At a small monument near the former ghetto, where tens of thousands of Jews were killed by Germans and Latvian fascists, our delegation laid a wreath from the State of Israel.

We were received by the chairman of the Supreme Council, Anatoliyjs Gorbunovs, after an exchange of notes on diplomatic relations. Gorbunovs asked us to trust his government to do everything in its power to identify and punish Latvians guilty of war crimes. The question the journalists had for me when I came out was, when would Israel appoint and send its first ambassador. In fact, the decision had not been taken and there was a debate on the relative merits of Vilnius versus Riga, finally resolved in favour of Riga due to its central geographical location. Israel could not afford to simultaneously open three independent embassies and had to settle for one. The logistics were as difficult in Riga as elsewhere. There were no houses available for chancelleries or residences but the Latvian government, already courted by the Europeans for all available space, nevertheless offered us several options, one of which we took, after considerable delay.

One of the outstanding and interesting members of the Latvian cabinet we met during our stay was Raymond Pauls, a musician and composer who had become the Minister of Culture. A man with very wide horizons and active in Riga and in the Soviet Union in music and drama, he was interested in promoting Jewish

---

* A league of free German port cities dealing in trade.

education and told us of his ambitious plans, which, for lack of funds, were not being implemented at that time. In fact, the small Jewish community was taking care of its own needs, with the help of foreign Jewish organizations and Israel. The associations in my mind regarding this city of liberal and democratic traditions before the nationalistic takeover of 1934, were such that I almost felt I had lived there before, and I would certainly like to go back to it some day.

We had a number of meetings with Latvian writers and journalists and discussed future cooperation. After 1945 a very large Russian population had settled in Latvia. Most of this population is probably industrial and agricultural proletariat, but must have included some interesting and outstanding people. No meetings were arranged with them, however, and I could see in this the hand of the Latvian authorities, who sought to limit the rights and privileges of this population, causing a dilemma regarding Latvia's future relations with Russia.

Due to the acute shortage of gasoline which restricted flights to two a week, the Latvian government put at our disposal automobiles to travel the 700 kilometres from Riga to Vilnius, our next stop. Aliza, Israel Mey-Ami, Danny Meggido from the East European division and I all piled into the cars and made the trip at night, conscious of the superiority of the Baltic roads over the Russian ones. The next day, before the now customary exchange of documents, I was received by Vitautas Landsbergis, the chairman of the Supreme Council, who spoke to me of the long association his country has had with the Jews and the economic and political connection Lithuania wished to have with Israel. I raised the question of the war criminals, and he promised to look into the individual records. However, the president was known for his very strong nationalistic tendencies. I sensed in Landsbergis a strong resistance to our wish of treating this question with the adequacy it merited. This topic would remain on the agenda for a long time to come.

One of the more pleasant duties that fell to me on this trip was the presentation of a medal and honorary Israeli citizenship to an 85-year-old woman: Bronja Straufis, who with her husband Jozas, had saved 27 Jews from the Nazis, at considerable risk to their own lives. There are numerous other deserving souls who acted in the same spirit and put their families at risk. Many have been sought out and their courage in Nazi times acknowledged.

Our delegation went out to visit the old Jewish quarter of Vilnius, much of it turned into a ghetto by the Nazis who led the Jews out to be slaughtered in the thousands. Today, there is no visible sign of the inferno, no element of architecture that might lead the eye and the mind five decades back. Seeing the clean, well-kept, white-washed houses and the quiet streets, I was struck with the scene's surrealism and its incomprehensibility. Could it happen again? There are no guarantees it will not, as recent events in other countries have shown.

From Vilnius we travelled the many miles it took to cross the snow-covered landscape of forested hills along the Baltic shore to reach Tallin. The capital of Estonia, another Hanseatic city, has a fine port, many old Germanic buildings, narrow streets and a decidedly non-Russian cast of life. I remembered how impressed I was on my first visit there, in March 1989, when the biting cold forced my security officer Ehud Balsar and me to stop every hour in our walk through the town, to warm up in one of the many small coffee shops along the way. The contrast with Moscow, which had no similar establishments, was conspicuous.

Lennart Mery, a historian and ethnographer who had been suddenly elevated to political stardom as minister of foreign affairs with the advent of Estonian independence, was no stranger to the diplomatic world. His father had been a diplomat, who had filled posts in Paris and Berlin and, after the Soviet takeover of Estonia in 1941, was exiled with his family to far Siberia. Soon after our visit to Tallin, Mery was elected to the presidency.

Mery had a poignant comment on Estonia's Ministry of Foreign Affairs: he remarked that his ministry had the same relation to politics as a giraffe to Saturn's rings. They had received no archives, no agreements, no staff from the Soviets and had to begin everything from scratch. In our conversation he dwelt principally on the very complex economic picture of his country, with its rapid and determined departure from the Soviet ruble zone. They were left with no energy sources, no finances to speak of, no trade and no great prospects for the future. At the same time, they had 50,000 Russian soldiers quartered in their cities.

With greater proximity to Europe and Finland, to which they are linguistically related, the Estonians turned out to be luckier than their Baltic neighbours. They have gone farther in their economic reforms than other Baltic countries. They have attained better results, but the cost of reconversion to the market economy has been heavy, and political pressure has increased to slow the rapid passage from the former socialist system. Estonia's Russian population, some 40 per cent of the total population, will remain a serious source of friction with Russia.

The Jews of Estonia are a relatively new community. Under the tsars, Estonia was part of Imperial Russia and consequently outside the Pale, the area of settlement permitted to Jews. Not entirely realizing the implication of his words, Lennart Mery told me this was one of the main reasons why there had not been a Jewish problem and anti-Semitism in Estonia, as opposed to both Latvia and Lithuania. Mery himself displayed a feeling of concern for the Jews of Siberia, where he had grown up. He admonished us not to forget the Jews of Birobidzhan who, he said, ought to be helped to re-establish their community and become the independent entity they always wanted to be. I had, in fact, maintained contact with this community throughout my stay in Moscow. They had even dispatched a representative to the new embassy, 11 time zones away from their city, to congratulate us on the re-establishment of diplomatic relations.

We took the flight back to Moscow from Tallin, but not before we sat long hours at the airport, waiting for the Estonian aircraft to be refuelled in Moscow in preparation for its flight to Tallin. This was a pointed reminder to new Air Estonia of its dependence on Russian goodwill.

DAVID LEVY COMES TO MOSCOW

Toward the end of January 1992, I had set up a number of meetings with the heads of states in Uzbekistan, Kazakhstan and Azerbaijan to establish diplomatic relations. This had to be postponed in view of David Levy's imminent visit to Moscow for the opening phase of the multilateral conference between Israel and the Arab states.

This 'second track' of the Madrid conference concerned the subject of economic relations between Israel and the Arabs. The preparations had all been made outside Moscow, mainly in Washington, but it had been decided to have the initial meeting in Moscow as a symbol of Soviet co-sponsorship of the peace process.

Boris Yeltsin now wore the mantle of leadership, yanked from the shoulders of his erstwhile rival, Mikhail Gorbachev, and every visiting foreign leader wanted to get acquainted with the Russian president. I left no stone unturned in trying to arrange a meeting between Yeltsin and Levy. At one point, the new head of presidential protocol, Yuri Zagainov, sounding irritated with the many requests, told me Yeltsin was unavailable to anyone because of ongoing meetings and discussions about the internal situation with the army and the Defence Ministry. Yeltsin finally agreed to meet with the group of ministers who had arrived in Moscow for the Mideast multilateral conference. He was due also to see the Japanese Foreign Minister, privately, on the same day. After a brief appearance before the participants of the conference, Yeltsin disappeared from view and was rumoured to have taken off to his dacha or to some other unknown destination. The Japanese minister, who arrived in the expectation of hearing Yeltsin's position on the Kuril Islands, had to leave without seeing the Russian president. No plausible explanation was furnished. Later we were to witness other, sudden disappearances.

The Moscow conference was a precursor to many similar meetings yet to come, and it opened on a note of high expectation for close contacts and the likelihood of cooperation on a practical level between Israel and the Arabs. A preparatory group from Israel, almost as large as the one that had gone to Madrid, was sent out of Jerusalem, and the Aerostar Hotel where I was now permanently staying was taken over by our crews. Dan Kurzer of the State Department arrived from Washington and a number of discussions were held in my rooms with Moshe Raviv, a senior Foreign Ministry official, to clear up the question of whether James Baker had authorized the inclusion of Palestinians living outside the occupied territories in the conference.

David Levy was on his way back from an official visit to China and as he came in on his El Al flight, he was mobbed by reporters who plied him with questions about his China visit and the Moscow conference. We could see Levy was highly pleased with his venture into China, and especially with how he had 'given it to those crafty Chinamen'.

The day before the opening of the conference I organized a meeting with US Ambassador Robert Strauss. He told Levy outright that greater care should be taken by the government of Israel on the subject of building settlements in the territories, otherwise Israel would be running a very real danger of damaging its relations with the American Jewish community. Levy listened with attention to what Strauss was saying and did not make any forceful comments. The next day the whole story appeared in *Yediot Aharonot*, in an article by Shimon Shiffer, who was not in Moscow at the time, but to whom the somewhat embarrassing information was leaked by one of the very few people present at the meeting.

The conversation with Bob Strauss was followed by an official pre-conference meeting with Andrei Kozyrev, who had been put in charge of foreign affairs for the Russian Federation after the collapse of the Soviet Union. David Levy was received in the sumptuous neo-gothic Morozov residence, built and decorated by prominent Russian artists before the Revolution and turned by the Soviets into their official Foreign Ministry reception centre*. David Levy explained Israel's peace initiative but had to listen to a barrage of questions on the settlements and the West Bank from Kolotusha and Derkovsky, whom Kozyrev had inherited from the now defunct Soviet Ministry of Foreign Affairs.

The conference opened on 28 January in the colonnaded interior of the House of Trade Unions, formerly the Russian Noblemen's Association. Professor Yaacov Frenkel, the head of the Bank of Israel, David Ivry, the director-general of our Ministry of Defence, and Yossi Hadass, director-general of the Ministry of Foreign Affairs, were all there, generating a high level of tension around them and vying for the next day's headlines in the Israeli press. David Kimche had also gotten an appointment to the Israeli team and tried hard to strike up a conversation with some of the Arab

---

* This building was destroyed in a fire in 1995

delegates. There was an undignified scramble for the forward seats in the Israeli delegation when the conference came to order. As I had gotten up to greet Amru Musa, the Egyptian minister of foreign affairs, who had been my colleague at the UN in New York, I had to return to the last chair of our delegation's back row.

After Andrei Kozyrev and James Baker made their opening remarks, the alphabetical list finally reached Israel. David Levy made a conciliatory statement. Bob Strauss told me he had 'taken the high road'. But there were slight embarrassments. The Jordanians were confused: did Levy say the Jordan River was the border line between Israel and Jordan or did he say the Jordan Valley? In fact, Levy said river, but the text that we had circulated in Arabic had said valley and we spent some time straightening that out. These circumstances notwithstanding, it was highly interesting to hear, perhaps for the first time in the annals of Middle Eastern diplomacy, positive statements on the future of the Middle East, made by representatives of the Arabs and of Israel in each other's presence. There was an additional point, related to current affairs: strong Arab criticism of an Arab country, Iraq, for its responsibility in the Gulf War. The strongest critic was Saudi Arabia, not a bit embarrassed to speak up in the presence of the official Israeli delegation. The conference promised greater advances in the future on disarmament, economic development and environment, which came under its collective heading. The first open, ground-breaking meeting between Israelis and Arabs in an international conference devoted to the Middle East seemed to have been a success and its continuation assured.

As David Levy's assistants had no idea what would please their chief in Moscow, I set up two meetings that I thought might interest him: with Shevardnadze and Gorbachev. Shevardnadze came in with his close adviser and confidant, Sergei Tarasenko, who had been head of political research at the Soviet ministry and had been consequently, a colleague of mine. Tarasenko was a man whose knowledge and versatility I had come to respect. Shevardnadze looked uncharacteristically ill at ease as he stepped out of an old and battered Volga automobile. The civil war in his native Georgia was claiming many casualties and fire had consumed many of Tbilisi's famous buildings. He appeared downcast. David Levy inquired about the situation in Georgia and in Russia, and noting Shevardnadze's worried tone assured him, with a certain touch of paternalism, that everything would work out well in the end.

The meeting with Gorbachev at his new Gorbachev Fund offices was rather more positive. The former president of the USSR radiated self-confidence. He spoke somewhat disparagingly of his successor. He told me he knew I had not submitted my credentials to Yeltsin yet, but who was Yeltsin to receive them? As to himself, he said he thought he resembled Moses. Levy commented that indeed, Moses had led the Jews for 40 years, preparing to bring a new generation of free men, rather than slaves, into the Holy Land. Levy gave the former president good marks. He said Gorbachev had done great things and that the world would remember him. 'Bravo!' he concluded. But Mikhail Sergeevich had intended something different: he was in the position God had put Moses in, observing the Promised Land from a distant mountain, but never actually getting there. Gorbachev's interest in the Bible seemed curious, but he explained it by the predilection Raisa had developed for the holy writ. The diplomats among the Israelis were charmed by Gorbachev's smiling, self-assured manner, his openness and good spirits. The journalists appeared more blasé, probably jaded by their profession.

As I accompanied David Levy to his plane he told me not to change my style and to avoid resembling the Foreign Ministry bureaucrats. I thought I shared the same wish. In the end, however, I had to contend with Levy's politics. The promised appointment to head the peace process in the ministry was forgotten as soon as Levy touched base with the staff in Jerusalem.

TEL AVIV UNIVERSITY ASSESSES SOVIET FOREIGN POLICY

In February 1992 Tel Aviv University's Cummings Center for Russian and East European Studies, together with the Institute of World History of the Russian Academy of Sciences, opened a conference on the history of Soviet foreign policy. Professors Gabriel Gorodetsky of Tel Aviv and Alexander Tchoubarian of Moscow organized this unusual get-together in Moscow to promote the study of post-revolutionary foreign policy — an area that had never been explored by a joint Israeli-Russian team. This was an occasion to reflect on the fact that in the field of foreign affairs, prominent Russian Jews like Trotsky, Maisky, Litvinov and others had played a leading role in Soviet foreign policy in the early days but were nowhere in evidence from the beginning of the Cold War, and well into the days of perestroika, when I arrived in Moscow. The cooperation between Tel Aviv and Moscow had not begun with the conference, but represented the fruit of contacts developed over time. As I inaugurated this event, I thought it was encouraging to see a communality of interests between Israeli and Russian scholars.

The Israeli Ministry of Sciences and the Soviet Academy of Sciences had already established a mutual programme of contacts and cooperation, begun with Ezer Weizmann's visit in 1990. In spite of all the money invested in it, the project had not really taken off. The reason was probably poor management and extraneous interests that had crept into the programme. The heads of the Soviet academy seemed to consider this agreement an excellent opportunity to visit Israel with their wives for 'a period of rest', an activity to which the ministry inexplicably acquiesced. More could and should have been done.

CREDENTIALS AT ST CATHERINE'S HALL

Finally, in early February 1992, the date was set for the presentation of my credentials to President Yeltsin. I went through the brief speech I was to make, and asked the embassy officials who would accompany me to check their shirts and ties. As the boat-like government Zil arrived to fetch us all to the Kremlin, I remembered Uri Lubrani's story of his presentation of credentials to Haile Selassie in Addis-Ababa. When the imperial Rolls-Royce arrived from the palace to fetch the ambassador, Uri was still fighting the neck buttons of his stiffly starched collar and the cuff-links of the white tie attire he had to put on to go to the palace. As customary on these occasions, the chief of imperial protocol alighted to invite the ambassador to mount the vehicle, whereupon Uri's German shepherd attacked the Ethiopian official, unceremoniously tearing his trousers and stopping short of biting off the man's leg only after much persuasive physical restraining. Following this short interlude, everyone smiled, strenuously, as they took off for the palace. Midway, Uri realized that his credentials were not in his leather briefcase and the whole procession, together with the outriders, returned to the residence where, after an exhaustive search, the official papers were discovered, hidden among the watercolours of Uri's five-year-old daughter, Nili.

On this occasion we made sure there were no dogs in sight and even meticulously cleaned the chancellery doorstep of the mud and snow that was carried in by hundreds of daily visitors. Israel Mey-Ami, Avi Idan, Yossi Bendor, Garry Koren and I stepped into the slightly worn official Zil and arrived without incident at the Kremlin. We took off our winter coats and faced what the French call *l'escalier d'honneur*, the parade stairway. The protocol herald proclaimed: 'The Ambassador of the State of Israel', as I began mounting the steps. A pair of stiffly saluting soldiers in blue parade uniforms stood on every third step, and it seemed as if the army had sent in a whole platoon to welcome me on my way. Evidently, our progress had to be strictly orchestrated as similar, staggered functions were taking place with the new Chinese and Nepalese ambassadors, but Russian protocol managed it with exquisite exactitude and grace. We dallied but a moment before the massive oak doors of St Catherine's Hall were thrown open and I perceived opposite me, at the other end of the very large, white taffeta-upholstered room, the president of Russia, Boris Yeltsin. After a moment's hesitation we began advancing toward each other and stood at attention at a designated spot. I read out my speech: '... historical and cultural ties link our two countries, horizons for understanding and cooperation ...'. The newspapermen who had loyally accompanied me later claimed I was very nervous, but I am certain now, as I was then, that our three Israeli reporters were far shakier than I.

After this brief ceremony, the still photographs and the television cameras, I was invited to join the president for a glass of champagne. Yeltsin opened with a monologue. This was merely a formal meeting, he began, and he promised we would find the time to sit down together again for a substantial conversation. Russia is going through a very critical period, the months of February and March will be extremely difficult. Russia and Israel, he remarked, should endeavour to repair the damage done to their relations, try to approach each other and work more closely. The world must help Russia in its difficult days, otherwise the world itself might suffer. The conservative forces were breathing down his neck, he said, but the new regime must not fail. I asked the president to take special care against the rise of anti-Semitism. Yeltsin replied that Jews had been living in Russia for a long time. This was their country. Why should they not live well in it? he asked rhetorically. He knew the emigration had been massive, but hoped it would start falling off. In Brezhnev's time, over 340,000 Jews had left the Soviet Union. He hoped less Jews would leave, and that those who remained would participate in rebuilding Russia and trust in its future.

I was pleasantly surprised, not at the fact that Yeltsin had been well-briefed, but that he did not seem to have difficulty in retaining the details of Jewish life and emigration in Russia. Yeltsin was smiling and looked decidedly alert and well-groomed, exactly as Ambassador Bob Strauss described from a meeting he had had with him. Although I did not keep Yeltsin long, I came away with a very favourable impression of the Russian president, whom I had met twice on previous occasions, but now found to be more self-assured and relaxed. I thought he would not take a position against us.

There was a small party at Nativ's Information Centre, with many friends and colleagues present. Chana and Marc Winer were there as well as David Kulits, Miki Federman and Yossi Myman, who had come to sign a large building contract in Moscow. Shoshi Perry and Yuli Nudelman were there as well, two comrades-in-arms who had been struggling with me in the Ukraina Hotel days to get established, albeit in trade rather than in diplomacy. Amnon Kapeliuk and Avi Raz of the Hebrew press, and Michael Karpin of Israeli television were there too, and I could tell they were as excited as I, over this last lap in my long journey towards attaining Israel's rightful place in Moscow's diplomatic colony. The embassy staff included Esther and David Bartov, stalwarts of the old

Moscow embassy, now running Nativ's Moscow office. They were all there, to the last man and woman, some recalling the first humble days of our beginnings. It was a restrained but warm celebration of our common achievement and I could not have asked for more.

25 · From Bukhara to Ararat

The time had come to make a journey to Central Asia. We had been in contact with these republics over a number of months to coordinate our trip, and after many false starts we set out for the new sovereign republic of Uzbekistan in mid-February 1992, to establish diplomatic relations. Our official visit to the Uzbek capital, Tashkent, had not yet been finalized when we started out from Moscow. In the interim, I intended to make a private visit to the ancient city of Bukhara, with its old Jewish community, an area suffused with the Iranian culture that I longed to experience once again.

Aliza and had already paid our respects to the Jewish community and the splendid architectural and historical sites of Samarkand in summer 1990. There the great conqueror, Tamerlane, lies buried in a mosque in the city which he turned into his capital — a meeting place of great minds and artists in the fourteenth century. The Jews have inhabited these lands for over two thousand years. We were lucky enough to be invited to several weddings that took place there in the open gardens of well-to-do Jewish families. The traditions, the synagogues, the Persian wedding music, the rich food combining rice and the many herbs and fruits of Central Asia all brought back memories of Iran.

Russia penetrated into Central Asia in the 1860s. Up until 1917 there were no well-defined internal borders within that region. The Khiva and Kokand Khanates and the Bukhara Emirate united people of various ethnic origins into a country loosely called Turkmenistan, ruled and administered after a fashion by the emir of Bukhara. The emirs were notoriously rapacious and cruel, as depicted in *A Thousand and One Nights*. In the small museum in the Ark, the Bukhara stronghold and palace, I saw the knives with which the emir personally slit the throats of dangerous criminals.

When Soviet rule over this vast territory was established in the early 1920s, the area was divided up by the 1923 Soviet Constitution into three republics: Uzbek, Turkmen and Tajik. The borders were said to have been drawn along ethnic lines but in fact they were haphazard, since there were no territorially defined conglomerations. Internally, power was divided among clans and cliques and territorial interests. The main separation is actually linguistic, between the Turkic and Farsi languages. There is a considerable Tajik population in Uzbekistan; and more Tajiks in Afghanistan than in the country that bears their name. As long as the Soviets administered these republics with an iron hand, the smouldering ethnic rivalries were kept largely in check. With sovereignty, the linguistic, cultural and now national differences threaten to perpetuate political instability. Yet with all the difficulties the three republics have run into, a single undivided Turkmenistan would have, in this period of history, been far easier prey for Iranian fundamentalism and could have presented a greater threat to its neighbours.

We arrived in Bukhara late at night. When I awakened at dawn I could see from my window minarets and towers, mosques and *maidans*, the shapes and colours that I remembered from Iran's dividing line between the desert and the sown. The huge pale sky spread its canopy over the dusty city with its uniform, subdued tones. The large central square stood out in its bleak communist architecture, a parade ground bordered by the massive Communist Party headquarters, office blocks closing around it. Gul Chehreh Khanum (the flower-faced lady, in Tajik), a pretty and intelligent young guide, took us to the bazaar, its workshops and stalls. Across from the Great Mosque, near the edge of a large pool used for ritual ablutions, there was a sculpture of Khajeh Nasreddin, the legendary Middle Eastern sage-buffoon, riding his donkey. The sculpture of the donkey and its master was a sacrilege, a violation of the Islamic injunction against graven images. Its presence here would have been unthinkable in the days of observant Islam, prior to the communist regime.

Gul Chehreh took us to see the Ark — the Bukharan fortress where the emir had both his administrative offices and his private quarters. The harem had been restored to its former splendour of stucco work and coloured tiles, and it contained a large collection of magnificent *suzani* needlework pieces. Outside, in summer, a large pool of water used to be the favourite frolicking grounds of the numerous wives and concubines of the emir. He would sit on a small balcony observing the scene below, picking his companion for the day (or the night). Our guide said the emir would indicate his preference by throwing a pomegranate toward the lady who attracted his fancy. From the distance where he sat, he must have been endowed with keen eyesight and possessed of a strong pitching arm.

Avnon Yaacobi, the head of the Jewish community and the district financial auditor, accompanied us to the chairman of Bukhara's executive committee, a sort of mini-governor of the city. Mavlon Rahmanov spoke to us about agricultural cooperation and growing cotton using drip irrigation. Irrigation was a favourite subject in this country, which had used up the waters of its mighty river, the Amu Darya, to grow cotton for the Soviet Union, thus denying the Aral Sea the inflow of one of its two tributaries and causing an environmental disaster. Rahmanov's main interest, as that of his many colleagues across Central Asia, was to attract investments from abroad. He was certain that Israel, being the country of the Jews, could invest more than many others.

Yaacobi took us to the Jewish quarter, the *mahalla*, where Jews have lived for many centuries. In my childhood I had many friends in Tehran's Jewish ghetto, and the sights and odours in Bukhara took me back a good 50 years. We saw a number of synagogues, some going back centuries into the history of the community. Many of the homes were built according to a traditional pattern of a single-storey house rising from its garden. I asked Yaacobi how the community had fared under communism. 'Communism? Oh yes, they'd heard about it', he said jocularly. The Jewish community did not suffer from overt interference into its affairs. Business was pretty slow though. He added that most Jews studied professions, in which they usually excelled.

I wanted to visit Khiva, another city of great historical interest, but the Uzbek Foreign Ministry's chief of protocol, Adham Rasulov, was against it and insistence was useless. An hour before our departure to Tashkent I asked Yossi Bendor to double-check the programme of our visit and see if the meetings we had set up with President Islam Karimov and others would take place. Yossi came back with a long face: Rasulov said the whole programme of our visit was cancelled, no meetings with the president or with the minister of foreign affairs, no exchange of notes on diplomatic relations. Yaacobi let me use his direct telephone line to contact the embassy in Moscow and I asked Mey-Ami to have the Uzbek representative in Russia talk to his people in Tashkent. At the airport, an hour later, before our flight to the Uzbek capital, I called Rasulov from a public phone. The connection was bad and I had to shout, with the whole airport intently listening in. We were on our way to accomplish what we had agreed to do, I bellowed into the receiver. Rasulov did not promise anything but said I would be welcome in Tashkent, and so we took off.

Rasulov was at the airport: he had worked everything out. The day after our arrival was the Sabbath and we could not ride in a car, since it was forbidden by Jewish law. So we walked from our hotel to the Ministry of Foreign Affairs. I had signed the notes on diplomatic relations the previous day at the airport to avoid having to do it on a Sabbath. The minister, Ubaidallah Abdulrazakov, put his signature to them as well, and we had a long conversation, now as mutually recognized diplomats. The minister had been an editor before his appointment and talked about Uzbekistan's plans for the future. In response to my question, he said the government had not yet decided if the country would go over to the Arabic script, which was seen as a very strong vehicle for Muslim fundamentalism.

At this time in early 1992, Turkey was still perceived in Central Asia as a bridgehead for western influence and a guide for dealing with the nascent Islamic movement. The Turkish government was eager to gain a position of influence in Central Asia and wished to convince the republics to adopt a secular constitution, like Turkey, to prevent fundamentalist Islam gaining ground. President Islam Karimov and the heads of the other Central Asian and the Azerbaijan governments, mindful of the winds blowing across their borders from Iran, were interested in close links with Turkey, a country which they felt had enormous economic potential. Turkey proposed to create a common Turkic market between Central Asia, Azerbaijan and itself, to handle what was seen as promising trade with the outside world. The problem of the alphabet was thus an extremely important one. The minister told me the country had passed from Arabic to Latin script in 1922 and to Cyrillic in 1938. Another change would be problematic and costly. The greatest Uzbek poet, Alisher Navoi, used the Arabic script, the minister remarked. A year later, after much debate, the Uzbeks decided to follow the Turkish example and adopted the Latin script.

The problem of fundamentalist Islam spreading in the Fergana valley and in the other areas of Uzbekistan was brought home to us again when we were told President Karimov was out on a tour of the Fergana, in connection with disturbances, and could receive us only several days later. We were lucky to have arrived just in time to meet the foreign minister, who was due to leave the same evening. We used the time to visit the central mosque and inspect an ancient Koran, written in the Kufic script and dating from the beginnings of Islam in the tenth century. It was kept in a large safe and shown only to the privileged. There was a great deal of vigorous activity around the area of the mosque, many *madrasas* (religious schools) had been set up to teach youths the traditional ritual and Koranic laws. It was clear that great efforts were being made to reanimate the religious establishment.

Uzbekistan had had a Jewish population of over 150,000, but the community was rapidly shrinking. Both the Ashkenazi group, which had settled there after the Second World War, and the local, traditional Sephardic population, were emigrating. The Uzbek Jews, when I visited them in their synagogue in Tashkent, protested against the fact that the Jewish Agency was prepared to transport only a few hundred kilograms of their belongings. Everything must be air freighted or transported to Israel free of charge, they insisted. I tried to explain that Israeli apartments, in which they would live, did not have sufficient space to house the belongings they had collected over many years, but I saw I was not getting through. Few of the older people were enthusiastic about emigration to Israel, but the younger generation was assiduously studying Hebrew. The various foreign Jewish organizations, the Orthodox Bnei Akiva, the Jewish Agency, Nativ — all had their hands full and hopes of immigration ran high.

RUSSIA LOSES ITS CHARM

On a few days' vacation in Israel after my Central Asian foray, I tried again to raise the subject of closer relations with Russia and the development of a base for long-term strategic interests. Director-General Hadass did not have the time or the inclination to get involved with the topic as he was engrossed in his endeavours to engage his minister's interest in running the ministry. I talked at length to Govrin about my project of inviting several rightist politicians and Russian Orthodox clergymen to Israel, which I had raised in the past. I even spoke to President Herzog about my feeling that the question of Russia and emigration had become a burdensome subject to Israeli policy-making bodies and politicians alike. Herzog said he agreed with me entirely and the subject deeply troubled him. He suggested I go on television to call the public's attention to this fact, but I found the suggestion impractical.

I expressed my concern in a meeting with Prime Minister Shamir who, as always, showed a lively interest in what I was saying but had nothing substantial to offer in the way of reawakening popular interest in immigration and preventing the continuation of the disunited and contradictory efforts of the many organizations involved: Nativ, the Jewish Agency, the World Orthodox movement and others. The director-general of the prime minister's office, Yosef Ben-Aharon, who was at this meeting, expressed his opinion that ultra-orthodox activism and education were not harmful, but I pointed out that it did reduce the status of Israel-oriented Hebrew education, which would be needed in Russia if emigration were to continue.

Shamir had by this time appointed a commission to review the Nativ-Jewish Agency dispute. The inquiry was highly restricted for fear of leaks. It was conducted by the late Michael Dagan, a former deputy-minister of agriculture and a loyal Shamir supporter. From the conversation I had with one of Dagan's assistants, I understood that the inquiry had already established the basic facts about the dramatis personae, their level of professionalism, their *modus operandi*, the resources put at their disposal and the goals involved. The end result was that the official reapportioning of immigration activity was foggy enough to require another official inquiry soon after the Labour Government came into power in 1992. The conclusions of the second review were similar. Even if a redivision of responsibility was established as a requirement by Prime Minister Rabin, Yitzhak Chofi, the former head of the Mossad, who conducted the inquiry, could not see a satisfactory means of accomplishing this. Perhaps the reason was that Chofi was primarily interested in having his findings correspond to Rabin's wishes, which did not seem to differ from those of his predecessor, Shamir. Israeli prime ministers want to keep the Russian emigration under their personal control, for internal political reasons. So, the conceptual problem of the immigration itself remains unresolved. There is no wisdom in having two agencies with two budgets doing the work of one.

I raised the question of a strategic reassessment of our relations with Russia in my discussions with the prime minister. Shamir declared himself in agreement with me but did not say what he thought we should actually do. There were other good examples of this ambiguous approach: Arkady Volsky, a very prominent Russian personality, on a visit to Israel, had asked Shamir for a large sum of money to help Russia out of its 'temporary' difficulties. In Moscow, Volsky had told me of his impression that the prime minister had made a promise in that regard. When I inquired, Shamir replied he had only said he would think about it.

On this occasion, Prime Minister Shamir mentioned the meeting he had had in his office with the Kazakh minister of agriculture, who had said his country, with a 50 per cent non-Kazakh population, was going to adopt its own brand of Zionism. To regain their majority, they would try to persuade fellow-Kazakhs residing outside the country, including China, to return to Kazakhstan. An official later told me the results of this policy were negligible: there was no proper government machinery or resources to ensure the success of such an enterprise and the motivation was, in any case, low. The Soviet Armenian Republic had also attempted to practice an ingathering of its Diaspora after the Second World War, but the results were disappointing.

Toward the second half of March, as we were preparing to set out for Kazakhstan to establish diplomatic relations, we received an increasing amount of information on the sale and theft of nuclear warheads from the former Soviet arsenal located in this republic. Some of these warheads were reportedly reaching Iran. Rumours on this subject were appearing in the Soviet press, but some came to me directly from Vice-President Rutskoi's staff, which was more disturbing. Rutskoi was involved in the sale of arms and on one of his junkets through Asia had offered Tehran some two billion dollars' worth of military equipment. My contacts in the Ministry of Foreign Affairs were denying it. At a private concert at the Netherlands Ambassador Joris Vos's residence, I met Deputy Foreign Minister Boris Kolokolov who was, at the time, charged with Middle East affairs. I inquired as to the veracity of this information and said it was a pity the Russians were continuing the policy of their predecessors. Kolokolov's wife, silent up to then, suddenly spoke up to say that Russians wanted to live, and in order to live they needed money. It was obvious that the pecuniary arguments were becoming more compelling by the day, as the Russian government sank lower into the financial and administrative quagmire left over from the Soviet Union.

AN ATOMIC REACTOR FOR WATER

At this juncture Israel was also trying to buy a nuclear reactor from Russia. It had become evident that with the increasing demands on our meagre water supplies, we were going to have to seek alternative sources. The only possibility open to us was to desalinate sea water. Israel had for many years been developing water desalination technologies, one of them, the Zarchin method, being more successful than others. There were two Israeli parties looking into this project, the minister of science, Yuval Ne'eman, and the Israeli businessman, Yaacov Nimrodi. They were not coordinating their efforts. In all known methods of desalination it is the energy factor that runs up the price of clean water. A nuclear plant, it was hoped, could produce the energy at relatively low cost for desalination and bolster the national electric grid as well. Nimrodi had had much experience in this area as his company had built a whole string of water desalination plants, running on cheap oil, on the Iranian shores and islands of the Persian Gulf before the Khomeini revolution. Both Ne'eman and Nimrodi visited Moscow and tried to line up contacts that would lead them to the purchase of the nuclear plant. Nimrodi had reached Rutskoi, and Ne'eman was operating through Academician Velikhov and the Ministry of Energy. Both attempts came to nought, in spite of the great interest the Russians displayed in the sale of such a plant, for financial reasons. The technological aspect was not always very clear to me. The Russians were offering different nuclear plants, whose installation would require additional western technology to make them safe and efficient. Insofar as I could judge, the Russians had not entirely resolved an internal debate on whether to go ahead and sell such plants to Israel. Perhaps it was the fear of alienating the Arab world. For whatever reason, this intriguing deal never went far beyond the initial talking stage, which was a pity, as it could have become a solid basis for of scientific and technological cooperation.

TIES WITH TAJIKISTAN

Since Tajikistan was in the throes of internal disorders in early April 1992, we decided by mutual agreement to perform the act of establishing relations at the Tajik Republic offices in Moscow, rather than risk an expedition to Dushanbe. Djamshed Karimov, First Deputy Premier, kept his word to me and was there for the occasion. We exchanged documents, talked about the situation in Dushanbe and quaffed champagne which, Karimov remarked, was even cooled for the occasion. It was an unsatisfactory alternative, but preferable to the repeated delays involved in coordinating a visit to the Tajik capital.

Several months later, we put this right by going to Dushanbe.

President Rahmon Nabiyev had not been able to control the political situation or dam the growing anarchy. A representative of the northern, industrialized region's interests, he could not adapt himself to the unexpected political developments whereby the backward and formerly neglected south and south-eastern Pamir region, were demanding a greater role in running the country. They had many grievances and were supported by Islamic fundamentalist movements from across the Afghan border. When I met Nabiyev he already looked distraught and beaten and died several months later, leaving the country in a state of worsening civil war. The minister of foreign affairs, Khodaberdi Khaliknazarov, a member of Pamir's Ismaili minority, had been a translator at the Soviet Embassy in Tehran before the breakup of the Soviet Union. I was surprised he agreed to see me, given his Islamic connections, but he appeared to be a reasonable person. He complained to me of his political weakness in relation to the former Soviet establishment which, he said, was still calling the shots.

A curious incident occurred during my talks with the Tajik leaders. When I rose to leave, after an hour's conversation in Farsi with the minister of foreign affairs, he said I spoke a good Tehrani dialect, implying that the Tajik version of Farsi is purer. Nevertheless, he asked me to grant an interview to national television. The next day, Deputy Prime Minister Karimov, at an official dinner in honour of our delegation, said the Iranian ambassador had called in with a protest. The government should not have allowed an Israeli representative, he had declared, to spread propaganda in Farsi over the official television channel.

The heads of the Tajik Jewish community were very concerned about the growing instability and were preparing to leave the country. I met them at my official guest residence, a former Communist Party dacha, but in the semi-darkness of a badly lit garden late at night. They were apprehensive about the political situation and the growing banditry in the countryside spreading to the capital city, where most of the community of 12,000 Jews lived. While the older generation opted for emigration to the United States where they had close relatives ready to receive them, the younger people wanted to emigrate to Israel. Nativ and the Jewish Agency each had an office in Dushanbe, which proved of great value when emigrants, on their way out of the country, had to be saved from the guerrilla bands of various persuasions.

The beginning of April 1992 was a critical time in Moscow, with Yeltsin under attack by the parliamentary opposition and many demonstrations in the streets. Unable to fully confront the rebellious conservatives in the parliament, Yeltsin dismissed Yegor Gaidar from his position as minister of finance. He also discharged his close collaborator Gennady Bourboulis. Both were kept in the government, Gaidar as first vice-premier and Bourboulis as secretary of state for special assignments. Doubts increased over the promised reforms. Ruslan Khasbulatov was spearheading another parliamentary rebellion, but the rising expectations of a decisive outcome to the crisis fizzled again. We could hardly do anything about these changes. Rather than continue a now aimless observation of the rapidly changing scene in Moscow and eager to extend our official contacts to the other emerging republics, I decided to travel. The Azeri capital, Baku, was next on our itinerary of new diplomatic relations and we set out for it in the first week of April.

SHADES OF A PERSIAN CHILDHOOD

My stepmother had grown up in Baku and I remembered her many nostalgic recollections of a cosmopolitan Russian-oriented city, with its theatres and orchestras, lovely parks and money-making oil rigs. Alfred Nobel had obtained a concession here at the end of the 1870s and Russian oil reigned supreme in the world until the discovery of oil in the western United States. The rapid development of Baku dates from the large investments of foreign and Russian oil-related capital at the end of the nineteenth century. The 1905 Revolution and the First World War and its fallout, saw great suffering and excesses in Baku and the surrounding countryside. During the 1917 Revolution a vortex of armies of all descriptions marched across the Caucasus, with Baku a prize fought over by the Germans, the Turks and the British. The Bolsheviks captured Baku in 1920 and dreams of Azerbaijani independence were dashed. The Soviet period, mainly under the first secretary of the Azerbaijan

Communist Party and Brezhnev's bosom friend, Gaidar Aliyev, was marked by stability and a relatively good life for many, although some suffered brutality and repression. This at least is what Baku old-timers fondly recall today. With the breakdown of Soviet rule and the Nagorno-Karabakh crisis, the political situation deteriorated. Armenians, who had inhabited this city for many years, were expelled and with the outbreak of war and growing internal dissension and disorder, the economy began stagnating. There was a political and constitutional crisis, the spoiled fruits of mismanaged sovereignty, characteristic of post-Soviet times.

Official protocol awaited us at the airport, as did Aaron Borisovitch, representing the Jewish community and serving as our patron and guide. We were driven through the barren and forlorn stretch of road bordered by abandoned rigs and oil-polluted waters to the heart of this windy city that I had heard so much about in my early childhood. The reality looked harsh. After a short break at the Government Hotel, we were taken to the Foreign Ministry. Hussein Sadikov, the foreign minister, signed the protocol of diplomatic relations and spoke to me of the Nagorno-Karabakh war, which seemed to override every other topic. There was no break in this theme from the time we landed. The Armenian advances on the front and the military threat to the town of Shusha were on everyone's lips. Sadikov was reluctant to support an exchange of exploratory missions to stake out mutual interests as a first step toward cooperation. It looked as though he was wary of criticism by pro-Islamic politicians. Sadikov did not show great interest in the problems of the distant Middle East. He said the Soviet garrison in Armenia was distributing heavy arms to Armenian fighters, who were using them against the Azerbaijan army. The minister also complained of Lebanese Armenians training fighters who reappeared in Karabakh, and expressed great concern over loss of territory to Armenia. He would not be drawn out on Syria's responsibility for the training Armenian fighters were receiving in the Lebanese Beka'a Valley or nearer to the Syrian border.

The gloomy preoccupation with the war was widespread. We were taken to a military cemetery with rows of fresh graves, bearing the images of the fallen. The granite slabs were covered with red carnations. There were also graves of Azeris killed by

Soviet troops on their entry into Baku in February 1990, to put down the severe outbreak of racial violence.

A happier encounter was with the minister of culture in his sumptuous office at the large Government House built by Gaidar Aliyev. The minister was a popular second-generation singer and his name, Polad Bul-Bul-Ogli (nightingale, in Azeri), was well deserved. Appointed by the new government, he stayed at his post for a number of years. He had many welcoming words to say, having been to Israel as a guest of the large Azeri colony resident there and having come away with warm memories of hospitality. The Jewish community in Baku had once numbered well over 35,000, but their ranks were rapidly diminishing because of emigration brought about by a feeling of insecurity and lack of economic prospects. Bul-Bul-Ogli said he regretted the days were past when Jews and Armenians as well as Azeris and Russians lived in perfect harmony, respected each other and never considered ethnic differences a barrier. I had heard many such statements, in various parts of the world, but somehow I tended to believe this minister. The evening before, at a dinner given by the Azeri-Israeli Friendship League, several outstanding Azeris spoke in the same vein. I was especially impressed by Zia Bunyatov, a Hero of the Soviet Union, an officer of the Russian Pankov armoured division that had participated in the capture of Berlin during the war. He was now a vice-president of the Azerbaijan Academy of Sciences. I noticed, nevertheless, that the Jews among the guests spoke in stronger patriotic terms and more often about the war against Armenia. I wondered if this was an unconscious desire to compensate for perceptions of inequality.

A very interesting subject that repeatedly came up for discussion in Baku, as well as in other meetings with Azeri Jews and non-Jews, was the Khazar legend. The Khazar Kingdom extended over a large territory stretching from the Caspian to the Black Sea, and from the Caucasus to the rivers Don and Volga, between the eighth and the thirteenth centuries. A Jewish scholar and statesman, Hasdai ibn-Shaprut, who lived in Muslim Spain in the tenth century, wrote to the Khazar King and inquired whether he was Jewish; he received a detailed and positive reply. One of the documents pertaining to the correspondence between the Jewish philosopher and the Khazar King is stored at the Leningrad Saltykov-Shchedrin Library, where I saw it, but had difficulty deciphering it. Many Azeris that I came across claimed descent from the Khazars, as did some of the Tat Jews who inhabit the area. Archeological finds of the era are not substantial enough to confirm or deny the existence of the Jewish Kingdom, but it is a definitely romantic and engaging story.

Bul-Bul-Ogli seemed completely free of any prejudice, and we had an interesting exchange on problems of the Baku Jews' cultural readaptation in Israel and the role they could play in the future as ambassadors of goodwill. We also discussed possibilities of cultural contacts. The minister spoke of his efforts to organize a mixed Jewish-Azeri youth choir, which would, among its other appearances, sing at the 500-year anniversary of the landing of Jews in Ottoman Turkey. President Herzog later told me of his official visit to Istanbul on this occasion and of the Azeri choir that had sung for him and the other guests, including President Turgut Ozal. On my second visit to Baku, in the autumn of 1992, Bul-Bul-Ogli invited me to a concert specially organized for our delegation and I could see that considerable effort had been put into the project by the Jewish community, Bul-Bul-Ogli's friend, Baku composer Vladimir Veinshtein and others.

While many Jews in Baku and in the larger cities are relative newcomers, there was a much older Jewish community living in the area from time immemorial: the Tats, who speak a mixture of Farsi and Hebrew rather than Azeri Turkish. The only large group which had not emigrated and was still almost intact was living in Kube, to the north of Baku near the Caspian Sea. Lev Bardani, the representative of the Jewish Agency, an Israeli from Georgia who knew the ways of Baku and had many acquaintances, chartered a helicopter to take us there. We landed amidst a large crowd of young people, forewarned and awaiting our arrival. The children took us captive, surprisingly asking us questions in Hebrew, and led us to the large welcoming party. The men all looked very solemn and wore large flat caps nicknamed 'landing-strips'. We immediately set out to see the town, famous for its ten very old synagogues, some of which we had noticed from the air before landing. In the world of Caucasian rugs Kube is well-known for the quality of its weave. Most of the Jews here have, for centuries, either woven rugs or dealt in their trade. The Jewish inhabitants of this far-flung town in a corner of the Caspian region were departing. They had chosen to leave their homes, trades, synagogues and cemeteries to settle in the land of their forefathers many generations removed.

As most of the synagogues had been turned by the Soviet government into warehouses or rug-weaving workshops, we went to the only two active ones. The doors were shut. Peeping through the windows I saw lamps and candelabra with dedications dating back to the middle of the nineteenth century. We flagged down one of the few cabs in town and went to see the cemetery. The stones dated from the nineteenth century. Reuben, an old man in an enormous cap and with a mouthful of gold teeth, volunteered as a guide. He said there was an ancient cemetery up in the hills. The Jews had lived there over 200 years ago but had had to flee, as they were threatened with slaughter by the surrounding Muslims and were saved only by the intercession of Fath Ali Khan, after whom they named a street in modern Kube. As we sat down in the tea-house to taste the excellent bread and white cheese, washed down with steaming tea, our hosts recounted what had happened in Kube after Israel's brilliant victory in 1967. The anger of the local Muslims was so great at the Israeli victory over the Arab armies that they wanted to slake their vengeance on the Jews. A young Jewish artillery colonel from the local military garrison placed his guns on the hill and threatened to shoot at any group who approached the slope to Kube. The Jews bought hunting rifles, the local mullahs counselled caution, and the pogrom was called off.

On our way back to the helicopter we noticed that every household had been turned inside out: kitchen utensils were immersed in cauldrons of boiling water for purification in the general cleanup that precedes every Passover, now only a week away. As we walked past the houses a woman busy with her dishes flashed a wide golden-toothed smile at Aliza, firmly hugged her to her breast and blessed her.

I wanted to pay my respects to the president of Azerbaijan, but Ayaz Mutalibov had resigned under the threat of a rebellion in the Supreme Soviet and gone off to Moscow. So I was taken to pay a courtesy call on Yagub Mamedov, who was actively standing in for the head of state. As I was about to enter his office, two worried military officers dressed in fatigues came out carrying maps. I understood that the military situation was not promising but Mamedov spoke with certitude of Azerbaijan's victory and appealed for global understanding and help. Azerbaijan was indeed in a difficult predicament. I expressed my country's sorrow at the loss of life and disruption of peace and told Mamedov that Israel knew what it meant to be at war. There was nothing we could substantially do in this conflict nor were we being asked to.

On a subsequent visit to Baku I met with Abulfaz Elchibey, who had come to power on an anti-communist ticket and on the strength of his personal honesty and idealism. Elchibey insisted on meeting me face-to-face. He declared himself a Zionist, which meant that he saw the dedication of Jews to their homeland as something natural and understandable. Elchibey was by profession a philologist. He was deeply upset by the attitude of the Soviet government to minorities, whether Jewish, Turkish, or otherwise, and thought that justice must be done to the Jews. Elchibey was probably too straightforward a man to last as a politician. He was brought down by a master of the art, Gaidar Aliyev, who had become a member of the Politburo under Brezhnev, largely through his superb cunning and *savoir faire*.

In Baku, the guns were firing, but the bazaars were open. Trade is in the blood of the Azeris. Still, the heavy pall of war over this country was clearly noticeable. The conflict would continue to undermine the lives of the Azeris. However difficult and painful the reality, many politicians I met in Baku seriously talked of an annexation of Iranian Azerbaijan to form a united, strong Azerbaijan. Many Azeris seemed to set great store in this visionary dream, whose chances of realization are slim. At least, the takeover of Azerbaijan by fundamentalist Iran has also failed. Gaidar Aliyev's advent to power in Baku and his concomitant bridling of the hyperactive political life which had begun spreading in the country, has returned Azerbaijan to the Russian fold, where it will stay, at least for a time.

We returned to Moscow for a day and flew to Alma-Ata. Kazakhstan, with its two and a half million square kilometres and its untold mineral wealth, black and yellow gold and much else, had been attracting foreign investors from the very first breath of its sovereignty. American, European and Asian transcontinental companies were marshalling their wares and enticing the Kazakhs with promises of financial help in exchange for concessions. Israeli firms too were interested but more in developing Kazakhstan's agriculture and introducing drip irrigation into its cotton fields. Nursultan Nazarbayev, the Kazakh president, was an important political figure in the Soviet Union as well as in his own country and had gained international respect for his determination in breaking away from the confining policies of the communist economy.

We landed early in the afternoon at the city's airport, on a plain nestling in the foothills of snow-capped Tyan Shan. We were taken to the official villa where, for lack of other accommodations, businessmen mingled with politicians and journalists who were visiting this city in increasing numbers. Israel Mey-Ami accompanied me on this trip, as did Alec Milman, who was to stay and represent us until such time as an ambassador was appointed. Amnon Kapeliuk of *Yediot Aharonot* came along us as well, promising to immortalize our visit in his paper.

The morning after our arrival we proceeded to the now familiar exchange of documents and a chat with the minister of foreign affairs, Tuleutay Suleimenov. We were then taken to the Supreme Soviet building to await the end of the session and meet the president. In a few minutes Nursultan Nazarbayev and a number of officials entered to take their seats along one side of a long wooden table, while our delegation sat at the other. The official Soviet emblem, carved in oak, still looked down benignly on the conference table. The prime minister, Sergei Tereshchenko, an Ukrainian, was on Nazarbayev's left. On his right sat the Kazakh Vice-President Yerik Assambayev, the minister of foreign affairs, the minister for foreign trade Sizdik Abishev (a very important economic figure in the cabinet) and several other high officials, all Kazakh. It was clear Nazarbayev was resolved to carry out his policy of de-Russification. Vice-Premier Oleg Soskovets soon left the Kazakhs to play a very influential role in Yeltsin's cabinet.

After words of greeting, we discussed the international

situation and the peace process, in which President Nazarbayev expressed a certain interest. We went on to projects of Israeli companies, the prospects of widening their activity and helping Kazakhstan obtain international credits. I invited the president to visit Israel and see with his own eyes what we had done in water conservation and in the growing of cotton and vegetables under drip irrigation. He could not promise to visit us very soon as he had a long list of invitations to the Far East and Europe, but he did send his prime minister. Two important Israeli companies dealing in the export of cotton-growing technology began operating in Kazakhstan after our government took steps to provide risk insurance. Their presence attracted additional groups and trade with the Kazakhs has been growing. One of the difficulties of operating in Kazakhstan is the bureaucratic red tape which slows operations, but projects have been successfully developing since the first exploratory stages.

I also asked the president about Chairman Arafat's visit. Nazarbayev said that some two weeks earlier he was suddenly informed that Arafat's airplane, unannounced, was approaching the Kazakh capital. Nazarbayev did not want to meet the chairman but was finally persuaded to drive out to the airport, to avoid inviting the importunate guest to stay. Arafat presented Nazarbayev with a golden sword, and went on his way. A day or two later, Arafat was involved in a plane crash in which his companions and the crew were killed and he was the sole survivor. News of the accident had reached the president's ears and he asked me about it, with a wry expression on his face.

THE GINSBURG COLLECTION

Between these bursts of activity to set up relations with far-flung republics, there were short respites in Moscow to take up the thread of embassy life. One notable intermission was the inauguration of an agreement between the Russian National Library in Moscow, formerly the Lenin Library, and the Hebrew University in Jerusalem. As I have already noted, the Soviet government had verbally agreed in the early 1920s to sell the

Ginsburg collection of Judaica, consisting of books and manuscripts, to the Hebrew University. Circumstances were such, however, that the plan was never carried out. In 1991, many months of exhaustive discussions over the possibility of renewing the pledge of sale having failed, Israel's National Library settled for a compromise of photographing the books. The Hebrew University provided special equipment and the work got underway in earnest, to be completed at the end of a year's intensive efforts. This material is now, at last, accessible to Hebrew scholars. The prolonged procrastination and resistance on the part of the Soviet government to this simple act was difficult to understand. The director of the Russian National Library, raising a glass of champagne at a brief ceremony, said he regretted the attitude shown in the past. The signing of the agreement marked the culmination of a long period of patient persistence on behalf of many individuals in Israel and elsewhere to bring this chapter to a close.

TO EREVAN AND ARARAT

After celebrating the Passover, Aliza, Yossi Bendor and I took off to establish relations with Armenia. The flight to Erevan had been repeatedly put off, but we finally coordinated a date with the Armenian government and landed at their capital toward the end of April 1992, at three o'clock in the morning, in pitch-blackness. Erik Hakopyan, an Armenian diplomat who spoke fluent Hebrew and who had been helping us with the preliminaries, was there with a number of his colleagues. We were escorted to the presidential compound and lodged in a comfortable villa.

We woke up to the singing of birds in the blazing sunshine of an early spring in mountainous country. Blooming cherry trees, as far as the eye could see, covered the terraces of a large garden reaching down into the gulley below our house. Armed guards stood lazily at the gates. Our villa was in an area which housed the head of state, the minister of foreign affairs and other top officials. The special advantage of these small houses was in the hot running water, of which the rest of the country was deprived, for lack of fuel. On our dining table we found large boxes of matzo (unleavened bread), and gefilte fish from California. We had our own supplies but we were touched by the gesture of the tiny Jewish community in Erevan, who wanted us to feel at home during the Passover week.

Rafi Ovanesyan, a strapping young international lawyer from Los Angeles, turned minister of foreign affairs, warmly greeted us at the Foreign Ministry and, as pre-arranged, signed with me the documents establishing diplomatic relations. The minister's father had been an important historian of Armenia's prolonged struggle for independence and Rafi Ovanesyan had given up a brilliant career to devote his energies to this first phase of Armenian sovereignty. Like many other Armenian officials, the minister expressed great admiration for Israel's achievements in regaining independence and establishing itself as a nation. He said the Armenians were interested in our economic and social experience and were eager to cooperate and share the knowledge we had accumulated in running our country. I had authority to offer some assistance to facilitate cooperation and, though very limited, it was accepted. I invited the foreign minister for a visit to Israel, which he never took advantage of, as some months later, apparently over matters pertaining to the continued Karabakh crisis, he resigned his post.

The mayor of Erevan, Ambartsum Gestelyan, had been one of the first initiators of the movement for separation from the Soviet Union and of the demand to grant Karabakh an independent status, detaching it from Azerbaijan. I had gotten acquainted with him in Moscow, on the eve of his trip to Jerusalem for an international mayors' conference. When we visited his office in Erevan he told us he had been extremely impressed with Teddy Kollek, the mayor of Jerusalem, and was already applying to Erevan some of the lessons he had learned from Teddy on collecting money for special projects. Gestelyan was a sociologist. He knew well the political map of the Soviet Union, had an incisive and clear mind and a pleasant and outgoing personality. Married to a Jewess, Ruth, he impressed us all with his tolerance and keen intelligence. It seemed to me, from my several conversations with him, that he was not in total agreement with the course of events in Karabakh. I thought he was not terribly pleased with the hijacking of the Karabakh movement by extremist Dashnak elements, who catapulted Armenia into a crippling military conflict, setting back the Armenian march toward economic and social development in the very first days of its newly won independence. Could not the war with Azerbaijan have been avoided? I thought Gestelyan and some other Armenians I met on this trip were troubled by these thoughts but were under great political strain and could not freely express their opinions.

The hills descending into the streets of Erevan were covered with houses built in soft shades of a multi-coloured volcanic rock called tuff. The rocky soil was interspersed with gardens, newly alive in the warming rays of the spring sun. The landscape reminded me of Jerusalem. As we ascended the steep steps of the presidential palace and entered Levon Ter-Petrosyan's office, I was sure the open and friendly atmosphere predominating in all of my meetings and discussions with the élite and the man-on-the-street in Armenia thus far, would characterize the meeting with the Armenian president. My expectations proved to be wrong.

Ter-Petrosyan was edgy and distant. The president reacted sceptically to my suggestion for widening the framework of our relations. Private Israeli and Jewish interests must first invest in the Armenian economy, he said. The president did not tell us which sectors he wanted us to invest in, but he wanted to slow down political relations and postpone cultural and technical contacts. Ter-Petrosyan added that he was due to fly to Syria in a few days and was sending Ovanesyan to the Gulf countries. He did not elaborate. The president then made another 'friendly' statement. He said he hoped Israel understood that the Armenians' participation in Arab terrorist acts against Israel was an attempt to survive. He did not develop this point but I surmised he was referring to acts of Armenian terrorists who were part of larger Arab organizations. It was true that among the most active terrorist groups operating from Lebanese and Syrian territory we sometimes came across Armenian names. I told Ter-Petrosyan we could neither understand nor condone such acts as they were being perpetrated against our security and we did not see any objective need for them from the Armenian point of view. As to investments, it would be difficult to persuade our citizens to invest in a country that intended to slow down relations before they even started. I then gave an exposé of our relations with the Arab world and the government's peace initiative, but the conversation trailed off into generalities. I presented some gifts from Israel, including an album on Jerusalem. Ter-Petrosyan remarked that the album would certainly please his wife.

I left Ter-Petrosyan's office in a subdued mood, wondering if his imminent trip to the Arab countries had interfered with our conversation. Ter-Petrosyan appeared uninterested in discussing Middle Eastern politics, which was not surprising as he had more immediate concerns. I thought he was probably going to ask the Arabs for loans and international help in the conflict with Azerbaijan. Ter-Petrosyan's father was a Syrian Armenian and one of the organizers of the Syrian Communist Party. Levon Ter-Petrosyan was himself born in Syria. All this was not a valid explanation for undiplomatic words, but it might have set the tone.

That evening, at an official dinner given by the foreign minister, I took Rafi Ovanesyan aside and told him about my meeting with the president. I asked him if he could enlighten me. Ovanesyan did not appear to have been briefed. He said he could not account for the president's attitude, but he must have been thinking of the interests of Armenians living in the Arab countries, or of the fact that his wife was Jewish, for which certain newspapers were attacking him. This sounded plausible.

News of my meeting with the president reached a number of high Armenian officials. Subsequent discussions with other ministers all started out with attempts to iron out the poor impression made on this first visit to Armenia of an Israeli delegation. Mayor Gestelyan also said not to be overly concerned with the interview with the president. He added that he would be coming to Moscow soon and would explain the situation, a reflection of the internal problems and the power struggle within Armenia.

The mayor personally took us on a visit to several interesting art museums including that of the painter Saranyan and that of the well-known, talented, eccentric Parajanyan. Gestelyan made us feel very much at home in his city and I could see there were many who related to him with great respect and fondness. He resigned his post a year after we visited Erevan. There were various rumours spread about the reasons that prompted this resignation, including insinuations of Gestelyan's involvement with the local mafia. There were also indications of political difficulties, some arising out of his marriage to a Jewish woman who could not totally bury her identity. Gestelyan went into business after his resignation. I was much upset to hear of his assassination, near his home, in December 1994. The murder was discussed in the Armenian Parliament, but responsibility for the crime was never established. Speculation tends to focus on the mafia or political motivations. Whatever the case, Armenia lost an outstanding young leader who could have continued serving it with great distinction.

An interesting part of our visit to Armenia was an audience we had with the head of the Armenian Orthodox Church, Vazgen I, in Echmiadzin, the Armenian Vatican. The Armenian Pope, a native of Romania, amiably talked to Aliza and me about the close connections the Armenians have had with Jerusalem. Armenia was baptized into Christianity at the beginning of the fourth century and soon afterwards monasteries and churches began going up in the city. The Armenian quarter in Jerusalem is well-known for its religious and educational activities and has maintained its special status in the city throughout the years. Echmiadzin Cathedral, a beautiful ancient building constructed according to an architectural plan that was to set the standards and lines for numerous Armenian churches throughout the Middle East, is situated some ten kilometres from Erevan. It was built on a lake, on a bed of straw, we were told. This ancient engineering technique preserved the cathedral from the recurrent earthquakes of this region, some of which have devastated Armenian cities in the past.

As we emerged from the Manoukyan rug museum near the cathedral, Mount Ararat came into full view, dominating a good portion of the clear, azure sky. A rough dirt track, leading from the edge of the asphalted road, trailed through a tall, half-open gate into the flowering orchards beyond. It pointed the way to the summit of the immense mountain, majestically rising from the fields in the distance to its flattened, snowy peak. Travelling in eastern Turkey, I had seen the other side of this mountain. There is an overpowering, mystical presence in this view, an authoritativeness that commands attention, a magic that brings back innate memories of antiquity. To the Armenians, Ararat is a unifying symbol of national hopes. To many it is a reminder of the story of Noah. Many expeditions failed to find his Ark but I could at least see how high the water must have stood, when the 40 days and nights of the Great Flood were finally over and a rainbow of hope appeared over the horizon.

In Erevan, Aliza and I searched out our composer friend Avet Terteryan and his wife Irina and spent an evening at their apartment. We could see with our own eyes the toll the fuel blockade had taken on the citizens of this country. The Terteryans looked as strong and defiant as always but it was clear the winter they had just lived through must have been punishing. In this connection, the US chargé d'affaires Rosemary Forsythe told me of the apprehension existing in Armenia, as well as outside its borders, about the possible reactivation of the Chernobyl-type atomic reactor located close to the Armenian capital. The reactor had been shut down for a number of years but with the sharp energy crisis, the opinion was that whatever the cost, the country could not sustain another such winter. The chances of explosion of this particular reactor were put at 40 per cent. I have since heard that the Armenian government has taken steps to begin the thorough preparations needed to start up the reactor, hoping for the best. If this plan is carried out it might threaten the entire Caucasus with a repetition of the Chernobyl disaster, the prevailing winds capable of carrying the radioactivity of a possible explosion around the world.

While I was engaged in the many meetings with Armenian officials, Aliza walked over on her own to meet Lucy, the wife of President Ter-Petrosyan, at her villa in the compound we were staying in. An elderly, well-dressed lady was at the landing, waiting. When Aliza asked her if the villa was that of the president, the lady nodded and said she was expecting the Israeli ambassador's wife to drive up. It turned out that the lady was the president's mother-in-law. Her name was Bracha and she addressed Aliza in a beautifully accented Hebrew which she had learned as a child at the Tarbut Hebrew gymnasium in Vilnius, one of the several schools in Lithuania and Latvia, well-known for their high standards of learning. Bracha said she wanted to meet the

Israeli ambassador and Aliza took her down to meet me. I spoke to her and marvelled at her Hebrew, still rich and fresh in spite of many years of disuse. She excused herself for not knowing Hebrew 'government' words such as ambassador and Parliament, not taught at her school in the 1930s, when Israel was but a distant dream.

The small Jewish community of Erevan, only about a thousand strong before the last phase of their emigration to Israel, was very animated over the visit of the Israeli delegation and received us officially in one of their apartments, plying us with Passover food and telling us about their hopes and expectations. They said they were very great patriots of Armenia, but the circumstances of their life were such that they wanted to hasten their emigration. I believe that most of this community has in fact departed from Erevan.

We all enjoyed our visit to Armenia. The similarity of our peoples' history and destiny, the shared hardiness and perseverance, the devotion to traditions, to learning and to things spiritual, fractiousness as a national characteristic, as well as the strong element of hope and determination which enabled both peoples to survive holocausts in the twentieth century, ought to have brought us closer together. It is a great pity that Armenian anti-Semitism still persists in some quarters and Armenian terrorists find their way into Arab organizations which commit acts of violence against Israel.

IN STRIFE-TORN GEORGIA

Jews are said to have been welcomed in Georgia, after the destruction of the First Temple, in the sixth century BC. Throughout these many years, Georgia purportedly has been free of anti-Semitism and Jews have dwelt among their neighbours in freedom and in peace. The Georgian Jews in Israel have maintained their traditions and are proud of their links with the old country. Strategically, Georgia has always been of great importance, with its domination of the Elbrus range, separating Europe from Asia; a country of deep valleys and swift mountain streams situated between the Black and the Caspian Seas.

It was well toward the end of May when we embarked on our last but one voyage to the new republics, this time to unsettled and war-torn Georgia. This was a journey I had wanted to make for a long time. A large group of officials awaited us at the Tbilisi airport. They included Sergei Tarasenko, Shevardnadze's close aide and adviser, who had followed him out of the Soviet Foreign Ministry into Georgia, the deputy-minister of foreign affairs and others. We were taken in hand by a young Foreign Ministry official, fluent in Hebrew, Timuri Yaacobashvili, who subsequently accompanied us on our visit. From the airport we proceeded to a large government compound which had hot running water, unlike the rest of the country, in the throes of an energy crisis, like Armenia. There was a loud bullfrog serenade as we descended from our cars. Early in the morning of the next day I was awakened by loud Georgian music blaring from a radio right under my window. It was the gardener, planting fruit trees, perhaps in haste to see his saplings bear fruit.

Georgian Foreign Minister Alexander Chikvaidze was the former Soviet ambassador to the Netherlands and had much international experience. He expounded on the catastrophic economic and political difficulties of his country. Industrial and agricultural production in Georgia had fallen by over 25 per cent. Georgians, ordinarily an industrious people, had no motivation to work, and hunger was stalking the country. Chikvaidze thought Israel could help stimulate Georgia's economy with its wide experience in similar circumstances and with its connections. I proffered Israel's help in training Georgian experts in various fields.

The minister was also a great lover of soccer. He inquired if we could organize bilateral matches. Israel's strength lay mostly in basketball, so I suggested we add that sport, as well. Only then did the minister sign the protocol of diplomatic relations and exchange notes.

The meeting with Prime Minister Tengiz Singua was unique. The prime minister was flanked by several colleagues, one of whom, the minister of defence, Tengiz Kitovani, was and still is well-known for his powerful political base. A painter and childhood friend of Gamsakhurdia (the elected president who was

373

later forced to flee), Kitovani was appointed to be head of the National Guard, which Gamsakhurdia abruptly disbanded, kindling the fiery enmity of his former supporter. An Israeli Georgian businessman had been attempting to buy arms and ammunition from Israel, giving Kitovani's name as a sponsor. When the foreign minister raised the question of small arms for the police, I said such requests must be handled only at government level, adding that of itself, this did not mean we would be able to provide them. At the meeting with the prime minister, the question of arms was raised by the foreign minister again and, when answering the query, I thought I was in fact talking to Kitovani, who remained silent throughout, watching me intently with his sharp, black eyes. The prime minister changed the subject to the economic and energy blockade by Russia. The civil war and the wars in South Ossetia and in Abkhazia were draining the country's resources, dividing it and delaying reconstruction.

The distance between the prime minister's office and the presidential palace was not great but we could see the burnt-out shells of many beautiful buildings, their black windows gaping upon Rustavelli Avenue below. The civil war had preceded the arrival of Shevardnadze and his election in Parliament as head of the State Council. The large president's office, formerly Communist Party headquarters, was dressed in grey granite and yellow tuff. It had been built by German prisoners of war and took many direct artillery hits from Gamsakhurdia's supporters but looked none the worse for wear. Tbilisi was handsome even in its dilapidation.

We were ushered into a large conference room and told to wait for Shevardnadze. He appeared a few minutes later from a small side-door. He looked gaunt. I had last seen him in Moscow, when I sat next to him at a presentation of *Uriel Acosta*, a play on a Jewish theme, performed by an excellent Georgian troupe.

Shevardnadze's first words were that he had just learned the supply of bread was down to one week. He had turned to the Turkish Foreign Minister, visiting Tbilisi, who immediately promised to send in 50,000 tons of wheat, without even consulting his government. The authorities would be certain to approve, he had said. The Russians had closed off the main 'military' road leading to Georgia and had again cut off the gas, supplied through a pipeline crossing Chechnya and Ossetia. Shevardnadze said he had complained to Vice-President Rutskoi, who, 'swearing like a trooper' crudely threatened to bomb Tbilisi if the Georgians did not desist from their intervention in South Ossetia. This pipeline was opened and closed again on many occasions, the Russians showing little concern for the plight of Georgians and Armenians. When I next saw Rutskoi in Moscow I told him of the great suffering that I had witnessed in Georgia and Armenia, as a result of the closure of the pipeline. Rutskoi again delivered a string of curses with regard to Shevardnadze's address, but said the blockade was being lifted.

Shevardnadze then went on to describe the situation that I had already witnessed: material difficulties and unsettled times, without any clear indication as to when the problems might be resolved. Three months earlier, in March, when Shevardnadze had decided to bow to the pressures exerted on him to accept his post, he was not terribly optimistic but thought his authority and reputation could help stabilize the country. The crisis, however, turned out to be far too complicated and had run too deep. It could not be dealt with on a purely Georgian level. Shevardnadze later felt obliged to invite the Russians back in order to force the warring factions to make a truce.

The civil war has died down a great deal but the inherent difficulties of this divided country still resist peacemaking. It is curious that the only period of relative calm Georgia enjoyed was under the Soviets, who controlled the tempestuous ambitions and rivalry of the many ethnic, tribal and social groups by the use of a ruthless system of administration. For more than 15 years, Shevardnadze headed that administration as party chief and minister of the interior. Now Georgia is more difficult to manage.

A very excited congregation awaited us at the large central synagogue in Tbilisi when we went to meet the Jewish community later in the day. The hall was packed with people who had come to welcome us, the first official representatives of the State of Israel, who had come to announce the establishment of diplomatic relations with the country these Jews had lived in for so many generations. This demonstration was not a mere act of curiosity. Obtaining a visa to Israel from Moscow had become an enormously difficult task, with the prices of plane tickets sky-high and flights rare. Everyone wanted to know how soon we would open a consulate in Tbilisi. We promised to do our best to expedite this, knowing how complicated this essentially bureaucratic and budgetary problem could in fact be. There were already people leaving the war-torn zone in Ossetia and Abkhazia, and Jewish Agency and Nativ officials were running great risks in evacuating the emigrants to the Georgian capital, which served as a clearing point. The first direct flight arranged by the Jewish Agency took off for Israel several days after our visit. Most of the Jews of Georgia are now resettled in Israel, and those who stayed behind in Abkhazia and Ossetia have been few.

As I was leaving the synagogue, a woman approached me to ask if I had spoken to Shevardnadze about her abducted 18-year-old son. I had indeed mentioned this matter and the Georgian leader had promised to severely punish the criminals, which was hardly helpful to the plight of the family. A day or two later I learned how complicated these cases were. The abductors had acted on behalf of the business rivals of the boy's father. They wanted him to give up his post as manager of a local bank. The boy's mother turned to me because she was an Israeli citizen. The case was finally resolved with the boy returned, and the father still working with the bank. These mafiosi tactics were rapidly spreading over the former Soviet Union.

Our meeting with the congregation at the synagogue was preceded by one with the Jewish leaders. Most of them were deeply rooted in the country, but intended to eventually emigrate, thus virtually bringing to an end the long story of Jewish settlement in Georgia. Dinner with the Jewish leaders followed a long session at the Georgian Academy of Sciences, whose president, Albert Tavkhelidze, invited us to discuss possible avenues of economic and academic cooperation.

On the flight back to Moscow on a very crowded plane, I fell into deep slumber only to be poked unceremoniously in the ribs by a man who demanded to know what Shevardnadze had said to me. When I asked what he wanted to know, he answered 'everything', which made me laugh, to the man's evident displeasure. This rude awakening suddenly made me realize how little I had seen of the immense country between the Baltic Sea and the Chinese border before my journey through its ten or more former republics. I could not claim to know a great deal more after my brief visits. Yet the distances, the leaders and the often clashing interests gave me a far better perception of the continental power that the Soviet Union had been. It was also an overview of the Jewish population, living in almost every distant corner of that immense empire. The Jews were pulling up their roots. Was this the final chapter of Jewish history in these lands? My instincts told me it was not.

26 · Winding Up

Alexander Rutskoi was the popular hero of Afghanistan and of the August crisis in 1991. Although he was a fighter pilot, everyone called him *rubaka* — a fearless Cossack, who gallops straight into an enemy squadron, chopping off heads right and left with his cavalry sabre. In fact, he had a gentler disposition and although quick to fly off the handle, seemed a reasonable man. What he lacked in his high government post of vice-president was experience. His advisers, often motivated by conflicting interests, were not always helpful. I had met the vice-president on numerous occasions and had good personal access to him.

Chafing at Rutskoi's frequent outbursts of criticism, President Yeltsin appointed him in February 1992 to head the agricultural land reform. Russia has always been in the hands of agricultural reformers, but has never been able to solve its age-old landowner-ship problems, nor to alleviate chronic food shortages. Rutskoi had busied himself in many directions, none of which had much to do with agriculture, but he took his brief very seriously and began making grandiose plans to put agriculture on the right track.

I sought Rutskoi's help on several occasions. As the Jewish Agency was operating in Russia without official authorization, I took Simcha Dinitz, the head of the agency, on a visit to Moscow to see Russian Premier Ivan Silaev, who agreed to support Dinitz's application. I hoped Rutskoi would help seal the decision and asked for an appointment with him. Dinitz and I had thus to listen attentively to Rutskoi's plans to privatize Russia's vast reserves of land while partially maintaining socialist agriculture. A good half-hour elapsed before we could get a word in, so convinced was the vice-president of his new panacea for Russia's perennial agricultural ills. Rutskoi readily promised support for the agency's juridical status in Russia and expressed the desire to visit Israel to see how it dealt with landownership. He added that he knew about anti-Semitism from personal experience. His mother, who lived in the city of Kursk, had had anti-Semitic graffiti painted on her door. This evidently implied that Rutskoi's mother was of Jewish origin, but we never could get that corroborated.

I undertook to provide an invitation for Rutskoi's trip to Israel. After a few weeks I met with his staff to coordinate a 'working visit' which was also to be sponsored by important Israeli business interests contemplating agricultural projects in Russia.

The vice-president arrived in April 1992 with his wife Ludmila for a stay of several days. The Russian Foreign Ministry bridled Rutskoi: Yuri Vorontsov, the Middle East authority, was in the vice-president's party. He kept to himself, but his presence was much in evidence. The Shamir government picked Ariel Sharon, a reserve general and minister of agriculture, to be Rutskoi's official host. On the first evening of his visit, Shaul Eisenberg gave a gentlemen-only dinner party for the vice-president and the business associates who accompanied him, highlighting the business interests that would accompany the group on its tour.

On a low-level flight in a small carrier to the north, I showed Rutskoi the topography of the country, comparing the map he held in his hands to the physical landmarks and explaining the strategic problems of the Golan Heights. I showed him the narrow strip of land separating the sea from the old pre-1967 borders. Rutskoi grasped the problems immediately. His eyes told him a great deal more than his ears had heard up to then. After landing, we spent the greater part of the day visiting agricultural research stations and kibbutzim, turkey farms, and meat and milk processing plants. He admired everything he saw and gave an interview to Russian television while biting into a juicy Israeli tomato. 'An excellent chaser', he said, 'why shouldn't the Russians have them too?'

The Rutskoi party was also taken to the Yad Vashem Holocaust memorial, which deeply impressed the vice-president, and to the Western Wall, where he was seen to shed a tear.

In Tel Aviv, Rutskoi was introduced to Yitzhak Rabin at the Labour Party headquarters. A bare two months were left until the elections, and Likud hecklers were outside the building, screaming at the top of their voices, while Rabin calmly proceeded to lay before Rutskoi the Labour Party plan for compromise and peace with the Arabs. There was no mistaking Rutskoi's opinion: he was for the other party, which did not want to give anything away. Before leaving the final meeting with Prime Minister Shamir, where we had signed a protocol on agricultural and technical cooperation, Rutskoi told Shamir he had heard we were preparing to give land away to the Arabs. This must not be done, he insisted. Israel was already a tiny country and if anything were given to the Arabs there would be demands for more. 'That's very interesting', Shamir said, thoughtfully.

Rutskoi believed in Israel's economic capabilities and brought several prominent Russian businessmen with him to talk about trade and investments in Russia. Shaul Eisenberg met and discussed the possibilities with Rutskoi and his friends, and contacts were maintained with the Russian vice-president after his return home. However, the Russian market was unreliable and danger-prone. Rutskoi's insistence that Israeli businesses enter Russia immediately and invest there, were not taken seriously by many Israelis. What appeared in the eyes of the Russians as a once-in-a-lifetime opportunity did not look attractive to the Israelis. It may have been a mistaken attitude, but it was safe.

In early May, barely back from his tour, Rutskoi came to our Independence Day celebrations and to the astonishment of Russian officials and foreign diplomats, embraced and kissed me on both cheeks. When I came to pay my respects, before leaving my post, I noticed a huge portrait of Peter the Great in Rutskoi's office. Evidently, Rutskoi sought to emulate Peter. Regretfully, his career ended in jail, after he had overrated his capacity in a confrontation with Yeltsin, in October 1994. Rutskoi was freed in a parliamentary amnesty and is preparing a comeback, together with the new Communist Party. He is still young, and remains popular in many quarters.

The day following our Independence celebrations, I gave an address at the Frunze Military Academy. I was told this was the first appearance of any foreign ambassador at the institution, which had trained the top commanders of the Soviet army for many years. Before passing into the lecture hall I was invited to spend a few minutes with the chief instructor. One of his walls was covered with a dozen schematic depictions of history's famous battles, including some fought in the Second World War. No one had to draw my attention to three plans showing actions fought by the Israeli army: against the Syrian forces on the northeastern coast of the Sea of Galilee in December 1955, the Six-Day War operations against the Golan Heights in 1967 and the crossing of the Suez Canal by Israeli forces in the Yom Kippur War in 1973.

I was greeted with respect and interest by a group of officers, mostly colonels. They listened intently to my words on the history of Israel's defence, its evolution and strategic needs. At the end of the lecture there was a number of questions, one of which was about Moshe Dayan, in their eyes still the legendary military hero of Israel's greatest victories. The question was, in which military academy in the Soviet Union had Dayan studied? I felt palpable disbelief among the audience when I assured them Dayan had never even visited the Soviet Union. I told them about the British officer Orde Wingate and the Russian Jew Yitzhak Sadeh, who had helped train the first military leaders, and about the Hagana, the underground army. They listened but appeared to think I was prevaricating. They seemed to think that such a capable general from a country settled by Russians could not have been anything but Russian-trained.

After my prolonged immersion in the Moscow scene I felt a change of environment would do me good. Parviz Nazarian, an old friend and one of the leaders of the Iranian Jewish community in Los Angeles, had been asking me for many months to lecture in Farsi about the great immigration saga. I was eager to see my old classmates, many from my grammar school days. I arranged for a few days' absence from Moscow, and Aliza and I flew to the west coast of the United States.

I was the main speaker at a gala dinner devoted to Israel's Day of Independence, at the Beverly Hilton. This Los Angeles audience took me back 52 years. There was a large number of people that I

381

had known in school in Tehran when I was eight to twelve years old, and others whom I had met when I was posted there as Deputy Chief of Mission before the Khomeini revolution.

At another engagement I was astounded to see, sitting in the front row, Dr. Matlub, my school principal (he must have been at least 90), who, at my father's behest, had 'taught me English'. His method consisted of making me stand up during recess and read out of a textbook: 'This is a flower. Say hello to John. The time is four o'clock'. I had absolutely no idea what the words meant. My interest in the exercise was mainly in the fact that Matlub took a liking to me. I thus enjoyed more consideration than my friends when punishment time would come around on Thursdays, or on other occasions when we were caught breaking the rules. We then had to hold out our palms and get struck with a flat wooden ruler. Matlub's ruler had a metal edge. I was not spared punishment, but the ruler landed on my palm gently — a blow not from the shoulder, but from considerably lower, which was low, indeed. Matlub was five feet, four inches tall. We would chant behind his back 'Matlub Kotole Zire Otole', which, roughly translated, meant 'Even under a car, Matlub can stand up to his full height.' There was considerable merriment around the millionaires' table in Los Angeles when I first revealed this private arrangement between myself and the school principal, 50 years back.

The Iranian Jews had lost most of their immovable property during and after the Khomeini upheaval, but I was glad to see how well they had done. In fact, the community in Los Angeles seemed to have changed little in the lifestyle it enjoyed under the Shah. The Iranian Jews seemed to be thriving, with many well-heeled professionals and businessmen, and their integration in the United States appeared to be a success.

When I returned to Moscow we had to tend urgently to the needs of the Moldovan Jews who were trapped in Transdnestria. Situated between the two new republics that had separated from the USSR, Moldova and Ukraine, Transdnestria,was fighting to get its own independence for a population of mixed Russian-Ukrainian-Moldovan background. This move was opposed by the new Moldovan Republic. As the conflict developed, heavy fighting broke out and thousands of people in the cities of Bendery and

Tiraspol found themselves under siege. The city of Bendery changed hands back and forth between the Moldovans and the forces of the Russian Fourteenth Army, located beyond the Dniester River toward Ukraine. Tens of thousands of residents, including most of the Jewish population, had to suddenly flee their homes. The Jewish Agency and Nativ first helped them get to Odessa, the Ukrainian port city nearby and later to Kishinev, the Moldovan capital. The American Joint Distribution Committee assisted in organizing camps in Odessa and taking care of the refugees in Kishinev.

Toward the end of June, with the crisis at its peak, I flew down to Moldova, to establish diplomatic relations with the new republic. Some of the refugees were ready to go to Israel; others hoped the fighting would soon die down, enabling them to regain their homes. It was impossible for the potential emigrants to get to Moscow for the necessary visas. We had no choice but to provide them with the permission for entry into Israel in the city of Kishinev, to which most of the refugees had fled.

The Moldovan President, Mircea Snegur, and his cabinet, most of whom I met, tried to help, including issuing temporary travel documents for emigrants whose background could not be definitively established. This was probably in the political interests of Moldova, but it ultimately saved lives. There were the usual bureaucratic difficulties among ourselves. On this occasion, too, we encountered excess zeal on the part of Nativ representatives who, entirely on their own initiative, had approached the Ukrainian government 'on behalf of the Israeli Embassy in Moscow'. Nativ had asked to evacuate the refugees, who were Moldovan citizens, on Ukrainian papers. The Ukrainians had declined. Accepting would have meant getting into an entirely unwarranted petty conflict with Moldova over privileges of sovereignty. In any case, most of the refugees did not wish to be evacuated; those who did could have easily done so through Kishinev. We opened a temporary consulate in the Moldovan capital and worked out an acceptable routine with the government agencies. The tragic circumstances in Bendery and Tiraspol continued for some time but we were now in a position to help any person to evacuate to Israel speedily, if he so desired.

RAISA AND MIKHAIL GORBACHEV IN ISRAEL

In June 1992, plans got under way to bring Mikhail Gorbachev on a visit to Israel. Only six months had elapsed since Gorbachev's resignation and his aureole had not entirely dimmed yet. The Haifa Technion announced it would make a gift of money to the Gorbachev Fund, in recognition of the former leader's contribution to humanity. Several universities desired to present him with honorary degrees and we wanted him to take the opportunity to see the country. On this occasion too, there were Israelis who wanted to appropriate the Gorbachev visit in their own interests, but we brushed them aside, more easily than in the past. The Israeli public looked forward to the former Soviet leader's visit with great enthusiasm. The date was set and a Swiss businessman, Nessim Gaon, generously responded to my request to loan his private jet for the occasion. Gorbachev's party included his wife Raisa, adviser Anatoly Cherniaev, the physicist Yuri Osipyan and the former Central Committee specialist on the Jews, Vladimir Tumarkin. I did not accompany Gorbachev as he was not travelling in an official capacity.

While waiting for Gorbachev's arrival at Moscow airport prior to take-off, I was approached by Alexander Yakovlev. I had seen him just a few days earlier, at the time of the presentation of his new book. He looked worried. He said I must do everything in my power to warn my government, as well as the president of the United States, of an impending outbreak of anti-Semitism. This time around, he said, it might turn out to be extremely dangerous for the Jews and harm Russia's relations with the West, as well. Yeltsin's government was not doing anything to prevent it, although they knew the direction these developments were taking. Did Gorbachev know about this and would he also talk about it with his influential friends? Yakovlev nodded in the direction of the plane and made an expressive gesture with the palm of his hand, suggesting it could not be counted on.

At that time a number of anti-Semitic statements had been made by the Pamyat group; the arch-conservatives and Communists were making a lot of noise in the press about 'the Jews', but it hardly presaged pogroms, as Yakovlev seemed to be warning. He was vague on the details and I surmised he knew more than he revealed, wondering why he was being evasive. I took his words at face value and consulted with our own staff as well as with the American and other western embassies. The general assessment was that the dangers were exaggerated and would not go beyond the vocal stage, which proved to be true.

In Israel, there were crowds around Gorbachev everywhere he went. Often, the public's reaction bordered on hysteria. Everyone wanted to thank him for the role he had played in opening the gates to Jewish emigration and changing the character of the Soviet Union. It was entirely unimportant what the exact nature of this leader's contribution was in the great transformations ascribed to him by popular opinion. He was looked upon as the symbol and the guiding light of a different and better world, inherited after the 70-year-old history of totalitarian Soviet power. He was relaxed, communicative and very engaging, and the crowds loved him.

I received the Gorbachev party when they returned to Moscow and accompanied them to a special VIP room at the airport. Yakovlev and Vadim Medvedev (ex-Politburo ideology chief) were there as well as a few members of the Gorbachev Fund. I asked for their impressions. Gorbachev said that up to that time he had thought his receptions in Germany were the warmest he had ever encountered. His trip to Israel had changed his mind, he said. The outpouring of feelings toward him and Raisa went beyond anything he had ever experienced. Raisa Gorbachev was also very moved by the religious aspect of their visit to the Holy Land, with the Sea of Galilee and Jerusalem being the high point of the tour for her. Wherever they went, they said, former Soviet citizens recognized and hailed them and gave them every sign of their appreciation for having been of help and having opened the gates.

ELECTIONS AND A NEW GOVERNMENT

In July Israel went to the polls. I was in Moscow at the time and waited for the results until early in the morning at Yossi Bendor's apartment with Masud Alikhani (a close friend from my Tehran days, who was doing business in Russia) and others. Late at night the forecast indicated a Labour victory. A new foreign policy and attitude toward the peace process were about to begin and perhaps change our lives. Not all of our group in Moscow were elated with the Labour victory. The majority of the embassy staff were former Soviet citizens and their sympathies were not necessarily with the victors. This attitude did not reflect the views of the majority of the Russian immigrants, who had voted for Labour, not so much because of their political inclinations, as out of general dissatisfaction with the reception they had gotten from the Shamir government. That, at least, was the feeling projected by the press. The immigration was thus beginning to affect domestic Israeli politics, beyond the struggle to open the gates of the Soviet Union.

On my next visit to Israel I went to see Shimon Peres, who was to become 'merely' minister of foreign affairs, to his visible disappointment. Peres complained that Rabin was about to hijack the peace negotiations and the glory that went with them. His feelings were no secret. I thought, however, that Peres would handle the economic aspect of the negotiations (referred to as the 'second track' in diplomatic lingo) to great advantage. This other direction could well develop to be as important as the political negotiations with the Palestinians and the Arab countries. Besides, no one could really close the door to Peres's participation in the political process. The results of the peace process, over time, would be greatly dependent on multi-faceted technical cooperation in the region. Peres agreed that this could prove to be true and asked me to write a paper on my suggestions for the reorganization of the ministry in view of the new tasks ahead, which I did.

Several days later, I was able to test Peres's reactions and intentions toward Russia. I asked Professor Gabriel Gorodetsky, the head of the Cummings Center for Russian Studies at Tel Aviv University to accompany me to a meeting with Peres, and both of us urged that greater attention be paid to Russia. Sophisticated use of opportunities in the economic and strategic fields could lead to better relations and personal contacts and ensure continuous, steady immigration. It might also make Russia into a potential ally, in view of the many interests we shared. Peres, who had in the meantime been invested as the foreign minister, looked distracted with the many concerns of his office and seemed to be paying little attention to the subject we were discussing. Russia and the former Soviet empire were not on the minister's mind.

In many ways, Gorodetsky and I agreed, the Russian question was slowly but surely descending the ladder of priorities: immigration was no longer a major issue; the Soviet superpower was but a past memory. The interest of the Israeli public toward a country which had been the source of great concern and hope, was dwindling. Governments are not in the habit of looking too far into the future to provide for rainy days ahead. Its ministers are too deeply drawn into the whirlpool of current politics at home and abroad. Our once defiant beginnings in Moscow, the stimulation of national challenges, the rising and falling wave of emigration, the restoration of relations and the emergence of new republics, were now all part of the historical record. It was the end of an era. This visit to Peres sobered me up considerably. My mission to Russia was reaching its conclusion. The time had come to return home.

In Moscow, 12 August brought back bitter memories for the Russian Jews. Some 40 years had elapsed since the day when a group of writers, poets scientists — members of the Anti-fascist Committee — were tried and shot on Beria's orders. This crime was committed some four years after the assassination of Solomon Mikhoels in 1948. Still ahead were the Doctors' Plot of 1953 and the strongly rumoured threat of mass deportations of the Jewish urban population into the heartland of Siberia, called off because of Stalin's death in March of that year. Moscow's Jewish organizations marked the day with an exhibition showing new documents on the trial and on Stalin's anti-Semitic policy. Mikhail Gorbachev was invited and attended the inauguration of the exhibition. Mayor Yuri Luzhkov and I addressed a large gathering commemorating the tragic events. In a reference to the growing number of Jews emigrating to Israel, Luzhkov said that the Russia that he had lived in all his life would not be the same without them.

SHIMON REMINISCES

Russia still had its attractions for some. I had been working hard to get a Russian invitation for an official visit by Shimon Peres, the new minister of foreign affairs. Although we were in the mid-summer lull, the Russian Foreign Ministry seemed too preoccupied with other international concerns to relate to this request. But I was in contact with a much friendlier Near East department and I thought our suggestion for a Peres visit was in good hands. The official who was now dealing with Israel, the Palestinians and Jordan was Vladimir Nosenko, formerly of the Oriental Institute. He had been a prolific writer on Israel and Zionism, in the unfriendly spirit required of specialists at the time. But he had changed course and become a defender of good relations with Israel. He had been transferred from IMEMO and posted to the new Russian Ministry of Foreign Affairs.

Early in August, Near East department head Kolotusha called me in to say Andrei Kozyrev was inviting Peres for a visit on 20 August; there were simply no other openings in the Russian official calendar and if the Israeli minister were not able to arrive, the visit would have to be put off for some time to come. Although no definite programme was mentioned, several calls to Peres's bureau chief, Avi Gil, confirmed that the Israeli foreign minister was interested. He was especially eager to confer with Yeltsin, and saw a photo opportunity which could be politically advantageous at that time. I had already made this request to the Russians, but the difficulties were great, even for the Russian Foreign Ministry. Besides, Yeltsin was not in Moscow. I had to set out on a veritable manhunt for the Russian president. It was the height of summer and Russians love long vacations in the month of August.

We finally tracked Yeltsin down to a dacha in the Crimea. I reached his head of protocol, Dmitri Rurikov, who consulted the president's schedule and said a meeting would in all likelihood be arranged when Peres was in Moscow. Several phone calls to Vice-President Rutskoi's assistant Andrei Fedorov, the only official available on the Kremlin staff, confirmed meetings with both the vice-president and the president.

Yuri Osipyan, a vice-president of the Academy of Sciences, promised to see to it that Peres got an honorary doctorate at the academy, although he feared the absence of the majority of the academy collegium might interfere with this act. Still, he hoped for the best.

On the eve of the minister's arrival, a late night call woke me at my hotel. Shimon? Yes, it was he. What kind of a visit was he going to have, who was he going to meet? The innuendo was unmistakable but he sounded pleased with what I told him. Would I mind if he brought the head of Nativ. Peres had seen my recommendations on the subject and agreed with them entirely (I had suggested Nativ be integrated in the Foreign Ministry, now that its secret mission was over). Peres wanted to put him in the proper disposition. I said I did not mind, on that premise.

Peres's visit started off with a meeting with Foreign Minister Kozyrev at the Morozov mansion. The discussion centred on an exposé by Peres of how the new government intended to handle the peace process. To Kozyrev's question of whether we would negotiate with the PLO, Peres responded that we were already having discussions with a Palestinian delegation, and that it was hardly necessary to change it into a purely terrorist representation, but that we would not check how 'kosher' the Palestinian delegation was. Kozyrev did not know the word. Peres also said the government was in a hurry, as a four-year term was not really very long. Kozyrev wanted to know if Israel would meet the Syrians on the issue of the Golan Heights. Peres asserted that we were open to any discussion, but would not simply return the Golan to a leader who had attacked Israel three times in a row.

In view of developments in 1994 it is interesting to recall Kozyrev's question regarding the relative strength of the PLO and Hamas. Peres remarked that the nearer we would get to peace, the stronger the PLO would become, and vice-versa. But fundamentalist movements, he added, are not all alike; each has its own agenda and aims. There was a great deal of money and corruption in the Middle East, Peres said, to which Kozyrev replied that the Soviet Union managed to have a great deal of corruption without any money.

In the end, the two ministers promised to cooperate on a number of subjects. Politically, Israel sought Russian help in transmitting to the Arabs the message that we were willing to take risks, but that there would be limitations on security issues. We wanted help with the Syrians. Economically, Israel wanted any assistance the Russians could provide in improving life in the

Middle Eastern region, so as to create a better framework for peace. Peres wanted to sign a communiqué on a general agreement of political understanding and cooperation with the Russians, but Kozyrev hedged. At that point Nimrod Novik, who was in the Peres party, rapidly composed a few lines resembling a statement of intent. The Russians agreed to let us read it out at the end of the official meeting.

In the encounter with Kozyrev, Peres, as is customary with him, flaunted his virtuosity in verbalizing abstract ideas. Russia cannot escape its greatness, Israel its small size; the Middle East possesses more territory than water; rain-bearing clouds do not go through customs; rockets do not stop at border crossings. The Russian minister gaped, but showed little interest in the Middle East. It seemed his thoughts were far away from the discussion. The Israeli minister expressed confidence in the future of Russia and said Israel wished to cooperate with it. Kozyrev nodded, approvingly.

A lunch followed in the pre-revolutionary setting of the Morozov dining hall, with its enormous fireplace under a fresh-looking Gobelin tapestry. The minister of culture, Yevgeny Sviridov, was there as was Golembiovsky, the editor of *Izvestiia*, a paper that had become independent and vaguely liberal. In his toast, Kozyrev said he welcomed Peres at the start of a new era of understanding. He also said the ambassador of Israel had done an extraordinary job of bringing the two countries closer, under very trying circumstances. Peres only blinked.

We proceeded to the Kremlin for a meeting with Rutskoi. He was not there. He was with Yeltsin, back from the Crimea. A half-hour passed. Peres started fretting and I was getting irritated. Peres wanted to leave but I kept him back. I took him to the Kremlin grounds to see the tsar-cannon, the greatest in its time but never fired, like the tsar-bell nearby, the greatest ever cast, but never tolled. We returned and waited another half-hour. I went to Yeltsin's office a third time to fetch Rutskoi. He came out just then, face perspiring, eyes blood-shot and brimming with tears of anger. He went into his office through a side door and it took him another few minutes to come to, evidently after a heated argument with the president. When we went in, Rutskoi was still totally overwhelmed and did not even have the decency to apologize. He shook hands and nonchalantly carried on although it was obvious his mind was elsewhere. The meeting with the president did not materialize, though it was scheduled right after the visit with Rutskoi. Peres asked why it had been cancelled. I said I did not know, although I suspected that after the row with Rutskoi, the president did not want to see anyone. I knew that he was never well-disposed toward seeing foreign ministers, but I could not share this bit of intelligence information with my minister of foreign affairs. And so, there was no photo opportunity and no photographic record in the Israeli press of a dramatic meeting between Yeltsin and Peres.

The next day, at a joint interview Yossi Bendor organized with the editors of Moscow newspapers and television, Peres shone, as always, and received excellent coverage. We took our minister to the old building of the Academy of Sciences, which prides itself on beautiful Russian neo-classical architecture and a massive table made of Karelian birch, on which Napoleon is purported to have worked when he occupied Moscow in 1812. At our meeting that morning, the academy lacked a quorum because of summer vacations, as Osipyan had predicted. The honorary doctorate was not delivered, but the president promised to present it to Peres in Israel in the autumn. Peres read a comprehensive lecture to the assembly on water desalination in Israel and asked for the academy's cooperation. He received kudos for his mastery of modern science.

That day's finale was a dinner I organized for Peres with the intellectuals of Moscow, where a gathering of some 50 writers, poets and other cultural stars, sat around him, each contributing his special talents. Bella Akhmadulina, the poetess, in a high state of nervous tension bordering on tears, recited a poem; so did the poet Voznesensky, with the Minister of Culture Sviridov looking on. Georgy Arbatov, the head of the USA and Canada Institute, had to catch a plane and left the gathering, which made Akhmadulina fly into a rage and make a political declaration against the establishment. Peres made a speech about the role of philosophy and literature in society; the guests regaled him with generous admiration and praise. Peres was pleased. He enjoys spending time with pundits and great spirits of the age.

At the synagogue on the Sabbath, the message of Peres's sermon was clear: emigration to Israel was the only solution. It would not be easy, he said, but things would work out in the end. This powerful message was also delivered to Jewish leaders and businessmen who called on Peres at his hotel later in the day.

Peres is an admirer of Leo Tolstoy, and he asked me to take him to the writer's Moscow home. This was on the Saturday after morning prayers. So as not to break the Sabbath, we walked the seven kilometres that separated Tolstoy's house from the synagogue. Peres was deeply impressed and even enlightened the director of the museum on some obscure detail of Tolstoy's writing career.

The following day we headed for Belorus* to visit Peres's birthplace. The Belorus government quartered the Peres party in a Minsk suburb, in a large villa called Zaslava. It was here that Leonid Brezhnev had entertained François Mitterand on a Belorussian bear hunt. We spent the next day meeting with the government and discussing plans for future cooperation, and visiting memorials to the Minsk ghetto (destroyed by the Nazis) and to the tens of thousands of Jews murdered in the Holocaust. Foreign Minister Kravchenko gave a lunch for Peres with leading intellectuals, poets, writers and historians. One guest, the sculptor Azgur, raised a toast to the Israeli foreign minister and said of himself that he was a communist and would descend to hell without changing his allegiance to the party. But Peres eclipsed them all with his erudition and the way he has with words. As we rode back through the suburbs of Minsk, on a grey and doleful afternoon, Peres looked out of the car at the run-down blocks of apartment houses, their neglected yards and the unkempt streets. He would not have been able to live there, he said.

Peres had asked to be taken to Volozhin, the site of a famous *yeshiva* near Minsk, where great rabbis as well as the Hebrew poet Bialik and others had studied the Talmud. Peres's grandfather and uncles used to frequent this *yeshiva* and were said to have been buried at the cemetery nearby. The shell of the building and its

---

* The new official name given the independent state which was formerly the Soviet Republic of Belorussia.

stars of David were still intact, but there was now a bakery inside. The cemetery was overgrown with weeds. Over a hundred Slavic-looking blonde villagers watched from a distance, loudly whispering to each other: 'He is looking for his grandfather's grave.' Peres discovered the tombstones of his uncle and other members of his family, the Perskis. He recited Kaddish, the prayer for the dead, and made a donation to clean the cemetery and repair the fence.

Not far from Volozhin is Vishnevo, the small town where Peres was born and raised until the age of 11, when he left for Palestine. Peres did not remember the location of his house. The village gently sloped down toward a stream, a tributary of the Berezina River. Peres looked around and asked where the felt factory had been. Few people remembered, as Vishnevo had been burnt down by the Germans. Several older people tried to position the landmarks. It was tough going and I began to suspect we would never discover the house. But Peres had a transcendental glow in his eyes and I knew then that he would find it. Up and down the main street we all trudged, with hundreds of town-dwellers trailing behind, looking into the apple orchards and among the cherry trees. I lost Peres for a few moments and then saw people rushing into a small clearing. Sure enough, there he stood, transfixed, near an old, covered well. That was the well they had drawn water from. His parents' house had disappeared. But the other house on the lot was that of his grandfather, with whom he had been very close.

Television cameras pointed their large glass eyes at Peres. He had come to see the land of his childhood, he said, to remember the taste of its fruit, the smell of its freshly-baked bread and the coolness of the water in its river. 'What are you thinking of at this moment?' the journalists barked. 'I remember my mother's lullaby.' And suddenly, Israel's minister of foreign affairs began singing, in Russian: 'I remember, I recall / How my mother loved me / And how over and over again / She so tenderly spoke to me / ...' And he trailed off. The lyrics are well known. They tell of a mother's admonition to her son Vanya not to keep bad company, lest he be led away, shackled in irons, to hard labour in Siberia. That same evening, Peres's lullaby was carried into every town and hamlet of the former Soviet Union, as the population tuned in to Russian television. This lullaby alone was worth a thousand pages of *hasbara* (an Israeli euphemism for propaganda). It carried a simple, human message of the bond that unites the Jews and the Russians, despite the cruelties and hardships of the past.

Parting with Peres at Moscow airport, I told him I saw no reason for my continuing in Russia, now that all of the aims set out had been fulfilled. Peres asked me to stay on, but I asked to be relieved, soon. He promised to look into it and reply in a few weeks' time.

A FINAL GUEST

Nativ had organized a parting trip to Russia for Yitzhak Shamir, their direct and ever-supportive, if passive, taskmaster. It was in Shamir's Foreign Ministry that I had begun working as head of political research. Shamir was always accessible, his door always open, his attention to my assessments and reports undivided — an important trait that other foreign ministers lacked. He may have brought his habits from his old desk at the Mossad. Though he regularly received reports from his alma mater and from army intelligence, as all ministers of foreign affairs before and after him, he heeded our advice as well, even though we were the junior partners in the intelligence community. This was a position that I fought hard to maintain with Peres. When Shamir became prime minister, I was repeatedly invited to state my views at sessions of the cabinet. I felt I had the benefit of an objective and receptive listener there as well.

Shamir was accompanied on this trip by his wife, Shulamit, smiling more generously, now that her husband had shed the burdens of his high office. This was not an official visit, but I felt duty bound to accord the Shamirs almost the same honours as I would if he had been the prime minister. I took him to see a number of important personalities, arranged for the mayor of Moscow to give him an official dinner, and gave him a party myself, well-attended by a number of politicians and leaders of the business community, such as Konstantin Borovoy, the head of the commodities exchange, Vladimir Ressin, the vice-mayor of

Moscow, Chana and Marc Winer of McDonald's, the Khakshuris, a prominent business family and many others. Diplomats were there too, a demonstration of respect and interest that must have pleased my former prime minister. Shamir was in a very relaxed, indulgent mood, edged with a trace of irony.

Shamir, like Peres, wanted to see the country of his origins. After a quick visit to Kiev, we went to see the area in which he had been born and grew up, not far from the birthplace of Shimon Peres. Although Shamir was only a former prime-minister, he was accorded great deference by Belorus officials, who organized welcoming receptions everywhere he went. In contrast to Peres, Shamir seemed to have little patience for nostalgia, relating to the sights and the courtesies with indifference and humour.

There was a comfortable bench in the yard of the villa where Shamir was lodged. A round pool with a small fountain and flower beds around gave this small space the aura of a comfortable resort. He asked me to sit down with him and tell him about the Soviet and the Russian scene and how we related to it. We spent a whole afternoon talking about emigration and the future of Jews in Russia. Shamir also wanted to hear about the political prognosis of the country inherited from the communist colossus. He seemed to know Russian history, especially its chapters on anarchists and terrorists in the pre-revolutionary era. I remember how he once prompted Gromyko, who was trying to remember the name of a Russian populist movement which had slipped his memory, the Narodniki. Shamir always listened intently, if he was not too tired (he had been known to doze off). This time he asked a whole string of questions, which I tried to answer.

I talked to Shamir about the impossible position his close aides had at times put me in, carelessly delegating quacks and private persons to bear political messages to Soviet leaders and misrepresenting the state. I recalled his passivity about the festering sore of rivalry between the two immigration agencies, that could have harmed the future of immigration. I was not expecting any comment or explanation from Shamir, but he said, after sadly shaking his head, that he would see to it that these situations never recurred. That was fine, I thought, but I was due to leave, and he knew it, and Shamir was not prime minister any longer.

Before bidding farewell, I took most of my friends and colleagues at the embassy on a grand tour of Siberia and the Russian Far East. We visited Irkutsk, on the shores of beautiful Lake Baikal and we called on the Jewish community at Birobidzhan, Stalin's Jewish Autonomous Republic. There, as everywhere else in the vast space between the Polish border and the Pacific Ocean, Jews were on the move, preferring the uncertainties of a life in their own country to the possible repetitions of the past in the territories of the former USSR.

My timetable remained jam-packed right up to my departure from Moscow, but the adrenaline-charged novelty of the first four years had gone. On a last visit to Jerusalem before taking leave of Russia, I briefed the late General Haim Bar-Lev, a former chief of staff and general secretary of the Labour Party, who was to take over my now well-worn seat behind the desk on Bolshaia Ordynka. I returned to Moscow to part with the many friends I was leaving behind. At the end of October 1992 a regular El Al flight took me back home, where I arrived early on a crisp autumn morning, the sun rising in the hills of Judea.

Postscriptum

How fortunate is he who visited this Earth
At its conclusive, crucial hour,
For he was summoned by the gods
To partake of a splendid feast
And witness the performance of an Elysian drama.

Fyodor Tyutchev

More than three years have elapsed since I left Russia in my formal capacity. I have returned several times. To the outside observer that I have now become, it seems that the country is going through a painful adjustment to the post-communist phase. The positive changes introduced over recent years have reawakened hope, but democracy is a new notion in the annals of the Russian state and will need time to strike roots into its soil. Those who have inherited or taken over political power are building the infrastructure to maintain it in their hands. It is difficult to predict the nature of the regime that will lead Russia into the twenty-first century.

Moscow looks neater, many of its houses repaired and repainted; the streets are clogged with cars; many stores have been privatized and stocked with imported goods. Some have come into money and enjoy the new bounty that life is providing. Others are struggling and despondent, especially outside the bigger cities. The embassy on Bolshaia Ordynka has diplomats and officials running a large, well-ordered establishment. No milling crowds on its grounds, no more anxious phone calls in the middle of the night asking for *vizovs*, no important visitors coming to be photographed with prospective immigrants. The bubbles have gone out of the champagne, and that is as it should be.

The six-hundred thousand immigrants who have passed through the gates of the embassy are still in the throes of their integration into the very different lifestyle and mores of their new country. The problematics of absorbing a large new population emerging from a different political and social culture have been considerable. Great efforts have been invested in their integration. No country could have done more. But for the newcomers, life has been difficult and often confusing. They have been forced by circumstances to abandon their past and begin anew. Still, few really regret their decision and fewer still dream of going back. The memory of the old country is dimming. In a few years, the people who left the Soviet Union will have become an integral part of Israeli life.

Relations with Russia have been renewed, but the once exciting prospects have been replaced by drab reality. Russia and Israel have been separately engaged in all-consuming activities, one endeavouring to rebuild its society, the other valiantly searching to end the decades of war in the Middle East. With obstacles removed and the larger part of the potential reservoir drained, immigration from Russia has become a secondary issue for Israel; and Israel, in spite of continuing curiosity of the media, is outside Russia's present orbit of political concerns. The small window of opportunity that opened up for a serious reconsideration of mutual interests after the fall of communism, is slowly closing. Neither country has had the foresight, or the patience to formulate a strategic view of future connections. Current affairs and pragmatism have overshadowed long-range considerations.

In spite of the great dissimilarities in land mass and international importance, population and wealth, both Russia and Israel are faced with a similar threat of fundamentalist Islam. Russia and Israel are strategic neighbours and might need each other's support in this regard. The two countries could forge stronger ties of cultural and economic cooperation as well, for the infrastructure and the interest are readily available and could be used to good advantage.

Do the remnants of Russian and Ukrainian Jewry have the

potential to develop into autonomous, eventually viable communities? A great deal would depend on the two countries involved, their economic and social development and whether they can provide the stability and tolerance necessary for the life of a Jewish minority. At this stage, it would be a grave error of judgment to dismiss the future importance and influence of Jews in Russia and Ukraine. In time, perhaps in the life of a single generation, we might see their re-establishment, with thriving and purposeful leadership. These communities will, in any case, continue to be a source of immigration to Israel for a number of years to come.

Seventy years of communism dealt a severe blow to Jewish life in the USSR. The rebirth of Judaism in the Soviet Union, the mass exodus of the Jews to Israel in the years of perestroika, are as miraculous as the demise of the Red Empire itself. In the tumultuous years of the twentieth century, a century of world wars and bloody revolutions, perhaps the biggest, most spectacular change was brought about without a shot being fired.

I was fortunate to have witnessed these great events. But as I look ahead to the advent of the next century, I am curious as to the nature of the life that awaits Russia. Optimists among the Russians like to quote Pushkin's verse: 'Where autocracy lies broken/ Russia will rise from her long sleep...' The more cynical remember Nekrasov, another poet, who said: 'Fate has bestowed upon us good intentions/ But their fulfilment is not within our reach.'

Glossary

aliyah	immigration to Israel
Bolshaia Ordynka	street address of the Israeli Embassy in Moscow
Lishkat HaKesher (Lishka)	a liaison bureau established in 1953 as part of the Israeli Prime Minister's office to deal with problems of Jews inside the eastern bloc countries; the Lishka was responsible for maintaining contacts with the Jewish population in the USSR
Nativ	code name for Lishkat HaKesher, meaning 'the route'
nomenklatura	official roster of hierarchy and privilege under the Soviet system
oleh	immigrant to Israel
OVIR	Otdel viz i registratsii, Visa and Registration Department, Soviet Ministry of the Interior
prisoners of Zion	Soviet Jews refused the right of emigration and incarcerated by the Russian authorities
refusenik	a Jew denied permission to emigrate from the USSR because of supposed knowledge of official secrets
UPDK	the directorate affiliated with the Soviet Foreign Ministry, responsible for Servicing the Diplomatic Corps,
vizov	an official application by foreign relatives, inviting a Soviet citizen to reside abroad; served as a basis for granting permission to emigrate; initially only Israeli *vizov*s were accepted and exit permission granted only to countries other than Israel. In 1989, OVIR began accepting *vizov*s from any country, which increased the number of potential emigrants to the West
yeshiva	a school for advanced talmudic study

Index

Envoy to Moscow

Kravchuk, Leonid, 319–20; and
Babi Yar memorial service, 319;
career background, 319
Kremer, Gideon, 273
Krichevsky, Ilya, 295, 298
Kryuchkov, Victor, 192, 296
Kube, 361–2
Kuibyshev (Saratov), 27
Kulik, Gennady, 111
Kulits, David, 346
Kurchatov Atomic Energy
Institute, 112
Kuril islands, 138
Kurzer, Dan, 340
Kuwait (*see also* Gulf War), 244
Kuznetsov, Felix, 162
Kyrgyzstan (*see also* Bishkek),
289–90
Kyrill, Archbishop, 257

Labour Party, 193, 385
Landsbergis, Vitautas, 337
Lanschoot, Robert, 93
Latvia (*see also* Riga), 336; Jewish
education in post-Soviet, 336
Lautman, Dov, 322
Law of Return, 102
Lebanon, 279, 283
Lebedev, Igor, 253
Leibler, Isi J., 72, 74, 75
Lenin, V. I., 131, 135, 164, 165, 306
Leningrad, 29; description of, 30–1;
Jews in, 32
Leningrad Conservatory, 272
Lenin in Zurich, 165
'Let My People Go', 174
Levin, Aliza, 79, 366, 371
Levin, Aryeh, arrives in Moscow
(1988) xx, 1–11; childhood in
Tehran, 10, 31, 199, 272, 350, 382,
385; diplomatic service in Iran,
289; diplomatic service in
Rwanda, xix; diplomatic service
at UN, 12–13; establishes
relations with Armenia, 367;
with Azerbaijan, 359; with
Estonia, 338; with Georgia, 373;
with Kazakhstan, 364; with
Latvia, 336; with Lithuania,

337–8; with Moldova, 383; with
Tajikistan, 356; with Ukraine,
332–4; with Uzbekistan, 351;
family background, xvii–xix;
205–6; and Gorbachev trip to
Israel, 384; invested as consul-
general, 256; leaves
ambassadorial post in Moscow,
394, 396; and media, 60–1, 246,
260–2, 263–4, 265, 326, 357;
meets with Shevardnadze in
Moscow, 57; meets with
Shevardnadze in Tbilisi, 375-7;
meets with Yeltsin, 80, 345–7;
visits Baltic States 330–1, 336–9;
visits Central Asia and the
Caucasus, 348–77
Levin, Ishai, 276, 325
Levin, Michal, 276, 313
Levin, Yael, 79, 128, 129
Levitin, Michael, 125, 289
Levy, David, 242–7, 255;
announces renewal of relations
with USSR, 324; becomes foreign
minister, 242; at General
Assembly (1990), 243; in
Moscow, 339–43; and settlement
of immigrants in occupied
territories, 211; statement at
Multilateral Conference, 342;
visit to China, 340
Levy-Bessmertnykh meeting, 279
Levy-Gorbachev meeting in
Moscow, 343
Levy-Pankin meeting at UN, 317
Levy-Shevardnadze meeting at
UN, 244–6, 342
Lewis, Victor, 7, 262, 263
and KGB, 263
Libya, 146, 193
Ligachev, Yegor, 218
Likhachev, Dmitri, 252
Likud government (*see also* Arens,
Moshe; Levy, David; Shamir,
Yitzhak), 88
Likud party, 12, 66, 68, 149, 193,
242
Lishkat Hakesher (*see* Nativ)
Literaturnaia gazeta, 161, 162, 163